# Contents

# The Evolution of Canadian Literature in English 1914-1945

# The Evolution of Canadian Literature in English 1914-1945

Edited by
**George L. Parker**

Holt, Rinehart and Winston of Canada, Limited
Toronto                                    Montreal

Distributed in the United States of America by Winston Press, Minneapolis

Library of Congress Catalog Card Number: 73-310

Distributed in the United States of America by Winston Press,
25 Groveland Terrace, Minneapolis, Minnesota 55403

**Other Titles in the Series**

The Evolution of Canadian Literature in English: Beginnings to 1867
Edited by Mary Jane Edwards, Carleton University, Ottawa

The Evolution of Canadian Literature in English 1867-1914
Edited by Mary Jane Edwards; Paul Denham, University of Saskatchewan;
and George L. Parker, Royal Military College of Canada, Kingston, Ontario

The Evolution of Canadian Literature in English 1945-1970
Edited by Paul Denham

General Editor:
Mary Jane Edwards
Assistant Professor,
Department of English,
Carleton University,
Ottawa.

Printed in Canada
1  2  3  4  5          77  76  75  74  73

# Preface

*Evolution of Canadian Literature 1914-1945* is one of a series of four anthologies which trace the development of Canadian literature in English from its beginnings in the eighteenth century to its manifestations in the nineteen-seventies. As one volume in a series, it follows a format adopted for all four anthologies. Each has an Introduction which attempts to tell the story of Canadian literature in English during a specific period of time and to relate this story to contemporary events and developments in life and in literature both in Canada and abroad. A brief introduction describing the author's life and works precedes the selection from each writer. Only items complete in themselves are included. Each anthology contains poetry, fiction, and other kinds of writing.

This anthology covers a particularly stormy period in life and literature. Most of the authors represented lived through the First World War, the Great Depression, and the Second World War. These events changed Western European and North American life and transformed their literatures. Echoes of these cultural shocks sound through many of the selections in this anthology.

But while this anthology covers the period 1914-1945, and certainly well represents works written and published during this time, half the authors in this book are still writing. Dorothy Livesay's "Ballad of Me", for example, was published in *The Unquiet Bed* (1967). The writers represented who are now deceased have died relatively recently. Many of them published some of their most impressive works after the Second World War. E.J. Pratt, who died in 1964, did not publish *Towards the Last Spike* until 1952.

Thus, although the historical period George Parker describes in the Introduction is that of 1914-1945, the literature he anthologizes often is quite contemporary in its date of publication. One might add that all of it is contemporary irrelevant of its date of publication. The agonies of war, drought, and depression are as present today as they were a generation ago. "Eden" still seems remote.

Ottawa,
August, 1972

Mary Jane Edwards

v

# Acknowledgments

I wish to thank the staff of the Royal Military College of Canada Massey Library and the staff of the Queen's University Lorne Pierce Special Collections for their help. My thanks also to Glen W. Hunter and particularly Thomas B. Vincent for reading the manuscript and making helpful suggestions. Special thanks to Mrs. Dorothy E. Rowe who typed the manuscript for me.

GLP

Raymond Knister. "Poisons", "The Plowman", "Plowman's Song", "The Hawk", "Night Walk", "October Stars", "Quiet Snow", "Change". Reprinted from *The Collected Poems* of Raymond Knister, The Ryerson Press, by permission of McGraw-Hill Ryerson Limited. "Mist-Green Oats" from *The Midland*, VIII (August-September 1922), pp. 254-276. Reprinted by permission of Mrs. Christy Grace.

Dorothy Livesay. "Reality", "Green Rain", "Day and Night", "Lorca", "Prelude for Spring", "Fantasia", "In Time of War", "Of Mourners", "On Looking into Henry Moore", "Ballad of Me". Reprinted from *Collected Poems, Two Seasons* by Dorothy Livesay, McGraw-Hill Ryerson Limited, by permission of Dorothy Livesay. "Call My People Home". Reprinted from *Collected Poems, Two Seasons* by Dorothy Livesay, McGraw-Hill Ryerson Limited, by permission of McGraw-Hill Ryerson Limited. "Winter". Reprinted from *Selected Poems* by Dorothy Livesay, The Ryerson Press, by permission of Dorothy Livesay. "Corbin — A Company Town Fights for Its Life". Reprinted from *New Frontier* (April 1936), by permission of Dorothy Livesay.

Anne Marriott. "The Wind Our Enemy". By permission of the author, Anne Marriott McLellan.

E.J. Pratt. "Newfoundland", "The Shark", "The Highway", "Erosion", "The Depression Ends", "Silences", "The Truant", "Towards the Last Spike", "Myth and Fact" from *Collected Poems* by E.J. Pratt, by permission of The Macmillan Company of Canada Limited.

Thomas H. Raddall. "Winter's Tale" from *The Pied Piper of Dipper Creek and Other Tales* by Thomas H. Raddall. Reprinted by permission of The Canadian Publishers, McClelland and Stewart Limited, Toronto. This story first appeared in the January 1936 issue of *Blackwood's Magazine*. "At the Tide's Turn" from *The Wedding Gift and Other Stories* by Thomas H. Raddall. Reprinted by permission of The Canadian Publishers, McClelland and Stewart Limited, Toronto.

Sinclair Ross. "The Lamp at Noon", "The Outlaw" from *The Lamp at Noon* by Sinclair Ross. Reprinted by permission of The Canadian Publishers, McClelland and Stewart Limited, Toronto.

W.W.E. Ross. "The Diver", "If Ice", "Reality", "Fish", "Rocky Bay", "On the Supernatural", "This Form", "Apparition" from *Shapes and Sounds* by W.W.E. Ross. With a Portrait by Dennis Burton, a Memoir by Barry Callaghan, and an Editorial Note by Raymond Souster and John Robert Colombo, 1968, Longman Canada Limited.

B.K. Sandwell. "The Boom" from *The Diversions of Duchesstown and Other Essays* by B.K. Sandwell. Used by permission of J.M. Dent & Sons (Canada) Limited.

F.R. Scott. "March Field", "Efficiency", "The Canadian Authors Meet", "Grey Morning", "Saturday Sundae", "Armageddon", "Trans Canada", "Bedside", "Lakeshore", "A Grain of Rice", "Eden", "W. L.M.K.", "All the Spikes but the Last". For permission to reprint, thanks are due to the author, F.R. Scott.

A.J.M. Smith. "The Lonely Land", "News of the Phoenix", "Sea Cliff", "A Hyacinth for Edith", "The Plot against Proteus", "The Archer", "The Sorcerer", "Business as Usual (1946)", "Fear as Normal (1954)" from *Poems New & Collected* by A.J.M. Smith. Reprinted by permission of the publisher, Oxford University Press, Canadian Branch. "Universal Peace (19 — )", "The Bird" from *Collected Poems* by A.J.M. Smith. Reprinted by permission of the publisher, Oxford University Press, Canadian Branch.

F.H. Underhill. "Some Reflections on the Liberal Tradition in Canada" from *In Search of Canadian Liberalism* by Frank H. Underhill, by permission of The Macmillan Company of Canada Limited.

W.P. Wilgar. "Poetry and the Divided Mind in Canada". Originally appeared in *The Dalhousie Review*, XXIV (October 1944), pp. 266-271. Reprinted with permission of *The Dalhousie Review*, Halifax, Canada.

The Evolution of Canadian Literature in
English 1914-1945

# Introduction

A major problem for Canadian writers has been the task of dealing with their experiences in unique and distinctive ways. This problem is not confined to Canada, of course, and it is one that often tends to be resolved by reference to the ways in which other societies formulate their experiences into art. Not surprisingly, then, in shaping their vision and ideas about a national literature, Canadian writers have used measuring rods imported chiefly from Great Britain and the United States, whose literatures are among the glories of the western world. In order to provide a background for the works in this Anthology, the Introduction will explore some of the social and artistic questions which gave a special tone to the literature published in Canada between 1914 and 1945.[1] That era, enclosed by two major wars, contained a series of national and international events which impressed themselves on Canadian writers.

The first significant watershed for change at home and abroad was the Great War of 1914-1918. Of 628,000 people in the armed forces, 425,000 went overseas — an impressive number for a nation of approximately eight million. The most famous poem of the War, Colonel John MacRae's (1872-1918) "In Flanders Fields", echoed the war attitudes of many people in the British nations — the semi-religious nature of the conflict, the nobility of sacrifice, and the tragedy of lost young lives:

> In Flanders fields the poppies blow
>    Between the crosses, row on row,
>    That mark our place; and in the sky
>    The larks, still bravely singing, fly
> Scarce heard amid the guns below.
>
> We are the Dead. Short days ago
> We lived, felt dawn, saw sunset glow,
>    Loved and were loved, and now we lie,
>         In Flanders fields.
>
> Take up our quarrel with the foe:
> To you from failing hands we throw
>    The torch; be yours to hold it high.
>    If ye break faith with us who die
> We shall not sleep, though poppies grow
>         In Flanders fields.

As a consequence of her military role at Ypres, Passchendale, and particularly at Vimy Ridge, and the industrial expansion at home, many Canadians emerged from the War proud of their record, certain that the Victorian Age had finally ended in Canada, and convinced that Canada was a nation at last. In 1919, for example, Sir Robert Borden went off to Versailles to demand, and receive, a separate seat for Canada in international councils.

In the years immediately after the War, neither the bad feelings over French Canada's disinclination to jump on the military bandwagon nor rising labour problems (particularly bitter in the Spring 1919 Winnipeg Strike) could dampen nationalism or the belief in a new world around the corner. A new language of social reform was in the air: there was talk of public ownership, unemployment and health insurance, and old age pensions. Although there was a depression in 1920-21, by the mid-1920s a wave of prosperity, like those of the 1850s and 1890s, swept the land. Oil fields were discovered in Alberta, giant hydro-projects were undertaken, the newsprint industry was expanded, and new mining ventures in Quebec, Ontario, and British Columbia opened the northern frontier to twentieth-century society and technology. Despite the nationalistic fervour and industrial development of the 1920s, however, some historians now see it as a decade when change in Canada was sometimes more apparent than real. In *Dominion of the North* (1957), Donald Creighton explains:

> At first it almost seemed as if the demands and requirements of these new ideals would cause a revolution in Canadian politics, both internal and external. But the lurid appearances of 1919 were highly deceptive. Far from departing on new adventures, Canada had returned slowly but persistently to the traditions of the past.[2]

One symptom of Canada's return to a traditional, comfortable middle way was the election in 1921 of the Liberal Government under William Lyon Mackenzie King. The domination of Canadian politics by this astute politician for the longest period of any Prime Minister in Commonwealth history has been explained thus by Frank Underhill:

> There are two ultimate reasons for Mr. King's long success in Canadian politics. They both rest upon marked characteristics of our Canadian community. One is our Canadian preference, in spite of the clearness of our physical climate, for living constantly in a mental haze. We never make issues clear to ourselves. We never define our differences, so that they can be understood clearly or reconciled . . . . Mr. King is obviously the most complete personification of the national Canadian characteristic who has ever appeared in our public life . . . . The other main reason for Mr. King's long predominance is Canadian disunity. We have never been in any deep sense a united people. We have not overcome the difficulties of geography, and we are as far from reconciling the difficulties of race as we were a hundred years ago.[3]

A second major event which influenced Canada between 1914 and 1945 was the Great Depression, which began with the crash of Wall Street in 1929 and which lasted throughout the 1930s. Canada was severely injured because its economy was dependent upon the export of primary staple products. The hardest hit were fishermen, lumbermen, farmers, and the unemployed workers who had been laid off in "an effort to reduce output rather than to lower prices".[4] Western farmers suffered even more than most Canadians when severe droughts between 1931 and 1937 covered the Prairies. The psychic effects of the Depression and drought lasted for almost a generation in parts of the West.

Federal and provincial governments responded too slowly and too late in their efforts to ameliorate social conditions. By the middle of the decade, however, the federal government undertook to set up social-security laws, to improve labour laws, and to exercise some government control over economic conditions. In these same years three important publicly-owned corporations were created: Trans Canada Air Lines, the Canadian Broadcasting Corporation, and the National Film Board.

One of the most important developments of the 1930s, however, was the emergence of new political parties, particularly in the West. These included the Social Credit Party founded in Alberta in 1932 and the Co-operative Commonwealth Federation — the CCF — founded in Regina in 1933. Its birth, announced by the "Regina Manifesto" whose author was Frank Underhill, not only provided Canada with its most effective "third party" but also with a philosophical basis for reform in all spheres of Canadian life. Although the Party (now renamed the New Democratic Party) has never formed a federal government, it has been elected on the provincial level in Saskatchewan, Manitoba, and British Columbia.

Looking back at the Depression in 1941, B. K. Sandwell observed that ultimately it might have a beneficial effect:

> The depression indeed will probably be found, in due time, to have done more to bring Canada to a state of mental maturity than anything else. It has abolished the attitude of smug satisfaction which prevailed too widely before 1930, and which assumed that the Dominion had no serious problems except those of reconciling French and English views as to its destiny and reducing the burden of interest on unprofitable railways. It is now realized that the condition of a large part of the wage-working and agricultural classes is unsatisfactory through no fault of their own, that the system of extensive seasonal employment with little or no effort to correlate winter and summer jobs is extremely wasteful. . . . [5]

Other events of the 1930s were also forcing Canadians out of their attitudes of "smug satisfaction". The growing fascist tendencies in the political life of Germany and Italy and the Spanish Civil War made the strongest impressions on the imagination of Canadians. But the influences from the United States — permanent factors, really — increased enormously in these years. There was growing economic control of Canadian firms, including the Canadian book industry, and there was a steady flow of American magazines, movies, and radio programs across the border. The metropolis, to Canadians looking for jobs or fulfillment of fantasies, was an American one — New York, Chicago, Minneapolis, Los Angeles.

World War II (1939-1945) both ended the Depression and provided at least temporary solutions to other problems facing Canadians. As "total war", it brought full employment and prosperity. New industries and factories sprang up to meet the allied demands for munitions and war equipment, and until the end of 1941 Canada was the second largest power on the allied side. By the War's end the nation of twelve million saw one million men and women in uniform, and once again the forces gave a good account of themselves, particularly in Italy and in Normandy. Like the Great War, it brought about a new feeling of shared effort among all groups, united in their support of a War to help annihilate fascism. And while old problems like the hesitancy of French Canada to join in European wars was raised again and new problems like the arrogant treatment of the Japanese on the West Coast were created, these were

3

generally smoothed out and rationalized away as Canadians in 1945 looked forward once again to a time of peace.

While the history of Canadian literature from 1914 to 1945 is chiefly one of Canadian writers responding to both the traditional questions about what Canadian literature ought to be and to the immediate social, economic, and political problems facing all Canadians, the Canadian writer in this period also had a special set of problems. These had to do with the economics and politics of publishing. The maple-leaf boosterism for which the 1920s are so often derided was certainly a factor in economic life, but in literary circles the casual equation of Art with Merchandise had rather insidious effects in book publishing. Since 1900, the Canadian publishing trade had expanded rapidly, and phenomenal sales during the War convinced several firms that they could now play a more active role in aiding literature. Furthermore, for a generation, poets such as Drummond and Service, and novelists such as Gilbert Parker, Ralph Connor, and Lucy Maud Montgomery had held their own in the international best-seller markets. But in a country which lacked a strong tradition of literary effort pursued regardless of sales or royalties, the effects of the best-seller syndrome were more pernicious than in the United States or Great Britain. While some Canadian writers like Mazo de la Roche succeeded in getting their works produced by the commercial publishers, others, particularly poets and short story writers, found book publishers (with the honourable exception of Lorne Pierce at Ryerson) increasingly shy of taking chances on their works, especially after 1925.

In the 1890s Lampman and Carman were able to publish in the large-circulation journals of both Canada and the United States; in the 1920s avant-garde poets like F. R. Scott and A.J.M. Smith found the popular magazines closed to them and uninterested in their art. One reaction to the lack of publishing outlets for the Canadian writer in Canada was the appearance of a number of little magazines. Louis Dudek provides a succinct account of the little magazine's role:

> The literary magazine of this type marks a stage in the history of printing, a retreat into intimate, or *cénacle*, publication, after the extreme extension of literacy and printing for mass audiences: it is also the stage at which printing and paper became economically available for such private and limited publication. In literary terms, it is the embattled literary reaction of intellectual minority groups to the commercial middle-class magazines of fiction and advertising which had evolved in the nineteenth century.[6]

In Canada these little magazines were established some decades after their appearance abroad. A.J.M. Smith's and F. R. Scott's *McGill Fortnightly Review* (1925-1927) and *The Canadian Mercury* (1928-1929) are considered the forerunners. The 1930s, surprisingly, did not develop the promise of the 1920s. Perhaps Depression economics explains this absence; perhaps, also, the fact that the twenties poets were establishing themselves in their professional careers explains the situation. However, the appearance of *Contemporary Verse* (1941-1952) in Vancouver, *Preview* (1942-1945) and *First Statement* (1942-1945) in Montreal, and *The Fiddlehead* (1945-    ) in Fredericton encouraged a little magazine tradition in Canada which has shown no tendency since then to disappear in spite of the comings and goings of individual titles.

If the new Canadian writers of the 1920s and 1930s worried over ways to publish their works, they worried even more over questions which had to do with the form and content of their poetry, fiction, and criticism. First, as new writers in a tradition, they had to decide either to accept or reject a tradition which included the poetic influences of Lampman, Carman, and Roberts, images of Canadian life popularized in the fiction of Parker, Connor, Montgomery, and Service, and critical theories stemming from Matthew Arnold's (1822-1888) contention that poetry should be a criticism of life and from Hippolyte Taine's (1828-1893) idea that art was the product of a special time, place, and race. On the whole, the younger writers rebelled against this tradition. Calling even those writers who were still among the living not merely Victorian, but neo-Victorian, Quasi-Victorian, and Pseudo-Victorian,[7] they judged them guilty of all the defects of the Victorianism they loathed: sentimentality, cliché language, prettifying regionalism, sexual repression, and an absence of self-consciousness about art.

Much of their wrath — F. R. Scott's poem "The Canadian Authors Meet" is a good illustration of it — was directed towards the writers, newspaper reviewers, and literary journalists who clustered around the Canadian Authors' Association. This society was founded in 1919 to persuade Parliament to pass a Copyright Act which would be consistent with the Berne Convention (1886) and the latest Imperial Copyright Act (1910). Its first four years were successfully devoted to such an end, and anyone who publishes a book in this country must be grateful for the Association's accomplishments. But the CAA became a mutual-admiration society, concerned not only with the economics of publishing but seduced by the jargon of business life into pushing Can. Lit. as a commodity to be morally and financially supported. The Association's mouthpiece, *The Canadian Bookman* (1919-    ), demonstrates clearly the distance between the lip-service paid to Parnassus and the claims of the market place.

Nevertheless, the elder generation was not as Victorian as their accusers imagined. For instance, John Murray Gibbon (1874-1952), the first President of the CAA, welcomed the New Poetry, praising it for its anti-Victorian elements:

> It would be a great thing for Canadian literature if it kept pace with the times instead of lingering in the drawing rooms of the early Victorians. The times are moving. Dynasties are falling, being swept away. The whole world is aflame with a war against the over-bearing tyranny of military caste. So too with poetry, where metrical rhyming forms are only the shibboleth of imaginary rank, of imaginary finish and style, of imaginary caste.[8]

In 1919, Gibbon was 45 (the same age as Robert Frost) and a sympathetic outsider to new currents.

Nor did the more famous members of the older generation fail to support the new young writers. Here is Charles G. D. Roberts' perceptive opinion of Callaghan in 1931:

> Mr. Morley Callaghan is reported as having declared himself a humble disciple of Mr. Hemingway — as having learned his art from Mr. Hemingway. If this be so, the disciple has on many accounts excelled the master. Compare the two novels, *Strange Fugitive* and *The Sun Also Rises*. The latter is marred by eccentricities in the vogue at the moment. You find yourself skipping whole pages of conversation whose only purpose is to display the reiterant [sic] of the drunken mind. Able as it is in many respects the book will hardly, I think, survive a change of fashion. It carries too great a burden of mere words. Mr. Callaghan's story, on the other hand, carries no such burden. There is not a superfluous word in it. The style is clear, bare, efficient. It is modernism — the subject matter is very "modern". But it has sanely avoided the modern fault of striving after

effect. It does not date itself; and it may well appear as readable a hundred years hence as it does today.[9]

Now Roberts, who is himself Canada's first "modern", cannot be faulted for his inability to see that the vogue set by Hemingway would provide the next generation of writers with a new style, tone, and even subject matter. Thus his comments on Hemingway do not invalidate those on Callaghan, and it is to Roberts' credit that he did perceive something unique about the young Canadian. For years Callaghan's admirers have told us that he was unappreciated in Canada, which is to confuse an author's sales with his critical reputation.

Ironically, Leo Kennedy's "The Future of Canadian Literature" (1928), one of the bitterest attacks on the CAA by a young poet, ends up at the same point where the Association's editorials were aimed. He explains how young writers can avoid the seductions of the best-seller market:

> ... they will approach the task of expression fortified by new ideas and original conceptions; they will learn the lesson of all precursors, discovering in a western grain field, a Quebec *maison*, or a Montreal nightclub, a spirit and a consciousness distinctly Canadian. Just as the writers of the United States today are inclined to segregate, with Frost expressing New Hampshire and Sandburg exploiting Chicago, so I believe these younger Canadians when properly fledged will embrace this practice, and write each of the soul and scene of his community. Only Whitman has comprehensively surveyed the whole American scene, and what is better in the American consciousness. Only a Canadian Whitman, and by that I mean a man of his genius and spiritual breadth, will correctly interpret the whole Canadian consciousness. Since Whitmans are purely accidents of birth, and may not be specifically begotten, these younger Canadians will continue their work of enlightenment and propagation, each striving at all times to be the national literary *obermensch*, and in due course will serve as a fitting background for this inevitable man.[10]

There is nothing here in this implicit evolutionary view that any cultured Canadian since the 1890s could not agree with. The point of quoting Kennedy at length is to suggest that most Canadian writers of his period were similarly concerned with the relation between a national literature, an organic culture, and the political framework of that literature.

When the new writers of the 1920s and 1930s rejected the traditions of Canadian literature which they had inherited and failed to see that some of these were their own, they were forced to search for new language, new forms, and new content for their work. They found new models for their poetry and fiction and new polemics for their criticism in several literary movements which had been influencing western culture from the late nineteenth and early twentieth century. And they discovered new, and old, writers who helped them express their social and political ideas in ways which suited their sensibilities.

The most important international poetry movement that affected younger Canadian poets was Imagism, whose principles were embodied in the Imagist Manifesto of *Des Imagistes* (1915).[11] The Imagists advocated simplicity and directness in language, the use of appropriate forms for content, and absolute freedom in subject matter. Virtually every important statement about poetry made in Canadian criticism until well into the 1950s paraphrased these articles of faith. A second movement, the Symbolist, although dating back to the 1890s as a romantic reaction to realism, also

6

exerted some influence on many of the younger poets of the post-War years. Symbolism's characteristic technique is to use a complex and private set of symbols to give expression to the artist's emotional responses. Because it is usually concerned with creating an interior world, the pattern of a symbolist work is usually non-sequential and a-logical.[12] The principles of these two movements were the basis for what the post-War generation meant by the terms *New Poetry* and *Modernism*, and the terms will be used in these senses throughout this Anthology.

The chief foreign poets who influenced Canadians were the American T. S. Eliot (1888-1965), the Irishmen William Butler Yeats (1865-1939) and James Joyce (1882-1941), and the Welshman Dylan Thomas (1914-1953). The most important English influences came from Gerard Manley Hopkins (1884-1889), whose poems were first published in 1918, and from W. H. Auden (1907-    ). All made significant experiments with language, rhythm, and form, and all developed highly personal styles which tended to overwhelm younger poets in their formative years. To an extent, all were "obscure" in that their writings never had the wide popularity enjoyed by some Victorian poems. Besides these modern influences, the poetry of the Jacobean period (1603-1649), itself a troubled, anxious era, held a new importance for its "metaphysical" qualities.

The only Americans who had a strong influence in Canada (apart from Eliot, who seemed "British" to his contemporaries) were William Carlos Williams (1883-1963) Marianne Moore (1887-    ). Raymond Knister and W.W.E. Ross, the two Canadians most sensitive to American poetry, were recognized by Americans in the 1920s as part of the vanguard, but, ironically, the two poets were more or less neglected by Canadians. It has only been in the 1960s that Knister and Ross have been accorded the honour of being the first New Poets in Canada.

The liberating influences of Yeats, Joyce, Eliot, Sandburg, and Williams cannot be understressed. In a land where the popular poetic forms of the Victorian Age still lingered, the free verse of the Imagists allowed for positive experiments with diction, cadence, and form. In a land where the diluted spirit of the Pre-Raphaelites and the Celtic Nineties still flourished, it was heartening to have lively and rebellious foreign contemporaries to follow. In a society which had no native critical theories, the flexible Imagist Manifesto was a godsend. In short, it was possible to find one's way in a new land with charts and instruments from abroad. W.W.E. Ross's "This Form Expresses Now" is itself a poetic illustration of the aims of the New Poetry.

In fiction, the new styles appeared more emphatically and sooner in the short story than in the novel. The new modes of realism, naturalism, and even symbolism were taken over by Knister and Callaghan in the early twenties, so that their short stories reflected almost simultaneously the techniques found in stories by James Joyce, Katherine Mansfield, Sherwood Anderson, and Ernest Hemingway. Although Grove's and Callaghan's novels certainly reflect new techniques in the craft of the novel, the influences of Henry James, Joseph Conrad, and Hemingway were slower to appear in the Canadian novel. But both Callaghan's *Strange Fugitive* (1928) and Sinclair Ross's *As For Me and My House* (1941), with their regard for shape, organization, and point of view, were evidence of a new kind of Canadian novel.

The fiction writers of the 1920s and 1930s liked to think they were the first to use realism in Canadian writing, but the technique of realism had been used effectively long before this period. The realism of Knister and Callaghan in short stories, and Dorothy Livesay (in her sketch "Corbin — A Company Town Fights For its Life") was new in that it "rendered" situations, removed the author from the story, and thus effected a kind of detachment in the narrative. That is, the author was at pains to keep from making direct moral judgments on his characters, but permitted the reader to form his own judgment on the basis of the evidence presented by the characters' actions and speech. In effect, the new realism of the 1920s meant a more self-conscious concern for craftmanship as well as a broader choice of subject matter than the earlier sentimentalized and genteel realistic fiction would allow. Even the romance fiction of Mazo de la Roche and Thomas Raddall was not unaffected by realism: in one way, by dispensing with the sentimentalism which also cluttered so much regionalist fiction (whether realistic or romantic) Miss de la Roche and Raddall were able to use realism to give accurate pictures of the worlds they depicted and thereby to raise the reputation of romance fiction.

Naturalism was a philosophy of scientific determinism in which the individual was motivated not by his own free will (or by the free will endowed in him by God) but by the forces of his biological makeup and his social environment. Grove, Knister, Sinclair Ross, and Callaghan certainly used a number of devices associated with literary naturalism, but in none of their stories do we find a character totally at the mercy of his heredity and environment. Indeed, they seemed to be taking the Darwinian ideas of biological evolution and the Spencerian notions about the survival of the fittest in the social jungle and juxtaposing these with human will, reason, and endurance.

In literary criticism, too, there were new movements. Well into the 1940s the most respected criticism was made by academics whose concepts had come from an earlier time: among these, Pelham Edgar's chapter on "English-Canadian Literature" in the *Cambridge History of English Literature,* Vol. XIV (1916) and Ray Palmer Baker's *A History of English-Canadian Literature to the Confederation* (1920) are good illustrations of the nineteenth-century historical and biographical approach to literature. Logan and French's *Highways of Canadian Literature* (1924), on the other hand, is an example of the excesses of pigeon-holing and of treating a colonial literature as if it contained the glories of the Elizabethan age. The three critics who helped change not only literary criticism but the teaching and the writing of literature were A.J.M. Smith, W.L. Collin, and E.K. Brown.

Smith called for higher critical standards and artistic craftsmanship equal to that expected in British and American literature. His criterion was not the Canadianness of a work but its artistry. He attacked poets who wrote of the "far north and the wild west and the picturesque east, seasoning well with allusions to the Canada goose, fir trees, maple leaves, snowshoes, northern lights, etc".[13] At the same time, Smith called for a work of art which would be both "successful and obscene", and for a philosophical criticism which would clarify the framework in which Canadian poets were working. Collin was the first critic to use symbolist terminology in order to criticize the New Poetry in Canada as exemplified in *New Provinces* (1936), an anthology that contained selections by Pratt, Smith, F. R. Scott, Dorothy Livesay, A. M. Klein, and

8

Robert Finch. E. K. Brown applied the best nineteenth-century standards to the evaluation of our poetry and fiction, and was instrumental in developing a terminology for the criticism of the novel. These men were by no means working alone, as even the most cursory survey of *The Canadian Forum* during the 1930s will indicate. Moreover, younger critics like Northrop Frye, Desmond Pacey, and Marshall McLuhan were beginning their criticism during the 1940s, but the impact of these three was to be felt in the years after World War II.

Out of the critical discussions of the inter-War decades there developed a dispute about the cosmopolitan-metaphysical and native-realist traditions of Canadian poetry. For years, A.J.M. Smith had been playing with these categories (see his "Rejected Preface"[14] to *New Provinces*). Then in 1943 he made the classification explicit, and a little too neat, in his Preface to *The Book of Canadian Poetry*. In the first group he placed himself; in the second he placed Raymond Knister. But a problem arose: where would one place Dorothy Livesay, whose poetry is a mixture of both traditions? Smith's theory provoked from John Sutherland a different kind of anthology, *Other Canadians, An Anthology of the New Poetry in Canada, 1940-1946* (1947), and a Preface that stressed North American diction and the open forms defended by William Carlos Williams, and practiced by three younger poets, Irving Layton, Louis Dudek, and Raymond Souster. The basis of the dispute, however, could not always be determined according to politics, literary friendships and quarrels, or even poetic practice. Significantly, both Smith and Sutherland later modified their extreme stances on this polarity. Perhaps, in fact, the distinguishing mark of Canadian writers was their ability to effect a compromise between the cosmopolitan-native poles and to be genuinely eclectic. One sees this at work in Pratt's ability to be both learned and colloquial; in Smith's ability to shift between the seventeenth-century metaphysical effects and the Group-of-Seven northern landscapes; in Sandwell's ease in either the drawing room or the hunting shack; in Klein's allusions to the Jewish past and to the French-Canadian present; in Dorothy Livesay's ability to be elegiac or syncopated.

The period covered by this Anthology closes at a point when three critics summed up their views of Canadian poetry. In 1943 E. K. Brown published *On Canadian Poetry*, a survey of the work of Lampman, Duncan Campbell Scott, and Pratt. Brown's introductory chapter on "The Problem of A Canadian Literature" is so perceptive that it has yet to be superseded, in spite of further studies of that problem. An earlier version of that chapter is included in this Anthology. In the same year, A.J.M. Smith published his important anthology, *The Book of Canadian Poetry*, which quickly became the standard text in university courses where a few hardy academic pioneers attempted to lay the groundwork for a systematic evaluation of Canadian writing. Smith's 1926 call for a critic of broad vision seemed to have been answered by Brown's book, Smith's own Preface, and Northrop Frye's lengthy discussion of Smith's anthology, a review which attempted to see patterns and motifs characteristic of the poetic mind of the country. Unfortunately for prose fiction, there was not and still is not a satisfactory anthology nor a thorough critical evaluation of fiction writing, although there were signs through the 1960s of growing critical interest in individual writers and general fictional patterns.

To assess the achievements of the poets, novelists, and critics between 1914 and 1945 is not the simplest task. The younger writers of this era did, as we have seen, rebel against much of what they considered wrong, or Victorian, in the work of their immediate predecessors in Canada. Thus, they not only freed themselves of what they thought was an unusable past but they also forced themselves out into a world of new literary movements and more modern writers. Two of their achievements stem from those exercises of rebellion and search. They brought the language, form, and content of Canadian literature and criticism up to date with other national literatures. They also shaped those new influences so that they could be used to talk about important issues of Canadian and international life. Thus, for example, Knister in "Poisons" and Raddall in *Winter's Tale* explore some effects of World War I on Canada and Canadians. F. R. Scott imagines an even more frightening kind of conflict in "Armageddon". E. J. Pratt, Sinclair Ross, and Anne Marriott, among others, agonize over the hardships of the Depression. In "Lorca" Dorothy Livesay responds to the shooting of the Spanish poet during his country's Civil War. A. M. Klein suffers through the persecutions of the Jews by the Nazis in World War II. E. J. Pratt wonders in "Myth and Fact" when in the twentieth century "fact" became harder to understand than "myth". All these writers, furthermore, register their loneliness and confusion as they face those and other contemporary problems.

Beyond these themes, however, there are five characteristics in this literature which we must consider: the metaphysical background; the predominant techniques; the use of landscape; the apprenticeship theme; and the duality in the Canadian attitude towards itself. For it is in their handling of these characteristics between 1914 and 1945 that the Canadian writers showed most clearly both their modernism and their continued participation as Canadians in the evolution of several traditional aspects of our literature.

One background element, somewhat nebulous but nonetheless pervasive, is the metaphysical framework in which Canadian writers have habitually worked. This is the liberal tradition. This phrase has many connotations and certainly different uses in discussions of politics than it has in discussions of culture. Liberalism was the dominant world-view in Canada in the late nineteenth and early twentieth centuries: it was an optimistic view of man, asserting that he was by nature good, and explaining evil as a social force which could be eradicated from society by rational principles, especially when applied to education, technology, and economics. Since the widespread acceptance of liberalism paralleled the advances made in the biological and chemical sciences, many nineteenth-century men associated liberalism with progress in the biological, social, economic, and cultural spheres. The liberal view of history saw civilization ascending, stage by stage, towards the earthly utopia of the twentieth century. But world wars, concentration camps, bigger bombs, and disorder in the streets are not that utopia, and consequently liberalism has been blamed for producing catastrophes. This is of course a simplification of a very complex cultural movement which is perhaps the most influential tradition to develop out of Renaissance Christian beliefs of man and society.

Among those Canadians in the later nineteenth century who espoused liberalism were not only politicians such as Edward Blake and Sir Wilfrid Laurier but writers such as Charles G. D. Roberts and Ralph Connor. In contrast to the earlier acceptance of liberalism, Canadian writers of the 1920s to 1940s reflected their dissatisfaction with this view of society. The older men like Sandwell retained their liberalism to the end of their lives; as committed liberals, however, Sandwell and Underhill always criticized the directions in which liberalism moved. Neither denied the existence of evil nor saw liberalism as a general panacea for all ills, nor did they ever become deceived by the excesses of flag-day rhetoric. Among their contemporaries, Pratt always tempered his liberalism with his Christian belief. Grove's tragic vision, on the other hand, was not a specifically liberal nor Christian one.

The younger writers questioned liberalism in stronger terms, probably because the Depression occurred during their formative years. Callaghan and Smith rejected liberalism for more conservative opinions of man's nature and his society. Neither was orthodox in his religion, but both accepted a Christian framework as a means of defining human dilemmas. F. R. Scott and Dorothy Livesay, whose fathers were good post-Victorian liberals, made an almost logical move towards socialism, but their emphasis was less on doctrinaire politics than on the humanitarianism which Canadian socialism, like British Fabianism, borrowed from its nineteenth-century evangelical protestant background. The only position which Canadian writers were not attracted to was an extreme right-wing stance.

The most prevalent technique which writers experimented with was the use of the "fragment", or brief piece. Again and again, poets such as Isabella Valency Crawford and James Reaney, Mrs. Moodie and Leonard Cohen, short story writers such as Leacock and Margaret Laurence, and essayists such as Haliburton and Marshall McLuhan have shown their preference for an organization which may be termed fragmented or mosaic. Their success with these forms meant that they were often able to make a virtue out of what might easily have been an artistic defect. Among poems manifesting these techniques are Pratt's *Towards the Last Spike*, Dorothy Livesay's *Day and Night*, and Anne Marriott's *The Wind Our Enemy*. Grove, Callaghan, MacLennan, and Mazo de la Roche have used this technique in their novels.

The other prominent technique was the documentary style — again, the Canadian writer has found this style compatible since colonial days although the term itself is of recent origin. The documentary approach lovingly records things as they are: Goldsmith's early Nova Scotian village, Roberts' New Brunswick countryside, Sara Jeannette Duncan's late nineteenth-century Elgin, Knister's rural Ontario, Callaghan's and Souster's mid-town Toronto, Sinclair Ross's drought-ridden Prairies, Ethel Wilson's West Coast cities and forests; all these settings capture the feeling of a particular time and place. Indeed, some of the most notable Canadian successes in the arts, from Mrs. Moodie's *Roughing it in the Bush* (1952) to the creations of the National Film Board and the CBC, have used this technique. The mixing of fact and fiction, or treating fiction as fact, or vice-versa, is of course a characteristic of realism, and is not unrelated to the widespread use of pictorial and photographic effects in nineteenth-century writing. The documentary is also related to the chronicle, another fictional form which Canadian writers as different as Grove and Raddall have used in order to send their protagonists on psychic journeys of identity.

Landscape remained a prominent element in our writing; Canadians were still aware of the hundreds of miles of trees, swamps, and barrens between them and the north pole. The sense of awesome space was there too, not only to the north, but in the oceans, on the prairie horizons, and on any highway. In Pratt and Grove we see it treated in a grand, cosmic way, as a force against which human skills can be pitted. The imagists and symbolists were still fascinated by the surfaces of the northern world, even though they gave a twentieth-century sensibility to their vision by the use of contemporary biological, geological, and technological imagery. But the poets of the 1920s and 1930s no longer viewed the natural world as embodying an immanent, benevolent spirit: while Lampman could borrow this notion from Wordsworth, Lampman's successor in Ontario, Raymond Knister, did not see nature this way. For many poets the landscape still had a mythological function, either to suggest a private, poetic interior (as in Dorothy Livesay) or to suggest social patterns (as in Pratt and F. R. Scott). However it was used, landscape still retained its regional associations for most Canadian poets.

A dominant theme in the fiction of the age was the apprenticeship or education pattern. Many stories and novels treated the growth of the adolescent, or young adult, or immigrant as he confronted new experiences. This pattern also appeared in the writings of McCulloch, Mrs. Moodie, and Sara Jeannette Duncan, and continues to preoccupy such writers as Ethel Wilson, W. O. Mitchell, and Mordecai Richler. A similar theme was the innocent's awareness of frustration, evil, and death in the world. A third related theme was the quest pattern. Curiously enough, exile was not a prominent theme, in spite of Callaghan's, Glassco's, Knister's, and Grove's life-experiences. The protagonist's destiny, moreover, was seen in terms of his society, rather than outside of it, so that if there was temporary alienation or exile, the protagonist returned to his society or family, instead of lighting out for the territory and staying there. Callaghan's *They Shall Inherit the Earth* (1936) is a good illustration of the way these themes are worked out. Furthermore, in stressing the importance of choice in their protagonist's lives, the writers associated the choice with sacrifice of personal things for a larger good: one finds Pratt, Callaghan, Sinclair Ross, Grove, and Raddall making this point frequently.

Perhaps the most complex and persistent element in the Canadian psyche is the awareness of dualities and the need to live with them. One can point to the history of Canada, as does R. E. Watters,[15] to find our society rife with polarities, of which the pulls between the United States and Great Britain are the best known; or within Canada, to the French-English, east-west, federal-provincial tensions. There is a duality in the two predominant views of modern man, the liberal-humanist (which derives from Western religious beliefs) and the Marxist-deterministic (which stems from certain social and scientific theories of the last century). Finally, the most puzzling duality — the persistence of those negative Canadian definitions of ourselves, usually in terms of our closest neighbour. This seems to be the most frustrating game of all. But it turns out to be not anti-Americanism (which only the Americans can play), but the least non-American factor in the Canadian psyche. Perhaps, as Hugh MacLennan once argued, we respond the way we do because our founding groups — French, English loyalist, Scots — all found themselves on the losing side a long time ago.[16]

Applying the negative approach, then, we find the following. We do not have a sense of impending catastrophe about to overwhelm the Western world, nor do we pessimistically believe that pollution and population growth will swamp us. We have never found an enemy we could turn into a monster. Because we framed no infallible national dreams, we have experienced no disillusioning nightmares when things go sour. We have had no revolution, and, despite the Rebellions of 1837 and 1885, we have had no civil disruptions such as Ireland, for instance, has experienced. No matter how seriously the two language-groups have disagreed, French-English tensions have not turned into a full-scale racial conflict. American stereotypes such as the Crocketts, the cowboys, and the gangsters which entertain us do not belong to us for purposes of identity. Rather, compare them with the Champlains, the Mounties, and the Maurice Richards who have impressed themselves on the Canadian consciousness. Or compare American responses to Chicago 1968 with Canadian responses to October 1970. Even that traumatic event failed to produce mythic figures in either the unfortunate victim or in the romantic terrorists, and the journalists have yet to convince us that we all passed beyond innocence and smugness at that time. Indeed, the very lack of immoderate actions as the outcome of that tense month is typically Canadian. And when we turn to our literature we find these dualities — whether explicit or implicit — reflected in Haliburton, Sara Jeannette Duncan, Leacock, Raddall, Klein, Birney, MacLennan, Richler, and Margaret Avison.

Robert Weaver, in reviewing *Callaghan's Short Stories* (1959),[17] noted that the stories were quieter, more human, less optimistic, than most American fiction; he used Callaghan's stories as evidence that Canadians are far less hopeful about altering circumstances than Americans, and Weaver attributed this to our European way of accepting life. Here, then, is another duality — or an ambivalent strength. Even if we prefer to avoid that term *optimistic* with its vague philosophical connotations, there is an openness about the Canadian spirit, a freshness of vision, to be found in our writing. It is a feeling that there are still possibilities in our lives and that there is a future before us: not a dream to be made real, but a way to be traced out, step by step, in an almost matter-of-fact attitude. The writers in this Anthology, like earlier and later Canadian writers, have a quality of temperate fortitude which is perhaps their most unique Canadian quality of all.

## Footnotes

[1] The best available literary histories are Desmond Pacey, *Creative Writing in Canada*, 2nd edition (Toronto: Ryerson, 1961); and Carl Klinck (ed.), *Literary History of Canada* (Toronto: University of Toronto Press, 1965).

[2] Donald Creighton, *Dominion of the North* (Toronto: Macmillan, 1957), p. 486. I am indebted to Creighton's work for the historical background used in this Introduction.

[3] Frank Underhill, "The Close of an Era: Twenty-five Years of Mr. Mackenzie King", in *In Search of Canadian Liberalism* (Toronto: Macmillan, 1960), p. 118.

[4] Creighton, *op. cit.*, p. 487.

[5] B. K. Sandwell, *The Canadian Peoples* (Toronto: Oxford, 1941), pp. 118-19.

[6] Louis Dudek, "The Role of the Little Magazines in Canada", *The Canadian Forum*, XXXVIII (July 1958), p. 76. Also reprinted in Louis Dudek and Michael Gnarowski's *The Making of Modern Poetry in Canada* (Toronto: Ryerson, 1967), p. 206.

[7] Quoted by Leo Kennedy in "The Future of Canadian Literature", in *The Making of Modern Poetry in Canada*, p. 36. First printed in *The Canadian Mercury* (December 1928).

[8] John Murray Gibbon, "Rhymes With and Without Reason", in *The Making of Modern Poetry in Canada*, p. 20. First printed in *The Canadian Bookman* (January 1919).

[9] Charles G. D. Roberts, "A Note on Modernism", in *Open House*, ed. by William Arthur Deacon and Wilfred Reeves (Ottawa: Graphic Publishers, 1931), pp. 23-24.

[10] Leo Kennedy, "The Future of Canadian Literature", in *The Making of Modern Poetry in Canada*, p. 37.

[11] The Imagist Manifesto is reprinted in Glenn Hughes, *The Imagist Movement* (London: Bowes & Bowes, 1960), pp. 39-40.

[12] Useful discussions of Symbolism will be found in Arthur Symons, *The Symbolist Movement in Literature* (London: Heinemann, 1899); W. B. Yeats, "The Symbolism of Poetry" from *Essays and Introductions* (London: Macmillan, 1961); and Edmund Wilson, *Axel's Castle* (New York: Scribner's, 1931).

[13] A.J.M. Smith, "Wanted — Canadian Criticism", *Canadian Forum*, VIII (April 1928), p. 600. Also reprinted in *The Making of Modern Poetry in Canada*, p. 32.

[14] A.J.M. Smith, "A Rejected Preface", *Canadian Literature*, No. 24 (Spring 1965), pp. 6-9.

[15] R. E. Watters, "A Special Tang: Stephen Leacock's Canadian Humour", *Canadian Literature*, No. 5 (Summer 1960), p. 25.

[16] Hugh MacLennan, "The Canadian Character", in *Cross-Country* (Toronto: Collins, 1949), pp. 9-10.

[17] Robert Weaver, "Stories by Callaghan", *Canadian Literature*, No. 2 (Autumn 1959), p. 70.

# B. K. Sandwell

*Bernard Keble Sandwell (1876-1954) was born in Ipswich, England, raised in Canada, and educated at Upper Canada College, where Stephen Leacock was one of his teachers. After his graduation from the University of Toronto in 1897, Sandwell began a literary career which for its variety has been equalled by few writers in this country. He was dramatic editor for the Montreal* Herald *from 1905 to 1911 and editor of* The Financial Times *during the war years. From 1919 to 1923, while he taught economics at McGill, he was active in organizing The Canadian Authors' Association and publishing* The Canadian Bookman. *He was head of the Queen's University English Department from 1923 to 1925. Finally, from 1932 to 1951, Sandwell, as Editor-in-Chief of* Saturday Night, *turned it into one of the nation's most influential journals. Among numerous honours bestowed on him was his election in 1925 as a Fellow of the Royal Society of Canada. Sandwell's literary essays can be found in* The Privacity Agent and Other Modest Proposals *(1928) and a posthumous collection edited by Robertson Davies,* The Diversions of Duchesstown and Other Essays *(1955).*

*Canada between the two world wars was a society ripe for the moralist and satirist, and Sandwell, like his friend Leacock, provided through his essays a jaunty, sometimes flippant, but always elegant, analysis of the manners of those decades. Because his satire depicts human nature through its social relationships, this mode permits a writer's contemporaries as well as future readers to accept him as a pleasant entertainer and, ironically, to reject him as a serious critic of their attitudes. Nevertheless, Sandwell's essays on upper-middle-class life isolate the two chief objects of his attack: the pretensions of a provincial society whose notions of culture are second-hand imports from England and the United States; and the indiscriminate acceptance of materialistic values as promoted by the businessman, the booster, and the educationalist.*

*Sandwell uses techniques which are characteristically Leacockian, surely his tribute to the older man's works.*[1] *Sandwell's essays have a gentle, ironic tone, and, partly critical, partly sympathetic attitude to the objects under investigation. His essays often approach the sketch or short story — as in the Duchesstown Diversions — in their use of narrative, characterization, and dialogue, and tend to unfold around a key metaphor. The Sandwell* persona *(sometimes known as Charles Charteris) is a brother to Leacock's* personae, *the informal, apparently naive man who sees deeper* into human nature than he admits. The persona is intelligent and imaginative enough to recognize the value of culture, even with its pretentiousness, while at the same time, he yearns for the pleasures of the golf course and the fishing hole. In short, this Canadian persona has the ability to resolve conflicts of interest and of values and, in fact, is Sandwell's means of impressing an implied ethical norm on his readers.

Despite his deference to Leacock, Sandwell is not merely an imitator of his mentor; his philosophical point of view is that of the "liberal humanist",[2] to use Robertson Davies' phrase. Sandwell referred to himself as a nineteenth-century man in The Gods in Twilight.[3] Thus, he implied his acceptance of liberal assumptions about individualism and progress, although near the end of his life he was unhappy about the drift of western democracies towards authoritarianism. Such attitudes shape his ironic and pragmatic views: he is an observer who is conservative enough to retain what is valuable, and flexible enough to question and reject those systems of thought or action which obscure the truth. According to Brandon Conron, Sandwell's norm was

> "the good old days", his own role that of laudator temporis acti. Sandwell's ideal is not to be found in any one era, however; it is rather that utopia where reason, common sense, and justice prevail. It is an ideal implied rather than described, and it lurks behind his every incisive criticism of twentieth century life.[4]

### Footnotes

[1]David Legate describes in his Stephen Leacock (Toronto: Doubleday, 1970), pp. 49, 61, how Bernard Sandwell had once tried to dissuade Leacock from publishing the pieces which were to become Literary Lapses, but later helped Leacock find a Montreal publisher for Sunshine Sketches.
[2]Robertson Davies, Introduction to Sandwell's Diversions of Duchesstown and Other Essays (Toronto: Dent, 1955), p. xi.
[3]B. K. Sandwell, The Gods in Twilight (Vancouver: University of British Columbia Publications, 1948), p. 8.
[4]Brandon Conron, "Essays and Autobiography" in Literary History of Canada (Toronto: University of Toronto Press, 1965), p. 613.

# The Boom

I was back in Duchesstown the other day. I noted a perceptible change in the atmosphere of the place — the kind of change one might observe in a tortoise suffering from a mild form of scarlet fever. The inhabitants seemed to move a little more briskly, with a keener look in their eyes. In the market-place, however, the agriculturists from the surrounding country looked as depressed as ever, so I gathered that whatever was happening was purely municipal and did not affect the price of potatoes. I was right.

There is a boom on in Duchesstown. A real-estate boom. It is the sixth since Confederation. You never could buy a house in Duchesstown for less than forty times its net annual rental; and now you can't buy one for seventy times. The Duchesstowners will rent their houses for almost nothing (they have to, or leave them empty, which is bad for the plumbing), but they will not sell them at any price that has any relation to their income-producing value. It is part of the creed of the Duchesstowner that Duchesstown will one day be one of the great industrial and commercial centres of the Dominion, and that when that great day comes the owners of property in Duchesstown will at last enter into their reward. Meanwhile they complain bitterly that there is no market for Duchesstown real estate. They are right. Nobody will buy property there, at the Duchesstown prices, except Duchesstowners, and they already have all that they can carry, and a bit more. Outsiders will not take on house property which, if continuously rented to the best possible tenants, would bring a net return of three per cent on the purchase price.

The boom seems to be based on the fact that the railway which runs through the far corner of the municipal area of Duchesstown, and is connected with the inhabited part by a fleet of taxicabs, has recently put on an additional fast train. This train, like all other trains, stops at Duchesstown to allow the engine to be wiped down and the passengers to buy buns and coffee at the railway restaurant. Its users are mostly through passengers between the Atlantic ports and the Upper Lakes territory. But the facts remain that it does stop at Duchesstown, that it is a nice fast train with lots of chair-cars and a diner, and that it certainly adds materially to the facilities for getting into (and out of) the city. Hence the boom.

I heard about it from my aunt. She wrote asking me to come up for a week-end. Not being very busy, and the Montreal golf-links being still very wet, I went, and arrived early Thursday afternoon. Contrary to custom, my aunt met me with her own car.

"We are going for a little spin round the town," she said, as she rescued me from the fourteen taxicab drivers who were fighting for the other two Duchesstown passengers.

"Show me all the changes," I said. "You know I haven't been here for over a year."

"Yes," said my aunt. "That corner there is where they are going to build the new Presbyterian Church for the people who broke off from the Old Central Presbyterian on account of its going into Union. We have two new churches this year — both splits. There is Mrs. Willie Calhoun's new garage; I see it's closed, so I expect the instalment people have seized the car again. And there is the new Lotus Blossom Tea Room, upstairs over the typewriter shop. They tell me that the theological students and the girls from St. Adela's dance there till one in the morning. I am afraid Duchesstown is changing greatly, and not always for the better."

"Is it the tea or the lotuses that does it?" I asked, in genuine curiosity. But my aunt, while an observer and recorder of social phenomena, is not a student of their inner meaning. She paid no attention to my enquiry.

"What I really brought you out here to see is my three dear little cottages on the waterfront. You remember them? There they are, behind the two big elms. You know, I've been trying for ever so long to sell them for eighteen thousand for the lot, and I want your advice. I'm beginning to think that's far too low. I was talking to the Hon. Mr. McKeltie the other day — our member, you know — and he says the reason why

17

Duchesstown property is so hard to sell is because we property-owners ask so little for it that people think we have no faith in our own city. He was all through the Calgary boom, you know, before he came back to Duchesstown, and he says that what started the boom was the way the Calgary people put up the prices on their own land until everybody else began to think it must really be worth something."

My aunt paused here and sighed, and I thought I heard the chauffeur sigh with her. And I recalled that some years ago a very diplomatic young salesman, who was supposed to be related by marriage to the Hon. Mr. McKeltie and so to have access to all sorts of cabinet secrets, had unloaded on the people of Duchesstown practically the whole of a township about nineteen miles north-east of Calgary, on which they have been paying wild-land taxes ever since. I remembered that Uncle John had been one of the most hopeful investors. The chauffeur, I now surmised, was in the deal too.

"There they are," said my aunt. "Aren't they beautiful? I really think I ought to ask twenty-four thousand. I don't believe it's patriotic to ask less." And she looked questioningly at me.

"Well," I said, "perhaps if you could get Lawren Harris to paint 'em. . . . Yes, they certainly are very picturesque. But do you people here buy your real estate on an aesthetic valuation? Because we don't in Montreal. You should see our latest apartment house on the Mountain. Looks like a cross between a garbage incinerator and a gasometer, but the best people are flocking into it, and I hear the contractor made half a million. What rent do your works of art here stand you in?"

"Thirty dollars a month each. But what has that to do with it?"

"And how much do they cost you for repairs and taxes?"

"Oh, I don't do any repairs. The tenant is supposed to look after that. But — "

I do not often snort at my aunt, but at this point I had to. The Duchesstowners, or some of them, in order to kid themselves into the conviction that they are really getting bank interest on their money invested in local property, have adopted the policy of contracting in their leases that the tenant, instead of the landlord, shall do all the repairs. The rent is naturally a little lower than in an ordinary lease, but the landlord fondly assures himself that he is getting all of it, minus only the municipal taxes. He goes on imagining this until, more or less simultaneously, the tenant moves out and the house begins to fall down — for it need hardly be said that no tenant ever really does any repairs. Why should he? He pins or sews or wires the house together so that it will last until the day he gets out, and that is all. The landlord has then to spend about a third of the value of the house fixing it up. Usually he finds seven or eight leaks in the roof, which the tenant has "repaired" by the efficient method of putting bath-tubs under them to catch the drip. Duchesstown is one of the few places where second-hand portable tin bath-tubs, such as the British officers are reputed to have used in the Boer War, have a regular market value, especially in early spring.

"But the city is growing," objected my aunt. "Two new ministers of religion and their families; and a new professor at the Theological College; and a new grocer; and a new undertaker."

"On the other hand," I objected, "two of your banks have merged, closing one branch and removing one manager and one clerk. And the wife of one of the other ministers has left him and joined the Unitarians."

18

"Oh, but she doesn't count," said my aunt joyfully. "We fired him immediately for letting his wife join the Unitarians, and now we have a new man with quite a large family. And then those additional trains — they must make some difference."

The next afternoon Uncle John was making motions towards taking me out to play golf (the Duchesstown links dry very rapidly), when my aunt intervened. "You cannot take him this afternoon," she said very positively.

"But my dear . . . "

"I told you that one of the chief reasons why I wanted him here this week-end was for him to attend Dr. McGeoghegan's lecture on Savonarola. If you think your wretched golf . . . "

As we motored across the park to the Theological College, my aunt became so apologetic and consolatory that I feared it was going to be even worse than I had supposed.

"There will be *quite* a large number of lantern slides," she said, "and he is *supposed* to get through by six o'clock so that people can get home to dinner. Even if he begins promptly at half-past four the lecture can hardly last more than an hour and a quarter, taking out the time for the pictures. But I was determined the poor dear man should have an audience. I have personally telephoned to thirty-seven women and made them promise to attend, and several of them are going to bring their husbands. I knew I should never be able to get John to go, so I thought of you. And really a distinguished stranger adds even more to the appearance of the audience than one's own local husband. You see, he is a terribly bad lecturer, and for the last three years they haven't allowed him in these extension courses at all, and they say the students won't go to his regular courses, and the poor man is getting quite depressed. I do feel so sorry for him. . . . And besides, I think if we can only get him in a really good humour I can sell him my three little cottages on the water-front."

The Rev. Dr. McGeoghegan was a small man with sparse hair, sparse whiskers, and sparse ideas. His voice was reminiscent of that of a grackle in early spring. It developed early that he had a moderately high opinion of Savonarola (whom he pronounced with an accent on each of the o's, so that it sounded like a new brand of soap), and that this was due to a brief visit to Florence, which had convinced him that Savonarola's estimate of the immorality of Florentine art was perfectly sound. He had a large audience, most of whom looked at my aunt in a reproachful way as if she were in some manner responsible for their troubles, which perhaps she was.

At the beginning of the lecture Dr. McGeoghegan announced that owing to a misunderstanding on the part of the janitor the room had not been darkened, and it would therefore be necessary to defer the pictures until the close of the lecture, by which time nature might have performed what the janitor had neglected. The audience therefore resigned itself to an hour or so of unmitigated Savonarola. But they were too optimistic. Dr. McGeoghegan had had this lecture on Savonarola in his system for several years, and it had grown like a cancer. This might well be his only opportunity for getting it out. He began by giving a history of the Renaissance. This had already been covered by four preceding lectures in the same course, but I subsequently learned that these four lecturers had all more or less approved of the Renaissance, whereas Dr.

19

McGeoghegan disapproved of it entirely. This was followed by a synopsis of a novel by George Eliot, of which the lecturer also disapproved.

The body of the lecture, however, consisted of the reading of a great number of passages of the most fervid kind from Savonarola's sermons. I could see as he read them that he felt himself to be a second Savonarola, debarred from the brilliant career and glorious martyrdom of the first only by the fact that the age was not suited to great preaching. But in actual fact there were several other things that kept the Rev. McGeoghegan from a Savonarolian career, and would have kept him even if he had lived in Florence under the Medici. One of them was his complete inability to put his feelings into his voice. He was obviously very fond of these sonorous utterances, but he read them like the town-crier reading the list of lost-and-found articles for the day — and at the end of a hard day of town-crying at that. Nor was the limitation merely physical. The poor man was a mass of inhibitions, which prevented him from giving free vent to any of his aspirations. He wanted to be a Savonarola, but still more he wanted to attract as little attention as possible, to be the perfect norm of a theological professor. In college politics he was relentlessly opposed to anybody who exhibited the slightest sign of conspicuous qualities; he was the natural leader of the ultra-professorial group in the Faculty, or rather (for they needed no leading, since they never moved forward) he stood in the forefront of that faction, face set rigidly against all progress and indeed all change.

While these reflections were passing through my mind, the sermons of Savonarola squeaked on. They croaked until ten minutes to six. They were still grating on the atmosphere at six. At ten minutes past six the janitor, who was up in the gallery waiting to manipulate the pictures, was making loud noises with benches and things, and trying to get the lecturer's attention by turning on the lantern light. And still Savonarola squawked on. At six-twenty a lady in the back row tried to sneak out, and would have succeeded if she had not dropped her umbrella. At six-thirty Savonarola ended, the lights went out, and the pictures began.

It had been Dr. McGeoghegan's intention to do quite a lot of talking about each picture, and he had a large wand with which to point out the interesting features. Each picture was to stay on until he rapped with this wand on the platform. But the janitor was not having any. He had another lecture to prepare for at eight o'clock, and he had a grievance about the pictures anyhow, for nobody had told him that there were going to be pictures at the McGeoghegan lecture until it was too late to prepare for them; and he was very hungry. I should have explained earlier that Dr. McGeoghegan, in addition to his other disqualifications for the role of Savonarola, had a form of asthma which necessitated his breaking any long sentence in two in order to gasp for air. The janitor, of course, knew all about this peculiarity, but pretended to think that these pauses were an indication that the good doctor had finished talking about the picture on the screen and wanted another one. The lecturer at first tried to regain control of the proceedings by rapping frantically on the platform with the wand; but this merely enabled the janitor to move on to a third and then a fourth picture.

The pictures were dim, the lantern was poor, the hall was very dark. All around us were the sounds of people escaping stealthily from their long imprisonment and hastening homewards to their overdue supper. Duchesstown sups at six-thirty sharp.

The Rev. Dr. McGeoghegan, absorbed in his duel of wills with the janitor, knew nothing of their flight. My aunt groaned, but not audibly enough for anybody to hear except myself.

"There won't be a soul left but us if he doesn't close up soon," she said in my ear. "And he will think there hasn't been anybody else here the whole time." The lantern meanwhile was going through the history of Florence like a Cook's tour of Americans from the Middle West, only faster. Dr. McGeoghegan was pointing out the significance of the fourth picture back from the one now on the screen. The Principal of the College tiptoed out, kicking my hat into the aisle. I was too depressed to care.

About seven the lights came on. There remained the Principal's wife (whom he had forbidden to leave), my aunt, myself, and in the gallery the janitor. The lecturer came waveringly and tentatively down from the platform, like somebody coming out of chloroform. He grasped my aunt by the hand. When he was not using pulpit English, his voice had a rich, almost Highland accent, and his sibilants hissed fiercely.

"I deed not realice that there were s-so few people pres-sent," he said. "It is var-ry dis-scouraching, iss it not?"

My aunt fairly purred with sympathy, and a long conversation ensued, of which I could make out only that the good Dr. McGeoghegan was getting more and more mollified, until he finally almost beamed. The words "cottages" and "balance on mortgage" drifted into the conversation, which ended in the lecturer being driven to his house in my aunt's car. . . .

At dinner the roast was badly overdone. At first we supposed that that was the reason for Uncle John's atrocious temper. But we learned better.

"That man McGeoghegan of yours is a pestilential nuisance," he sputtered after a while. "You know that McKeltie and I have been trying to round up the Duchesstown holdings in McKeltie's Calgary subdivision, so as to be able to turn over the whole block to a new golf club. We offered everybody concerned a nice little fair profit; but your old brute of a McGeoghegan — "

"John, I will not have you speak in that way of an ordained clergyman, even if he is only a theological lecturer."

"Well, your McGeoghegan, then, must have got wind of what we were up to. Anyhow he holds us up for twenty-five thousand for his miserable lots for which he only gave ten, and we were offering him fifteen. And to-day McKeltie and I decided to give the old skinflint his price, and believe me I'm mad about it. It takes all the velvet off my share of the job, and you won't get your fur coat next winter either."

"Oh, I don't know," said my aunt. "I sold him my cottages to-day for twenty-four thousand. And I could have got the whole twenty-five if you had only told me."

The Duchesstown *Advocate-Register* told the story of the cottages (but not of the Calgary lots) next week under the heading: "Record Prices for Duchesstown Property; Great Real Estate Boom Now Fully Under Way; Estimated Increase in Value of All City Property Is Placed by Experts at Thirty Million Dollars."

Distinctly, there is a boom on in Duchesstown.

# Mazo de la Roche

*Mazo de la Roche (1879-1961) was born in Toronto and was raised there and in surrounding towns. After studying art for a short time, she lived for some years on a fruit and livestock farm near Clarkson, on the shores of Lake Ontario. Her cottage was on the large estate, "Benares", the model for "Jalna" in the Whiteoak series. Here she worked at her craft, writing short stories and novels. When* Jalna *won the Atlantic-Little Brown Award in 1927, her days of hardship were over and her popularity was assured thereafter. In 1929 she and her favourite cousin Caroline Clement moved to England where they lived for ten years and adopted an orphaned brother and sister. She spent the last twenty years of her life in Toronto. Miss de la Roche had one of the largest and most loyal reading publics of any modern author and is today perhaps the Canadian writer best known in Europe.*

*Her reputation rests on her series of thirteen novels chronicling the hundred years of an Anglo-Irish matriarch, Adeline Whiteoak, and her numerous descendants. This family lives at "Jalna", an English-style country estate on Lake Ontario, named after the Indian town where Adeline's husband had been posted with the British Army. The tracing of family activities and traits through several generations is a kind of fictional equivalent of the nineteenth- and twentieth-century interest in psychological and sociological investigations. Ultimately, the characters take on mythic proportions as we meet them again and again. The world of the Whiteoaks is a fictional creation on the order of the family dynasties created by John Galsworthy in* The Forsyte Saga *and William Faulkner in his Yoknapatawpha County, Mississippi stories. The CBC-TV series begun in the winter of 1972 has revived interest in the Jalna books.*

*Miss de la Roche claimed that her other novels were overlooked by the critics and readers.[1] Certainly,* Possession *(1923),* Delight *(1926), and* Growth of a Man *(1938) reveal the same careful structuring and character delineation that made the Jalna books so readable and popular. In her other stories are recurring situations which deal with the inexplicable nature of love, the daily lives of domestic animals, and the adventurous world as seen through the eyes of children.*

*What is unique in Mazo de la Roche is the erotic, sensuous style and the vigourous quality of her writing which were entirely new in Canadian fiction. It is a poetic style, moreover, in its use of animal metaphors to suggest freedom, energy, and violence. This style is her way of viewing life as a struggle, where destructive forces are in* constant conflict. At the same time, her fictional world vibrates with passions and sensations. Her writing is, in short, extremely tactile.

Mazo de la Roche could use realism when it suited her purposes, but compared to the way in which Callaghan, Grove, and Knister used realism, it seems more accurate to judge her stories within the framework of romance; that is, to see the people and the animals as types, no matter how individualized they are. Although romance tends, furthermore, to idealize human types and to see them as part of a larger pattern of life, the psychological truth of a character or situation is still evident, even if the story seems too contrived or neat. Indeed, Mazo de la Roche writes in the tradition of the well-made story: it may evoke a mood or reveal the essence of a character, but it remains faithful to the notion of plot.

Since hers is a world of violence, aggression, and destruction, the author accepts these things not merely as inexplicable, absurd, or chaotic, but as part of the pattern of life and death. In her concern for plot, then, there is a typical nineteenth-century acceptance of sequence and logic, even if the characters themselves can see no logic. For example, in "The Sacred Bullock", the white bullock holds a fascination for the boy which he himself does not understand. In ancient Mediterranean religions, the bull was a symbol of royalty and an animal sacred to the gods responsible for the storm clouds and the harvests. Moses chastized the Israelites in the desert for worshipping the golden calf, which probably represented Baal to them (Exodus XXXII:4). In this story, de la Roche, like other modern writers who have been interested in the forces represented by pagan divinities, presents an age-old situation: the mysterious attraction to an object whose claims go beyond respect and even involve death.

The dangers of writing animal stories are threefold: the author may be escaping his obligation to deal with human affairs; the animals may be too humanized and therefore neither real animals nor satisfactory emblems of human ethics (such as Aesop's animals are); or they may be sentimentalized. Mazo de la Roche skirts all these dangers, although she can describe their struggles with some feeling, as in "The Ninth Life", the story of a pregnant cat. Like Charles G. D. Roberts before her, de la Roche has observed her domesticated creatures minutely. Behind the animal story is the implicit belief that the animals share the earth with us, and that their ways should be of interest to us.

**Footnote**

[1]Useful background information will be found in the following places: Desmond Pacey, Introduction to Delight (Toronto: McClelland and Stewart, 1961). Also: Ronald Hambleton, Mazo de la Roche of Jalna (Toronto: General Publishing, 1966).

# The Sacred Bullock

Hoi! Hoi!" Young Davey shouted, as he and the dog, which was a mixture of several breeds and combined the intelligence of all of them, drove the little bullocks along the rocky path toward the pasture where they were to be fattened for market.

"Hoi! Hoi!" he shouted, even when it was not necessary, for he liked the sound of his own voice in the desolate place, and his brain was so empty that a single word like "hoi" meant much to it.

The great barren hills in the heart of Wales, that seemed to have upheaved themselves from the bowels of the earth, might have been expected to have dwarfed the figure of a man driving a dozen bullocks before him, with a dog at his heels, but they did not. He, in his heavy boots, thick corduroys, with his broad shoulders and plunging walk, looked massive, towering above the little beasts he drove, like some powerful prehistoric man. On their part they looked soft and weak, their sturdy legs not yet accustomed to the rough paths, their eyes timid as they looked over their shoulders at the dog.

Beyond and beyond, the hills reared their rocky heads, their shoulders shaggy with bracken. Beyond and beyond, they crouched and sank like receding waves. There were always the endless variety and endless monotony of the hills. Up and up the morning sun showed its face among them, lifting their veils of mist, casting their dim shadows into the valleys. In the most fertile of the valleys was the farm where young Davey worked. From this height you could see its stone walls and its two chimneys. He looked down at it and, for a moment, the faces of the two who lived there came into his mind. Then it was empty again and he shouted "Hoi, hoi!" to the bullocks and drove them along the path.

The two who lived there were a farmer named Owen and his daughter Glennys. Twenty years ago Owen had come home from the War, blinded. He had married the girl who had been waiting for him, and two years later she had died in giving birth to his daughter. All these years he had been worked for, waited on, by a married couple, but last summer the husband had strained his back. It was little he would be able to do for a long while, so young Davey came from a distant farm to help. He was so strapping, so willing, that Owen liked the sound of him about the place. He asked Glennys to tell him what the boy looked like.

"I wish you could see him," said Glennys, laughing; "he's a funny-looking boy!"

"Ugly to look at?"

"Well, not exactly, but he has a thick neck and a high head and he has tow-colored hair in curls on the top of his head and his eyelashes are almost white."

"He sounds ugly and not a bit like a Welshman."

"Oh, he's Welsh!" laughed Glennys. "He can't speak a word of English."

"I like his voice," said Owen. "I wish he spoke oftener. And I like the sound of his step."

Young Davey slept in an attic room under a roof that sloped to the floor. There was nothing but a bed in the room, and an old iron-bound chest for his clothes. He owned a quite good coat which he wore when he went to church, but the heels were always out

24

of his socks. He owned a Bible in very fine print, but he could not read. He washed himself in a shed at the back of the house. All his life he had washed with coarse yellow soap, but now Glennys gave him a piece of pink soap with a scent to it. It had only cost tuppence, but to him it seemed luxurious and he was careful not to be extravagant with it.

He was happy as he drove the little bullocks along the track. He shouted "Hoi, hoi!" loudly and felt the strength of his power over them as they ran and stumbled, not knowing what they were expected to do. Far below he saw the farmhouse, looking very grey and small. Then his mind returned to the bullocks, which were to be fattened for the market, and he called to the dog to harry them up the path to the pasture.

The pasture lay on a plateau against the side of a ruined Abbey. Owen had had the piece of sheltered rich land fenced in and the grass grew thick and strong here. A protecting hill rose on the north and the walls of the Abbey kept off the cold east wind. It was said that in olden times the monks had their garden here and that a richness had been left in the soil that would forever nourish what grew there.

"Hoi! Hoi!" Davey shouted at the little beasts and they crowded in at the gate, looking with frightened eyes at the dog who just touched their legs with his teeth.

There was one bullock that was not so obedient as the others. He turned and faced Davey with a wondering look and lowered his head, with its little coral pink bumps of horn, toward the dog. Davey had noticed him before and now he had a good look at him.

He was white, with a peculiar milky whiteness above his pink skin. The others were red, or red with a patch of white. But he was white all over and it gave him a look of purity and innocent power. There was a bunch of white curls on his crown, rather like Davey's. His tail ended in a white ringlet. Only his great liquid eyes, that seemed to see but a short way, were of a midnight blue.

"Hoi!" shouted Davey. "Hoi!" And waved his staff.

The dog barked sharp orders at the bullock. It wheeled and went after the others.

Davey could not keep his eyes off it. As it bent its massive little head to graze he stood staring at it, admiring it. It was shy but not timid. He filled his hand with its curly topknot, ran his hands over its silky sides, appraised it for the good beef it would put on to its sturdy frame. It stretched its neck, its wet pink nose following his fingers, its underlip thrust out in its instinct for sucking.

The bullocks had been bought by Owen for fattening. Twice a week he asked Davey how they were getting on.

"They're putting on the fat wonderful," said Davey. "There's a white one."

"Oh. Is he a good one?"

Davey laughed. "He's the best. He looks like a regular little — " He could not talk for laughing because Glennys was in the room and the sight of her filled him with confusion.

Christmas was past. It was January and a misty sunlight, not without warmth in it, slanted across the hills. Owen said: —

"I think I'll go up the path and see the beasts."

"He can't see them," thought Davey. "He means feel them." And he chuckled to himself.

25

"All right, Father," said Glennys. "Shall we go now? Davey could come with us, couldn't you, Davey?"

She looked so beautiful to him, standing in the dim room, with the fairness of her skin and the darkness of her hair and her large grey eyes, that his legs felt heavy and his head light. He twisted his fingers together and looked at her from under his white lashes, not able to speak.

Owen was on his feet, groping for the peg where his cap hung. He did not like being helped, so the boy and girl watched while he found it and put it on his head. He led the way through the door and along the cobbled path. At the end of it he stopped and threw up his head.

"What's that I smell?" he asked.

"Snowdrops," said Glennys. "It's wonderful how you can smell them, Father. Their scent is so faint."

Owen smiled proudly. It filled him with pride to do some things better than other people could. Glennys picked a few of the flowers and put them into his hand. He laid his other hand on her arm.

Davey led the way up the steep rough path, up and up, his strong legs springing before them, the rags dangling from his coat, the dog pressing close after him. He was so eager to show off the bullocks that he could scarcely endure to wait for Owen's slower steps. The sheep grazing on the hillside moved closer to each other, for they seldom saw so many people. A faint baa came from their midst. It came from the first lamb of the season, who stood peering between the bodies of the sheep that were a woolly barrier between him and the world.

" 'Tis a new lamb," said Davey. "The ewe dropped it yesterday. There'll be more before sundown."

The lamb cried out again, his close-curled wool shaking with the strength of his baa. Suddenly he dived under his mother and bunted the milk from her udder with his curly head. His cry had gone through Owen with the piercing sweetness of the first voice of spring.

"I wish I could see the lamb," he said.

Glennys led him on up the path. The ruin of the Abbey rose before them, the broken arch of grey stone, the crumbling tower solid against the fragility of the wintry-blue sky. Through the windows Glennys saw the little bullocks grazing in what had been the chapel.

The bullocks raised their heads and stared meditatively through the windows at the group approaching. Then, as though with calculated design, they passed through the narrow door of the chancel into the open pasture — all but one.

This was the white bullock, and he stood motionless on the delicately carved altar stone that had fallen and now lay sunk in the grass.

"Oh, lovely!" cried Glennys. "Doesn't he look lovely there?"

"Who? Where?" demanded Owen, turning his face impatiently from side to side.

"The white bullock. He's like the sacred bull of pagan times. The sacrificial bull."

"Is he getting fat?" asked Owen.

"He's best of them all," said Davey. He was smiling in pride because of the girl's surprise. He strode to the bullock and grasped him by the curly topknot and drew him toward Owen. He came docilely, stepping daintily over the grass, but his eyes were two luminous globes turning in courage and pride.

Owen passed his hands over him. "What a silky hide!" he said. "Yes, he's putting on the flesh."

"What a pity he has to be killed!" said Glennys. "He looks so lovely here. I'd like to keep him. . . . He looks sacred."

"You're a foolish girl," said Owen, pressing her arm against his side.

"The beast should be saved for breeding," muttered Davey in Owen's ear.

"Hmph, well, he just came with the lot I bought. Take me to the others."

They passed through the door and found the little herd in a russet clump among the bracken. The white bullock followed them. Even when they were far down the path he stood staring after them. He watched their movements contemplatively till they were out of his sight. Then he returned to his companions but never seemed entirely to belong to them.

The remembrance of the visit Glennys had paid to the ruin was always coming into Davey's mind. "She got a surprise, she did!" he would chuckle, and he would wonder if ever she would come to see the bullock again. He would pull and push him till he got him on the altar stone, then he would stand gazing at him in wonder and admiration.

The bullock soon learned that he was singled out for attention but he scarcely had to learn it, for he was not timid like the others. He watched for Davey's comings and pressed forward to get the hay he spread on the ground or to thrust his nose first into the bucket of meal. Davey would lead him into the chancel and strew his share on the altar because that was where he had stood on the day Glennys had praised him.

One day she showed Davey a picture in an old book of a sacred bull. His horns rose out of a chaplet of flowers, and young girls and youths, in Greek dress that showed their lovely limbs, danced in procession after him. They had musical instruments in their hands and vine leaves in their hair. Davey had never seen a book like this before. He took it reverently and, as he looked from the picture to her face and back again, a smile lighted his face and a tremor ran through him. He asked, in his Welsh tongue: —

"Was there really times like that — in the world once?"

"Of course there were!"

"I wish I'd lived then."

"Oh, Davey, you would have looked funny among the Greeks!" Then her eyes swept him appraisingly and she added — "Well, from the neck down, you'd have looked all right. Yes, the Greek tunic would have suited you."

He did not understand but he stared at the picture, trying to draw sense from it. He was ashamed of the fervor of feeling that swept over him. A rich color rose from his neck and flooded his boyish cheeks.

"I'm going to sew a patch on your coat," said Glennys, "and darn your socks."

He looked at her, startled by the fervor in him. He pushed the book into her hands and clattered up the stairs to his attic. From the chest he took his clean pair of socks that had both heels worn through, and hid them under the mattress of his bed. He found pins and pinned up the tear on his sleeve. "She'll not mend for me whatever," he said, the tears filling his eyes.

But when he hung the coat on a peg in the kitchen while he cleaned out the stable

27

she took it down and mended the tear, and when he next looked in the chest there were the socks folded together, with neat darns on the heels. He held the socks to his breast and his heart throbbed like an engine against them.

He could not thank her, but when they met in the passage he said: —

"You'd ought to come and see the white bullock, how he's growing."

"So I should," she answered, her face bright in the dim passage. "I'll come to-day."

Do you think your father will come too?" he asked timidly.

"No. He's tired. He's been out all the morning. I shall come alone."

She saw the muscles about his mouth quiver and his eyes turn away, as though he were afraid to let her see into them. She had a sudden feeling of power. Yet the power was tremulous with something strange. Ought I to go alone with Davey? she wondered. It may seem too familiar. Yet surely I can go to look at my father's beasts when he can't see them himself!

As they passed through the garden he said: —

"You ought to bring some flowers to make the bullock one of them things — what you said — for his head."

Glennys laughed. "Davey, you are romantic!"

"What's that?"

"Oh, having pretty ideas about flowers and old-time customs and all that."

"We could take some daffydils."

"We shall do no such thing."

She spoke a little sharply and there was silence between them as they mounted the steep path. But the March wind was so sportive and so scented with new growth, the clouds were so white and so flowing, that before they reached the plateau they were laughing into each other's eyes for joy in the little lambs that played all about them.

The lambs were strewn over the hillside, white and weak and gay. They broke into sudden sidewise darts. They flung out their woolly legs in an abandon of play. Forehead to forehead they tried their infant strength against each other. The sheep watched them with no maternal pride, no responsive gayety. Their cold eyes and flat pale cheeks were bent toward the grass and they forgot that they ever had been lambs.

The white bullock was not with the others that came to meet Davey.

"Where is the white bullock?" Glennys asked.

"You wait and see."

He led her into the Abbey and there, standing on the altar stone, was the massive little beast, his eyes luminous for the feed that would be strewn there, his hoof gently pawing the stone.

"I've never seen anything like it!" cried Glennys. "It's wonderful! Have you bewitched him, Davey, or has he bewitched you?"

"Hoi! Hoi!" shouted Davey to the bullock, and he strewed a little meal on the altar stone.

"How clean and white he is!" she said.

"I brush him. He's like that beast in the picture you showed me. He's sacred."

"But he's for the market."

"Don't tell your father how he thrives, will you? I'd like to keep him a little longer."

28

Glennys felt troubled as she looked at Davey standing there in his strength and his ignorance. He was like the white bullock. He was aloof and belonged to another age. They were like the lonely hills and the wind-swept stones of the Abbey. She went to the beast's side and laid her hand on his shoulder. He swung his head on his thick neck to touch her with his tongue. She saw how his little horns were growing so that they arched above his curly pate, smooth and sharp and threatening. But his eyes were gentle, she thought. As she looked into their blue-black depths, she saw no intelligence there, just an overwhelming instinct.

"Isn't it strange," she said, "how the monks once lived here? Do you ever think of them, Davey, and imagine what their life was like?"

"Monks!" he said. "Who were they?"

"Don't tell me that you haven't heard of the monks who built the Abbey?"

"I haven't heard." He looked at her dumbly, his hands clasping the smooth sickle of the bullock's horn, and she noticed how luminous his eyes were and the pulse that beat in his strong neck.

"The monks built the Abbey seven hundred years ago. They built it for worship."

"Worship?"

"Yes. Worship of God and prayer. That part out there, where the other bullocks are grazing, was the cloister."

"Did the monks live alone here? Without women?"

"Yes. They were holy men."

"Touch me," he said, moving closer to her. "Lay your hand on me — like on the bullock."

She spoke to him in a high clear voice: —

"How did you think the Abbey came to be here?"

"I though it had always been."

"But it had to be *built*!"

"Put your hand on me." He came still closer. "Like on the bullock." She could see the white glimmer of his skin under his shirt.

She turned pale and moved quickly away from him. "I made a mistake, coming up here with you," she said.

The bullock moved through the space between them and pressed through the narrow priests' door into the cloisters among the others. Glennys turned her back, trembling with fear, and walked swiftly out of the ruin. But Davey did not follow her. He stood looking after her through the broken arch of a window, till she was only a midget descending into the valley. Then he followed the bullock and laid his mouth against the place where her hand had lain on the animal's side. Tears fell from his eyes and he sought to make something clear, that he might understand, out of the confusion in his mind.

Spring had come too soon. Now, in the middle of March, winter came back for a space. The hills turned savage and bleak. The snow came down in thick flakes and was blown in drifts against the iron of the hills. When the young lambs saw it falling they knew it for their enemy and ran out bravely to meet it, stamping on it with their little hoofs, flattening the flakes into the ground. But the lambs were weak. They could not stamp all day long and, after a while, they crept under the warmth of their mothers' wool and huddled there.

The ewes watched the snow coming down for two days, standing close together, their cold eyes without apprehension or compassion for their lambs. Then they sank to their knees and the drifts began to bury them. Davey worked all day shoveling them out of the snow, dragging them up to their feet. The sweat poured from him and he took a slab of bread and cheese from his pocket and ate it, leaning on his spade.

That night the snow came down harder than ever. Davey did not wait for daylight but was out of bed in the bitter cold dawn, staring through the leaded panes of the attic into the terrible white fortifications of the hills.

Glennys had not spoken to him since the scene in the ruin, but now he clumped in his hobnailed boots to her door and rapped.

"If the sheep are to be saved," he said, "you must come and help me."

"I'll come at once," she answered.

"What is the matter?" shouted Owen from his room.

"It's the snow!" she called back. "I must go with Davey to help with the sheep."

"Oh, curse this sciatica of mine!" cried Owen. "I should be going too!"

"Don't worry, Father. We shall save them."

With a scarf wrapped round her head and neck she plodded up the hill after Davey, placing her feet in the holes his feet had made in the snow. He carried the two spades and she a basket with sandwiches in it and a thermos of cocoa. He felt a fire of strength in him as he struggled upward, knowing she was close behind. He leaped through the drifts, eager to show off his strength.

A great mound marked where the sheep huddled. Davey and Glennys ran to it and began frantically to dig. The sheep were uncovered, stretched on their sides, their pale tongues lolling, their white eyelashes motionless over their pale eyes. Sometimes they lay heaped on top of each other. Then the ones at the bottom were dead. Most of the lambs lay dead, some with noses close to the ewes' udders. There had been more than thirty lambs. Now there were just three. Davey dragged the living sheep to their feet and supported them, but they gave him no look of gratitude, or pleasure at the lambs that lived, or pity for the ones that were dead. They stood humbly, gently, waiting for the life to come back into them.

"Don't cry so," said Davey.

"I can't help it," answered Glennys. "The lambs were so sweet." She was holding the weakest of the three living ones in her arms. He was the only black one and his little black face lay on her breast. She was so hot that she had thrown back the scarf and her fine hair clung to her head in a dark mass.

Davey looked at her kneeling there in the snow and his mind was clouded and dark, like the sky overhead. His speech came thickly.

"Stop your crying, and pull your scarf on your head. You'll take cold."

She smiled a little at the authority of his words. She dried her eyes on the corner of her scarf but she did not cover her head.

"I'm so hot," she said, "I should die if I covered my head."

Davey threw down his spade and strode to her. Before she could stop him he took her scarf in his hands and drew it close over her head.

"You shall keep your hair covered!" he said thickly. As he returned to his digging, he kept on saying, "You shall keep it covered. You shall . . . "

30

They worked in silence then, digging out the sheep. The black lamb's dam was dead and no living ewe would suckle it. Perhaps it was because of its color but, weak as they were, they gave pale hatred to it out of their eyes and would not let down their milk.

At last Glennys was so tired that the spade fell from her hands. The sweat trickled down her face.

"You stop digging and drink some cocoa," said Davey. "I can finish the job. Look at the sun. There's a change coming."

A mildness was in the air. In one place, like a tunnel in the clouds, the pale sun peered through. A breeze stole up from the south. The black lamb's fleece began to curl closely.

"Yes, I must rest for a bit," she said. "My back aches. Look! The sun is really coming out."

"Rest in the stable," Davey said. "It's nice in there."

"The stable?"

He pointed, with his spade, to the ruin. "I call that the stable."

She laughed. It was the first time she had laughed that day and, when he saw her white teeth and her lips parted and the escaped black lock on her forehead, he felt the joy of her nearness almost unbearable.

She thought — "If he follows me into the Abbey I will go out at the other side. I will not be alone with him in there." With the lamb in her arms she went through the snow, which was not so deep on the plateau, into the Abbey. Here it was sheltered and the sun poured between the delicate stone arches and filled the ruin with an ethereal beauty.

Glennys laid the lamb on her skirt. She unwrapped the scarf from her head and covered the lamb with it. She had found a corner with clean straw in it and she laid her food on the carved top of a fallen column. She did not let her mind dwell on the sheep and lambs that had died but on those that had been saved. She wet her finger in the cocoa and the lamb beside her sucked it.

Then she saw the bullock appear in the narrow doorway that opened into the chancel. He stood looking in at her, the crescents of his horns bent above his curly poll, his forelegs thick and short beneath the bulk of his strong breast.

He stood staring at her in surprise. She could hear the breath blowing in his wide nostrils. He pressed through the door and she wondered if she ought to be afraid of him. There was the lamb's little head, showing above the scarf. Perhaps the bullock had it in his mind to harm the lamb.

He came closer. His glowing yet senseless eyes moved insolently in their sockets. His coat glistened, the long hair silky like fur. He stared at her and at the lamb. Now she gave a loud clear scream and struck at him with her fist.

Davey came leaping through the snow. He shouted: —

"Don't be afraid! He means no harm. Look now, he does just what I tell him!"

But the bullock pushed Davey aside with his shoulder and thrust his wet nostrils against the girl's breast. "He means no harm!" shouted Davey and caught him by the horns and swung him away.

Glennys watched the two of them wrestling together. Whether there was anger or just mischief in the bullock, she could not tell. Now he swung Davey from side to side, as though he would hurl him off. Now Davey bent the beast's proud neck and pushed him closer to the door. Now he had the upper hand. The bullock was thrust outside the Abbey. A heavy wooden bar closed the entrance.

Davey was laughing but his breath came in harsh gasps. He dropped to his knees beside Glennys. "It's a pity he frightened ye," he said, "for he means no harm."

"I wasn't frightened," she answered, "except for the lamb. That was why I screamed for you."

His love poured from his eyes and she began to rise, but he put out his hand and held her by the skirt. "Hold me," he said, "like you did the lamb. Hold me in your arms."

Glennys tore herself from him and ran out of the Abbey. She ran through the deep snow down the hillside, putting her feet into the holes made by his. "How dared he! I hate him! I hate him!" she said over and over again. Yet her anger was so mixed with love that she could not tell one from the other.

After a while Davey carried the lamb into the kitchen. He said gruffly: —

"Is the lamb to die, or will you feed it?"

"I have warm milk in a bottle, waiting for it," she answered gently.

She took the lamb from him and laid it on the warm hearth. "Oh, pretty, pretty, pretty!" she whispered to it, and it sucked from the bottle with all its might.

Its body warm, its stomach full of warm milk, it soon began to totter about the kitchen, putting its pert face into every corner and, as it felt its strength return, gamboling as it would in a meadow.

Before long Owen sent for a cattle buyer to look at the bullocks. He needed money for his season's work. But, on the morning, Davey told him that one of the bullocks, the white one it was, should be held back for a little. It had been struck by a stone falling from the tower of the Abbey and hadn't thrived for a bit, but it would be all right.

Owen told the drover to have a look at it, in any case. But it was not with the others and Davey said that it was shut in the stable.

"What stable?" asked the drover.

"Oh, a stable," answered Davey, vaguely. "He isn't ready for killing yet."

When the eleven red bullocks had been herded away, Davey let down the bar and the white bullock stepped out of the chancel, in his pride and his beauty. He raised his head toward the April sky and the round white clouds that drifted across it were not whiter than he.

Now Davey had him all to himself. The hills stretched, wave upon wave, hump upon hump, to the horizon and, on this hill, he and the white bullock were alone together. Davey did not ask himself why he loved the beast, why the thought of his being butchered was more than he could bear. He did not ask himself why he doted on his beauty and fed him delicately and kept fresh straw for him to lie on. In some mysterious way the beast now bore the burden of Davey's love for Glennys. Davey would put both arms about him and press his forehead to the place where her hand had lain.

But since their bout of wrestling the bullock was not so docile as he had been. Now, when Davey approached, he swung his tail and pawed the tender grass. There was a challenge in his eyes, even while he did what he was bid. He was restless, always moving in and out of the Abbey, throwing up his head and distending his nostrils against the wind. He seemed to be always expecting some fresh service from Davey. He did not move sedately, as the other bullocks had, but with force and arrogance.

Owen kept asking about him and Davey always said — "He's better, but not fit for killing."

Davey had grown sullen and scarcely looked at Glennys. But she looked at him more and more often.

The farm laborer whose back had been strained was now well and able to work. Owen paid off Davey and told him he could go.

"This is the end of it all," thought Davey, in the chaos of his mind. From the garden he stole spring flowers and carried them to the ruin of the Abbey. With his thick hands he made them into a wreath and placed it on the bullock's head.

"Now," he said, "you are like the sacred bull in the picture. . . . "

Davey was to leave the farm that day, but when evening came he had not returned to the house for his box, which stood packed, waiting on the doorstep.

"Wherever can the boy be?" asked Owen, again and again.

Suddenly Glennys said she would go and look for him.

"Let the man go," said Owen.

"No, Father, I shall go myself!"

She climbed the hill, in the golden evening light. In the Abbey, on the altar stone, she found Davey lying dead. Near by the white bullock was quietly grazing. The crescents of his horns rose above a chaplet of spring flowers and the points of his horns were red with blood.

# Frederick Philip Grove

*Frederick Philip Grove (1879-1948) is one of the few Canadian writers who has successfully dealt with tragedy. The tragic novelist should have an awareness of both good and evil at work in the universe, a sense of the interrelation between the individual and society, and an ability to create a protagonist who can err greatly, suffer deeply, and yet arrive at the truth of his situation by accepting his responsibility with dignity. Whether his novels are set in the Prairies or in industrial Ontario, Grove establishes through his description of landscapes a natural equivalent for the passionate actions and desperate failures of his protagonists. Moreover, he has created some of the finest portraits of immigrant European life, with its dreams, quests, and compromises, that early twentieth-century North American literature can offer. While he is best known for his eight novels and his autobiography, he is also an essayist of some power. As a short-story writer, however, he is extremely uneven, for many of his published stories read like unpolished first drafts.[1]*

*Grove's autobiography* In Search of Myself *(1946) may turn out to be fiction also. Since the 1920s most critics of Grove have, not unnaturally, accepted his version of his European birth and early years; however, recent investigations by Douglas Spettigue indicate that Grove probably fictionalized his early life for reasons we cannot yet fathom, although his artistic impulses in part may account for the reshaping of real events. According to Spettigue,[2] Grove may have been born in Germany around 1879, and may have come to America in 1909 (but not at the age of twenty, as Grove claimed). He may also have known a life of hardship in different parts of the United States. At any rate, around 1912 he settled in Manitoba, took up school teaching until 1924, got married in 1914, and turned to writing around 1919. In 1929 the Groves moved permanently to a farming district near Simcoe, Ontario. His wife Catherine was a great companion, encouraging him to write and giving him the freedom to do so by her own teaching; nevertheless, he was forced to supplement his income by lectures and editorial work. In spite of the poor sales and the criticism of sexual candour in his novels, Grove always had a small, appreciative audience who recognized his genius.[3] In 1934 he was awarded the Lorne Pierce Medal for literature and in 1941 was elected to the Royal Society of Canada.*

*"Skies and Scares" is the sixth of seven carefully integrated autobiographical essays in Grove's first published work,* Over Prairie Trails *(1922). In 1917-18, while Catherine Grove taught at Falmouth, Manitoba, Grove was at a school in Gladstone, about*

fifty miles to the south; these pieces are a record of his weekend homeward trips. They are not only absorbing accounts in themselves of pre-automobile travel in the Prairie winters, but they present us with a persona of Grove which is very similar to his fictional protagonists, especially Abe Spalding of Fruits of the Earth (1933). As teacher-husband-father, braving the elements with his buggy and two horses, Grove reveals a defiant and fighting spirit that can take on either the village society or the winter world with equal vigour and that may be defeated but will never be humiliated. Furthermore, Grove, carefully documenting the look and the feel of the landscape, records his fascinated response to this world. These descriptions contribute to the mood of panic and near catastrophe which prevail in "Skies and Scares".

The essays in Over Prairie Trails are not of course tragic themselves, but in them is the stuff of the heroic and the tragic. Human will and human action must contest with the irrational forces in the universe, represented by the beautiful and destructive snow, the glittering stars, the violent winds, and even human passions themselves. These irrational forces turn up again in "Snow" (1932), Grove's finest short story. Although it seems to be the quintessence of naturalistic writing, particularly in the fatalism of the old Altmans, Grove is also rendering their endurance and dignity in the face of unpleasant truth. Hence, what appears to be the reverse of the aggressive, even arrogant, spirit which prevails in Grove's novels is in actuality a complementary attitude which views life not pessimistically but with stoicism.

### Footnotes

[1] Some of Grove's short stories have been edited by Desmond Pacey in Tales From the Margin (Toronto: McGraw-Hill Ryerson, 1971).
[2] Douglas Spettigue, Frederick Philip Grove (Toronto: Copp Clarke, 1969). See Chapter I.
[3] Desmond Pacey, Frederick Philip Grove (Toronto: Ryerson, 1970). This has a selection of critical pieces and book reviews about Grove's novels.

# Skies and Scares

We had had a "soft spell" over a week end, and on Monday it had been followed by a fearful storm — snowstorm and blizzard, both coming from the southeast and lasting their traditional three days before they subsided. On Thursday, a report came in that the trail across the wild land west of Bell's corner was closed completely — in fact, would be impassable for the rest of the winter. This report came with the air of authority; the man who brought it knew what he was talking about; of that I had no doubt. For the time being, he said, no horses could possibly get through.

That very day I happened to meet another man who was habitually driving back and forth between the two towns. "Why don't you go west?" he said. "You angle over anyway. Go west first and then straight north." And he described in detail the few difficulties of the road which he followed himself. There was no doubt, he of all men should certainly know which was the best road for the first seventeen miles. He had come in from that one-third-way town that morning. I knew the trails which he described as summer-roads, had gone over them a good many times, though never in winter; so, the task of finding the trail should not offer any difficulty. Well and good, then; I made up my mind to follow the advice.

On Friday afternoon everything was ready as usual. I rang off at four o'clock and stepped into the hall. And right there the first thing went wrong.

Never before had I been delayed in my start. But now there stood three men in the hall, prominent citizens of the town. I had handed my resignation to the schoolboard; these men came to ask me that I reconsider. The board, so I had heard, was going to accept my decision and let it go at that. According to this committee the board did not represent the majority of the citizens in town. They argued for some time against my stubbornness. At last, fretting under the delay, I put it bluntly. "I have nothing to reconsider, gentlemen. The matter does no longer rest with me. If, as I hear, the board is going to accept my resignation, that settles the affair for me. It must of necessity suit me or I should not have resigned. But you might see the board. Maybe they are making a mistake. In fact, I think so. That is not my business, however." And I went.

The time was short enough in any case; this cut it shorter. It was five o'clock before I swung out on the western road. I counted on moonlight, though, the fickle luminary being in its first quarter. But there were clouds in the north and the weather was by no means settled. As for my lights, they were useless for driving so long as the ground was completely buried under its sheet of snow. On the snow there form no shadows by which you can recognize the trail in a light that comes from between the two tracks. So I hurried along.

We had not yet made the first three miles, skirting meanwhile the river, when the first disaster came. I noticed a rather formidable drift on the road straight ahead. I thought I saw a trail leading up over it — I found later on that it was a snowshoe trail. I drove briskly up to its very edge; then the horses fell into a walk. In a gingerly kind of way we started to climb. And suddenly the world seemed to fall to pieces. The horses disappeared in the snow, the cutter settled down, there was a sharp snap, I fell back — the lines had broken. With lightning quickness I reached over the dashboard down to the whiffletrees and unhooked one each of the horses' traces. That would release the others, too, should they plunge. For the moment I did not know what they were doing. There was a cloud of dustdry snow which hid them. Then Peter emerged. I saw with horror that he stood on Dan who was lying on his side. Dan started to roll over; Peter slipped off to the right. That brought rebellion into Dan, for now the neck yoke was cruelly twisting his head. I saw Dan's feet emerging out of the snow, pawing the air: he was on his back. Everything seemed convulsed. Then Peter plunged and reared, pulling Dan half-ways up; that motion of his released the neckyoke from the pole. The next moment both horses were on their feet, head by head now, but facing each other, apparently trying to pull apart; but the martingales held. Then both jumped clear of the cutter and the pole; and they plunged out, to the rear, past the cutter, to solid ground.

I do not remember how I got out; but after a minute or so I stood at their heads, holding them by the bridles. The knees of both horses shook, their nostrils trembled; Peter's eye looked as if he were going to bolt. We were only a hundred yards or so from a farm. A man and a boy came running with lanterns. I snapped the halter ropes into the bit rings and handed the horses over to the boy to be led to and fro at a walk so as to prevent a chill; and I went with the man to inspect the cutter. Apparently no damage was done beyond the snapping of the lines. The man, who knew me, offered to lend me another pair, which I promptly accepted. We pulled the cutter out backwards, straightened the harness, and hitched the horses up again. It was clear that, though they did not seem to be injured, their nerves were on edge.

The farmer meanwhile enlightened me. I mentioned the name of the man who had recommended the road. Yes, the road was good enough from town to town. This was the only bad drift. Yes, my adviser had passed here the day before; but he had turned off the road, going down to the river below, which was full of holes, it is true, made by the ice-harvesters, but otherwise safe enough. The boy would go along with his lantern to guide me to the other side of the drift. I am afraid I thought some rather uncharitable things about my adviser for having omitted to caution me against this drift. What I minded most, was, of course, the delay.

The drift was partly hollow, it appeared; the crust had thawed and frozen again; the huge mass of snow underneath had settled down. The crust had formed a vault, amply strong enough to carry a man, but not to carry horse and cutter.

When in the dying light and by the gleam of the lantern we went through the dense brush, down the steep bank, and on to the river, the horses were every second ready to bolt. Peter snorted and danced, Dan laid his ears back on his head. But the boy gave warning at every open hole, and we made it safely. At last we got back to the road, I kept talking and purring to the horses for a while, and it seemed they were quieting down.

It was not an auspicious beginning for a long night-drive. And though for a while all things seemed to be going about as well as I could wish, there remained a nervousness which, slight though it seemed while unprovoked, yet tinged every motion of the horses and even my own state of mind. Still, while we were going west, and later, north into the one-third-way town, the drive was one of the most marvellously beautiful ones that I had had during that winter of marvellous sights.

As I have mentioned, the moon was in its first quarter and, therefore, during the early part of the night high in the sky. It was not very cold; the lower air was quiet, of that strange, hushed stillness which in southern countries is the stillness of the noon hour in midsummer — when Pan is frightened into a panic by the very quiet. It was not so, however, in the upper reaches of the atmosphere. It was a night of skies, of shifting, ever changing skies. Not for five minutes did an aspect last. When I looked up, after maybe having devoted my attention for a while to a turn in the road or to a drift, there was no trace left of the picture which I had seen last. And you could not help it, the sky would draw your eye. There was commotion up there — operations were proceeding on a very vast scale, but so silently, with not a whisper of wind, that I felt hushed myself.

A few of the aspects have persisted in my memory, but it seems an impossible task to sketch them.

I was driving along through open fields. The trail led dimly ahead. Huge masses of snow with sharp, immovable shadows flanked it. The horses were very wide awake. They cocked their ears at every one of the mounds; and sometimes they pressed rump against rump, as if to reassure each other by their mutual touch.

About halfway up from the northern horizon there lay a belt of faintest luminosity in the atmosphere — no play of northern lights — just an impalpable paling of the dark blue sky. There were stars, too, but they were not very brilliant. Way down in the north, at the edge of the world, there lay a long, low-flung line of cloud, black, scarcely discernible in the light of the moon. And from its centre, true north, there grew out a monstrous human arm, reaching higher and higher, up to the zenith, blotting the stars behind it. It looked at first — in texture and rigid outline — as the stream of straw looks that flows from the blower of a threshing machine when you stand straight in its line and behind it. But, of course, it did not curve down. It seemed to stretch and to rise, growing more and more like an arm with a clumsy fist at its end, held unconceivably straight and unbending. This cloud, I have no doubt, was forming right then by condensation. And it stretched and lengthened till it obscured the moon.

Just then I reached the end of my run to the west. I was nearing a block of dense poplar bush in which somewhere two farmsteads lay embedded. The road turned to the north. I was now exactly south of and in line with that long, twenty-mile trail where I had startled horses, rabbit, and partridge on the last described drive. I believe I was just twenty-five miles from the northern correction line. At this corner where I turned I had to devote all my attention to the negotiating of a few bad drifts.

When I looked up again, I was driving along the bottom of a wide road gap formed by tall and stately poplars on both sides — trees which stood uncannily still. The light of the moon became less dim, and I raised my eyes. That band of cloud — for it had turned into a band now, thus losing its threatening aspect — had widened out and loosened up. It was a strip of flocculent, sheepy-looking, little cloudlets that suggested curliness and innocence. And the moon stood in between like a goodnatured shepherd in the stories of old.

For a while I kept my eyes on the sky. The going was good indeed on this closed-in road. And so I watched that insensible, silent, and yet swift shifting of things in the heavens that seemed so orderly, pre-ordained, and as if regulated by silent signals. The clouds lost their sheeplike look again; they became more massive; they took on more substance and spine, more manliness, as it were; and they arranged themselves in distinct lines. Soldiers suggested themselves, not soldiers engaged in war, but soldiers drilling in times of peace, to be reviewed, maybe, by some great general. That central point from which the arm had sprung and which had been due north had sidled over to the northwest; the low-flung line along the horizon had taken on the shape of a long wedge pointing east; farther west it, too, looked more massive now — more like a rather solid wall. And all those soldier-clouds fell into a fan-shaped formation — into lines radiating from that common central point in the northwest. This arrangement I have for many years been calling "the tree." It is quite common, of course, and I read it with great confidence as meaning "no amount of rain or snow worth mentioning." "The tree" covered half the heavens or more, and nowhere did I see any large reaches of clear sky. Here and there a star would peep through, and the moon seemed to be

38

quickly and quietly moving through the lines. Apparently he was the general who reviewed the army.

Again there came a shifting in the scenes. It looked as if some unseen hands were spreading a sheet above these flocculent clouds — a thin and vapoury sheet that came from the north and gradually covered the whole roof of the sky. Stars and moon disappeared; but not, so far, the light of the moon; it merely became diffused — the way the light from an electric bulb becomes diffused when you enclose it in a frosted globe. And then, as the sheet of vapour above began to thicken, the light on the snow became dim and dimmer, till the whole of the landscape lay in gloom. The sheet still seemed to be coming, coming from the north. But no longer did it travel away to the south. It was as if it had brought up against an obstacle there, as if it were being held in place. And since there was more and more of it pressing up — it seemed rather to be pushed now — it telescoped together and threw itself into folds, till at last the whole sky looked like an enormous system of parallel clothes-lines over all of which one great, soft, and loose cloth were flung, so that fold after fold would hang down between all the neighbouring pairs of lines; and between two folds there would be a sharply converging, upward crease. It being night, this arrangement, common in grey daylight, would not have shown at all, had it not been for the moon above. As it was, every one of the infolds showed an increasingly lighter grey the higher it folded up, and like huge, black udders the outfolds were hanging down. This sky, when it persists, I have often found to be followed within a few days by heavy storms. To-night, however, it did not last. Shifting skies are never certain signs, though they normally indicate an unsettled condition of the atmosphere. I have observed them after a blizzard, too.

I looked back over my shoulder, just when I emerged from the bush into the open fields. And there I became aware of a new element again. A quiet and yet very distinct commotion arose from the south. These cloth-clouds lifted, and a nearly impalpable change crept over the whole of the sky. A few minutes later it crystallised into a distinct impression. A dark grey, faintly luminous, inverted bowl stood overhead. Not a star was to be seen above, nor yet the moon. But all around the horizon there was a nearly clear ring, suffused with the light of the moon. There, where the sky is most apt to be dark and hazy, stars peeped out — singly and dimly only — I did not recognize any constellation.

And then the grey bowl seemed to contract into patches. Again the change seemed to proceed from the south. The clouds seemed to lift still higher, and to shrink into small, light, feathery cirrus clouds, silvery on the dark blue sky — resembling white pencil shadings. The light of the moon asserted itself anew. And this metamorphosis also spread upward, till the moon herself looked out again, and it went on spreading northward till it covered the whole of the sky.

This last change came just before I had to turn west again for a mile or so in order to hit a trail into town. I did not mean to go on straight ahead and to cut across those radiating road lines of which I have spoken in a former paper. I knew that my wife would be sitting up and waiting till midnight or two o'clock, and I wanted to make it. So I avoided all risks and gave my attention to the road for a while. I had to drive through a ditch and through a fence beyond, and to cross a field in order to strike that road which led from the south through the park into town. A certain farmstead was my landmark. Beyond it I had to watch out sharply if I wanted to find the exact spot where according to my informant the wire of the fence had been taken down. I found it.

To cross the field proved to be the hardest task the horses had had so far during the night. The trail had been cut in deep through knee-high drifts, and it was filled with firmly packed, freshly blown-in snow. That makes a particularly bad road for fast driving. I simply had to take my time and to give all my attention to the guiding of the horses. And here I was also to become aware once more of the fact that my horses had not yet forgotten their panic in that river drift of two hours ago. There was a strawstack in the centre of the field; at least the shape of the big, white mound suggested a strawstack; and the trail led closely by it. Sharp shadows showed, and the horses, pricking their ears, began to dance and to sidle away from it as we passed along its southern edge.

But we made it. By the time we reached the park that forms the approach to the town from the south, the skies had changed completely. There was now, as far as my eye would reach, just one vast, dark-blue, star-spangled expanse. And the skies twinkled and blazed down upon the earth with a veritable fervour. There was not one of the more familiar stars that did not stand out brightly, even the minor ones which you do not ordinarily see oftener than, maybe, once or twice a year — as, for instance, Vega's smaller companions in the constellation of the Lyre, or the minor points in the cluster of the Pleiades.

I sometimes think that the mere fact of your being on a narrow bush-road, with the trees looming darkly to both sides, makes the stars seem brighter than they appear from the open fields. I have heard that you can see a star even in daytime from the bottom of a deep mine-pit if it happens to pass overhead. That would seem to make my impression less improbable, perhaps. I know that not often have the stars seemed so much alive to me as they did that night in the park.

And then I came into the town. I stayed about forty-five minutes, fed the horses, had supper myself, and hitched up again.

On leaving town I went for another mile east in the shelter of a fringe of bush; and this bush kept rustling as if a breeze had sprung up. But it was not till I turned north again, on the twenty-mile stretch, that I became conscious of a great change in the atmosphere. There was indeed a slight breeze, coming from the north, and it felt very moist. Somehow it felt homely and human, this breeze. There was a promise in it, as of a time, not too far distant, when the sap would rise again in the trees and when tender leaflets would begin to stir in delicate buds. So far, however, its more immediate promise probably was snow.

But it did not last, either. A colder breeze sprang up. Between the two there was a distinct lull. And again there arose in the north, far away, at the very end of my seemingly endless road, a cloud-bank. The colder wind that sprang up was gusty; it came in fits and starts, with short lulls in between; it still had that water-laden feeling, but it was now what you would call "damp" rather than "moist" — the way you often feel winter-winds along the shores of great lakes or along sea-coasts. There was a cutting edge to it — it was "raw." And it had not been blowing very long before low-hanging, dark, and formless cloud-masses began to scud up from the north to the zenith. The northern lights, too, made their appearance again about that time. They formed an arc very far to the south, vaulting up behind my back, beyond the zenith. No streamers in them, no filtered rays and streaks — nothing but a blurred luminosity high above the clouds and — so it seemed — above the atmosphere. The northern lights have moods, like the clouds — moods as varied as theirs — though they do not display them so often nor quite so ostentatiously.

We were nearing the bridge across the infant river. The road from the south slopes down to this bridge in a rather sudden, s-shaped curve, as perhaps the reader remembers. I still had the moonlight from time to time, and whenever one of the clouds floated in front of the crescent, I drove more slowly and more carefully. Now there is a peculiar thing about moonlight on snow. With a fairly well-marked trail on bare ground, in summertime, a very little of it will suffice to indicate the road, for there are enough rough spots on the best of trails to cast little shadows, and grass and weeds on both sides usually mark the beaten track off still more clearly, even though the road lead north. But the snow forms such an even expanse, and the trail on it is so featureless that these signs are no longer available. The light itself also is too characterless and too white and too nearly of the same quality as the light reflected by the snow to allow of judging distances delicately and accurately. You seem to see nothing but one vast whiteness all around. When you drive east or west, the smooth edges of the tracks will cast sharply defined shadows to the north, but when you drive north or south, even these shadows are absent, and so you must entirely rely on your horses to stay on the trail. I have often observed how easily my own judgment was deluded.

But still I felt so absolutely sure that I should know when I approached the bridge that, perhaps through over-confidence, I was caught napping. There was another fact which I did not take sufficiently into account at the time. I have mentioned that we had had a "soft spell." In fact, it had been so warm for a day or two that the older snow had completely iced over. Now, much as I thought I was watching out, we were suddenly and quite unexpectedly right on the downward slope before I even realized that we were near it.

As I said, on this slope the trail described a double curve, and it hit the bridge at an angle from the west. The first turn and the behaviour of the horses were what convinced me that I had inadvertently gone too far. If I had stopped the horses at the point where the slope began and then started them downward at a slow walk, we should still have reached the bridge at too great a speed; for the slope had offered the last big wind from the north a sheer brow, and it was swept clean of new snow, thus exposing the smooth ice underneath; the snow that had drifted from the south, on the other hand, had been thrown beyond the river, on to the lower northern bank; the horses skidded, and the weight of the cutter would have pushed them forward. As it was, they realized the danger themselves; for when we turned the second curve, both of them stiffened their legs and spread their feet in order to break the momentum of the cutter; but in spite of the heavy calks under their shoes they slipped on all fours, hardly able to make the bend on to the bridge.

They had to turn nearly at right angles to their last direction, and the bridge seemed to be one smooth sheet of ice. The moon shone brightly just then; so I saw exactly what happened. As soon as the runners hit the iced-over planks, the cutter swung out sideways; the horses, however, slipping and recovering, managed to make the turn. It was a worth-while sight to see them strike their calks into the ice and brace themselves against the shock which they clearly expected when the cutter started to skid. The latter swung clear of the bridge — you will remember that the railing on the east-side was broken away — out into space, and came down with a fearful crash, but right side up, on the steep north bank of the river — just at the very moment when the horses reached the deep, loose snow beyond which at least gave them a secure footing. They had gone along the diagonal of the bridge, from the southwest corner, barely clearing the rail, to the northwest corner where the snow had piled in to a depth of from two to five feet on the sloping bank. If the ground where I hit the bank had been bare, the cutter would have splintered to pieces; as it was, the shock of it seemed to jar every bone in my body.

It seemed rather a piece of good luck that the horses bolted; the lines held; they pulled me free of the drift on the bank and plunged out on the road. For a mile or two we had a pretty wild run; and this time there was no doubt about it, either, the horses were thoroughly frightened. They ran till they were exhausted, and there was no holding them; but since I was on a clear road, I did not worry very much. Nevertheless, I was rather badly shaken up myself; and if I had followed the good advice that suggested itself, I should have put in for some time at the very next farm which I passed. The way I see things now, it was anything rather than safe to go on. With horses in the nervous condition in which mine were I could not hope any longer to keep them under control should a further accident happen. But I had never yet given in when I had made up my mind to make the trip, and it was hard to do so for the first time.

As soon as I had the horses sufficiently in hand again, I lighted my lantern, got out on the road, and carefully looked my cutter over. I found that the hardwood lining of both runners was broken at the curve, but the steel shoes were, though slightly bent, still sound. Fortunately the top had been down, otherwise further damage would have been sure to result. I saw no reason to discontinue the drive.

Now after a while — when the nervousness incident upon the shock which I had received subsided — my interest in the shifting skies revived once more, and again I began to watch the clouds. The wind was squally, and the low, black vapour-masses overhead had coalesced into a vast array of very similar but yet distinct groups. There was still a certain amount of light from the moon, but only just enough to show the texture and the grouping of the clouds. Hardly ever had I seen, or at least consciously taken note of a sky that with its blackness and its massed multitudes of clouds looked so threatening, so sinister, so much like a battle-array. But way up in the northeast there were two large areas quite suffused with light from the north. They must have been thin cloud-layers in whose upper reaches the northern lights were playing. And these patches of light were like a promise, like a word of peace arresting the battle. Had it not been for these islands of light, I should have felt depressed when I looked back to the road.

We were swinging along as before. I had rested the horses by a walk, and to a casual observer they would have seemed to be none the worse for their fling at running away.

But on closer scrutiny they would again have revealed the unmistakable signs of nervous tension. Their ears moved jerkily on the slightest provocation. Still, the road was good and clear, and I had no apprehensions.

Then came the sudden end of the trail. It was right in front of a farm yard. Clearly, the farmer had broken the last part of the road over which I had come. The trail widened out to a large, circus-shaped flat in the drifts. The snow had the ruffled appearance of being thoroughly tramped down by a herd of cattle. On both sides there were trees — wild trees — a-plenty. Brush lined the narrow road gap ahead; but the snow had piled in level with its tops. This had always been rather a bad spot, though the last time I had seen it the snow had settled down to about half the height of the shrubs. I stopped and hesitated for a moment. I knew just where the trail had been. It was about twenty-five feet from the fence of the field to the east. It was now covered under three to four feet of freshly drifted-in snow. The drift seemed to be higher towards the west, where the brush stood higher, too. So I decided to stay as nearly as I could above the old trail. There, even though we might break through the new snow, the older drifts underneath were likely to be firm enough.

We went ahead. The drift held, and slowly we climbed to its summit. It is a strange coincidence that just then I should have glanced up at the sky. I saw a huge, black cloud-mass elbowing its way, as it were, in front of those islands of light, the promise of peace. And so much was I by this time imbued with the moods of the skies that the disappearance of this mild glimmer sent a regret through my very body. And simultaneously with this thrill of regret there came — I remember this as distinctly as if it had been an hour ago — the certainty of impending disaster. The very next moment chaos reigned. The horses broke in, not badly at all; but as a consequence of their nervous condition they flew into a panic. I held them tight as they started to plunge. But there was no guiding them; they were bound to have things their own way altogether. It seemed as if they had lost their road-sense, too, for instead of plunging at least straight ahead, out on the level trail, they made, with irresistible bounds and without paying the slightest attention to the pull of the lines, towards the east. There the drift, not being packed by any previous traffic, went entirely to pieces under their feet. I had meanwhile thrown off my robes, determined at all costs to bring them to a stop, for I knew, if I allowed them to get away with me this time, they would be spoiled for any further drives of mine.

Now just the very fraction of a second when I got my feet up against the dashboard so as to throw my whole weight into my pull, they reared up as if for one tremendous and supreme bound, and simultaneously I saw a fence post straight under the cutter pole. Before I quite realized it, the horses had already cleared the fence. I expected the collision, the breaking of the drawbar and the bolting of the horses; but just then my desperate effort in holding them told, and dancing and fretting they stood. Then, in a flash, I mentally saw and understood the whole situation. The runners of the cutter, still held up by the snow of the drift which sloped down into the field and which the horses had churned into slabs and clods, had struck the fence wire and, lifting the whole of the conveyance, had placed me, cutter and all, balanced for a moment to a nicety, on top of the post. But already we began to settle back.

I felt that I could not delay, for a moment later the runners would slip off the wire and the cutter fall backward; that was the certain signal for the horses to bolt. The very paradoxicality of the situation seemed to give me a clue. I clicked my tongue and, holding the horses back with my last ounce of strength, made them slowly dance forward and pull me over the fence. In a moment I realized that I had made a mistake. A quick pull would have jerked me clear of the post. As it was, it slowly grated along the bottom of the box; then the cutter tilted forward, and when the runners slipped off the wire, the cutter with myself pitched back with a frightful knock against the post. The back panel of the box still shows the splintered tear that fence post made. The shock of it threw me forward, for a second I lost all purchase on the lines, and again the horses went off in a panic. It was quite dark now, for the clouds were thickening in the sky. While I attended to the horses, I reflected that probably something had broken back there in the cutter, but worst of all, I realized that this incident, for the time being at least, had completely broken my nerve. As soon as I had brought the horses to a stop, I turned in the knee-deep snow of the field and made for the fence.

Half a mile ahead there gleamed a light. I had, of course, to stay on the field, and I drove along, slowly and carefully, skirting the fence and watching it as closely as what light there was permitted.

I do not know why this incident affected me the way it did; but I presume that the cumulative effect of three mishaps, one following the other, had something to do with it; the same as it affected the horses. But more than that, I believe, it was the effect of the skies. I am rather subject to the influence of atmospheric conditions. There are not many things that I would rather watch. No matter what the aspect of the skies may be, they fascinate me. I have heard people say, "What a dull day!" — or, "What a sleepy day!" — and that when I was enjoying my own little paradise in yielding to the moods of cloud and sky. To this very hour I am convinced that the skies broke my nerve that night, that those incidents merely furnished them with an opportunity to get their work in more tellingly.

Of the remainder of the drive little needs to be said. I found a way out of the field, back to the road, drove into the yard of the farm where I had seen the light, knocked at the house, and asked for and obtained the night's accommodation for myself and for my horses.

At six o'clock next morning I was on the road again. Both I and the horses had shaken off the nightmare, and through a sprinkling, dusting fall of snow we made the correction line and finally home in the best of moods and conditions.

# Snow

Towards morning the blizzard had died down, though it was still far from daylight. Stars without number blazed in the dark-blue sky which presented that brilliant and uncompromising appearance always characterizing, on the northern plains of America, those nights in the dead of winter when the thermometer dips to its lowest levels.

In the west, Orion was sinking to the horizon. It was between five and six o'clock.

In the bush-fringe of the Big Marsh, sheltered by thick but bare bluffs of aspens, stood a large house, built of logs, white-washed, solid — such as a settler who is still single would put up only when he thinks of getting married. It, too, looked ice-cold, frozen in the night. Not a breath stirred where it stood; a thin thread of whitish smoke, reaching up to the level of the tree-tops, seemed to be suspended into the chimney rather than to issue from it.

Through the deep snow of the yard, newly packed, a man was fighting his way to the door. Arrived there, he knocked and knocked, first tapping with his knuckles, then hammering with his fists.

Two, three minutes passed. Then a sound awoke in the house, as of somebody stirring, getting out of bed.

The figure on the door-slab — a medium-sized, slim man in sheepskin and high rubber boots into which his trousers were tucked, with the ear-flaps of his cap pulled down — stood and waited, bent over, hands thrust into the pockets of the short coat, as if he wished to shrink into the smallest possible space so as to offer the smallest possible surface to the attack of the cold. In order to get rid of the dry, powdery snow which filled every crease in his foot-gear and trousers, he stamped his feet. His chin was drawn deep into the turned-up collar on whose points his breath had settled in the form of a thick layer of hoar frost.

At last a bolt was withdrawn inside.

The face of a man peered out, just discernible in the starlight.

Then the door was opened; in ominous silence the figure from the outside entered, still stamping its feet.

Not a word was spoken till the door had been closed. Then a voice sounded through the cold and dreary darkness of the room.

"Redcliff hasn't come home. He went to town about noon and expected to get back by midnight. We're afraid he's lost."

The other man, quite invisible in the dark, had listened, his teeth chattering with the cold. "Are you sure he started out from town?"

"Well," the new-comer answered hesitatingly, "one of the horses came to the yard."

"One of his horses?"

"Yes. One of those he drove. The woman worked her way to my place to get help."

The owner of the house did not speak again. He went, in the dark, to the door in the rear and opened it. There, he groped about for matches, and, finding them, lighted a lamp. In the room stood a big stove, a coal-stove of the self-feeder type; but the fuel used was wood. He opened the drafts and shook the grate clear of ashes; there were two big blocks of spruce in the fire-box, smouldering away for the night. In less than a minute they blazed up.

The new-comer entered, blinking in the light of the lamp, and looked on. Before many minutes the heat from the stove began to tell.

45

"I'll call Bill," the owner of the house said. He was himself of medium height or only slightly above it, but of enormous breadth of shoulder: a figure built for lifting loads. By his side the other man looked small, weakly, dwarfed.

He left the room and, returning through the cold bare hall in front, went upstairs.

A few minutes later a tall, slender, well-built youth bolted into the room where the new-comer was waiting. Bill, Carroll's hired man, was in his underwear and carried his clothes, thrown in a heap over his arm. Without loss of time, but jumping, stamping, swinging his arms, he began at once to dress.

He greeted the visitor. "Hello, Mike! What's that Abe tells me? Redcliff got lost?"

"Seems that way," Mike said listlessly.

"By gringo," Bill went on. "I shouldn't wonder. In that storm! I'd have waited in town. Wouldn't catch me going out over the marsh in that kind of weather!"

"Didn't start till late in the afternoon," Mike Sobotski said in his shivering way.

"No. And didn't last long, either," Bill agreed while he shouldered into his overalls. "But while she lasted . . . "

At this moment Abe Carroll, the owner of the farm, re-entered, with sheep-skin, fur cap, and long, woollen scarf on his arm. His deeply lined, striking, square face bore a settled frown while he held the inside of his sheep-skin to the stove to warm it up. Then, without saying a word, he got deliberately into it.

Mike Sobotski still stood bent over, shivering, though he had opened his coat and, on his side of the stove, was catching all the heat it afforded.

Abe, with the least motion needed to complete dressing, made for the door. In passing Bill, he flung out an elbow which touched the young man's arm. "Come on," he said; and to the other, pointing to the stove, "Close the drafts."

A few minutes later a noise as of rearing and snorting horses in front of the house. . .

Mike, buttoning up his coat and pulling his mitts over his hands, went out.

They mounted three unsaddled horses. Abe leading, they dashed through the new drifts in the yard and out through the gate to the road. Here, where the shelter of the bluffs screening the house was no longer effective, a light but freshening breeze from the north-west made itself felt as if fine little knives were cutting into the flesh of their faces.

Abe dug his heels into the flank of his rearing mount. The horse was unwilling to obey his guidance, for Abe wanted to leave the road and to cut across wild land to the south-west.

The darkness was still inky-black, though here and there, where the slope of the drifts slanted in the right direction, starlight was dimly reflected from the snow. The drifts were six, eight, in places ten feet high; and the snow was once more crawling up their flanks, it was so light and fine. It would fill the tracks in half an hour. As the horses plunged through, the crystals dusted up in clouds, flying aloft over horses and riders.

In less than half an hour they came to a group of two little buildings, of logs, that seemed to squat on their haunches in the snow. Having entered the yard through a gate, they passed one of the buildings and made for the other, a little stable; their horses snorting, they stopped in its lee.

Mike dismounted, throwing the halter-shank of his horse to Bill. He went to the house, which stood a hundred feet or so away. The shack was even smaller than the stable, twelve by fifteen feet perhaps. From its flue-pipe a thick, white plume of smoke blew to the south-east.

Mike returned with a lantern; the other two sprang to the ground; and they opened the door to examine the horse which the woman had allowed to enter.

The horse was there, still excited, snorting at the leaping light and shadows from the lantern, its eyes wild, its nostrils dilated. It was covered with white frost and fully harnessed, though its traces were tied up to the back-band.

"He let him go," said Mike, taking in these signs. "Must have stopped and unhitched him."

"Must have been stuck in a drift," Bill said, assenting.

"And tried to walk it," Abe added.

For a minute or so they stood silent, each following his own gloomy thoughts. Weird, luminous little clouds issued fitfully from the nostrils of the horse inside.

"I'll get the cutter," Abe said at last.

"I'll get it," Bill volunteered. "I'll take the drivers along. We'll leave the filly here in the stable."

"All right."

Bill remounted, leading Abe's horse. He disappeared into the night.

Abe and Mike, having tied the filly and the other horse in their stalls, went out, closed the door and turned to the house.

There, by the light of a little coal-oil lamp, they saw the woman sitting at the stove, pale, shivering, her teeth a-chatter, trying to warm her hands, which were cold with fever, and looking with lack-lustre eyes at the men as they entered.

The children were sleeping; the oldest a girl, on the floor, wrapped in a blanket and curled up like a dog; four others in one narrow bed, with hay for a mattress, two at the head, two at the foot; the baby on, rather than in, a sort of cradle made of a wide board slung by thin ropes to the pole-roof of the shack.

The other bed was empty and unmade. The air was stifling from a night of exhalations.

"We're going to hunt for him," Mike said quietly. "We've sent for a cutter. He must have tried to walk."

The woman did not answer. She sat and shivered.

"We'll take some blankets," Mike went on. "And some whisky if you've got any in the house."

He and Abe were standing by the stove, opposite the woman, and warming their hands, their mitts held under their arm-pits.

The woman pointed with a look to a home-made little cupboard nailed to the wall and apathetically turned back to the stove. Mike went, opened the door of the cupboard, took a bottle from it, and slipped it into the pocket of his sheep-skin. Then he raised the blankets from the empty bed, rolled them roughly into a bundle, dropped it, and returned to the stove where, with stiff fingers, he fell to rolling a cigarette.

Thus they stood for an hour or so.

47

Abe's eye was fastened on the woman. He would have liked to say a word of comfort, of hope. What was there to be said?

She was the daughter of a German settler in the bush, some six or seven miles north-east of Abe's place. Her father, an oldish, unctuous, bearded man had, some ten years ago, got tired of the hard life in the bush where work meant clearing, picking stones, and digging stumps. He had sold his homestead and bought a prairie-farm, half a section, on crop-payments, giving notes for the equipment which he needed to handle the place. He had not been able to make it 'a go.' His bush farm had fallen back on his hands; he had lost his all and returned to the place. He had been counting on the help of his two boys — big, strapping young fellows who were to clear much land and to raise crops which would lift the debt. But the boys had refused to go back to the bush; they could get easy work in town. Ready money would help. But the ready money had melted away in their hands. Redcliff, the old people's son-in-law, had been their last hope. They were on the point of losing even their bush farm. Here they might perhaps still have found a refuge for their old age — though Redcliff's homestead lay on the sand-flats bordering on the marsh where the soil was thin, dreadfully thin; it drifted when the scrub-brush was cleared off. Still, with Redcliff living, this place had been a hope. What were they to do if he was gone? And this woman, hardly more than a girl, in spite of her six children!

The two tiny, square windows of the shack began to turn grey.

At last Abe, thinking he heard a sound, went to the door and stepped out. Bill was there; the horses were shaking the snow out of their pelts; one of them was pawing the ground.

Once more Abe opened the door and gave Mike a look for a signal. Mike gathered the bundle of blankets into his arms, pulled on his mitts, and came out.

Abe reached for the lines; but Bill objected.

"No. Let me drive. I found something."

And as soon as the two older men had climbed in, squeezing into the scant space on the seat, he clicked his tongue.

"Get up there!" he shouted, hitting the horses' backs with his lines. And with a leap they darted away.

Bill turned, heading back to the Carroll farm. The horses plunged, reared, snorted, and then, throwing their heads, shot along in a gallop, scattering snow-slabs right and left and throwing wing-waves of the fresh, powdery snow, especially on the lee side. Repeatedly they tried to turn into the wind, which they were cutting at right angles. But Bill plied the whip and guided them expertly.

Nothing was visible anywhere; nothing but the snow in the first grey of dawn. Then, like enormous ghosts, or like evanescent apparitions, the trees of the bluff were adumbrated behind the lingering veils of the night.

Bill turned to the south, along the straight trail which bordered Abe Carroll's farm. He kept looking out sharply to right and left. But after a while he drew his galloping horses in.

"Whoa!" he shouted, tearing at the lines in see-saw fashion. And when the rearing horses came to a stop, excited and breathless, he added, "I've missed it." He turned.

"What is it?" Abe asked.

"The other horse," Bill answered. "It must have had the scent of our yard. It's dead . . . frozen stiff."

A few minutes later he pointed to a huge white mound on top of a drift to the left. "That's it," he said, turned the horses into the wind, and stopped.

To the right, the bluffs of the farm slowly outlined themselves in the morning greyness.

The two older men alighted and, with their hands, shovelled the snow away. There lay the horse, stiff and cold, frozen into a rocklike mass.

"Must have been here a long while," Abe said.

Mike nodded. "Five, six hours." Then he added, "Couldn't have had the smell of the yard. Unless the wind has turned."

"It has," Abe answered and pointed to a fold in the flank of the snow-drift which indicated that the present drift had been superimposed on a lower one whose longitudinal axis ran to the north-east.

For a moment longer they stood and pondered.

Then Abe went back to the cutter and reached for the lines. "I'll drive," he said.

Mike climbed in.

Abe took his bearings, looking for landmarks. They were only two or three hundred feet from his fence. That enabled him to estimate the exact direction of the breeze. He clicked his tongue. "Get up!"

And the horses, catching the infection of a dull excitement, shot away. They went straight into the desert of drifts to the west, plunging ahead without any trail, without any landmark in front to guide them.

They went for half an hour, an hour, and longer.

None of the three men said a word. Abe knew the sand-flats better than any other; Abe reasoned better than they. If anyone could find the missing man, it was Abe.

Abe's thought ran thus. The horse had gone against the wind. It would never have done so without good reason; that reason could have been no other than a scent to follow. If that was so, however, it would have gone in as straight a line as it could. The sand-flats stretched away to the south-west for sixteen miles with not a settlement, not a farm but Redcliff's. If Abe managed to strike that line of the scent, it must take him to the point whence the horses had started.

Clear and glaring, with an almost indifferent air, the sun rose to their left.

And suddenly they saw the wagon-box of the sleigh sticking out of the snow ahead of them.

Abe stopped, handed Bill the lines, and got out. Mike followed. Nobody said a word.

The two men dug the tongue of the vehicle out of the snow and tried it. This was part of the old, burnt-over bush land south of the sand-flats. The sleigh was tightly wedged in between several charred stumps which stuck up through the snow. That was the reason why the man had unhitched the horses and turned them loose. What else, indeed, could he have done?

The box was filled with a drift which, toward the tail-gate, was piled high, for there three bags of flour were standing on end and leaning against a barrel half-filled with small parcels the interstices between which were packed with mealy snow.

Abe waded all around the sleigh, reconnoitring; and as he did so, wading at the height of the upper edge of the wagon-box, the snow suddenly gave way beneath him; he broke in; the drift was hollow.

A suspicion took hold of him; with a few quick reaches of his arm he demolished the roof of the drift all about.

And there, in the hollow, lay the man's body as if he were sleeping, a quiet expression, as of painless rest, on his face. His eyes were closed; a couple of bags were wrapped about his shoulders. Apparently he had not even tried to walk! Already chilled to the bone, he had given in to that desire for rest, for shelter at any price, which overcomes him who is doomed to freeze.

Without a word the two men carried him to the cutter and laid him down on the snow.

Bill, meanwhile, had unhitched the horses and was hooking them to the tongue of the sleigh. The two others looked on in silence. Four times the horses sprang, excited because Bill tried to make them pull with a sudden twist. The sleigh did not stir.

"Need an axe," Mike said at last, "to cut the stumps. We'll get the sleigh later."

Mike hitched up again and turned the cutter. The broken snow-drifts through which they had come gave the direction.

Then they laid the stiff, dead body across the floor of their vehicle, leaving the side doors open, for it protruded both ways. They themselves climbed up on the seat and crouched down, so as not to put their feet on the corpse.

Thus they returned to Abe Carroll's farm where, still in silence, they deposited the body in the granary.

That done, they stood for a moment as if in doubt. Then Bill unhitched the horses and took them to the stable to feed.

"I'll tell the woman," said Mike. "Will you go tell her father?"

Abe nodded. "Wait for breakfast," he added.

It was ten o'clock; and none of them had eaten since the previous night.

On the way to Altmann's place in the bush, drifts were no obstacles to driving. Drifts lay on the marsh, on the open sand-flats.

Every minute of the time Abe, as he drove along, thought of that woman in the shack: the woman, alone, with six children, and with the knowledge that her man was dead.

Altmann's place in the bush looked the picture of peace and comfort: a large log-house of two rooms. Window-frames and door were painted green. A place to stay with, not to leave. . . .

When Abe knocked, the woman, whom he had seen but once in his life, at the sale where they had lost their possessions, opened the door — an enormously fat woman, overflowing her clothes. The man, tall, broad, with a long, rolling beard, now grey, stood behind her, peering over her shoulder. A visit is an event in the bush!

"Come in," he said cheerfully when he saw Abe. "What a storm that was!"

Abe entered the kitchen which was also dining- and living-room. He sat down on the chair which was pushed forward for him and looked at the two old people, who remained standing.

Suddenly, from the expression of his face, they anticipated something of his message. No use dissembling.

50

"Redcliff is dead," he said. "He was frozen to death last night on his way from town."

The two old people also sat down; it looked as if their knees had given way beneath them. They stared at him, dumbly, a sudden expression of panic fright in their eyes.

"I thought you might want to go to your daughter," Abe added sympathetically.

The man's big frame seemed to shrink as he sat there. All the unctuousness and the conceit of the handsome man dwindled out of his bearing. The woman's eyes had already filled with tears.

Thus they remained for two, three minutes.

Then the woman folded her fat, pudgy hands; her head sank low on her breast; and she sobbed, "God's will be done!"

# E. J. Pratt

*Edwin John Pratt (1883-1964) was born in Western Bay, Newfoundland and educated at Methodist College, St. John's. After several years of teaching school and working as a student minister in Newfoundland, he left in 1907 for Toronto where he attended Victoria College. He received his B.A. in 1911, his M.A. in 1912, his B.D. in 1913, and his Ph.D. in 1917, all from the University of Toronto. In 1913, he was ordained in the Methodist Ministry, but never held a congregational charge; Peter Buitenhuis suggests that this is partly because Pratt experienced a crisis of belief.[1] Rather than pursue a career in the Church, Pratt accepted a post as English teacher at Victoria College, where he remained from 1919 until his retirement in 1953. He was Editor of* Canadian Poetry Magazine *from 1936 to 1942. The Governor General's Award for Poetry was given to Pratt three times, for* The Fable of the Goats *(1937), for* Brébeuf and his Brethren *(1940), and for* Towards the Last Spike *(1952). Among the honours he received were election to the Royal Society of Canada (1930) and the Lorne Pierce Medal for distinguished service to Canadian literature (1940). In the 1946 King's Honours, he was made a Commander of the Order of St. Michael and St. George.*

*Although Pratt's poetic career reaches well into the twentieth century (1917-1952), a careful study of his poems indicates that his ideals and values were shaped by his responses to late nineteenth-century questions. It is not surprising, then, that his interest in late nineteenth-century scientific and religious thought provides most of the central motifs in his poetry: the evolutionary process as central metaphor;[2] the polarity between mechanistic and vital forces; and the fascination with energy and violence, whether directed towards good or evil ends.*

*This late nineteenth-century vision by no means keeps Pratt from dealing with the affairs of the twentieth century; indeed, his imagery suggests how profoundly twentieth-century man is still grappling with the social and political questions raised by the post-Romantic world. Furthermore, Pratt's awareness of his own times is fully evident in the treatment of his subjects. One of his favourite subjects is the sea. In works like "The Ice-Floes" and* The Titanic *(1935), he describes the part it plays in the lives of Newfoundlanders, fishermen, and sailors. It is not simply a destructive force, however, for it is an object against which men can test their ability to survive and to adapt, and it is an agent which challenges their inventions and technology. During the 1930s, his interest turned to the international tensions growing in the human community. Like the sea, these tensions can provoke the best and the worst in men, and*

Pratt's fascination with struggle appears in parables like the early work, Titans *(1927)*, The Fable of the Goats *(1937), and the wartime poem* Dunkirk *(1941).* Brébeuf and His Brethren *(1940) indicates a new area of interest — Pratt's attraction to the Canadian past as a subject for presenting human struggles in national and mythic terms. Hence, Pratt's use of geological, biological, and technological imagery is both an acknowledgement of his nineteenth-century background and his ability to describe twentieth-century life in appropriate terminology. But at the centre of Pratt's vision of man is his acceptance of Christ's life and death as the crossroads events of history.*

*While Pratt was equally skilled in writing short lyrics and long narratives, his shorter pieces (such as "The Highway" and "Silences") provide a concise statement of the themes that preoccupy Pratt in the longer narratives (such as* The Titanic, Brébeuf and His Brethren *and* Towards the Last Spike*). What we do not immediately see in the shorter pieces is Pratt's mythologizing imagination at work on Canadian history. The poet shapes from fact, rather than from legend, his stories of missionaries, sailors, politicians, and railway builders, whose individual fortitude and shared efforts — even when tragic — gave universal meaning to particular events. Pratt's narratives celebrate the Canadian virtues of coping with the environment by compromising with it, of acknowledging the need for group enterprise, and of admitting that life is hard but not disillusioning. His treatment of national myths is in the great tradition of Homer, Virgil, and the* Beowulf *poet, each of whom used the history of his people in order to praise those virtues which his contemporaries valued. Pratt's myth-making powers are as brilliantly exploited in comic poems as they are in heroic poems. Narratives such as* The Witches Brew *(1925) and* Titans *(1926) often puzzle readers who are not prepared to accept comedy and fantasy as legitimate modes for serious subjects and solid craftsmanship.*[3]

*Nevertheless, few poets can match Pratt for his exuberant diction and high spirits. As Northrop Frye has observed,*[4] *Pratt developed a narrative line supple enough to shift from comic to tragic to epic, and dramatic enough — within the mosaic structures of the long poems — to sustain suspense and develop conflicts. Furthermore, his lines are both colloquial and learned in a characteristic North American manner, and are thus free of the stifling Shakespearean and Miltonic echoes in the lines of so many Victorian poets. The discovery and use of this line relates Pratt to the twentieth-century movements concerned with language and metre as the basis of poetic art.*

## Footnotes

[1]*Peter Buitenhuis, Introduction to* Selected Poems of E.J. Pratt *(Toronto: Macmillan, 1968), p. xiv.*

[2]Ibid., *p. xiii.*

[3]*For an account of Pratt's critical reputation up to 1959, see Earle Birney, "E. J. Pratt and His Critics", in* Our Living Tradition, *2nd and 3rd Series, Edited by R. L. McDougall (Toronto: University of Toronto Press, 1959), pp. 123-147.*

[4]*Northrop Frye, Introduction to E. J. Pratt's* Collected Poems, *2nd Ed. (Toronto: Macmillan, 1958), pp. xiv-xv.*

# Newfoundland

Here the tides flow,
And here they ebb;
Not with that dull, unsinewed tread of waters
Held under bonds to move
Around unpeopled shores—
Moon-driven through a timeless circuit
Of invasion and retreat;
But with a lusty stroke of life
Pounding at stubborn gates,
That they might run
Within the sluices of men's hearts,
Leap under throb of pulse and nerve,
And teach the sea's strong voice
To learn the harmonies of new floods,
The peal of cataract,
And the soft wash of currents
Against resilient banks,
Or the broken rhythms from old chords
Along dark passages
That once were pathways of authentic fires.

*Red is the sea-kelp on the beach,*
*Red as the heart's blood,*
*Nor is there power in tide or sun*
*To bleach its stain.*
*It lies there piled thick*
*Above the gulch-line.*
*It is rooted in the joints of rocks,*
*It is tangled around a spar,*
*It covers a broken rudder,*
*It is red as the heart's blood,*
*And salt as tears.*

Here the winds blow,
And here they die,
Not with that wild, exotic rage
That vainly sweeps untrodden shores,
But with familiar breath
Holding a partnership with life,
Resonant with the hopes of spring,
Pungent with the airs of harvest.
They call with the silver fifes of the sea,

They breathe with the lungs of men,
They are one with the tides of the sea,
They are one with the tides of the heart,
They blow with the rising octaves of dawn,
They die with the largo of dusk,
Their hands are full to the overflow,
In their right is the bread of life,
In their left are the waters of death.

*Scattered on boom*
*And rudder and weed*
*Are tangles of shells;*
*Some with backs of crusted bronze,*
*And faces of porcelain blue,*
*Some crushed by the beach stones*
*To chips of jade;*
*And some are spiral-cleft*
*Spreading their tracery on the sand*
*In the rich veining of an agate's heart;*
*And others remain unscarred,*
*To babble of the passing of the winds.*

Here the crags
Meet with winds and tides—
Not with that blind interchange
Of blow for blow
That spills the thunder of insentient seas;
But with the mind that reads assault
In crouch and leap and the quick stealth,
Stiffening the muscles of the waves.
Here they flank the harbours,
Keeping watch
On thresholds, altars and the fires of home,
Or, like mastiffs,
Over-zealous,
Guard too well.

*Tide and wind and crag,*
*Sea-weed and sea-shell*
*And broken rudder—*
*And the story is told*
*Of human veins and pulses,*
*Of eternal pathways of fire,*
*Of dreams that survive the night,*
*Of doors held ajar in storms.*

# The Shark

He seemed to know the harbour,
So leisurely he swam;
His fin,
Like a piece of sheet-iron,
Three-cornered,
And with knife-edge,
Stirred not a bubble
As it moved
With its base-line on the water.

His body was tubular
And tapered
And smoke-blue,
And as he passed the wharf
He turned,
And snapped at a flat-fish
That was dead and floating.
And I saw the flash of a white throat,
And a double row of white teeth,
And eyes of metallic grey,
Hard and narrow and slit.

Then out of the harbour,
With that three-cornered fin
Shearing without a bubble the water
Lithely,
Leisurely,
He swam—
That strange fish,
Tubular, tapered, smoke-blue,
Part vulture, part wolf,
Part neither — for his blood was cold.

# The Highway

What aeons passed without a count or name,
Before the cosmic seneschal,
Succeeding with a plan
Of weaving stellar patterns from a flame,
Announced at his high carnival
An orbit — with Aldebaran!

And when the drifting years had sighted land,
And hills and plains declared their birth
Amid volcanic throes,
What was the lapse before the marshal's hand
Had found a garden on the earth,
And led forth June with her first rose?

And what the gulf between that and the hour,
Late in the simian-human day,
When Nature kept her tryst
With the unfoldment of the star and flower—
When in her sacrificial way
Judaea blossomed with her Christ!

But what made *our* feet miss the road that brought
The world to such a golden trove,
In our so brief a span?
How may we grasp again the hand that wrought
Such light, such fragrance, and such love,
O star! O rose! O son of Man?

# Erosion

It took the sea a thousand years,
A thousand years to trace
The granite features of this cliff,
In crag and scarp and base.

It took the sea an hour one night,
An hour of storm to place
The sculpture of these granite seams
Upon a woman's face.

# The Depression Ends

If I could take within my hand
The rod of Prospero for an hour,
With space and speed at my command,
And astro-physics in my power,
Having no reason for my scheme
Beyond the logic of a dream
To change a world predestinate
From the eternal loom of fate,
I'd realize my mad chimera
By smashing distaff and the spinner,
And usher in the golden era
With an apocalyptic dinner.
I'd place a table in the skies
No earthly mind could visualize:
No instruments of earth could bound it—
'Twould take the light-years to go round it.
And to this feast I would invite
Only the faithful, the elect—
The shabby ones of earth's despite,
The victims of her rude neglect,
The most unkempt and motley throng
Ever described in tale or song.
All the good lads I've ever known
From the twelve winds of sea and land
Should hear my shattering bugle tone
And feel its summoning command.
No one should come who never knew
A famine day of rationed gruel,
Nor heard his stomach like a flue
Roaring with wind instead of fuel:
No self-made men who proudly claim
To be the architects of fame;
No profiteers whose double chins
Are battened on the Corn-Exchange,
While continental breadlines range
Before the dust of flour-bins.
These shall not enter, nor shall those
Who soured with the sun complain
Of all their manufactured woes,
Yet never had an honest pain:
Not these — the well-groomed and the sleeked,
But all the gaunt, the cavern-cheeked,

The waifs whose tightened belts declare
The thinness of their daily fare;
The ill-starred from their natal days,
The gaffers and the stowaways,
The road-tramps and the alley-bred
Who leap to scraps that others fling,
With luck less than the Tishbite's, fed
On manna from the raven's wing.

This dinner, now years overdue,
Shall centre in a barbecue.
Orion's club — no longer fable—
Shall fall upon the Taurus head.
No less than Centaurs shall be led
In roaring pairs forth from their stable
And harnessed to the Wain to pull
The mighty carcass of the bull
Across the tundras to the table,
Where he shall stretch from head to stern,
Roasted and basted to a turn.
I'd have the Pleiades prepare
Jugged Lepus (to the vulgar *hare*),
Galactic venison just done
From the corona of the sun,
Hoof jellies from Monoceros,
Planked tuna, shad, stewed terrapin,
And red-gut salmon captured in
The deltas of the Southern Cross.
Devilled shrimps and scalloped clams,
Flamingoes, capons, luscious yams
And cherries from Hesperides;
And every man and every beast,
Known to the stars' directories
For speed of foot and strength of back,
Would be the couriers to this feast—
Mercury, Atlas, Hercules,
Each bearing a capacious pack.
I would conscript the Gemini,
Persuading Castor to compete
With Pollux on a heavy wager,
Buckboard against the sled, that he,
With Capricornus could not beat
His brother mushing Canis Major.
And on the journey there I'd hail
Aquarius with his nets and pail,

And Neptune with his prong to meet us
At some point on the shores of Cetus,
And bid them superintend a cargo
Of fresh sea-food upon the Argo—
Sturgeon and shell-fish that might serve
To fill the side-boards with *hors d'oeuvres.*

And worthy of the banquet spread
Within this royal court of night,
A curving canopy of light
Shall roof it myriad-diamonded.
For high above the table head
Shall sway a candelabrum where,
According to the legend, dwelt a
Lady seated in a chair
With Alpha, Beta, Gamma, Delta,
Busy braiding up her hair.
Sirius, the dog-star, shall be put
Immediately above the foot,
And central from the cupola
Shall hang the cluster — Auriga,
With that deep sapphire-hearted stella,
The loveliest of the lamps, Capella.

For all old men whose pilgrim feet
Were calloused with life's dust and heat,
Whose throats were arid with its thirst,
I'd smite Jove's taverns till they burst,
And punch the spigots of his vats,
Till flagons, kegs and barrels all
Were drained of their ambrosial
As dry as the Sahara flats.
For toothless, winded ladies who,
Timid and hesitating, fear
They might not stand the barbecue
(Being so near their obsequies),
I'd serve purees fresh from the ear
Of Spica with a mild ragout—
To satisfy the calories—
Of breast of Cygnus stiffened by
The hind left leg of Aries,
As a last wind-up before they die.
And I would have no wardens there,
Searching the platters for a reason
To seize Diana and declare

60

That venison is out of season.
For all those children hunger-worn
From drought or flood and harvest failing,
Whether from Nile or Danube hailing,
Or Yangtze or the Volga born,
I'd communize the total yields
Of summer in the Elysian fields,
Gather the berries from the shrubs
To crown souffles and syllabubs.
Dumplings and trifles and *éclaires*
And roly-polies shall be theirs;
Search as you may, you will not find
One dash of oil, one dish of prunes
To spoil the taste of the macaroons,
And I would have you bear in mind
No dietetic aunt-in-law,
With hook-nose and prognathic jaw,
Will try her vain reducing fads
Upon these wenches and these lads.
Now that these grand festivities
Might start with holy auspices,
I would select with Christian care,
To offer up the vesper prayer,
A padre of high blood — no white
Self-pinched, self-punished anchorite,
Who credits up against his dying
His boasted hours of mortifying,
Who thinks he hears a funeral bell
In dinner gongs on principle.
He shall be left to mourn this night,
Walled in his dim religious light:
Unto this feast he shall not come
To breathe his gloom. No! rather some
Sagacious and expansive friar,
Who beams good-will, who loves a briar,
Who, when he has his fellows with him
Around a board, can make a grace
Sonorous, full of liquid rhythm,
Boom from his lungs' majestic bass;
Who, when requested by his host
To do the honours to a toast,
Calls on the clan to rise and hold
Their glasses to the light a minute,
Just to observe the mellow gold
And the rare glint of autumn in it.

Now even at this hour he stands,
The benison upon his face,
In his white hair and moulded hands,
No less than in his spoken grace.
"We thank thee for this table spread
In such a hall, on such a night,
With such unusual stores of bread,
O Lord of love! O Lord of light!
We magnify thy name in praise
At what thy messengers have brought,
For not since Galilean days
Has such a miracle been wrought.
The guests whom thou hast bidden come,
The starved, the maimed, the deaf, and dumb,
Were misfits in a world of evil,
And ridden hard by man and devil.
The seven years they have passed through
Were leaner than what Israel knew.
Dear Lord, forgive my liberty,
In telling what thou mayst not know,
For it must seem so queer to thee,
What happens on our earth below:
The sheep graze on a thousand hills,
The cattle roam upon the plains,
The cotton waits upon the mills,
The stores are bursting with their grains,
And yet these ragged ones that kneel
To take thy grace before their meal
Are said to be thy chosen ones,
Lord of the planets and the suns!
Therefore let thy favours fall
In rich abundance on them all.
May not one stomach here to-night
Turn traitor on its appetite.
Take under thy peculiar care
The infants and the aged. Bestow
Upon all invalids a rare
Release of their digestive flow,
That they, with health returned, may know
A hunger equal to the fare,
And for these mercies, Lord, we'll praise
Thee to the limit of our days."


He ended. The salubrious feast
Began: with inundating mirth

It drowned all memories of earth:
It quenched the midnight chimes: nor ceased
It till the wand of Prospero,
Turning its magic on the east,
Broke on a master charm, when lo!
Answering the summons of her name,
Fresh from the surf of Neptune came
Aurora to the Portico.

# Silences

There is no silence upon the earth or under the earth like the
        silence under the sea;
No cries announcing birth,
No sounds declaring death.
There is silence when the milt is laid on the spawn in the weeds
        and fungus of the rock-clefts;
And silence in the growth and struggle for life.
The bonitoes pounce upon the mackerel,
And are themselves caught by the barracudas,
The sharks kill the barracudas
And the great molluscs rend the sharks,
And all noiselessly—
Though swift be the action and final the conflict,
The drama is silent.

There is no fury upon the earth like the fury under the sea.
For growl and cough and snarl are the tokens of spendthrifts
        who know not the ultimate economy of rage.
Moreover, the pace of the blood is too fast.
But under the waves the blood is sluggard and has the same
        temperature as that of the sea.

There is something pre-reptilian about a silent kill.

Two men may end their hostilities just with their battle-cries.
"The devil take you," says one.
"I'll see you in hell first," says the other.

And these introductory salutes followed by a hail of gutturals
and sibilants are often the beginning of friendship, for
who would not prefer to be lustily damned than to be
half-heartedly blessed?
No one need fear oaths that are properly enunciated, for they
belong to the inheritance of just men made perfect,
and, for all we know, of such may be the Kingdom of
Heaven.
But let silent hate be put away for it feeds upon the heart of the
hater.
Today I watched two pairs of eyes. One pair was black and the
other grey. And while the owners thereof, for the space
of five seconds, walked past each other, the grey
snapped at the black and the black riddled the grey.
One looked to say — "The cat,"
And the other — "The cur."
But no words were spoken;
Not so much as a hiss or a murmur came through the perfect
enamel of the teeth; not so much as a gesture of
enmity.
If the right upper lip curled over the canine, it went unnoticed.
The lashes veiled the eyes not for an instant in the passing.
And as between the two in respect to candour of intention or
eternity of wish, there was no choice, for the stare was
mutual and absolute.
A word would have dulled the exquisite edge of the feeling,
An oath would have flawed the crystallization of the hate.
For only such culture could grow in a climate of silence,—
Away back before the emergence of fur or feather, back to the
unvocal sea and down deep where the darkness spills its
wash on the threshold of light, where the lids never
close upon the eyes, where the inhabitants slay in
silence and are as silently slain.


# The Truant


"What have you there?" the great Panjandrum said
To the Master of the Revels who had led
A bucking truant with a stiff backbone
Close to the foot of the Almighty's throne.

64

"Right Reverend, most adored,
And forcibly acknowledged Lord
By the keen logic of your two-edged sword!
This creature has presumed to classify
Himself — a biped, rational, six feet high
And two feet wide; weighs fourteen stone;
Is guilty of a multitude of sins.
He has abjured his choric origins,
And like an undomesticated slattern,
Walks with tangential step unknown
Within the weave of the atomic pattern.
He has developed concepts, grins
Obscenely at your Royal bulletins,
Possesses what he calls a will
Which challenges your power to kill."

"What is his pedigree?"

"The base is guaranteed, your Majesty—
Calcium, carbon, phosphorus, vapour
And other fundamentals spun
From the umbilicus of the sun,
And yet he says he will not caper
Around your throne, nor toe the rules
For the ballet of the fiery molecules."
"His concepts and denials — scrap them, burn them—
To the chemists with them promptly."

                                          "Sire,

The stuff is not amenable to fire.
Nothing but their own kind can overturn them.
The chemists have sent back the same old story—
'With our extreme gelatinous apology,
We beg to inform your Imperial Majesty,
Unto whom be dominion and power and glory,
There still remains that strange precipitate
Which has the quality to resist
Our oldest and most trusted catalyst.
It is a substance we cannot cremate
By temperatures known to our Laboratory.' "

And the great Panjandrum's face grew dark—
"I'll put those chemists to their annual purge,
And I myself shall be the thaumaturge

To find the nature of this fellow's spark.
Come, bring him nearer by yon halter rope:
I'll analyse him with the cosmoscope."

Pulled forward with his neck awry,
The little fellow six feet short,
Aware he was about to die,
Committed grave contempt of court
By answering with a flinchless stare
The Awful Presence seated there.

The ALL HIGH swore until his face was black.
He called him a coprophagite,
A genus *homo*, egomaniac,
Third cousin to the family of worms,
A sporozoan from the ooze of night,
Spawn of a spavined troglodyte:
He swore by all the catalogue of terms
Known since the slang of carboniferous Time.
He said that he could trace him back
To pollywogs and earwigs in the slime.
And in his shrillest tenor he began
Reciting his indictment of the man,
Until he closed upon this capital crime—
"You are accused of singing out of key,
(A foul unmitigated dissonance)
Of shuffling in the measures of the dance,
Then walking out with that defiant, free
Toss of your head, banging the doors,
Leaving a stench upon the jacinth floors.
You have fallen like a curse
On the mechanics of my Universe.

"Herewith I measure out your penalty—
Hearken while you hear, look while you see:
I send you now upon your homeward route
Where you shall find
Humiliation for your pride of mind.
I shall make deaf the ear, and dim the eye,
Put palsy in your touch, make mute
Your speech, intoxicate your cells and dry
Your blood and marrow, shoot
Arthritic needles through your cartilage,
And having parched you with old age,
I'll pass you wormwise through the mire;

And when your rebel will
Is mouldered, all desire
Shrivelled, all your concepts broken,
Backward in dust I'll blow you till
You join my spiral festival of fire.
Go, Master of the Revels — I have spoken."

And the little genus *homo*, six feet high,
Standing erect, countered with this reply—
"You dumb insouciant invertebrate,
You rule a lower than a feudal state—
A realm of flunkey decimals that run,
Return; return and run; again return,
Each group around its little sun,
And every sun a satellite.
There they go by day and night,
Nothing to do but run and burn,
Taking turn and turn about,
Light-year in and light-year out,
Dancing, dancing in quadrillions,
Never leaving their pavilions.

"Your astronomical conceit
Of bulk and power is anserine.
Your ignorance so thick,
You did not know your own arithmetic.
We flung the graphs about your flying feet;
We measured your diameter—
Merely a line
Of zeros prefaced by an integer.
Before we came
You had no name.
You did not know direction or your pace;
We taught you all you ever knew
Of motion, time and space.
We healed you of your vertigo
And put you in our kindergarten show,
Perambulated you through prisms, drew
Your mileage through the Milky Way,
Lassoed your comets when they ran astray,
Yoked Leo, Taurus, and your team of Bears
To pull our kiddy cars of inverse squares.

"Boast not about your harmony,
Your perfect curves, your rings

67

Of *pure and endless light* — 'Twas we
Who pinned upon your Seraphim their wings,
And when your brassy heavens rang
With joy that morning while the planets sang
Their choruses of archangelic lore,
'Twas we who ordered the notes upon their score
Out of our winds and strings.
Yes! all your shapely forms
Are ours — parabolas of silver light,
Those blueprints of your spiral stairs
From nadir depth to zenith height,
Coronas, rainbows after storms,
Auroras on your eastern tapestries
And constellations over western seas.

"And when, one day, grown conscious of your age,
While pondering an eolith,
We turned a human page
And blotted out a cosmic myth
With all its baby symbols to explain
The sunlight in Apollo's eyes,
Our rising pulses and the birth of pain,
Fear, and that fern-and-fungus breath
Stalking our nostrils to our caves of death—
That day we learned how to anatomize
Your body, calibrate your size
And set a mirror up before your face
To show you what you really were — a rain
Of dull Lucretian atoms crowding space,
A series of concentric waves which any fool
Might make by dropping stones within a pool,
Or an exploding bomb forever in flight
Bursting like hell through Chaos and Old Night.

"You oldest of the hierarchs
Composed of electronic sparks,
We grant you speed,
We grant you power, and fire
That ends in ash, but we concede
To you no pain nor joy nor love nor hate,
No final tableau of desire,
No causes won or lost, no free
Adventure at the outposts — only
The degradation of your energy
When at some late

Slow number of your dance your sergeant-major Fate
Will catch you blind and groping and will send
You reeling on that long and lonely
Lockstep of your wave-lengths towards your end.

"We who have met
With stubborn calm the dawn's hot fusillades;
Who have seen the forehead sweat
Under the tug of pulleys on the joints,
Under the liquidating tally
Of the cat-and-truncheon bastinades;
Who have taught our souls to rally
To mountain horns and the sea's rockets
When the needle ran demented through the points;
We who have learned to clench
Our fists and raise our lightless sockets
To morning skies after the midnight raids,
Yet cocked our ears to bugles on the barricades,
And in cathedral rubble found a way to quench
A dying thirst within a Galilean valley—
No! by the Rood, we will not join your ballet."


## Towards the Last Spike

It was the same world then as now — the same,
Except for little differences of speed
And power, and means to treat myopia
To show an axe-blade infinitely sharp
Splitting things infinitely small, or else
Provide the telescopic sight to roam
Through curved dominions never found in fables.
The same, but for new particles of speech—
Those algebraic substitutes for nouns
That sky cartographers would hang like signboards
Along the trespass of our thoughts to stop
The stutters of our tongues with their equations.

As now, so then, blood kept its ancient colour,
And smoothly, roughly, paced its banks; in calm
Preserving them, in riot rupturing them.

Wounds needed bandages and stomachs food:
The hands outstretched had joined the lips in prayer—
*"Give us our daily bread, give us our pay."*
The past flushed in the present and tomorrow
Would dawn upon today: only the rate
To sensitize or numb a nerve would change;
Only the quickening of a measuring skill
To gauge the onset of a birth or death
With the precision of micrometers.
Men spoke of acres then and miles and masses,
Velocity and steam, cables that moored
Not ships but continents, world granaries,
The east-west cousinship, a nation's rise,
Hail of identity, a world expanding,
If not the universe: the feel of it
Was in the air — *"Union required the Line."*
The theme was current at the banquet tables,
And arguments profane and sacred rent
God-fearing families into partisans.
Pulpit, platform and floor were sounding-boards;
Cushions beneath the pounding fists assumed
The hues of western sunsets; nostrils sniffed
The prairie tang; the tongue rolled over texts:
Even St. Paul was being invoked to wring
The neck of Thomas in this war of faith
With unbelief. Was ever an adventure
Without its cost? Analogies were found
On every page of history or science.
A nation, like the world, could not stand still.
What was the use of records but to break them?
The tougher armour followed the new shell;
The newer shell the armour; lighthouse rockets
Sprinkled their stars over the wake of wrecks.
Were not the engineers at work to close
The lag between the pressured and the valves?
The same world then as now thirsting for power
To crack those records open, extra pounds
Upon the inches, extra miles per hour.
The mildewed static schedules which before
Had like asbestos been immune to wood
Now curled and blackened in the furnace coal.
This power lay in the custody of men
From down-and-outers needing roofs, whose hands
Were moulded by their fists, whose skins could feel
At home incorporate with dolomite,

70

To men who with the marshal instincts in them,
Deriving their authority from wallets,
Directed their battalions from the trestles.


THE GATHERING


*("Oats — a grain which in England is generally given
to horses, but in Scotland supports the people." —
Dr. Samuel Johnson. "True, but where will you find
such horses, where such men?" — Lord Elibank's
reply as recorded by Sir Walter Scott.)*


Oatmeal was in their blood and in their names.
Thrift was the title of their catechism.
It governed all things but their mess of porridge
Which, when it struck the hydrochloric acid
With treacle and skim-milk, became a mash.
Entering the duodenum, it broke up
Into amino acids: then the liver
Took on its natural job as carpenter:
Foreheads grew into cliffs, jaws into juts.
The meal, so changed, engaged the follicles:
Eyebrows came out as gorse, the beards as thistles,
And the chest-hair the fell of Grampian rams.
It stretched and vulcanized the human span:
Nonagenarians worked and thrived upon it.
Out of such chemistry run through by genes,
The food released its fearsome racial products:—
The power to strike a bargain like a foe,
To win an argument upon a burr,
Invest the language with a Bannockburn,
Culloden or the warnings of Lochiel,
Weave loyalties and rivalries in tartans,
Present for the amazement of the world
Kilts and the civilized barbaric Fling,
And pipes which, when they acted on the mash,
Fermented lullabies to *Scots wha hae*.


Their names were like a battle-muster — Angus
(He of the Shops) and Fleming (of the Transit),
Hector (of the *Kicking Horse*), Dawson,
"Cromarty" Ross, and Beatty (Ulster Scot),
Bruce, Allan, Galt and Douglas, and the "twa"—

Stephen (Craigellachie)* and Smith (Strathcona)—
Who would one day climb from their Gaelic hide-outs,
Take off their plaids and wrap them round the mountains.
And then the everlasting tread of the Macs,
Vanguard, centre and rear, their roving eyes
On summits, rivers, contracts, beaver, ledgers;
Their ears cocked to the skirl of Sir John A.,
The general of the patronymic march.

*(Sir John revolving round the Terms of Union with
British Columbia. Time, late at night.)*

Insomnia had ripped the bed-sheets from him
Night after night. How long was this to last?
Confederation had not played this kind
Of trickery on him. That was rough indeed,
So gravelled, that a man might call for rest
And take it for a life accomplishment.
It was his laurel though some of the leaves
Had dried. But this would be a longer tug
Of war which needed for his team thick wrists
And calloused fingers, heavy heels to dig
Into the earth and hold — men with bull's beef
Upon their ribs. Had he himself the wind,
The anchor-waist to peg at the rope's end?
'Twas bad enough to have these questions hit
The waking mind: 'twas much worse when he dozed;
For goblins had a way of pinching him,
Slapping a nightmare on to dwindling snoozes.
They put him and his team into a tug
More real than life. He heard a judge call out—
"Teams settle on the rope and take the strain!"
And with the coaches' *heave*, the running welts
Reddened his palms, and then the gruelling *backlock*
Inscribed its indentations on his shoulders.
This kind of burn he knew he had to stand;
It was the game's routine; the other fire
Was what he feared the most for it could bake him—
That white dividing rag tied to the rope
Above the centre pole had with each heave
Wavered with chances equal. With the backlock,

*"Stand Fast, Craigellachie," the war-cry of the Clan Grant, named after a rock in the Spey Valley, and used as a cable message from Stephen in London to the Directors in Montreal.

72

Despite the legs of Tupper and Cartier,
The western anchor dragged; the other side
Remorselessly was gaining, holding, gaining.
No sleep could stand this strain and, with the nightmare
Delivered of its colt, Macdonald woke.


Tired with the midnight toss, lock-jawed with yawns,
He left the bed and, shuffling to the window,
He opened it. The air would cool him off
And soothe his shoulder burns. He felt his ribs:
Strange, nothing broken — how those crazy drowses
Had made the fictions tangle with the facts!
He must unscramble them with steady hands.
Those Ranges pirouetting in his dreams
Had their own knack of standing still in light,
Revealing peaks whose known triangulation
Had to be read in prose severity.
Seizing a telescope, he swept the skies,
The north-south drift, a self-illumined chart.
Under Polaris was the Arctic Sea
And the sub-Arctic gates well stocked with names:
Hudson, Davis, Baffin, Frobisher;
And in his own day Franklin, Ross and Parry
Of the Canadian Archipelago;
Kellett, McClure, McClintock, of *The Search*.
Those straits and bays had long been kicked by keels,
And flags had fluttered on the Capes that fired
His youth, making familiar the unknown.
What though the odds were nine to one against,
And the Dead March was undertoning trumpets,
There was enough of strychnine in the names
To make him flip a penny for the risk,
Though he had palmed the coin reflectively
Before he threw and watched it come down *heads*.
That stellar path looked too much like a road map
Upon his wall — the roads all led to market—
The north-south route. He lit a candle, held
It to a second map full of blank spaces
And arrows pointing west. Disturbed, he turned
The lens up to the zenith, followed the course
Tracked by a cloud of stars that would not keep
Their posts — Capella, Perseus, were reeling;
Low in the north-west, Cassiopeia
Was qualmish, leaning on her starboard arm-rest,
And Aries was chasing, butting Cygnus,

Just diving. Doubts and hopes struck at each other.
Why did those constellations look so much
Like blizzards? And what lay beyond the blizzards?

'Twas chilly at the window. He returned
To bed and savoured soporific terms:
*Superior*, the *Red River, Selkirk, Prairie,*
*Port Moody* and *Pacific.* Chewing them,
He spat out *Rocky* grit before he swallowed.
*Selkirk!* This had the sweetest taste. Ten years
Before, the Highland crofters had subscribed
Their names in a memorial for the Rails.
Sir John reviewed the story of the struggle,
That four months' journey from their native land—
The Atlantic through the Straits to Hudson Bay,
Then the Hayes River to Lake Winnipeg
Up to the Forks of the Assiniboine.
He could make use of that — just what he needed,
A Western version of the Arctic daring,
Romance and realism, double dose.
How long ago? Why, this is '71.
Those fellows came the time Napoleon
Was on the steppes. For sixty years they fought
The seasons, 'hoppers, drought, hail, wind and snow;
Survived the massacre at Seven Oaks,
The "Pemmican War" and the Red River floods.
They wanted now the Road — those pioneers
Who lived by spades instead of beaver traps.
Most excellent word that, pioneers! Sir John
Snuggled himself into his sheets, rolling
The word around his tongue, a theme for song.
Or for a peroration to a speech.


THE HANGOVER AT DAWN

He knew the points that had their own appeal.
These did not bother him: the patriot touch,
The Flag, the magnetism of explorers,
The national unity. These could burn up
The phlegm in most of the provincial throats.
But there was one tale central to his plan
(The focus of his headache at this moment),
Which would demand the limit of his art—
The ballad of his courtship in the West:
Better reveal it soon without reserve.

74

## THE LADY OF BRITISH COLUMBIA

Port Moody and Pacific! He had pledged
His word the Line should run from sea to sea.
*"From sea to sea"*, a hallowed phrase. Music
Was in that text if the right key were struck,
And he must strike it first, for, as he fingered
The clauses of the pledge, rough notes were rasping—
*"No Road, No Union"*, and the converse true.
East-west against the north-south run of trade,
For California like a sailor-lover
Was wooing over-time. He knew the ports.
His speech was as persuasive as his arms,
As sinuous as Spanish arias—
Tamales, Cazadero, Mendecino,
Curling their baritones around the Lady.
Then Santa Rosa, Santa Monica,
Held absolution in their syllables.
But when he saw her stock of British temper
Starch at ironic sainthood in the whispers—
*"Rio de nuestra señora de buena guia,"**
He had the tact to gutturalize the liquids,
Steeping the tunes to drinking songs, then take
Her on a holiday where she could watch
A roving sea-born Californian pound
A downy chest and swear by San Diego.

Sir John, wise to the tricks, was studying hard
A fresh proposal for a marriage contract.
He knew a game was in the ceremony.
That southern fellow had a healthy bronze
Complexion, had a vast estate, was slick
Of manner. In his ardour he could tether
Sea-roses to the blossoms of his orchards,
And for his confidence he had the prime
Advantage of his rival — *he was there.*

## THE LONG-DISTANCE PROPOSAL

A game it was, and the Pacific lass
Had poker wisdom on her face. Her name
Was rich in values — *British;* this alone

---

*"River of Our Lady of Safe Conduct."*

75

Could raise Macdonald's temperature: so could
*Columbia* with a different kind of fever,
And in between the two, *Victoria*.
So the *Pacific* with its wash of letters
Could push the Fahrenheit another notch.
She watched for bluff on those Disraeli features,
Impassive but for arrowy chipmunk eyes,
Engaged in fathoming a contract time.
With such a dowry she could well afford
To take the risk of tightening the terms—
*"Begin the Road in two years, end in ten"*—
Sir John, a moment letting down his guard,
Frowned at the Rocky skyline, but agreed.

*(The Terms ratified by Parliament, British
Columbia enters Confederation July, 1871, Sand-
ford Fleming being appointed engineer-in-chief of
the proposed Railway, Walter Moberly to co-
operate with him in the location of routes. "Of
course, I don't know how many millions you have,
but it is going to cost you money to get through
those canyons." — Moberly to Macdonald.)*

THE PACIFIC SCANDAL

*(Huntingdon's charges of political corruption
based on correspondence and telegrams rifled from
the offices of the solicitor of Sir Hugh Allan, Head
of the Canada Pacific Company; Sir John's defence; and the appearance of the Honourable
Edward Blake who rises to reply to Sir John at 2
a.m.)*

BLAKE IN MOOD

Of all the subjects for debate here was
His element. His soul as clean as surf,
No one could equal him in probing cupboards
Or sweeping floors and dusting shelves, finding
A skeleton inside an overcoat;
Or shaking golden eagles from a pocket
To show the copper plugs within the coins.
Rumours he heard had gangrened into facts—
Gifts nuzzling at two-hundred-thousand dollars,
Elections on, and with a contract pending.

The odour of the bills had blown his gorge.
His appetite, edged by a moral hone,
Could surfeit only on the Verities.


*November 3, 1873*

A Fury rode him to the House. He took
His seat, and with a stoic gloom he heard
The Chieftain's great defence and noted well
The punctuation of the cheers. He needed all
The balance of his mind to counterpoise
The movements of Macdonald as he flung
Himself upon the House, upon the Country,
Upon posterity, upon his conscience.
That plunging played the devil with Blake's tiller,
Threatened the set of his sail. To save the course,
To save himself, in that five hours of gale,
He had to jettison his meditation,
His brooding on the follies of mankind,
Clean out the wadding from his tortured ears:
That roaring mob before him could be quelled
Only by action; so when the last round
Of the applause following the peroration
Was over, slowly, weightily, Blake rose.

A statesman-chancellor now held the Floor.
He told the sniffing Commons that a sense
Keener than smell or taste must be invoked
To get the odour. Leading them from facts
Like telegrams and stolen private letters,
He soared into the realm of principles
To find his scourge; and then the men involved,
Robed like the Knights of Malta, Blake undressed,
Their cloaks inverted to reveal the shoddy,
The tattered lining and bare-threaded seams.
He ripped the last stitch from them — by the time
Recess was called, he had them in the dock
As brigands in the Ministry of Smells,
Naked before the majesty of Heaven.

For Blake recesses were but sandwiches
Provided merely for cerebral luncheons—
No time to spread the legs under the table,
To chat and chaff a while, to let the mind
Roam, like a goblet up before the light

77

To bask in natural colour, or by whim
Of its own choice to sway luxuriously
In tantalizing arcs before the nostrils.
A meal was meant by Nature for nutrition—
A sorry farinaceous business scaled
Exactly to caloric grains and grams
Designed for intellectual combustion,
For energy directed into words
Towards proof. Abuse was overweight. He saw
No need for it; no need for caricature,
And if a villainous word had to be used,
'Twas for a villain — keen upon the target.
Irrelevance was like a moral lesion
No less within a speech than in a statute.
What mattered it who opened up the files,
Sold for a bid the damning correspondence—
That Montreal-Chicago understanding?
A dirty dodge, so let it be conceded.
But *here* the method was irrelevant.
Whether by legal process or by theft,
The evidence was there unalterable.
So with the House assembled, he resumed
Imperial indictment of the bandits.
The logic left no loopholes in the facts.
Figures that ran into the hundred-thousands
Were counted up in pennies, each one shown
To bear the superscription of debasement.

Again recess, again the sandwiches,
Again the invocation of the gods:
Each word, each phrase, each clause went to position,
Each sentence regimented like a lockstep.
The only thing that would not pace was time;
The hours dragged by until the thrushes woke—
Two days, two nights — someone opened a window,
And members of the House who still were conscious
Uncreaked their necks to note that even Sir John
Himself had put his fingers to his nose.

*(The appeal to the country: Macdonald defeated:
Mackenzie assumes power, 1874.)*

A change of air, a drop in temperature!
The House had rarely known sobriety
Like this. No longer clanged the *Westward Ho!"*

And quiet were the horns upon the hills.
Hard times ahead. The years were rendering up
Their fat. Measured and rationed was the language
Directed to the stringency of pockets.
The eye must be convinced before the *vision*.
*"But one step at a time,"* exclaimed the feet.
It was the story of the hen or egg;
Which came before the other? *" 'Twas the hen,"*
Cried one; *"undoubtedly the hen must lay
The egg, hatch it and mother it." "Not so,"*
Another shouted, *" 'Twas the egg or whence
The hen?"* For every one who cleared his throat
And called across the House with Scriptural passion—
*"The Line is meant to bring the loaves and fishes,"*
A voting three had countered with the question—
*"Where are the multitudes that thirst and hunger?"*
Passion became displaced by argument.
Till now the axles justified their grease,
Taught coal a lesson in economy.
All doubts here could be blanketed with facts,
With phrases smooth as actuarial velvet.

For forty years in towns and cities men
Had watched the Lines baptized with charters, seen
Them grow, marry and bring forth children.
Parades and powder had their uses then
For gala days; and bands announced arrivals,
Betrothals, weddings and again arrivals.
Champagne brimmed in the font as they were named
With titles drawn from the explorers' routes,
From Saints and Governors, from space and seas
And compass-points — Saints Andrew, Lawrence, Thomas,
Louis and John; Champlain, Simcoe; Grand Trunk,
Intercolonial, the Canadian Southern,
Dominion-Atlantic, the Great Western — names
That caught a continental note and tried
To answer it. Half-gambles though they were,
Directors built those Roads and heard them run
To the sweet silver jingle in their minds.

The airs had long been mastered like old songs
The feet could tap to in the galleries.
But would they tap to a new rhapsody,
A harder one to learn and left unfinished?
What ear could be assured of absolute pitch
To catch this kind of music in the West?

The far West? Men had used this flattering name
For East or but encroachment on the West.
And was not Lake Superior still the East,
A natural highway which ice-ages left,
An unappropriated legacy?
There was no discord in the piston-throbs
Along this Road. This was old music too.
That northern spine of rock, those western mountains,
Were barriers built of God and cursed of Blake.
Mild in his oaths, Mackenzie would avoid them.
He would let contracts for the south and west,
Push out from settlement to settlement.
This was economy, just plain horse-sense.
The Western Lines were there — American.
He would link up with them, could reach the Coast.
The Eagle and the Lion were good friends:
At least the two could meet on sovereign terms
Without a sign of fur and feathers flying.
As yet, but who could tell? So far, so good.
Spikes had been driven at the boundary line,
From Emerson across the Red to Selkirk,
And then to Thunder Bay — to Lake Superior;
Across the prairies in God's own good time,
His plodding, patient, planetary time.

Five years' delay: surveys without construction;
Short lines suspended, discord in the Party.
The West defrauded of its glittering peaks,
The public blood was stirring and protesting
At this continuous dusk upon the mountains.
The old conductor off the podium,
The orchestra disbanded at the time
The daring symphony was on the score,
The audience cupped their ears to catch a strain:
They heard a plaintive thinning oboe-A
That kept on thinning while slow feeble steps
Approached the stand. Was this the substitute
For what the auditorium once knew—
The maestro who with tread of stallion hoofs
Came forward shaking platforms and the rafters,
And followed up the concert pitch with sound
Of drums and trumpets and the organ blasts
That had the power to toll out apathy
And make snow peaks ring like Cathedral steeples?
Besides, accompanying those bars of music,

There was an image men had not forgotten,
The shaggy chieftain standing at his desk,
That last-ditch fight when he was overthrown,
That desperate five hours. At least they knew
His personal pockets were not lined with pelf,
Whatever loot the others grabbed. The words
British, the West instead of South, the Nation,
The all-Canadian route — these terms were singing
Fresher than ever while the grating tones
Under the stress of argument had faded
Within the shroud of their monotony.

*(Sir John returns to power in 1878 with a National
Policy of Protective Tariff and the Transcontinental.)*

Two years of tuning up: it needed that
To counterpoint Blake's eloquence or lift
Mackenzie's non-adventurous common sense
To the ignition of an enterprise.
The pace had to be slow at first, a tempo
Cautious, simple to follow. Sections strewn
Like amputated limbs along the route
Were sutured. This appealed to sanity.
No argument could work itself to sweat
Against a prudent case, for the terrain
Looked easy from the Lake to the Red River.
To stop with those suspensions was a waste
Of cash and time. But the huge task announced
Ten years before had now to start afresh—
The moulding of men's minds was harder far
Than moulding of the steel and prior to it.
It was the battle of ideas and words
And kindred images called by the same name,
Like brothers who with temperamental blood
Went to it with their fists. Canyons and cliffs
Were precipices down which men were hurled,
Or something to be bridged and sheared and scaled.
Likewise the Pass had its ambiguous meaning.
The leaders of the factions in the House
And through the country spelled the word the same:
The way they got their tongue around the word
Was different, for some could make it hiss
With sound of blizzards screaming over ramparts:
The Pass — the Yellowhead, the Kicking Horse—

Or jam it with *coureur-de-bois* romance,
Or join it to the empyrean. Eagles,
In flight banking their wings above a fish-stream,
Had guided the explorers to a route
And given the Pass the title of their wings.
The stories lured men's minds up to the mountains
And down along the sandbars of the rivers.
Rivalling the *"brown and barren"* on the maps,
Officially *"not fit for human life"*,
Were vivid yellows flashing in the news—
*"Gold in the Cariboo,"* *"Gold in the Fraser."*
The swish of gravel in the placer-cradles
Would soon be followed by the spluttering fuses,
By thunder echoing thunder; for one month
After Blake's Ottawa roar would Onderdonk
Roar back from Yale by ripping canyon walls
To crash the tons by millions in the gorges.

The farther off, as by a paradox
Of magnets, was the golden lure the stronger:
Two thousand miles away, imagined peaks
Had the vacation pull of mountaineering,
But with the closer vision would the legs
Follow the mind? 'Twas Blake who raised the question
And answered it. Though with his natural eyes
Up to this time he had not sighted mountains,
He was an expert with the telescope.

THE ATTACK

Sir John was worried. The first hour of Blake
Was dangerous, granted the theme. Eight years
Before, he had the theme combined with language.
*Impeachment* — word with an historic ring,
Reserved for the High Courts of Parliament,
Uttered only when men were breathing hard
And when the vertebrae were musket-stiff:
High ground was that for his artillery,
And *there*, despite the hours the salvos lasted.
But *here* this was a theme less vulnerable
To fire, Macdonald thought, to Blake's gunfire,
And yet he wondered what the orator
Might spring in that first hour, what strategy
Was on the Bench. He did not mind the close
Mosaic of the words — too intricate,

82

Too massive in design. Men might admire
The speech and talk about it, then forget it.
But few possessed the patience or the mind
To tread the mazes of the labyrinth.
Once in a while, however, would Blake's logic
Stumble upon stray figures that would leap
Over the walls of other folds and catch
The herdsmen in their growing somnolence.
The waking sound was not — *"It can't be done";*
That was a dogma, anyone might say it.
It was the following burning corollary:
*"To build a Road over that sea of mountains."*
This carried more than argument. It was
A flash of fire which might with proper kindling
Consume its way into the public mind.
The House clicked to the ready and Sir John,
Burying his finger-nails into his palms,
Muttered — *"God send us no more metaphors
Like that — except from Tory factories."*

Had Blake the lift of Chatham as he had
Burke's wind and almost that sierra span
Of mind, he might have carried the whole House
With him and posted it upon that sea
Of mountains with sub-zeros on their scalps,
Their glacial ribs waiting for warmth of season
To spring an avalanche. Such similes
Might easily glue the members to their seats
With frost in preparation for their ride.
Sir John's *"from sea to sea"* was Biblical;
It had the stamp of reverent approval;
But Blake's was pagan, frightening, congealing.
The chieftain's lips continued as in prayer,
A fiercely secular and torrid prayer—
*"May Heaven intervene to stop the flow
Of such unnatural images and send
The rhetorician back to decimals,
Back to his tessellated subtleties."*
The prayer was answered for High Heaven did it.
The second hour entered and passed by,
A third, a fourth. Sir John looked round the House,
Noticed the growing shuffle of the feet,
The agony of legs, the yawn's contagion.
Was that a snore? Who was it that went out?
He glanced at the Press Gallery. The pens

83

Were scratching through the languor of the ink
To match the words with shorthand and were failing.
He hoped the speech would last another hour,
And still another. Well within the law,
This homicidal master of the opiates
Loosened the hinges of the Opposition:
The minds went first; the bodies sagged; the necks
Curved on the benches and the legs sprawled out.
And when the Fundy Tide had ebbed, Sir John,
Smiling, watched the debris upon the banks,
For what were yesterday grey human brains
Had with decomposition taken on
The texture and complexion of red clay.

*(In 1880 Tupper lets contract to Onderdonk for
survey and construction through the Pacific Section of the mountains. Sir John, Tupper, Pope,
and McIntyre go to London to interest capital but
return without a penny.)*

Failing to make a dent in London dams,
Sir John set out to plumb a reservoir
Closer in reach. He knew its area,
Its ownership, the thickness of its banks,
Its conduits — if he could get his hands
Upon the local stopcocks, could he turn them?
The reservoir was deep. Two centuries
Ago it started filling when a king
Had in a furry moment scratched a quill
Across the bottom of His Royal Charter—
*"Granting the Governor and His Company
Of Gentlemen Adventurers the right
Exclusive to one-third a continent."*
Was it so easy then? A scratch, a seal,
A pinch of snuff tickling the sacred nostrils,
A puff of powder and the ink was dry.
Sir John twisted his lips: he thought of London.
Empire and wealth were in that signature
For royal, princely, ducal absentees,
For courtiers to whom the parallels
Were nothing but chalk scratches on a slate.
For them wild animals were held in game
Preserves, foxes as quarry in a chase,
And hills were hedges, river banks were fences,
And cataracts but fountains in a garden

84

Tumbling their bubbles into marble basins.
Where was this place called Hudson Bay? Some place
In the Antipodes? Explorers, traders,
Would bring their revenues over that signet.
Two centuries — the new empire advanced,
Was broken, reunited, torn again.
The *fleur-de-lis* went to half-mast, the *Jack*
To the mast-head, but fresher rivalries
Broke out — Nor'-Westers at the Hudson's throat
Over the pelts, over the pemmican;
No matter what — the dividends flowed in
As rum flowed out like the Saskatchewan.

The twist left Sir John's lips and he was smiling.
Though English in ambition and design,
This reservoir, he saw there in control
Upon the floodgates not a Londoner
In riding breeches but, red-flannel-shirted,
Trousered in homespun, streaked and blobbed with seal-oil,
A Scot with smoke of peat fire on his breath—
Smith? Yes: but christened Donald Alexander
And loined through issue from the Grants and Stuarts.

To smite the rock and bring forth living water,
Take lead or tin and transmute both to silver,
Copper to gold, betray a piece of glass
To diamonds, fabulize a continent,
Were wonders once believed, scrapped and revived;
For Moses, Marco Polo, Paracelsus,
Fell in the same retort and came out *Smith*.
A miracle on legs, the lad had left
Forres and Aberdeen, gone to Lachine—
*"Tell Mr. Smith to count and sort the rat-skins."*
Thence Tadoussac and Posts off Anticosti;
From there to Rigolet in Labrador,
A thousand miles by foot, snowshoe and dog-sled.
He fought the climate like a weathered yak,
And conquered it, ripping the stalactites
From his red beard, thawing his feet, and wringing
Salt water from his mitts; but most of all
He learned the art of making change. Blankets,
Ribbons and beads, tobacco, guns and knives,
Were swapped for muskrat, marten, fox and beaver.
And when the fur trade thinned, he trapped the salmon,
Canned it; hunted the seal, traded its oil

85

And fertilized the gardens with the carcass.
Even the melons grew in Labrador.
What could resist this touch? Water from rock!
Why not? No more a myth than pelts should be
Thus fabricated into bricks of gold.

If rat-skins, why not tweeds? If looms could take
Raw wool and twill it into selling shape,
They could under the draper's weaving mind
Be patterning gold braid:
                    So thought George Stephen.

His legs less sturdy than his cousin Donald's,
His eyes were just as furiously alert.
His line of vision ran from the north-west
To the Dutch-held St. Paul-Pacific Railway.
Allied with Smith, Kitson and Kennedy,
Angus, Jim Hill and Duncan McIntyre,
Could he buy up this semi-bankrupt Road
And turn the northern traffic into it?
Chief bricklayer of all the Scotian clans,
And foremost as a banking metallurgist,
He took the parchments at their lowest level
And mineralized them, roasted them to shape,
Then mortared them into the pyramid,
Till with the trowel-stretching exercise
He grew so Atlas-strong that he could carry
A mountain like a namesake on his shoulders.

*(The Charter granted to The Canadian Pacific
Railway, February 17, 1881, with George Stephen
as first President . . . One William Cornelius Van
Horne arrives in Winnipeg, December 31, 1881,
and there late at night, forty below zero, gives vent
to a soliloquy.)*

Stephen had laid his raw hands on Van Horne,
Pulled him across the border, sent him up
To get the feel of northern temperatures.
He knew through Hill the story of his life
And found him made to order. Nothing less
Than geologic space his field of work,
He had in Illinois explored the creeks
And valleys, brooded on the rocks and quarries.
Using slate fragments, he became a draughtsman,

Bringing to life a landscape or a cloud,
Turning a tree into a beard, a cliff
Into a jaw, a creek into a mouth
With banks for lips. He loved to work on shadows.
Just now the man was forcing the boy's stature,
The while the youth tickled the man within.
Companioned by the shade of Agassiz,
He would come home, his pockets stuffed with fossils—
Crinoids and fish-teeth — and his tongue jabbering
Of the earth's crust before the birth of life,
Prophetic of the days when he would dig
Into Laurentian rock. The Morse-key tick
And tape were things mesmeric — space and time
Had found a junction. Electricity
And rock, one novel to the coiling hand,
The other frozen in the lap of age,
Were playthings for the boy, work for the man.
As man he was the State's first operator;
As boy he played a trick upon his boss
Who, cramped with current, fired him on the instant;
As man at school, escaping Latin grammar,
He tore the fly-leaf from the text to draw
The contour of a hill; as boy he sketched
The principal, gave him flapdoodle ears,
Bristled his hair, turned eyebrows into quills,
His whiskers into flying buttresses,
His eye-tusks into rusted railroad spikes,
And made a truss between his nose and chin.
Expelled again, he went back to the keys,
To bush and rock and found companionship
With quarry-men, stokers and station-masters,
Switchmen and locomotive engineers.

Now he was transferred to Winnipeg.
Of all the places in an unknown land
Chosen by Stephen for Van Horne, this was
The pivot on which he could turn his mind.
Here he could clap the future on the shoulder
And order Fate about as his lieutenant,
For he would take no nonsense from a thing
Called Destiny — the stars had to be with him.
He spent the first night in soliloquy,
Like Sir John A. but with a difference.
Sir John wanted to sleep but couldn't do it:
Van Horne could sleep but never wanted to.

It was a waste of time, his bed a place
Only to think or dream with eyes awake.
Opening a jack-knife, he went to the window,
Scraped off the frost. Great treks ran through his mind,
East-west. Two centuries and a half gone by,
One trek had started from the Zuyder Zee
To the new Amsterdam. 'Twas smooth by now,
Too smooth. His line of grandsires and their cousins
Had built a city from Manhattan dirt.
Another trek to Illinois; it too
Was smooth, but this new one it was his job
To lead, then build a highway which men claimed
Could not be built. Statesmen and engineers
Had blown their faces blue with their denials:
The men who thought so were asylum cases
Whose monomanias harmless up to now
Had not swept into cells. His bearded chin
Pressed to the pane, his eyes roved through the west.
He saw the illusion at its worst — the frost,
The steel precision of the studded heavens,
Relentless mirror of a covered earth.
His breath froze on the scrape: he cut again
And glanced at the direction west-by-south.
That westward trek was the American,
Union-Pacific — easy so he thought,
Their forty million stacked against his four.
Lonely and desolate this. He stocked his mind
With items of his task: the simplest first,
Though hard enough, the Prairies, then the Shore
North of the Lake — a quantity half-guessed.
Mackenzie like a balky horse had shied
And stopped at this. Van Horne knew well the reason,
But it was vital for the all-land route.
He peered through at the South. Down there Jim Hill
Was whipping up his horses on a road
Already paved. The stations offered rest
With food and warmth, and their well-rounded names
Were tossed like apples to the public taste.

He made a mental note of his three items.
He underlined the Prairies, double-lined
The Shore and triple-lined *Beyond the Prairies*,
Began counting the Ranges — first the Rockies;
The Kicking Horse ran through them, this he knew;
The Selkirks? Not so sure. Some years before

88

Had Moberly and Perry tagged a route
Across the lariat loop of the Columbia.
Now Rogers was traversing it on foot,
Reading an aneroid and compass, chewing
Sea-biscuit and tobacco. Would the steel
Follow this trail? Van Horne looked farther west.
There was the Gold Range, there the Coastal Mountains.
He stopped, putting a period to the note,
As rivers troubled nocturnes in his ears.
His plans must not seep into introspection—
Call it a night, for morning was at hand,
And every hour of daylight was for work.

*(Van Horne goes to Montreal to meet the
Directors.)*

He had agenda staggering enough
To bring the sweat even from Stephen's face.
As daring as his plans, so daring were
His promises. To build five hundred miles
Upon the prairies in one season: this
Was but a cushion for the jars ahead.
The Shore — he had to argue, stamp and fight
For this. The watercourses had been favoured,
The nation schooled to that economy.
He saw that Stephen, after wiping beads
From face and forehead, had put both his hands
Deep in his pockets — just a habit merely
Of fingering change — but still Van Horne went on
To clinch his case: the north shore could avoid
The over-border route — a national point
If ever there was one. He promised this
As soon as he was through with buffalo-grass.
And then the little matter of the Rockies:
This must be swallowed without argument,
As obvious as space, clear as a charter.
But why the change in Fleming's survey? Why
The Kicking Horse and not the Yellowhead?
The national point again. The Kicking Horse
Was shorter, closer to the boundary line;
No rival road would build between the two.
He did not dwell upon the other Passes.
He promised all with surety of schedule,
And with a self-imposed serenity
That dried the sweat upon the Board Room faces.

NUMBER ONE

Oak Lake to Calgary. Van Horne took off
His coat. The North must wait, for that would mean
His shirt as well. First and immediate
This prairie pledge — five hundred miles, and it
Was winter. Failure of this trial promise
Would mean — no, it must not be there for meaning.
An order from him carried no repeal:
It was as final as an execution.
A cable started rolling mills in Europe:
A tap of Morse sent hundreds to the bush.
Where axes swung on spruce and the saws sang,
Changing the timber into pyramids
Of poles and sleepers. Clicks, despatches, words,
Like lanterns in a night conductor's hands,
Signalled the wheels: a nod put Shaughnessy
In Montreal: supplies moved on the minute.
Thousands of men and mules and horses slipped
Into their togs and harness night and day.
The grass that fed the buffalo was turned over,
The black alluvial mould laid bare, the bed
Levelled and scraped. As individuals
The men lost their identity; as groups,
As gangs, they massed, divided, subdivided,
Like numerals only — sub-contractors, gangs
Of engineers, and shovel gangs for bridges,
Culverts, gangs of mechanics stringing wires,
Loading, unloading and reloading gangs,
Gangs for the fish-plates and the spiking gangs,
Putting a silver polish on the nails.
But neither men nor horses ganged like mules:
Wiser than both they learned to unionize.
Some instinct in their racial nether regions
Had taught them how to sniff the five-hour stretch
Down to the fine arithmetic of seconds.
They tired out their rivals and they knew it.
They'd stand for overwork, not overtime.
Faster than workmen could fling down their shovels,
They could unhinge their joints, unhitch their tendons;
Jumping the foreman's call, they brayed *"Unhook"*
With a defiant, corporate instancy.
The promise which looked first without redemption
Was being redeemed. From three to seven miles
A day the parallels were being laid,

90

Though Eastern throats were hoarse with the old question—
Where are the settlements? And whence the gift
Of tongues which could pronounce place-names that purred
Like cats in relaxation after kittens?
Was it a part of the same pledge to turn
A shack into a bank for notes renewed;
To call a site a city when men saw
Only a water-tank? This was an act
Of faith indeed — substance of things unseen—
Which would convert preachers to miracles,
Lure teachers into lean-to's for their classes.
And yet it happened that while labourers
Were swearing at their blisters in the evening
And straightening out their spinal kinks at dawn,
The tracks joined up Oak Lake to Calgary.

NUMBER TWO

On the North Shore a reptile lay asleep—
A hybrid that the myths might have conceived,
But not delivered, a progenitor
Of crawling, gliding things upon the earth.
She lay snug in the folds of a huge boa
Whose tail had covered Labrador and swished
Atlantic tides, whose body coiled itself
Around the Hudson Bay, then curled up north
Through Manitoba and Saskatchewan
To Great Slave Lake. In continental reach
The neck went past the Great Bear Lake until
Its head was hidden in the Arctic Seas.
This folded reptile was asleep or dead:
So motionless, she seemed stone dead — just seemed:
She was too old for death, too old for life,
For as if jealous of all living forms
She had lain there before bivalves began
To catacomb their shells on western mountains.
Somewhere within this life-death zone she sprawled,
Torpid upon a rock-and-mineral mattress.
Ice-ages had passed by and over her,
But these, for all their motion, had but sheared
Her spotty carboniferous hair or made
Her ridges stand out like the spikes of molochs.
Her back grown stronger every million years,
She had shed water by the longer rivers
To Hudson Bay and by the shorter streams

To the great basins to the south, had filled
Them up, would keep them filled until the end
Of Time.

        Was this the thing Van Horne set out
To conquer? When Superior lay there
With its inviting levels? Blake, Mackenzie,
Offered this water like a postulate.
*"Why those twelve thousand men sent to the North?*
*Nonsense and waste with utter bankruptcy."*
And the Laurentian monster at the first
Was undisturbed, presenting but her bulk
To the invasion. All she had to do
Was lie there neither yielding nor resisting.
Top-heavy with accumulated power
And overgrown survival without function,
She changed her spots as though brute rudiments
Of feeling foreign to her native hour
Surprised her with a sense of violation
From an existence other than her own—
Or why take notice of this unknown breed,
This horde of bipeds that could toil like ants,
Could wake her up and keep her irritated?
They tickled her with shovels, dug pickaxes
Into her scales and got under her skin,
And potted holes in her with drills and filled
Them up with what looked like fine grains of sand,
Black sand. It wasn't noise that bothered her,
For thunder she was used to from her cradle—
The head-push and nose-blowing of the ice,
The height and pressure of its body: these
Like winds native to clime and habitat
Had served only to lull her drowsing coils.
It was not size or numbers that concerned her.
It was their foreign build, their gait of movement.
They did not crawl — nor were they born with wings.
They stood upright and walked, shouted and sang;
They needed air — that much was true — their mouths
Were open but the tongue was alien.
The sounds were not the voice of winds and waters,
Nor that of any beasts upon the earth.
She took them first with lethargy, suffered
The rubbing of her back — those little jabs
Of steel were like the burrowing of ticks
In an elk's hide needing an antler point,

Or else left in a numb monotony.
These she could stand but when the breed
Advanced west on her higher vertebrae,
Kicking most insolently at her ribs,
Pouring black powder in her cavities,
And making not the clouds but her insides
The home of fire and thunder, then she gave
Them trial of her strength: the trestles tottered;
Abutments, bridges broke; her rivers flooded:
She summoned snow and ice, and then fell back
On the last weapon in her armoury—
The first and last — her passive corporal bulk,
To stay or wreck the schedule of Van Horne.

NUMBER THREE

The big one was the mountains — seas indeed!
With crests whiter than foam: they poured like seas,
Fluting the green banks of the pines and spruces.
An eagle-flight above they hid themselves
In clouds. They carried space upon their ledges.
Could these be overridden frontally,
Or like typhoons outsmarted on the flanks?
And what were on the flanks? The troughs and canyons,
Passes more dangerous to the navigator
Than to Magellan when he tried to read
The barbarous language of his Strait by calling
For echoes from the rocky hieroglyphs
Playing their pranks of hide-and-seek in fog:
As stubborn too as the old North-West Passage,
More difficult, for ice-packs could break up;
And as for bergs, what polar architect
Could stretch his compass points to draught such peaks
As kept on rising there beyond the foothills?
And should the bastions of the Rockies yield
To this new human and unnatural foe,
Would not the Selkirks stand? This was a range
That looked like some strange dread outside a door
Which gave its name but would not show its features,
Leaving them to the mind to guess at. This
Meant tunnels — would there be no end to boring?
There must be some day. Fleming and his men
Had nosed their paths like hounds; but paths and trails,
Measured in every inch by chain and transit,
Looked easy and seductive on a chart.

The rivers out there did not flow: they tumbled.
The cataracts were fed by glaciers;
Eddies were thought as whirlpools in the Gorges,
And gradients had paws that tore up tracks.

Terror and beauty like twin signal flags
Flew on the peaks for men to keep their distance.
The two combined as in a storm at sea—
*"Stay on the shore and take your fill of breathing,*
*But come not to the decks and climb the rigging."*
The Ranges could put cramps in hands and feet
Merely by the suggestion of the venture.
They needed miles to render up their beauty,
As if the gods in high aesthetic moments,
Resenting the profanity of touch,
Chiselled this sculpture for the eye alone.

*(Van Horne in momentary meditation at the*
*Foothills.)*

His name was now a legend. The North Shore,
Though not yet conquered, yet had proved that he
Could straighten crooked roads by pulling at them,
Shear down a hill and drain a bog or fill
A valley overnight. Fast as a bobcat,
He'd climb and run across the shakiest trestle
Or, with a locomotive short of coal,
He could supply the head of steam himself.
He breakfasted on bridges, lunched on ties;
Drinking from gallon pails, he dined on moose.
He could tire out the lumberjacks; beat hell
From workers but no more than from himself.
Only the devil or Paul Bunyan shared
With him the secret of perpetual motion,
And when he moved among his men they looked
For shoulder sprouts upon the Flying Dutchman.

But would his legend crack upon the mountains?
There must be no retreat: his bugles knew
Only one call — the summons to advance
Against two fortresses: the mind, the rock.
To prove the first defence was vulnerable,
To tap the treasury at home and then
Untie the purse-strings of the Londoners,
As hard to loosen as salt-water knots—

That job was Stephen's, Smith's, Tupper's, Macdonald's.
He knew its weight: had heard, as well as they,
Blake pumping at his pulmonary bellows,
And if the speeches made the House shock-proof
Before they ended, they could still peal forth
From print more durable than spoken tones.
Blake had returned to the attack and given
Sir John the ague with another phrase
As round and as melodious as the first:
*"The Country's wealth, its millions after millions*
*Squandered* – LOST IN THE GORGES OF THE FRASER":
A beautiful but ruinous piece of music
That could only be drowned with drums and fifes.
Tupper, fighting with fists and nails and toes,
Had taken the word *scandal* which had cut
His master's ballots, and had turned the edge
With his word *slander*, but Blake's *sea*, how turn
That edge? Now this last devastating phrase!
But let Sir John and Stephen answer this
Their way. Van Horne must answer it in his.

INTERNECINE STRIFE

The men were fighting foes which had themselves
Waged elemental civil wars and still
Were hammering one another at this moment.
The peaks and ranges flung from ocean beds
Had wakened up one geologic morning
To find their scalps raked off, their lips punched in,
The colour of their skins charged with new dyes.
Some of them did not wake or but half-woke;
Prone or recumbent with the eerie shapes
Of creatures that would follow them. Weather
Had acted on their spines and frozen them
To stegosaurs or, taking longer cycles,
Divining human features, had blown back
Their hair and, pressing on their cheeks and temples,
Bestowed on them the gravity of mummies.
But there was life and power which belied
The tombs. Guerrilla evergreens were climbing
In military order: at the base
The *ponderosa* pine; the fir backed up
The spruce; and it the Stoney Indian lodge-poles;
And these the white-barks; then, deciduous,
The outpost suicidal Lyell larches
Aiming at summits, digging scraggy roots

95

Around the boulders in the thinning soil,
Till they were stopped dead at the timber limit—
Rock *versus* forest with the rock prevailing.
Or with the summer warmth it was the ice,
In treaty with the rock to hold a line
As stubborn as a Balkan boundary,
That left its caves to score the Douglases,
And smother them with half a mile of dirt,
And making snow-sheds, covering the camps,
Futile as parasols in polar storms.
One enemy alone had battled rock
And triumphed: searching levels like lost broods,
Keen on their ocean scent, the rivers cut
The quartzite, licked the slate and softened it,
Till mud solidified was mud again,
And then, digesting it like earthworms, squirmed
Along the furrows with one steering urge—
To navigate the mountains in due time
Back to their home in worm-casts on the tides.

Into this scrimmage came the fighting men,
And all but rivers were their enemies.
Whether alive or dead the bush resisted:
Alive, it must be slain with axe and saw,
If dead, it was in tangle at their feet.
The ice could hit men as it hit the spruces.
Even the rivers had betraying tricks,
Watched like professed allies across a border.
They smiled from fertile plains and easy runs
Of valley gradients: their eyes got narrow,
Full of suspicion at the gorges where
They leaped and put the rickets in the trestles.
Though natively in conflict with the rock,
Both leagued against invasion. At Hell's Gate
A mountain laboured and brought forth a bull
Which, stranded in mid-stream, was fighting back
The river, and the fight turned on the men,
Demanding from this route their bread and steel.
And there below the Gate was the Black Canyon
With twenty-miles-an-hour burst of speed.

(ONDERDONK BUILDS THE "SKUZZY" TO FORCE THE PASSAGE.)

Twas more than navigation: only eagles
Might follow up this run; the spawning salmon
Gulled by the mill-race had returned to rot
Their upturned bellies in the canyon eddies.

96

Two engines at the stern, a forrard winch,
Steam-powered, failed to stem the cataract.
The last resource was shoulders, arms and hands.
Fifteen men at the capstan, creaking hawsers,
Two hundred Chinese tugging at shore ropes
To keep her bow-on from the broadside drift,
The *Skuzzy* under steam and muscle took
The shoals and rapids, and warped through the Gate,
Until she reached the navigable water—
The adventure was not sailing: it was climbing.

As hard a challenge were the precipices
Worn water-smooth and sheer a thousand feet.
Surveyors from the edges looked for footholds,
But, finding none, they tried marine manoeuvres.
Out of a hundred men they drafted sailors
Whose toes as supple as their fingers knew
The wash of reeling decks, whose knees were hardened
Through tying gaskets at the royal yards:
They lowered them with knotted ropes and drew them
Along the face until the lines were strung
Between the juts. Barefooted, dynamite
Strapped to their waists, the sappers followed, treading
The spider films and chipping holes for blasts,
Until the cliffs delivered up their features
Under the civil discipline of roads.

RING, RING THE BELLS

*Ring, ring the bells but not the engine bells:*
*Today only the ritual of the steeple*
*Chanted to the dull tempo of the toll.*
*Sorrow is stalking through the camps, speaking*
*A common mother-tongue. 'Twill leave tomorrow*
*To turn that language on a Blackfoot tepee,*
*Then take its leisurely Pacific time*
*To tap its fingers on a coolie's door.*
*Ring, ring the bells but not the engine bells:*
*Today only that universal toll,*
*For granite, mixing dust with human lime,*
*Had so compounded bodies into boulders*
*As to untype the blood, and, then, the Fraser,*
*Catching the fragments from the dynamite,*
*Had bleached all birthmarks from her swirling dead.*

Tomorrow and the engine bells again!

THE LAKE OF MONEY

*(The appeal to the Government for a loan of*
*twenty-two-and-a-half million, 1883.)*

Sir John began to muse on his excuses.
Was there no bottom to this lake? One mile
Along that northern strip had cost — how much?
Eleven dollars to the inch. The Road
In all would measure up to ninety millions,
And diverse hands were plucking at his elbow.
The Irish and the Dutch he could outface,
Outquip. He knew Van Horne and Shaughnessy
Had little time for speeches — one was busy
In grinding out two thousand miles; the other
Was working wizardry on creditors,
Pulling rabbits from hats, gold coins from sleeves
In Montreal. As for his foes like Blake,
He thanked his household gods the Irishman
Could claim only a viscous brand of humour,
Heavy, impenetrable till the hour
To laugh had taken on a chestnut colour.
But Stephen was his friend, hard to resist.
And there was Smith. He knew that both had pledged
Their private fortunes as security
For the construction of the Road. But that
Was not enough. Sir John had yet to dip
And scrape farther into the public pocket,
Explore its linings: his, the greater task;
His, to commit a nation to the risk.
How could he face the House with pauper hands?
He had to deal with Stephen first — a man
Laconic, nailing points and clinching them.
Oratory, the weapon of the massed assemblies
Was not the weapon here — Scot meeting Scot.
The burr was hard to take; and Stephen had
A Banffshire-cradled *r*. Drilling the ear,
It paralysed the nerves, hit the red cells.
The logic in the sound, escaping print,
Would seep through channels and befog the cortex.

Sir John counted the exits of discretion:
Disguise himself? A tailor might do much;
A barber might trim down his mane, brush back
The forelock, but no artist of massage,

Kneading that face from brow to nasal tip,
Could change a chunk of granite into talc.
His rheumatism? Yet he still could walk.
Neuralgia did not interfere with speech.
The bronchial tubing needed softer air?
Vacations could not cancel all appointments.
Men saw him in the flesh at Ottawa.
He had to speak this week, wheedling committees,
Much easier than to face a draper's clerk,
Tongue-trained on Aberdonian bargain-counters.
He raised his closed left hand to straighten out
His fingers one by one — four million people.
He had to pull a trifle on that fourth,
Not so resilient as the other three.
Only a wrench could stir the little finger
Which answered with a vicious backward jerk.

The dollar fringes of one hundred million
Were smirching up the blackboard of his mind.
But curving round and through them was the thought
He could not sponge away. Had he not fathered
The Union? Prodigy indeed it was
From Coast to Coast. Was not the Line essential?
What was this fungus sprouting from his rind
That left him at the root less clear a growth
Than this Dutch immigrant, William Van Horne?
The name suggested artificial land
Rescued from swamp by bulging dikes and ditches;
And added now to that were bogs and sloughs
And that most cursèd diabase which God
Had left from the explosions of his wrath.
And yet this man was challenging his pride.
North-Sea ancestral moisture on his beard,
Van Horne was now the spokesman for the West,
The champion of an all-Canadian route,
The Yankee who had come straight over, linked
His name and life with the Canadian nation.
Besides, he had infected the whole camp.
Whether acquired or natural, the stamp
Of faith had never left his face. Was it
The artist's instinct which had made the Rockies
And thence the Selkirks, scenes of tourist lure,
As easy for the passage of an engine
As for the flight of eagles? Miracles
Became his thought: the others took their cue

99

From him. They read the lines upon his lips.
But miracles did not spring out of air.
Under the driving will and sweltering flesh
They came from pay-cars loaded with the cash.
So that was why Stephen had called so often—
Money — that lake of money, bonds, more bonds.

*(The Bill authorizing the loan stubbornly carries
the House.)*

DYNAMITE ON THE NORTH SHORE

The lizard was in sanguinary mood.
She had been waked again: she felt her sleep
Had lasted a few seconds of her time.
The insects had come back — the ants, if ants
They were — dragging *those* trees, *those* logs athwart
Her levels, driving in *those* spikes; and how
The long grey snakes unknown within her region
Wormed from the east, unstriped, sunning themselves
Uncoiled upon the logs and then moved on,
Growing each day, ever keeping abreast!
She watched them, waiting for a bloody moment,
Until the borers halted at a spot,
The most invulnerable of her whole column,
Drove in that iron, wrenched it in the holes,
Hitting, digging, twisting. Why that spot?
Not this the former itch. That sharp proboscis
Was out for more than self-sufficing blood
About the cuticle: 'twas out for business
In the deep layers and the arteries.
And this consistent punching at her belly
With fire and thunder slapped her like an insult,
As with the blasts the caches of her broods
Broke — nickel, copper, silver and fool's gold,
Burst from their immemorial dormitories
To sprawl indecent in the light of day.
Another warning — this time different.

Westward above her webs she had a trap—
A thing called muskeg, easy on the eyes
Stung with the dust of gravel. Cotton grass,
Its white spires blending with the orchids,
Peeked through green table-cloths of sphagnum moss.
Carnivorous bladder-wort studded the acres,

100

Passing the water-fleas through their digestion.
Sweet-gale and sundew edged the dwarf black spruce;
And herds of cariboo had left their hoof-marks,
Betraying visual solidity,
But like the thousands of the pitcher plants,
Their downward-pointing hairs alluring insects,
Deceptive — and the men were moving west!
Now was her time. She took three engines, sank them
With seven tracks down through the hidden lake
To the rock bed, then over them she spread
A counterpane of leather-leaf and slime.
A warning, that was all for now. 'Twas sleep
She wanted, sleep, for drowsing was her pastime
And waiting through eternities of seasons.
As for intruders bred for skeletons—
Some day perhaps when ice began to move,
Or some convulsion ran fires through her tombs,
She might stir in her sleep and far below
The reach of steel and blast of dynamite,
She'd claim their bones as her possessive right
And wrap them cold in her pre-Cambrian folds.

THREATS OF SECESSION

The Lady's face was flushed. Thirteen years now
Since that engagement ring adorned her finger!
Adorned? Betrayed. She often took it off
And flung it angrily upon the dresser,
Then took excursions with her sailor-lover.
Had that man with a throat like Ottawa,
That tailored suitor in a cut-away,
Presumed compliance on her part? High time
To snub him for delay — for was not time
The marrow of agreement? At the mirror
She tried to cream a wrinkle from her forehead,
Toyed with the ring, replaced it and removed it.
Harder, she thought, to get it on and off—
This like the wrinkle meant but one thing, age.
So not too fast; play safe. Perhaps the man
Was not the master of his choice. Someone
Within the family group might well contest
Exotic marriage. Still, her plumes were ruffled
By Blake's two-nights' address before the Commons:
Three lines inside the twenty-thousand words
Had maddened her. She searched for hidden meanings—

"Should she insist on those preposterous terms
And threaten to secede, then let her go,
Better than ruin the country." "Let her go,"
And "ruin" — language this to shake her bodice.
Was this indictment of her character,
Or worse, her charm? Or was it just plain dowry?
For this last one at least she had an answer.
Pay now or separation — this the threat.
Dipping the ring into a soapy lather,
She pushed it to the second knuckle, twirled
It past. Although the diamond was off-colour,
She would await its partner ring of gold—
The finest carat; yes, by San Francisco!

BACK TO THE MOUNTAINS

As grim an enemy as rock was time.
The little men from five-to-six feet high,
From three-to-four score years in lease of breath,
Were flung in double-front against them both
In years a billion strong; so long was it
Since brachiapods in mollusc habitats
Were clamping shells on weed in ocean mud.
Now only yesterday had Fleming's men,
Searching for toeholds on the sides of cliffs,
Five thousand feet above sea-level, set
A tripod's leg upon a trilobite.
And age meant pressure, density. Sullen
With aeons, mountains would not stand aside;
Just block the path — morose but without anger,
No feeling in the menace of their frowns,
Immobile for they had no need of motion;
Their veins possessed no blood — they carried quartzite.
Frontal assault! To go through them direct
Seemed just as inconceivable as ride
Over their peaks. But go through them the men
Were ordered and their weapons were their hands
And backs, pickaxes, shovels, hammers, drills
And dynamite — against the rock and time;
For here the labour must be counted up
In months subject to clauses of a contract
Distinguished from the mortgage-run an age
Conceded to the trickle of the rain
In building river-homes. The men bored in,
The mesozoic rock arguing the inches.

102

This was a kind of surgery unknown
To mountains or the mothers of the myths.
These had a chloroform in leisured time,
Squeezing a swollen handful of light-seconds,
When water like a wriggling casuist
Had probed and found the areas for incision.
Now time was rushing labour — inches grew
To feet, to yards: the drills — the single jacks,
The double jacks — drove in and down; the holes
Gave way to excavations, these to tunnels,
Till men sodden with mud and roof-drip steamed
From sunlight through the tar-black to the sunlight.

HOLLOW ECHOES FROM THE TREASURY VAULT

Sir John was tired as to the point of death.
His chin was anchored to his chest. Was Blake
Right after all? And was Mackenzie right?
*Superior* could be travelled on. Besides,
It had a bottom, but those northern bogs
Like quicksands could go down to the earth's core.
Compared with them, quagmires of ancient legend
Were backyard puddles for old ducks. To sink
Those added millions down that wallowing hole!
He thought now through his feet. Many a time
When argument cemented opposition,
And hopeless seemed his case, he could think up
A tale to laugh the benches to accord.
No one knew better, when a point had failed
The brain, how to divert it through the ribs.
But now his stock of stories had run out.
This was exhaustion at its coma level.
Or was he sick? Never had spots like these
Assailed his eyes. He could not rub them out—
Those shifting images — was it the sunset
Refracted through the bevelled window edges?
He shambled over and drew down the blind;
Returned and slumped; it was no use; the spots
Were there. No light could ever shoot this kind
Of orange through a prism, or this blue,
And what a green! The spectrum was ruled out;
Its bands were too inviolate. He rubbed
The lids again — a brilliant gold appeared
Upon a silken backdrop of pure white,
And in the centre, red — a scarlet red,

103

A dancing, rampant and rebellious red
That like a stain spread outward covering
The vision field. He closed his eyes and listened:
Why, what was that? 'Twas bad enough that light
Should play such pranks upon him, but must sound
Crash the Satanic game, reverberate
A shot fifteen years after it was fired,
And culminate its echoes with the thud
Of marching choruses outside his window:

*"We'll hang Riel up the Red River,*
*And he'll roast in hell forever,*
*We'll hang him up the River*
*With a yah-yah-yah."*

The noose was for the shot: 'twas blood for blood;
The death of Riel for the death of Scott.
What could not Blake do with that on the Floor,
Or that young, tall, bilingual advocate
Who with the carriage of his syllables
Could bid an audience like an orchestra
Answer his body swaying like a reed?
Colours and sounds made riot of his mind—
White horses in July processional prance,
The blackrobe's swish, the Métis' sullen tread,
And out there in the rear the treaty-wise
Full-breeds with buffalo wallows on their foreheads.

This he could stand no longer, sick indeed:
Send for his doctor, the first thought, then No;
The doctor would advise an oculist,
The oculist return him to the doctor,
The doctor would see-saw him to another—
A specialist on tumours of the brain,
And he might recommend close-guarded rest
In some asylum — Devil take them all,
He had his work to do. He glanced about
And spied his medicine upon the sideboard;
Amber it was, distilled from Highland springs,
That often had translated age to youth
And boiled his blood on a victorious rostrum.
Conviction seized him as he stood, for here
At least he was not cut for compromise,
Nor curried to his nickname Old Tomorrow.
Deliberation in his open stance,

104

He trenched a deep one, gurgled and sat down.
What were those paltry millions after all?
They stood between completion of the Road
And bankruptcy of both Road and Nation.
Those north-shore gaps must be closed in by steel.
It did not need exhilarated judgment
To see the sense of that. To send the men
Hop-skip-and-jump upon lake ice to board
The flatcars was a revelry for imps.
And all that cutting through the mountain rock,
Four years of it and more, and all for nothing,
Unless those gaps were spanned, bedded and railed.
To quit the Road, to have the Union broken
Was irredeemable. He rose, this time
Invincibility carved on his features,
Hoisted a second, then drew up the blind.
He never saw a sunset just like this.
He lingered in the posture of devotion:
That sun for sure was in the west, or was it?
Soon it would be upholstering the clouds
Upon the Prairies, Rockies and the Coast:
He turned and sailed back under double-reef,
Cabined himself inside an armchair, stretched
His legs to their full length under the table.
Something miraculous had changed the air—
A chemistry that knew how to extract
The iron from the will: the spots had vanished
And in their place an unterrestrial nimbus
Circled his hair: the jerks had left his nerves:
The millions kept on shrinking or were running
From right to left: the fourth arthritic digit
Was straight, and yes, by heaven, the little fifth
Which up to now was just a calcium hook
Was suppling in the Hebridean warmth.
A blessed peace fell like a dew upon him,
And soon, in trance, drenched in conciliation,
He hiccuped gently — *"Now let S-S-Stephen come!"*

*(The Government grants the Directors the right to
issue $35,000,000, guarantees $20,000,000, the
rest to be issued by the Railway Directors.
Stephen goes to London, and Lord Revelstoke,
speaking for the House of Baring, takes over the
issue.)*

105

SUSPENSE IN THE MONTREAL BOARD ROOM

Evening had settled hours before its time
Within the Room and on the face of Angus.
Dejection overlaid his social fur,
Rumpled his side-burns, left moustache untrimmed.
The vision of his Bank, his future Shops,
Was like his outlook for the London visit.
Van Horne was fronting him with a like visage
Except for two spots glowing on his cheeks—
Dismay and anger at those empty pay-cars.
His mutterings were indistinct but final
As though he were reciting to himself
The Athanasian damnatory clauses.
He felt the Receiver's breath upon his neck:
To come so near the end, and then this hurdle!

Only one thing could penetrate that murk—
A cable pledge from London, would it come?
Till now refusal or indifference
Had met the overtures. Would Stephen turn
The trick?
              A door-knock and a telegram
With Stephen's signature! Van Horne ripped it
Apart. Articulation failed his tongue,
But Angus got the meaning from his face
And from a noisy sequence of deductions:—
An inkstand coasted through the office window,
Followed by shredded maps and blotting-pads,
Fluttering like shad-flies in a summer gale;
A bookshelf smitten by a fist collapsed;
Two chairs flew to the ceiling — one retired,
The other roosted on the chandelier.
Some thirty years erased like blackboard chalk,
Van Horne was in a school at Illinois.
Triumphant over his two-hundred weight,
He leaped and turned a cartwheel on the table,
Driving heel sparables into the oak,
Came down to teach his partner a Dutch dance;
And in the presence of the messenger,
Who stared immobilized at what he thought
New colours in the managerial picture,
Van Horne took hold of Angus bodily,
Tore off his tie and collar, mauled his shirt,
And stuffed a Grand Trunk folder down his breeches.

106

*(The last gap in the mountains — between the
Selkirks and Savona's Ferry — is closed.)*

The Road itself was like a stream that men
Had coaxed and teased or bullied out of Nature.
As if watching for weak spots in her codes,
It sought for levels like the watercourses.
It sinuously took the bends, rejoiced
In plains and easy grades, found gaps, poured through them,
But hating steep descents avoided them.
Unlike the rivers which in full rebellion
Against the canyons' hydrophobic slaver
Went to the limit of their argument:
Unlike again, the stream of steel had found
A way to climb, became a mountaineer.
From the Alberta plains it reached the Summit,
And where it could not climb, it cut and curved,
Till from the Rockies to the Coastal Range
It had accomplished what the Rivers had,
Making a hundred clean Caesarian cuts,
And bringing to delivery in their time
Their smoky, lusty-screaming locomotives.

THE SPIKE

Silver or gold? Van Horne had rumbled *"Iron"*.
No flags or bands announced this ceremony,
No Morse in circulation through the world,
And though the vital words like Eagle Pass,
Craigellachie, were trembling in their belfries,
No hands were at the ropes. The air was taut
With silences as rigid as the spruces
Forming the background in November mist.
More casual than camera-wise, the men
Could have been properties upon a stage,
Except for road maps furrowing their faces.

Rogers, his both feet planted on a tie,
Stood motionless as ballast. In the rear,
Covering the scene with spirit-level eyes,
Predestination on his chin, was Fleming.
The only one groomed for the ritual
From smooth silk hat and well-cut square-rig beard
Down through his Caledonian longitude,
He was outstaturing others by a foot,
And upright as the mainmast of a brig.
Beside him, barely reaching to his waist,

107

A water-boy had wormed his way in front
To touch this last rail with his foot, his face
Upturned to see the cheek-bone crags of Rogers.
The other side of Fleming, hands in pockets,
Eyes leaden-lidded under square-crowned hat,
And puncheon-bellied under overcoat,
Unsmiling at the focused lens — Van Horne.
Whatever ecstasy played round that rail
Did not leap to his face. Five years had passed,
Less than five years — so well within the pledge.

The job was done. Was this the slouch of rest?
Not to the men he drove through walls of granite.
The embers from the past were in his soul,
Banked for the moment at the rail and smoking,
Just waiting for the future to be blown.

At last the spike and Donald with the hammer!
His hair like frozen moss from Labrador
Poked out under his hat, ran down his face
To merge with streaks of rust in a white cloud.
What made him fumble the first stroke? Not age:
The snow belied his middle sixties. Was
It lapse of caution or his sense of thrift,
That elemental stuff which through his life
Never pockmarked his daring but had made
The man the canniest trader of his time,
Who never missed a rat-count, never failed
To gauge the size and texture of a pelt?
Now here he was caught by the camera,
Back bent, head bowed, and staring at a sledge,
Outwitted by an idiotic nail.
Though from the crowd no laughter, yet the spike
With its slewed neck was grinning up at Smith.
Wrenched out, it was replaced. This time the hammer
Gave a first tap as with apology,
Another one, another, till the spike
Was safely stationed in the tie and then
The Scot, invoking his ancestral clan,
Using the hammer like a battle-axe,
His eyes bloodshot with memories of Flodden,
Descended on it, rammed it to its home.

\*          \*          \*          \*

The stroke released a trigger for a burst
Of sound that stretched the gamut of the air.

108

The shouts of engineers and dynamiters,
Of locomotive-workers and explorers,
Flanking the rails, were but a tuning-up
For a massed continental chorus. Led
By Moberly (of the Eagles and *this* Pass)
And Rogers (of *his own*), followed by Wilson,
And Ross (charged with the Rocky Mountain Section),
By Egan (general of the Western Lines),
Cambie and Marcus Smith, Harris of Boston,
The roar was deepened by the bass of Fleming,
And heightened by the laryngeal fifes
Of Dug McKenzie and John H. McTavish.
It ended when Van Horne spat out some phlegm
To ratify the tumult with *"Well Done"*
Tied in a knot of monosyllables.

Merely the tuning up! For on the morrow
The last blow on the spike would stir the mould
Under the drumming of the prairie wheels,
And make the whistles from the steam out-crow
The Fraser. Like a gavel it would close
Debate, making Macdonald's *"sea to sea"*
Pour through two oceanic megaphones—
Three thousand miles of *Hail* from port to port;
And somewhere in the middle of the line
Of steel, even the lizard heard the stroke.
The breed had triumphed after all. To drown
The traffic chorus, she must blend the sound
With those inaugural, narcotic notes
Of storm and thunder which would send her back
Deeper than ever in Laurentian sleep.


# Myth and Fact


We used to wake our children when they screamed;
We felt no fever, found no pain,
And casually we told them that they dreamed
And settled them in sleep again.

So easy was it thus to exorcise
The midnight fears the morning after.
We sought to prove they could not literalize
*Jack*, though the giant shook with laughter.

109

We showed them pictures in a book and smiled
At red-shawled wolves and chasing bruins—
Was not the race just an incarnate child
That sat at wells and haunted ruins?

We had outgrown the dreams, outrung the knells
Through voodoo, amulet and prayer,
But knew that daylight fastened on us spells
More fearful than Medusa's hair.

We saw the bat-companioned dead arise
From shafts and pipes, and nose like beagles
The spoors of outlaw quarry in the skies
Whose speed and spread made fools of eagles.

We shut our eyes and plugged our ears, though sound
And sight were our front-line defences,
The mind came with its folly to confound
The crystal logic of the senses.

Then turned we to the story-books again
To see that Cyclopean stare.
'Twas out of focus for the beast was slain
While we were on our knees in prayer.

Who were those giants in their climbing strength?
No reason bade us calibrate
These flying lizards in their scaly length
Or plumb a mesozoic hate.

The leaves released a genie to unbind
Our feet along a pilgrimage:
The make-believe had furnished to the mind
Asylum in the foliage.

Draw down the blinds and lock the doors tonight:
We would be safe from that which hovers
Above the eaves. God send us no more light
Than falls between our picture covers.

For what the monsters of the long-ago
Had done were nursery peccadilloes
To what those solar hounds in tally-ho
Could do when once they sniffed the pillows.

# F. H. Underhill

*Frank Hawkins Underhill (1889-1971) was born in Stouffville, Ontario and educated at the University of Toronto and Oxford:*

> *The Toronto of my student days (1907-11) was pretty well devoid of political ideas; but I had the advantage of working under one classical professor, Milner, who had a genius for stirring up interest in ideas, and under the history department of Wrong and the English department of Alexander . . . . The Oxford to which I went from Toronto seethed with politics. I was there (1911-14) in the exciting days of the House of Lords and Home Rule crisis, when everybody seemed to be a politician. My chief tutor in Greats was A.D. Lindsay who was a notorious socialist and whose wife went out addressing women's suffrage demonstrations . . . . I was swept off my feet by the iconoclastic wit and high spirits of Bernard Shaw's plays, I read H.G. Wells and the Webbs, and became a member of a Balliol Fabian group in which the leading spirit was G.D.H. Cole.* [1]

*Although trained in classics, Underhill returned from World War I to teach political science and history at the University of Saskatchewan and to involve himself in Prairie politics during the 1920s. His interest in politics continued when he moved to Toronto to teach history at the University of Toronto. He helped found the League for Social Reconstruction in 1932, wrote the first draft of the CCF Party's Regina Manifesto in 1933, and served for many years as an editorial contributor to* The Canadian Forum. *After his retirement from the University of Toronto in 1955, Underhill served as Curator of Laurier House in Ottawa from 1955 to 1959. He was elected Fellow of the Royal Society of Canada in 1949. His collected Essays,* In Search of Liberalism *(1960) received the Governor General's Award for Non-Fiction.*

*A Victorian liberal who espoused Fabian socialism without becoming a doctrinaire socialist, he continually goaded intellectuals and politicians into examining the principles behind their actions. Indeed, he undertook to change his generation of fellow academics from ivory-tower observers to activists. "Some Reflections on the Liberal Tradition in Canada", one of these undertakings, is typical of Underhill for several reasons. First, his style is candid, witty, and vigorous. Secondly, Underhill's concerns are by no means confined to the discipline of history, for his subject here is the philosophical basis of our culture and its impact on political, economic, and artistic life. Thus he argues that we should pay more attention to Canadian intellectual history as opposed to the emphasis on economic and political events in most text* books. Furthermore, he proposes that historical scholarship by Canadians must not be confined to the subject of Canada only, but to all areas of world history.

Thirdly, this timely paper (1946) is itself one of Underhill's contributions towards the as-yet-unwritten intellectual history of Canada. Liberalism here refers not merely to a specific political party, but encompasses the broader political and historical ramifications of the term. Throughout the nineteenth·century the liberal movement was defined by its optimistic, rational view of the biological and social possibilities inherent in human beings. But, for many men, liberalism became closely identified with the interests of laissez-faire capitalism and economic imperialism, a narrow view which in Underhill's eyes has dominated successive governments in Canada and the United States. For other men, liberalism posited a lofty ideal of liberty and democracy which has not been achieved by mid-twentieth century. As a result, liberalism since World War II has been increasingly criticized, sometimes in grossly inaccurate ways, for having brought not utopia but world wars, atom bombs, further racial inequities, and continued injustices.

Because liberalism has been the predominant tradition for the last century (filtering through every aspect of education and culture in the Canada of 1914, for instance), the philosophical framework behind much of the fiction and poetry of these anthologies has been determined by the writer's response to this tradition. Pratt and Sandwell have adhered to it; Callaghan and F.R. Scott have moved away from it. Far too little has been written about the background values that underlie the literature of our society: as Underhill observes, we lack an intellectual history. His essay is included here as a thoughtful statement about the philosophical currents shaping the Canadian consciousness in the century following the upheaval of 1837.

**Footnote**

[1] F. H. Underhill, In Search of Liberalism (Toronto: Macmillan, 1960), pp. ix-x.

# Some Reflections on the Liberal Tradition in Canada

(This paper was read by me as President of the Canadian Historical Association at its annual meeting in 1946.)

"The reader is about to enter upon the most violent and certainly the most eventful moral struggle that has ever taken place in our North American colonies. . . . That I was sentenced to contend on the soil of America with Democracy, and that if I did not overpower it, it would overpower me, were solemn facts which for some weeks had been perfectly evident to my mind." So wrote Sir Francis Bond Head in his *Narrative*,[1] the famous apologia for the policy of his governorship of Upper Canada. The issue as he saw it, and as his contemporaries in Canada saw it, was not merely whether the British North American colonies were to set up a responsible form of government; it was the much deeper one of whether they were to follow the example of the United States and commit themselves to achieving a democratic form of society. And good Sir Francis appealed with confidence to all right-thinking property-owning Englishmen against what he termed "the insane theory of conciliating democracy" as put into practice by the Colonial Office under the guidance of that "rank republican", Mr. Under-Secretary Stephen. No doubt, if the phrase had been then in use he would have accused Stephen, and Lord Glenelg and Lord Durham, of appeasement. In rebuttal of Durham's criticisms of the Upper Canada Family Compact he wrote:

> It appears from Lord Durham's own showing that this "Family Compact" which his Lordship deems it so advisable that the Queen should destroy, is nothing more nor less than that "social fabric" which characterizes every civilized community in the world. . . . "The bench", "the magistrates", "the clergy", "the law", "the landed proprietors", "the bankers", "the native-born inhabitants", and "the supporters of the Established Church" [these were the social groups which Durham had defined as composing the Family Compact] form just as much *"a family compact"* in England as they do in Upper Canada, and just as much in Germany as they do in England. . . . The *"family compact"* of Upper Canada is composed of those members of its society who, either by their abilities and character, have been honoured by the confidence of the executive government, or who by their industry and intelligence, have amassed wealth. The party, I own, is comparatively a small one; but to put the multitude at the top and the few at the bottom is a radical reversion of the pyramid of society which every reflecting man must foresee can end only by its downfall.[2]

Sir Francis' statement is as clear and as trenchant an enunciation of the anti-democratic conservative political philosophy of his day as could be quoted from the American conservatives who were fighting Jacksonian Democracy at this same time or from the English conservatives who were fighting the Reform Bill or Chartism. As we all know, this "moral struggle" over the fundamental principles on which society should be based, which Sir Francis correctly discerned as representing the real meaning of the Canadian party strife of the 1830s, was to be decided against him and his tory friends. The century since his *Narrative* was published has been, in the English-speaking world at least, a period of continuously developing liberal and democratic movements. Liberalism has merged into democracy. Today the people of Canada are recovering from the second world war within a generation in defence of democracy. Presumably, considering the sacrifices we have shown ourselves willing to make for the cause, we Canadians cherish passionately the liberal-democratic tradition which is our inheritance from the nineteenth century. Presumably, the growth of liberal-democratic institutions and ideas in our political, economic, and social life is one of the main themes in our Canadian history, just as it certainly is in the history of Great Britain and the United States, the two communities with which we have most intimately shared our experience.

Yet it is a remarkable fact that in the great debate of our generation, the debate which has been going on all over the western world about the fundamental values of

113

liberalism and democracy, we Canadians have taken very little part. We talk at length of the status which our nation has attained in the world. We have shown in two great wars that we can produce soldiers and airmen and sailors second to none. We have organized our productive resources so energetically as to make ourselves one of the main arsenals and granaries of democracy. We have achieved political autonomy and economic maturity. But to the discussion of those deep underlying intellectual, moral and spiritual issues which have made such chaos of the contemporary world we Canadians are making very little contribution.

Our Confederation was achieved at the very time in the nineteenth century when a reaction was beginning to set in against the liberal and democratic principles which, springing from eighteenth-century Enlightenment, had seemed up to that moment to be winning ever fresh victories. The liberal nationalism of the early part of the century was beginning to turn into something sinister, the passionate, exclusive, irrational, totalitarian nationalism that we know today. The optimistic belief in human equality and perfectibility was beginning to be undermined by new knowledge about man provided by the researches of biologists and psychologists. At the same time technological developments in mass production industries were building up a new social pyramid with a few owners and managers at the top and the mass of exploited workers at the bottom; and new techniques of mass propaganda still further emphasized this division of mankind into élite and masses. The freedom which our Victorian ancestors thought was slowly broadening down from precedent to precedent seemed to become more and more unreal under the concentrated pressure of capitalistic big business or of the massive bureaucratic state. In such surroundings, the liberal spirit does not flourish. And the more reflective minds of our day have been acutely aware that the mere winning of military victories under banners labelled "liberty" or "democracy" does not carry us very far in the solving of our deeper problems.

Canada is caught up in this modern crisis of liberalism as are all other national communities. But in this world-debate about the values of our civilization the Canadian voice is hardly heard. Who ever reads a Canadian book? What Canadian books are there on these problems? What have we had to say about them that has attracted the attention of our contemporaries or has impressed itself upon their imagination? In the world of ideas we do not yet play a full part. We are still colonial. Our thinking is still derivative. Like other peoples Canadians have of late expended a good deal of misdirected energy in endeavours to export goods without importing other goods in return. But we continue to import ideas without trying to develop an export trade in this field. We are in fact, as I have said, colonial. For our intellectual capital we are still dependent upon a continuous flow of imports from London, New York, and Paris, not to mention Moscow and Rome. It is to be hoped that we will continue to raise our intellectual standards by continuing to import from these more mature centres, and that we will never try to go in for intellectual autarchy. But international commerce in ideas as well as in goods should be a two-way traffic at least, and preferably it should be multilateral.

Incidentally, it is worth remarking in passing that one sign of this colonialism in our intellectual world is to be seen in the present state of Canadian historiography. The guild of Canadian historians confine their activities very largely to the writing of studies in local national history. South of the border American historians have long been demonstrating their intellectual equality by pouring out books on English and European and world history as well as on local subjects. But how little of this kind of research and writing has been done in Canada! During the past year we have lost one of our most distinguished colleagues, in the person of Professor Charles Norris Cochrane; and his book on *Christianity and Classical Culture* is a notable example of the sort of thing I mean. But one cannot think of many cases like this, in which we have asserted our full partnership in the civilization of our day by Canadian writing upon the great subjects of permanent and universal interest.

Now it seems to me — and this is more or less the main theme of the present rambling discursive paper — that this intellectual weakness of Canada is a quality which shows itself through all our history. In particular it is to be discerned in that process of democratization which is the most important thing that has happened to us, as to other kindred peoples, during the last hundred years. When we compare ourselves with Britain and the United States there is one striking contrast. Those two countries, since the end of the eighteenth century, have abounded in prophets and philosophers who have made articulate the idea of a liberal and equalitarian society. Their political history displays also a succession of practical politicians who have not merely performed the functions of manipulating and manoeuvring masses of men and groups which every politician performs, but whose careers have struck the imagination of both contemporaries and descendants as symbolizing certain great inspiring ideas. We in Canada have produced few such figures. Where are the classics in our political literature which embody our Canadian version of liberalism and democracy? Our party struggles have never been raised to the higher intellectual plane at which they become of universal interest by the presence of a Canadian Jefferson and a Canadian Hamilton in opposing parties. We have had no Canadian Burke or Mill to perform the social function of the political philosopher in action. We have had no Canadian Carlyle or Ruskin or Arnold to ask searching questions about the ultimate values embodied in our political or economic practice. We lack a Canadian Walt Whitman or Mark Twain to give literary expression to the democratic way of life. The student in search of illustrative material on the growth of Canadian political ideas during the great century of liberalism and democracy has to content himself mainly with a collection of extracts from more or less forgotten speeches and pamphlets and newspaper editorials. Whatever urge may have, at any time, possessed any Canadian to philosophize upon politics did not lead to much writing whose intrinsic worth helped to preserve it in our memory.

At least this is true of us English-speaking Canadians. Our French-speaking fellow citizens have shown a much greater fondness and capacity for ideas in politics than we have; but their writings, being in another language, have hardly penetrated into our English-Canadian consciousness.

We early repudiated the philosophy of the Manchester School; but in the long history of our Canadian "National Policy" it is difficult to find any Canadian exposition of the anti-Manchester ideas of a national economy, written by economist, business man, or politician, which has impressed itself upon us as worthy of preservation. Our history is full of agrarian protest movements, but the ordinary Canadian would be stumped if asked to name any representative Canadian philosopher of agrarianism. And the most notable illustration of this poverty of our politics at the intellectual level is to be found in the fact that while we were the pioneers in one of the great liberal achievements of the nineteenth century — the experiment of responsible government, which transformed the British Empire into the Commonwealth, and which has thrown fresh light in our own day on the possibility of reconciling nationalism with a wider international community — even in this field, in which our practical contribution was so great, there has arisen since the days of Joseph Howe no Canadian prophet of the idea of the Commonwealth whose writings seem inspiring or even readable to wider circles than those of professional historians.

This seeming incapacity for ideas, or rather this habit of carrying on our communal affairs at a level at which ideas never quite emerge into an articulate life of their own, has surely impoverished our Canadian politics. Every teacher of Canadian history has this fact brought home to him with each fresh batch of young students whom he meets. How reluctant they are to study the history of their own country! How eagerly they show their preference for English or European or (if they get the chance) for American history! For they instinctively feel that when they get outside of Canada they are studying the great creative seminal ideas that have determined the character of our modern world, whereas inside Canada there seem to be no ideas at issue of permanent or universal significance at all. I can myself still remember the thrill of appreciation with which as a university freshman I heard a famous professor of Greek[3] remark that our Canadian history is as dull as ditchwater, and our politics is full of it. Of course, there is a considerable amount of ditchwater in the politics of all countries; my professor was more conscious of it in Canada because he missed here those ideas which he found in the politics of classical Greece. And as far as I have been able to observe, young students of this present generation are still repelled by Canadian history because they find in it little more than the story of a half-continent of material resources over which a population of some twelve million economic animals have spread themselves in a not too successful search for economic wealth.

It will, of course, be said in answer to these mournful reflections upon the low quality of intellectual activity in Canadian politics that they are exaggerated and extreme. So I should like to buttress my position by referring to observations made at different times by students from the outer world upon the nature and quality of Canadian party politics. The name of Goldwin Smith comes to mind at once. He watched and studied Canadian politics continuously from the early 1870s to the early 1900s, applying to them the standards of an English Manchester liberal; and his verdict was adverse. He felt that Canadians after 1867 had failed to rise to their intellectual opportunities, that they had failed to grasp in their imagination the potentialities of the new nationality, that their political parties operated only to debase and pervert the discussion of public issues, and that in the absence of great guiding, inspiring ideas Canadian national statesmanship had degenerated into a sordid business of bargaining and manoeuvring amongst narrow selfish particularist interest groups. He took a certain sardonic pleasure in noting the skill with which Macdonald played this low game as contrasted with the clumsiness with which Mackenzie and Blake played it; but

116

he could see in it nothing but a low game after all. The obvious reply to Goldwin Smith is that he was embittered by the disappointment of his own ambitions and that his testimony is therefore to be discounted. But no one who studies the politics of the period 1867 to 1914 can be convinced that this is a wholly satisfactory defence against his criticisms.

At the period of the turn of the century, we were studied by another overseas observer who has given us the most penetrating and illuminating analysis of our politics that has yet been written by anyone, native or foreign. In 1907 André Siegfried published his book, *The Race Question in Canada*, and set forth the somewhat paradoxical conclusion that, while (to quote his opening sentence) "Canadian politics are a tilting ground for impassioned rivalries", they operated so as to suppress the intellectual vitality which would be the natural result of such a situation.

> Originally formed to subserve a political idea, these parties are often to be found quite detached from the principles which gave them birth, and with their own self-preservation as their chief care and aim. Even without a programme, they continue to live and thrive, tending to become mere associations for the securing of power, their doctrines serving merely as weapons, dulled or sharpened, grasped as occasion arises for use in the fight. . . . This fact deprives the periodical appeals to the voting public of the importance which they should have. . . . Whichever side succeeds, the country it is well known will be governed in just the same way; the only difference will be in the *personnel* of the Government. That is how things go save when some great wave of feeling sweeps over the Dominion, submerging all the pigmies of politics in its flood. In the intervals between these crises. . . . it is not the party that subserves the idea, it is the idea that subserves the party. Canadian statesmen . . . undoubtedly take longer views. They seem, however, to stand in fear of great movements of public opinion, and to seek to lull them rather than to encourage them and bring them to fruition. Thus, deliberately and not from shortsightedness, they help to promote the state of things which I have described. The reason for this attitude is easy to comprehend. Canada, with its rival creeds and races, is a land of fears and jealousies and conflicts. . . . Let a question involving religion or nationality be once boldly raised. . . and the elections will be turned into real political fights, passionate and sincere. This is exactly what is dreaded by far-sighted and prudent politicians, whose duty it is to preserve the national equilibrium. . . . They exert themselves, therefore, to prevent the formation of homogeneous parties, divided according to creed or race or class. The purity of political life suffers from this, but perhaps the very existence of the Federation is the price. The existing parties are thus entirely harmless. The Liberals and Conservatives differ very little really in their opinions upon crucial questions, and their views as to administration are almost identical. . . . They have come to regard each other without alarm: they know each other too well and resemble each other too closely.[4]

Mr. J. A. Hobson, the well-known English economist, published a little book about Canada at almost the same moment as M. Siegfried — *Canada Today*, which appeared in 1906. It also gives a rather unfavourable impression of Canadian politics, although the author's main interest was in the economic question of protection and the British preference.

More recently another great student of politics from overseas has given us his observations upon Canada. James Bryce had played an active part in the politics of his own country, had made himself intimately acquainted with the American Commonwealth, and applied to Canada a mind that was deeply learned in comparative politics. In his book, *Modern Democracies*, published in 1921, he devoted some chapters to the working of Canadian democracy.

Since 1867 the questions which have had the most constant interest for the bulk of the nation are . . . those which belong to the sphere of commercial and industrial progress, the development of the material resources of the country . . . — matters scarcely falling within the lines by which party opinion is divided, for the policy of *laissez-faire* has few adherents in a country which finds in governmental action or financial support to private enterprises the quickest means of carrying out every promising project. . . . The task of each party is to persuade the people that in this instance its plan promises quicker and larger results, and that it is fitter to be trusted with the work. Thus it happens that general political principles . . . count for little in politics, though ancient habit requires them to be invoked. Each party tries to adapt itself from time to time to whatever practical issue may arise. Opportunism is inevitable, and the charge of inconsistency, though incessantly bandied to and fro, is lightly regarded. . . . In Canada ideas are not needed to make parties, for these can live by heredity. . . . The people show an abounding party spirit when an election day arrives. The constant party struggle keeps their interest alive. But party spirit, so far from being a measure of the volume of political thinking, may even be a substitute for thinking. . . . In every country a game played over material interests between ministers, constituencies and their representatives, railway companies and private speculators, is not only demoralizing to all concerned but interferes with the consideration of the great issues of policy on a wise handling of which a nation's welfare depends. Fiscal questions, labour questions, the assumption by the State of such branches of industry as railroads or mines, and the principles it ought to follow in such works as it undertakes — questions like these need wide vision, clear insight, and a firmness that will resist political pressure and adhere to the principles once laid down. These qualities have been wanting, and the people have begun to perceive the want.[5]

This general failure of our Canadian politics to rise above a mere confused struggle of interest groups has been no doubt due to a variety of causes. In the middle of the twentieth century it is rather too late for us to keep harping on the pioneer frontier character of the Canadian community as the all sufficient answer to criticism. The young American republic which included a Jefferson and a Hamilton and a Franklin, not to mention many of their contemporaries of almost equal intellectual stature, was a smaller and more isolated frontier community than Canada has been for a long time; but it was already by the end of the eighteenth century the peer of Europe in the quality of its political thinking and was recognized as such. We still remain colonial in the middle of the twentieth century.

One reason for our backwardness, and the reason which interests me most at the moment, has been the weakness of the Radical and Reform parties of the Left in our Canadian history. A healthy society will consist of a great majority massed a little to the right and a little to the left of centre, with smaller groups of strong conservatives and strong radicals out on the wings. If these minority groups are not present in any significant force to provide a perpetual challenge to the majority, the conservatives and liberals of the centre are likely to be a pretty flabby lot, both intellectually and morally.

For this weakness of the Left in Canada, the ultimate explanation would seem to be that we never had an eighteenth century of our own. The intellectual life of our politics has not been periodically revived by fresh drafts from the invigorating fountain of eighteenth-century Enlightenment. In Catholic French Canada the doctrines of the rights of man and of Liberty Equality Fraternity were rejected from the start, and to this day they have never penetrated, save surreptitiously or spasmodically. The mental climate of English Canada in its early formative years was determined by men who were fleeing from the practical application of the doctrines that all men

118

are born equal and are endowed by their Creator with certain unalienable rights amongst which are life, liberty and the pursuit of happiness. All effective liberal and radical democratic movements in the nineteenth century have had their roots in this fertile eighteenth-century soil. But our ancestors made the great refusal in the eighteenth century. In Canada we have no revolutionary tradition; and our historians, political scientists, and philosophers have assiduously tried to educate us to be proud of this fact. How can such a people expect their democracy to be as dynamic as the democracies of Britain and France and the United States have been?

Then also it has never been sufficiently emphasized that our first great democratic upheaval a hundred years ago was a failure. In the United States, Jacksonian Democracy swept away most of the old aristocratic survivals and made a strong attack upon the new plutocratic forces. The Federalists disappeared; and their successors, the Whigs, suffered a series of defeats at the hands of triumphant Democracy. But the Canadian version of Jacksonian Democracy represented by the movements of Papineau and Mackenzie was discredited by the events of their abortive rebellions. And Canada followed the example of Britain rather than of the United States. Responsible government was a British technique of government which took the place of American elective institutions. Our historians have been so dazzled by its success that they have failed to point out that the real radicals in Canada were pushed aside in the 1840s by the respectable professional and property-owning classes, the "Moderates" as we call them; just as the working-class radicals in Britain, without whose mass-agitation the Reform Bill could not have been passed, were pushed aside after 1832 for a long generation of middle-class Whig rule. The social pyramid in Canada about which Sir Francis Bond Head was so worried in 1839 was *not* upset; and after a decade of excitement it was clear that the Reform government was only a business men's government. When Baldwin and LaFontaine were succeeded by Hincks and Morin this was so clear that new radical movements emerged both in Upper and in Lower Canada, the Grits and les Rouges.

Now in North America the essence of all effective liberal movements — I assume in this paper that liberalism naturally leads towards democracy — must be that they are attacks upon the domination of the community by the business man. This was what the Democratic party of Jackson and Van Buren was. As Mr. Schlesinger has recently been pointing out in his brilliant book, *The Age of Jackson*,[6] the effectiveness of the Jacksonians was due to the fact that their leading ideas about the relations of business and government came primarily not from the frontier farmers of the West but from the democratic labour movements in the big cities and their sympathizers amongst the urban intellectuals. Jefferson had been mainly interested in political democracy; Jackson tackled the problem of economic democracy in a society becoming increasingly industrialized. The social equality of the frontier has never given agrarian democrats a sufficient understanding of the problems of a society divided into the rich and the poor of an urban civilization. Here we seem to come upon an important explanation for the weakness of all Canadian radical movements from the 1830s to the end of the century. They were too purely agrarian. The only force that could ultimately overcome the Hamiltonians must, like them, have its base of operations in the cities.

Mr. Schlesinger has also pointed out that American conservatism was immensely strengthened when it transformed itself from Federalism to Whiggism. In the 1830s, as he puts it, it changed from broadcloth to homespun. "The metamorphosis revived it politically but ruined it intellectually. The Federalists had thought about society in an intelligent and hard-boiled way. The Whigs, in scuttling Federalism, replaced it by a social philosophy founded, not on ideas, but on subterfuges and sentimentalities."[7] But the Whigs learned the techniques of demagogy from the Jacksonians and set out to guide the turbulent new American democracy along lines that would suit the purposes of business. Surely we should remark that exactly the same metamorphosis took place just a little later in Canadian conservatism. The clear-cut anti-democratic philosophy of Sir Francis Bond Head and the Family Compact Tories was as obsolete and out-of-place in the bustling Canada of the 1850s as Federalism had been in the United States in the 1820s. The Macdonald-Cartier Liberal-Conservative party was American Whiggism with a British title. (And no doubt the British label on the outside added considerably to the potency of the American liquor inside the bottle.) The Liberal-Conservatives had made the necessary demagogic adjustments to the democratic spirit of the times; they had a policy of economic expansion to be carried out under the leadership of business with the assistance of government which was an almost exact parallel to Clay's Whig "American System". But there was no Jackson and no Jacksonian "kitchen cabinet" in Canada to counter this Liberal-Conservatism.

The Grits and les Rouges did not quite meet the needs of the situation. What Rougeism, with its body of ideas from the revolutionary Paris of 1848, might have accomplished we cannot say; for it soon withered under the onslaught of the Church. Grittism in Upper Canada was originally a movement inspired by American ideas, as its early fondness for elective institutions and its continuing insistence on "Rep by Pop" show. But Brown's accession tended to shift the inspiration in the British direction. Brown himself became more and more sentimentally British as he grew older. Moreover, as publisher of the *Globe*, he was a business man on the make, and Toronto was a growing business centre. As Toronto grew, and as the *Globe* grew, the original frontier agrarianism of the Grits was imperceptibly changed into something subtly different. As early as January 3, 1857 the *Globe* was declaring: "The schemes of those who have announced that Toronto must aspire no higher than to be 'the Capital of an Agricultural District' must be vigorously met and overcome." Brown defeated the radicals from the Peninsula in the great Reform convention of 1859, and by 1867 Grit leaders were more and more becoming urban business and professional men. A party which contained William McMaster of the Bank of Commerce and John Macdonald, the big wholesale merchant, was not likely to be very radical. Oliver Mowat, a shrewd cautious lawyer, was about to take over the direction of its forces in Ontario provincial politics; and its rising hope in the federal sphere was Edward Blake, the leader of the Ontario equity bar. Moreover, as Brown's unhappy experiences with his printers in 1872 were to show, the Reform party under *Globe* inspiration found difficulty in adjusting itself to the new ideas which industrialism was encouraging in the minds of the working class. Blake and Mowat, who dominated Canadian Liberal thinking after Brown, were not American democrats or radicals so much as English Whigs in their temperament, their training, and their political philosophy. For political equality and liberty they were prepared to fight; economic equality did not move them very deeply. And the same might be said about Laurier who succeeded them.

Another point worth noting is the effect of British influences in slowing down all movements throughout the nineteenth century in the direction of the democratization of politics and society. Inevitably, because of geographical proximity and the mutual interpenetration of the lives of the two North American communities, the urge towards greater democracy was likely to appear in Canada as an American influence; and since the survival of Canada as a separate entity depended on her not being submerged under an American flood, such influences were fought as dangerous to our Canadian ethos. Sir Francis Bond Head and the Tories of his time habitually used the words "democratic" and "republican" as interchangeable. Every Canadian movement of the Left in those days and since has had to meet accusations of Americanism, and in proving its sound British patriotism it has been apt to lose a good deal of its Leftism. Canadian Methodism, for example, widely influenced by its American connections, was on the Reform side of politics until the Ryerson arrangement in the 1830s with the British Wesleyans put it on the other side.

When we get down to the Confederation period no one can fail to see how markedly the British influence gives a conservative tone to the whole generation of the Fathers. Later Canadians have had to reflect frequently on the sad fact that the "new nationality" was very imperfectly based upon any deep popular feeling. It has occurred to many of them, with the wisdom of hindsight, that Confederation would have been a much stronger structure had the Quebec Resolutions received the ratification of the electorate in each colony in accordance with American precedents. But the British doctrine of legislative sovereignty operated to override all suggestions that the people should be consulted; and Canadian nationality has always been weak in its moral appeal because "We the People" had no formal part in bringing it into being.

Similarly British example was effective in delaying the arrival of manhood suffrage in Canada till towards the end of the century, though the Americans had adopted it in the early part of the century. The ballot did not become part of Canadian law until sanctioned by British precedent in the 1870s. The Chancery Court which had long been a favourite object of radical attack in Upper Canada remained intact until jurists of the Mother Country had amalgamated the equity and common law jurisdictions there. And that strange constitutional device, the Canadian Senate, with its life appointees, was slipped into our constitution with the plea that appointment by the Crown was the British way of doing things. John A. Macdonald must have had his tongue in his cheek when he presented this Senate as a protector of provincial rights, its members being appointed by the head of the very federal government against which provincial rights were to be protected. In the privacy of the Quebec Conference, when they were constructing the second chamber, he had remarked to his fellow delegates: "The rights of the minority must be protected, and the rich are always fewer in number than the poor." One wonders what George Brown or Oliver Mowat, the Grit representatives, must have said at this point, or whether the secretary, who caught Macdonald's immortal sentence, failed to take down their comments. Generally speaking, the notable fact is that in all this era of constitution making, and of constitution testing in the decades just after 1867, the voice of democratic radicalism was so weak.

On the other hand, when Britain began to grow really democratic towards the end of the nineteenth century, her example seemed to have little effect upon Canadian liberalism. The two most significant features in internal British politics since the 1880s have been the rise of industrial labour to a share of power both in the economic and in the political fields, and the growing tendency towards collectivism in social policy. We are only beginning to enter upon this stage of development in Canada today. Throughout it has been the conservative trends in English life that we have usually copied. And one of the few sources of innocent amusement left in the present tortured world is to watch the growing embarrassment of all those professional exponents in Canada of the English way of doing things, now that the English way threatens to become less conservative.

Of course, the great force, by far the most important force, weakening liberal and democratic tendencies in Canada after 1867 was the rush to exploit the resources of a rich half-continent. This was the age in American history which Parrington has called "The Great Barbecue".

> The spirit of the frontier was to flare up in a huge buccaneering orgy. . . . Congress had rich gifts to bestow — in lands, tariffs, subsidies, favors of all sorts; and when influential citizens had made their wishes known to the reigning statesmen, the sympathetic politicians were quick to turn the government into the fairy godmother the voters wanted it to be. A huge barbecue was spread to which all presumably were invited. Not quite all, to be sure; inconspicuous persons, those who were at home on the farm or at work in the mills and offices were overlooked. . . . But all the important people, leading bankers and promoters and business men, received invitations. . . . To a frontier people what was more democratic than a barbecue, and to a paternal age what was more fitting than that the state should provide the beeves for roasting? Let all come and help themselves. . . . But unfortunately what was intended to be jovially democratic was marred by displays of plebeian temper. Suspicious commoners with better eyes than manners discovered the favoritism of the waiters, and drew attention to their own meager helpings and the heaped-up plates of the more favored guests.[8]

Parrington's description fits the Canadian situation also, though our barbecue did not get going in full force till after 1896. In the first generation after Confederation, Canadian Liberals wandered mostly in the deserts of opposition because they could not produce any policy which could match in attractiveness the economic expansionism of the Conservatives. They criticized the extravagant pace of Conservative policy, they denounced the corruption of the Macdonald system, they pointed with true prophecy to the danger of building up great business corporations like the C.P.R. which might become more powerful than the national government itself. But the spirit of the Great Barbecue was too strong for them. And when finally they did come into office under Laurier they gave up the struggle. The effort to control this social force of the businessman-on-the-make was abandoned. Their moral abhorrence of the methods of Macdonald gave place with a striking rapidity to an ever deepening cynicism. "You say we should at once set to reform the tariff," Laurier wrote to his chief journalistic supporter after the victory of 1896. "This I consider impossible except after ample discussion with the business men."[9] And until he made the fatal mistake of reciprocity in 1911, the Liberal government was conducted on the basis of ample discussion with the business men.

It is easy to say that this was inevitable in the circumstances of the time. And indeed the remarkable fact about the Canada of the turn of the century is the slowness of other social groups in acquiring political consciousness and organizing movements of revolt against government by business men. American populism was only faintly reflected amongst Canadian farmers until the 1920s. The Progressive movement which helped to bring Theodore Roosevelt and Woodrow Wilson to the White House seemed to cause few repercussions north of the border. Everybody in Canada in those days was reading the popular American magazines as they carried on the spectacular campaigns of the muckraking era against the trusts. But this fierce attack next door to us against the domination of society by big business stirred few echoes in Canadian public life. Our Canadian millionaires continued to die in the odour of sanctity. Canadian liberalism in the Laurier era was equally little affected by the contemporary transformation of the British Liberal party into a great radical social-reform movement.

What seems especially to have struck visitors from across the ocean was the absence of any effective labour movement in Canadian politics. Both André Siegfried from France and J. A. Hobson from England remarked upon this phenomenon in the books which they published in 1906. "When the workers of Canada wake up," said Hobson, "they will find that Protection is only one among the several economic fangs fastened in their 'corpus vile' by the little group of railroad men, bankers, lumber men and manufacturing monopolists who own their country."[10]

The Great Barbecue was still in full swing when these observers studied Canada. As I have said already, liberalism in North America, if it is to mean anything concrete, must mean an attack upon the domination of institutions and ideas by the business man. In this sense Canadian liberalism revived after 1918, to produce results with which we are all familiar. Amongst those results, however, we can hardly include any advance in the clarity or the realism of the liberal thinking of the so-called Liberal party, however much we may be compelled to admire its dexterity in the practical arts of maintaining itself in office. In the realm of political ideas its performance may be correctly described as that of going on and on and on, and up and up and up. But I am now touching upon present-day controversies. And, whatever latitude may be allowed to the political scientist, we all know that the historian cannot deal with current events without soiling the purity of his scientific objectivity.

In the meantime Canadian historians must continue to study and to write the history of their country. I have devoted these rambling remarks to the subject of political ideas because I have a feeling that Canadian historiography has come to the end of an epoch. For the past twenty or thirty years, most of the best work in Canadian history has been in the economic field. How different groups of Canadians made their living, how a national economy was built up, how the Canadian economy was integrated into a world economy, these topics have been industriously investigated; and we have been given thereby a new and a deeper understanding of the basis of our national life. The climax in this school of activity was reached with the publication of the Carnegie series on Canadian-American relations and of the various volumes connected with the Rowell-Sirois Report.

The best work in the Carnegie collection is for the most part on the economic side. And the volume, published during the past year, which crowns the series — Professor Bartlet Brebner's *North American Triangle* — can hardly be praised too highly for the skill and insight with which the author brings out the pattern of the joint Canadian-American achievement in settling the continent and exploiting its economic resources, and with which he explains the practical working of our peculiar North American techniques and forms of organization. But it is significant that he has little to say about the intellectual history of the two peoples, about education, religion, and such subjects; and especially about the idea of democracy as understood in North America. Materials from research on the intellectual history of Canada were not, as a matter of fact, available to him in any quantity. Volume I of the Rowell-Sirois Report is likewise a brilliant and, within its field, a convincing exercise in the economic interpretation of Canadian history. But it is abstract history without names or real flesh-and-blood individuals, the history of puppets who dance on strings pulled by obscure world forces which they can neither understand nor control; it presents us with a ghostly ballet of bloodless economic categories.

The time seems about due for a new history-writing which will attempt to explain the ideas in the heads of Canadians that caused them to act as they did, their philosophy, why they thought in one way at one period and in a different way at another period. Perhaps when we settle down to this task we shall discover that our ancestors had more ideas in their heads than this paper has been willing to concede them. At any rate, we shall then be able to understand more clearly the place of the Canadian people in the civilization of the liberal-democratic century which lies behind us.

## Footnotes

[1] Sir Francis Bond Head, *A Narrative* (London, 1839), p. 64.
[2] *Ibid.*, p. 464.
[3] Maurice Hutton, Principal of University College in the University of Toronto.
[4] André Siegfried, *The Race Question in Canada* (English translation, London, 1907), pp. 141-3.
[5] James Bryce, *Modern Democracies* (New York, 1921), I, pp. 471-505. Bryce's analysis was based mainly upon observations made before World War I.
[6] A. M. Schlesinger, Jr., *The Age of Jackson* (Boston, 1945).
[7] *Ibid.*, p. 279.
[8] Vernon Louis Parrington, *Main Currents in American Thought*, III, *The Beginnings of Critical Realism in America* (New York, 1930), p. 23.
[9] Laurier to Willison, the editor of the *Globe*, 29 June, 1896 (in the Willison papers in the Public Archives of Canada).
[10] J. A. Hobson, *Canada Today* (London, 1906), p. 47.

# W. W. E. Ross

William Wrightson Eustace Ross (1894-1966) was born in Peterborough, Ontario and educated at the University of Toronto. During his years as a student he made surveying trips to the Algonquin region and to the north shore of Lake Huron. After serving in World War I, Ross became a geophysicist at the Dominion Magnetic Observatory near Toronto. It can be argued that all these experiences helped to give Ross a vision and technique for looking at reality sharply, accurately, and unmetaphorically[1] and to make him "the first important modern Canadian poet writing in English".[2] There is no doubt that one of the most appealing characteristcs of Ross's poetry is his imagery of a hard, clear, northern landscape which reminds many readers of paintings by Lawren Harris and Tom Thomson. Ross himself referred to this northern quality when he spoke of "ambiance or poetic habit . . . . If this ambiance is generally acceptable as an image, or partial image, of a region or country, then the poet becomes a regional or national poet".[3] He was certain that the best poetry, even the "cosmopolitan" poetry of the 1920s, came out of specific rural or urban settings which the poet made his own.

But if Ross's strength as a poet comes from a specific landscape which he made his own, the assumptions behind Ross's poetry are those of Imagism, which stressed simplicity and compactness in diction, and which advocated a form and rhythm appropriate to the subject as well as to the times. Thus Ross sets forth his principles in "This Form Expresses Now". Ross places his emphasis on the verbs, nouns, and adjectives to create an elliptical, concentrated sentence. From this style, one gets a sense of the poetic experience as a process, rather than as an already completed action. His lines usually cannot be regularly scanned, although many of them have a variable number of unstressed syllables and usually two strong beats, thus:

> The iron rocks
> slope sharply down
> into the gleaming
> of northern water

The worth of a poem will not be evident in the isolation of one line, however, but in the cadence developed through the poem, and in the sustained tone and imagery. While many of the poems are realistic in their pinpointing of objects in the landscape, other lyrics such as "Reality" and "On the Supernatural" posit a reality beyond that of the physical universe. Indeed, the essence of Ross's poetry is what Barry Callaghan calls its "profound emotional and intellectual complexes"[4] which come mainly from the tensions established between its simple, almost classic, style and the vitality and restlessness of its subjects.

### Footnotes

[1] *Peter Stevens, "On W.W.E. Ross"*, Canadian Literature, No. 39 (Winter 1969), pp. 44, 52.
[2] *W.W.E. Ross, Experiment (Toronto: Contact Press, 1956), p. 23. Notes by Raymond Souster.*
[3] *W.W.E. Ross, "On National Poetry", The Canadian Forum, XXIV (July 1944), p. 88.*
[4] *Barry Callaghan, Memoir in W.W.E. Ross's Shapes and Sounds (Toronto: Oxford, 1968), p. 7.*

## The Diver

I would like to dive
Down
Into this still pool
Where the rocks at the bottom are safely deep,

Into the green
Of the water seen from within,
A strange light
Streaming past my eyes—

Things hostile;
You cannot stay here, they seem to say;
The rocks, slime-covered, the undulating
Fronds of weeds—

And drift slowly
Among the cooler zones;
Then, upward turning,
Break from the green glimmer

Into the light,
White and ordinary of the day,
And the mild air,
With the breeze and the comfortable shore.

# If Ice

                            If
ice shall melt
                        if
thinly the fresh
cold clear          water
running        shall make
grooves in the sides
of the ice;
if life return
            after death
or depart not at death,
then shall buds
burst into       May-
leafing, the blooms of May
appear like stars
on the brown dry
            forest-bed.


# Reality

In its green solidity
Very real is every tree;
Very clear is the outline
Of each one of the leaves that shine

In the sunlight. A cylinder
Is every trunk, and circular,
Nearly, does each leaf gleam.—
Earth, then, is not a dream.

The objects in the countryside
Are solid heavy and opaque.
The road runs resolutely on.
These exist. Let no mistake

Confuse the mind but there are here
Objects real and very clear;—
And yet this tree is designed free
From empire of geometry.

# Fish

A fish dripping
sparkling drops
of crystal water,
pulled from the lake;
long has it dwelt
in the cool water,
in the cold water
of the lake.

Long has it wandered
to and fro
over the bottom
of the lake
among mysterious
recesses
there in the semi-
light of the water;

now to appear
surprised, aghast,
out of its element
into the day;—
out of the cold
and shining lake
the fish dripping
sparkling water.

# Rocky Bay

The iron rocks
slope sharply down
into the gleaming
of northern water,
and there is a shining
to northern water
reflecting the sky
on a keen cool morning.

A little bay,—
and there the water
reflects the trees
upside down,
and the coloured rock,
inverted also
in the little
shining bay.

Above, on the rock,
stand trees, hardy,
gripping the rock
tenaciously.
The water repeats them
upside down,
repeats the coloured
rock inverted.

# On the Supernatural

We must affirm the supernatural
However doubtfully we have looked upon
Its bare existence in the time that's gone,
For it is ever near and ever real;
As we shall find. We love the natural.
The human reason seated on a throne,
Creator of kingdoms for itself alone,
Is conscious of no zone ethereal.
But to an end with all this lower view,
The cause illusory, vain and yet employed;—
Angels there are and kindly demons too,
Their throng, removed from faulty human sight,
In the unseen worlds as we should know in spite
Of natural explanation thin and void.

# This Form

This form expresses now.
At other times other forms.
Now, this form.
This form seems effective now.
It is monotonous, crude.
It may be called "primitive."
A primitive form.
No form, a lack of form.
Nevertheless, it expresses.
It is expressive now.
At other times other forms.
This form now. Expressive now.

# Apparition

Why did a grass-snake lustrous green
So sinuously glide
Out from the sumacs' sheltering screen
To come and pause beside
The pine tree by whose roots I sat
Astonished suddenly by that

Apparition from beyond
My world of everyday?
Its nimble tongue shot forth unbound
In rapid threatening play.
Its slim length twisted silently
As on the ground it softly lay—

When, doubling quickly, it returned
Upon its former track
As if a hostile glance had spurned
An innocent attack,
Refused whatever gift it brought—
Or what strange purpose was its thought.

# Raymond Knister

*Raymond Knister (1899-1932) was born near Comber, Ontario of German-Scottish parents, was educated at country schools and at Victoria College, Toronto, which he attended in 1919. After a three-year apprenticeship writing poems and stories, he left his father's farm for Chicago and Iowa City in the hope of finding work and friends congenial to his literary ambitions. This literary exile fortunately brought him into contact with the group centred around* The Midland *(Iowa City), one of the leading mid-Western little magazines of the 1920s. By 1926 he was back in Toronto freelancing, and the last five years of his life — a running battle against poverty — saw Knister's reputation grow as his poems and stories appeared in such quality journals as* This Quarter *(Paris),* Poetry *(Chicago), and* The Canadian Forum. *He also published an excellent anthology,* Canadian Short Stories *(1928), and a promising first novel,* White Narcissus *(1929). He was seeing through publication his prize-winning second novel,* My Star Predominant *(1934), at the time of his drowning.*

*In a letter Knister wrote, "Poetry is to make things real — those of the imagination, and those of the tangible world".[1] In the Foreword to his projected volume of poems,* Windfalls for Cider, *he further defined this idea:*

> *Birds and flowers and dreams are real as sweating men and swilling pigs. But the feeling about them is not always so real, anymore, when it gets into words. Because of that, it would be good just to place them before the reader, just let the reader picture them with the utmost economy and clearness, and let him be moved in the measure that he is moved by little things and great. Let him snivel, or be uncaring, or make his own poems from undeniable glimpses of the world.*
>
> *It would be good for the flowers and birds and dreams, and good for us. We would love them better and be more respectful. And we might feel differently about many things if we saw them clearly enough. In the end we in Canada here might have the courage of our experience and speak according to it only.[2]*

*Three points in this passage are pertinent to his concept of poetry. First, Knister hopes to be as accurate and truthful an artist as is possible with his subject, the rural life he knew so well from childhood. In this regard, Peter Stevens notes that for Knister, "the farmer imposing order on his land is the poet imposing order on his materials, but the material is unwieldy".[3] Stevens' observation points to the theme of tension in Knister's poetry: man versus the environment, the poet versus the elusive phrase, or in general, the conflict between Knister's desire to create art and his awareness of its burdens and frustrations. Secondly, the passage indicates Knister's* awareness that the tenets of Imagism would serve him as the basis for his artistic principles. Knister wishes to present his subject simply and pictorially, through what Robert Finch called "these bare, unmusical imagist lines".[4] Consequently, Knister's line is rarely metrical although his "free verse" style does not preclude rhyme or intricate sound-patterns. Thirdly, the second paragraph brings up a continuing problem for the North American artist: how to use the English language to reflect the particular spirit of the artist's time and place. This question has been more or less resolved by American writers, but Knister's generation was still dealing with it in Canada.

Knister's short stories (which remain uncollected) also draw on the author's familiarity with rural Ontario for their settings and characters. "Mist-Green Oats" is a typical Knister story, reflecting the slow-moving, monotonous life of that world, while revealing in Len's buried inner life the clash between his sense of duty and his yearning for escape. Typically, also, this story reflects the new post-war realistic depiction of rural life: a subject no longer sentimentalized but nonetheless treated sympathetically.

### Footnotes

[1] *Raymond Knister in a letter quoted by Dorothy Livesay in her Memoir in Raymond Knister's* Collected Poems *(Toronto: Ryerson, 1949), p. xxi.*
[2] Ibid., *pp. vii-viii.*
[3] *Peter Stevens, "The Old Futility of Art",* Canadian Literature, *No. 23 (Winter 1965), p. 51.*
[4] *Quoted by Dorothy Livesay in Knister's* Collected Poems, *p. xiii.*

# Poisons

Slow down the peach-rows drives Gil Alberts. He sits high
    on the weighty spray outfit, weighty with a heaviness
    alive, as it lurches and rolls through soft wet gravel to
    sniffle and spit for its firing engine and dogged groan
    and whine of pumps.

At each young tree he stops a moment, moving on slowly at
    once.

(The bay horses are long-haired and soft from the winter.
    Their two heaved breaths at each stopping rocks the
    machine a little. At each shout of Gil as the tree's
    finished they pull in their heads and stamp onward,
    sweat about the roots of their ears, hearing the relent-
    less bark and swift whine of engine and pump.)

Beside him is a yellow trumpet of fog from the gun, two
hundred pounds pressure of poison loosened on the
pink well-rooted young trees.

He thinks of a yellow green poison-cloud four years, four
thousand miles away, the sight through gas masks,
through slit of the swivelled gun, in the roar and the
rhythm unabolished by lurchings, as the tank gropes
forward.

At one side of him, now, wide strips of yellow green lie wet
on the gravel and dried grass of last summer along the
tree-rows.

As he turns at the long orchards and the sun makes a
rainbow halo of yellow-green poison.

Never forgetting, Gil Alberts keeps his well-timed pull of the
reins, his well-timed shout to the horses at the calls of
his brother as each tree's done. Rolling amid the bark
and sniffle and whine of engine and pump they pass
down another row, about them the hiss of poison to
pink young trees.

## The Plowman

All day I follow
Watching the swift dark furrow
That curls away before me,
And care not for skies or upturned flowers,
And at the end of the field
Look backward
Ever with discontent.
A stone, a root, a strayed thought
Has warped the line of that furrow—
And urge my horses 'round again.

Sometimes even before the row is finished
I must look backward;
To find, when I come to the end
That there I swerved.

133

Unappeased I leave the field,
Expectant, return.

The horses are very patient.
When I tell myself
This time
The ultimate unflawed turning
Is before my share,
They must give up their rest.

Someday, someday, be sure,
I shall turn the furrow of all my hopes
But I shall not, doing it, look backward.


# Plowman's Song

Turn under, plow,
My trouble;
Turn under griefs
And stubble.

Turn mouse's nest,
Gnawing years;
Old roots up
For new love's tears.

Turn, plow, the clods
For new thunder.
Turn under, plow,
Turn under.


# The Hawk

Across the bristled and sallow fields,
The speckled stubble of cut clover,
Wades your shadow.

Or against a grimy and tattered
Sky
You plunge.

Or you shear a swath
From trembling tiny forests
With the steel of your wings—

Or make a row of waves
By the heat of your flight
Along the soundless horizon.


# Night Walk

Wind, and the dark, and the cool
Momently, lightly, beat forth.
The cricket shrills.

The wind, so fleet, so gentle,
Erratically so steady,
Makes titillation
In leaves unseen:

Rhythmic, almost imperceptible
Ebb and flow among the pines,
Is the ceaseless, unabashed caressing
Heard by inland beaches
Of the inconstant wave.

Nearer, the used eye may see
Tall pines jostling
In mock sedateness
Against the near-black sky.

Ungraspable odour is the air
That haunts,
Reminds of itself.

My soul is steeped in calm.
Then,
Like the sudden unprompted
Chant of a bird
When all the woods
Are still,
I am drawn to cognizance
Of the myriads of men everywhere
Dumbly, unconsideringly striving
To shape their lives,
Asleep now.

## October Stars

Was it the frenzied whisper
Of covert wind to obdurate apple-boughs,
  (Leaves sheltering no more fruit)
Or the paled sky drawing in,
Or the peal of a shooting-star
Across the night?
Or did all these
And the tame apple-smell
Through the wind in your hair
Make me to long
For an end to life?

## Quiet Snow

The quiet snow
Will splotch
Each in the row of cedars
With a fine
And patient hand;
Numb the harshness,
Tangle of that swamp.
It does not say, The sun
Does these things another way.

Even on hats of walkers,
The air of noise
And street-car ledges
It does not know
There should be hurry.


# Change

I shall not wonder more, then,
But I shall know.

Leaves change, and birds, flowers,
And after years are still the same.

The sea's breast heaves in sighs to the moon,
But they are moon and sea forever.

As in other times the trees stand tense and lonely,
And spread a hollow moan of other times.

You will be you yourself,
I'll find you more, not else,
For vintage of the woeful years.

The sea breathes, or broods, or loudens,
Is bright or is mist and the end of the world;
And the sea is constant to change.

I shall not wonder more, then,
But I shall know.


# Mist-Green Oats

It was not until after he arrived home from taking his mother to the railway station
that he began to realize how tired he had become. "Now don't work too hard while
I'm away, Len," had been her last words on kissing him, and before he left the train.
While he was riding slowly homeward his thoughts had been busy hopping from one

detail to another of the morning's activities: of his coming up from the field at eleven o'clock and stabling the horses, of the bustlings of last-minute preparations, carrying the grips out and expostulating with his mother as she stood before the mirror straight and young-looking in her travelling-dress, of the stirring numbers of people about the station and the platform waiting and staring, who made him conscious of his Sunday coat, overalls and heavy shoes. And his mind had leaped on ahead of her to his cousins whom she would see, and what he thought to be their life in the remote city, as he pictured it from the two or three holidays he had passed there in the course of his childhood.

In the lane at the end of the barn when he arrived home his father was hitching his three-horse team together, square-framed and alike in size; and throwing a word now and then to Syd Allrow who was sitting hunched on the handles of his plow which lay on the ground behind his team of blacks. The boy nodded to Syd, and his father, seeing his look of surprise, said hurriedly, "Syd's helping us a day or two. Thought I'd get an early start. — Go right on in now, and have dinner. We'll be back in the apple orchard when you come."

The boy began to notice as he had not before that his father's face had become a little thin and bitten of apparently new wrinkles. The acute stridor of haste and the spring work, the heavy anxiety, the lack of help — he turned away when his father hastily came around to that side of the team. Walking toward the house he heard Syd make some inertly voiced remark or query.

The victuals were cold, but his dinner was awaiting him on the table in the kitchen. When a few minutes later he began to take the dishes away he left off abruptly, remembering that he should have time for such tasks in the evening, when the work outside was done. Then he recommenced and finished clearing the table, for Syd would be there, they would be hungry and wish to have supper as soon as possible after coming from the field.

As he moved about he was not oppressed now by a sense of haste, by a fear, almost, of something unknown threatening their determination which yet chivied and lured the men of farms through those ontreading days of late spring. The season had been retarded by late frosts and heavy rains at seeding time, and the later work, corn-planting and plowing, must be done quickly before the soil became intractable. Such conjunctures, with their own necessity, were at the source of what might in certain types of men evolve as a race against time as much for the sake of the race as for the prefigured prize. He mused.

This released sense must have come from the variation in the plan of the day. At this hour of the afternoon he was used to be in the field, or choring about the barn. Alone in the house Len Brinder's movements became slower as he made the turn from kitchen to pantry and back again. His mind went to the city toward which his mother was now speeding, where the streets and buildings and the spirit of them, which every one of the crowds about him seemed in a way to share, were wonderful from a distance of two years. It was impossible that the spirit and the crowds could mean anything but life rendered into different terms, understandable and entracing. Everyone appeared to be full of active keenness, a beauty, and, for all it was deceptive, no one appeared to work. Automatically he continued moving the dishes about.

138

His father and Syd were both finishing a round when he arrived at the end of the apple-orchard. The horses of their teams were already beginning to show wet about their flanks, despite their hardened condition. As they came toward him the heads of his father's three horses, which were pulling a two-furrow plow, bobbed unevenly, and their loud breaths produced a further and audible discord. The noses of Syd's black team were drawn in to their breasts, for they were pulling a walking-plow and the reins passed around their driver's back. There was little wind among the big mushroom-shaped appletrees.

"Well," said Sam Brinder from his seat, "Syd's finishing the lands for me. Do you want to strike them out? It will be pretty hard around those old trunks, though."

The boy did want to. — "Not much difference, is there?" — and at once turned his team into line. The absence of his father's accustomed brusque unconsciousness struck him readily enough as a blandness affected for the benefit of the neighbor.

The hardness of the ground astonished him. He wondered how he could have thought of anything else since leaving his plow in the morning. He was obliged to hold the handles at a wearying angle in going around the trunks of the big trees, and to twist it back to a normal position in the spaces between. White dust like a smoke burst forth from between the ground and the fresh soil falling heavy upon it. All along the orchard the spurting dust preceded him, thin portions rising with a little wisp of breeze about his face. When he reached the end of the long furrow he was almost panting from the wrestle. "This is going to be hard on horses," he said to himself. "The hottest day yet." The ground seemed to have become petrified since the day before. "I'll have to rest them oftener now, just after dinner. Later on we can go," he thought, as he turned again for the return on the other side of the trees.

It was necessary to plow two furrows around each row of trees before the big plow could be used. As the end of the orchard was reached each time the ground seemed harder and the boy's arms more stretched and tired. As the time passed the horses began to give signs of the strain. One of them would put his head down and make a forward rush, straightening the doubletree, while his mate seemed to hang back — then the other in turn dashed ahead, leaving his mate behind.

"Straighten 'em up there. Make 'em behave!" his father called from the riding-plow, and banished Len's own vexation with the team. He tried but languidly to bring it under control, while he thought, "It's the ground. The horses are all right. They're willing enough." Nothing could be more willing than a horse. He'd go until he dropped if the driver hadn't sense enough to pull him up, to keep him from foundering himself. It was the cursed soil. The plowing shouldn't have been put off so long. It needn't have been. Why couldn't they have left some of the manure-hauling, some of the pruning, and done this first? And other people were able to get men on some terms, why couldn't his father? Then, why must he take such a busy time as last week had been to go to the city to see about the mortgage? These questions were like arrows pointing a center in his thoughts: the feeling of being ill-used. Bad management was to blame, but he could not, yet, hold his father responsible, whom circumstances seemed to have rendered powerless. The boy's hat was sticking to his brow as though clamped there with some iron band driven down like hoops on a barrel.

Sam Brinder and Syd were talking at the end of the field. What did they have so important to talk about? They had been at the same spot when he started back from the other end. He didn't rest his horses that much. He was too interested in getting the work done to be so determined to take part in a confab. He would show them what he thought. He'd not give his horses half as much rest as they gave theirs. That would shame them, maybe, the lazy — "Ned! Dick! Get up here, you old — "

Tight-throated in the dust, wrestling bitterly with the stony soil, he went up and down the rows. These thoughts lasted him a long time and he forgot everything about him except the wrenching heavy plow and the rhythmic swinging singletrees and the creaking harness. Time and the sun seemed to stand still, breathless.

They started on again with a jerk when an hour later he heard his father hailing him through the trees.

"Go up and get us a pail of water," Sam Brinder called. "Your horses can stand the rest anyway, I guess."

"Well, I'm not thirsty, but if you are, of course — "

"We've been back here longer than you have, remember," his father added.

The boy looked at him, wrapped the lines about the plow-handles and went up the lane toward the well. Walking was queer alone now; easier, perhaps? It almost seemed to be done automatically, his body leaning slightly forward.

He went to the house, and brought the pail back to the well, drank slowly and gratefully of the cold water. . . .

He was walking down the lane at a moderate, stooped shouldered pace. The light summer clothes hung about his gaunt form. Well, the afternoon was going. Four o'clock when he had left the house. It might be nearly half-past four by the time he got back to work. Well, no. Five, ten minutes had gone now. Not more than ten more would pass, before he should have taken Syd and his father their drinks. Even at that; twenty minutes after four; the afternoon was going pretty well. . . . Syd would be for supper, of course. Kind of nice, they had been alone so much, since his older sister had left them and gone into an office in the city. Could it be as hot as this in the city, where one might go into the ice-cream parlors and the movie theatres? Different it would be, anyway.

In the orchard the sunlight seemed to pack the heat down below the boughs and above the earth. The boughs seemed to hold it there, and to make room in some way for more heat, which the sun still packed down. His feet in the heavy shoes seemed to be broiling; the socks hung loose about his thin ankles and over the hard unbendable uppers. The horses needed a rest, his father had said, eh? It was they who needed the rest! He'd give them rest enough, all right, from now on. At each end of the field. If his father didn't mind, why should he try to do more than his share?

"Well," said Syd as he reached for the dipper, standing in the furrow and looking up at him, "how you standing it?" At the unevadable reply, "Oh, all right," he added:

"Getting about enough of farming? I was that way myself for a while. Seems kinda hard work after going to high-school, I s'pose."

That was like him! When it was almost a year since Len had left high-school. "Oh, I'm used to it by now," the boy replied coldly.

Syd mopped his face with a patterned handkerchief, spat, swung a line, and said, "Well, I guess I'll have to be getting along. Boss'll be makin' the fur fly, if I don't." He

140

smiled at the joke, as a farmer's son himself, and independent of the whims of bosses. "So you're keeping batch now? I better not bother you for supper."

"Yes, you're to stay for supper. There's no trouble about that. Yes, mother thought she'd take a rest before the canning came on. . . . " He added, "Gone to the city," with a smile he suddenly felt was meant to appear brave.

"Tchka! Bill! Sam! Get outa here!"

His father said: "You'll have to go up a little earlier than us and get supper ready."

Len made no reply. Assent he felt was too miserably unnecessary, and he stood looking in silence back of the plow.

"Not making much of a job," said Brinder. "I got to stand on it most of the time. You got to be quick and keep shifting the levers. You got to have 'er just so. Some job, all right!"

As he walked across the scarred and lumpy headland the boy made an effort to feel at odds with his father, and to conjure an image proper to the aim. He saw him, a clipped-moustached and almost spruce figure, going away from the house to attend perhaps a meeting of school-trustees, to raise his voice among the other men. Trying to find in his memory cue for a critical attitude, Len began to wonder how he himself appeared to those about him, going through the gestures of daily living.

What were people made of anyway, he reflected, bitterly deprecatory — but extravagances, ludicrous to everyone but themselves.

The sweat was caked in salt upon the flanks of his horses when he got back to them. One horse's head was held in a natural position; the other's back and head were level, and its weight slouched on a hind leg.

Stiffly the three plodded on again. As one long round after another was made, night almost seemed to be getting farther away, rather than nearing them. To lean back in the lines as he found himself wanting to do and allow the plowtails to pull him along was impossible. The point would shoot up and the plow slide along the ground until he could get the horses stopped. In spite of him sometimes it did this, when it struck a stone or when it came to a packed area of ground, and then the boy had to drag its weight back several feet into its former position; shouting at the horses and pulling them back at the same time.

But at each end of the field he gave the team a long rest, sitting on the plow-handles as the clumsy implement lay on its side. He dangled his legs and moved his feet about in the heavy shoes. The soles were burning. Looking at the wrinkled tough leather, which seemed to form impenetrable bumps, he noticed that the toe of the right shoe was turned up on the outside with a seemingly immanent bend, given it by the slope of the furrow which he had for days been following. Every day the same! With the impressionableness of youth he could not believe that there had ever been a time at which he had not been tired out. Every day the same. The weariness of last night and of the night before, the same. But this day was far from spent yet. Tonight as well as the usual chores there would be work in the house.

He looked for a long time across the wide pasture at the end of the orchard. Several cattle were on its gently raised surface. Their feet seemed to be above the fence on the lower ground beyond them, which could be seen at either side of the rise. The sky was clear and high, and it seemed to give the cattle a lightness which should make possible

141

for them any feat. It looked as though they might with one fabulous jump easily clear the fence in the distance and be free. For what — free? They would break into the green oats or wet alfalfa and kill themselves. The boy sighed and raised the plow-handles again. Over in the midst of the trees sharp sweet notes of birdsong began to come, giving the place in his present mood a chilled look. The grass became pale before his eyes and the sunlight a little milder broke among the branches as among windy streaming snowflakes.

The horses pulled evenly now. They were going with a seemingly terrible swiftness. The boy staggered and strode along behind them, wrenching the plow as it threatened to jump to the surface. They found it easier, charging through so rapidly, or else they wanted to get each stint over as quickly as possible for the rest at the end of it. Stumbling and striding along behind, Len hated them. Boy and horses began to sweat more profusely. "They always get that way about this time. It must be getting late." The sun was shining in his eyes.

As he reached the end his father shouted across to him, and he stooped to undo the tugs.

It was when he reached the house that the desire came to him to take off his shoes. He seemed to have walked on lumpy plates of hot greasy iron for innumerable ages. He sat down and untied them slowly, and the mere loosening of the leathern laces made the feet ache relief. He walked about the cool kitchen oilcloth in his socks. Then a fancy struck him. He opened the screen-door and went out on the lawn. He shoved his feet along in the short grass and rubbed them against each other. Such immeasurable sweet pain he had never known. At first he could scarcely bear to raise his weary feet from the depth of the grass. Presently he would lift one at a time in a strange and heavy dance, for the pleasure it was of putting it down again among the cool soft blades. The lowering sun variegated the green of the different kinds of evergreen trees back of the house, of which he always confused the names. Something of beauty which, it seemed, must have been left out of it or which he had forgotten, appeared in the closing day. Something was changed, perhaps. He did not know how long he had been there, scrubbing his soles about like brushes in the grass, and regretfully hopping, until he remembered that the men would be coming in for their supper at any minute. Beginning to wonder whether anyone had witnessed his movements, he went into the house and relaced his shoes.

The men were eating their supper. After they had washed their hands and faces outside of the back door, throwing each dirty basinful away with a dripping hiss into the light breeze, they entered the house. Syd sat very straight on a chair by the wall, with his arms folded, and looked at nothing in particular. His black shirt was still open at the neck. Sam Brinder bustled about helping Len to complete the preparations. "Now, the eggs. How'll ye have the eggs — Syd?"

"Doesn't make any difference to me," Syd gravely replied.

"Come now, you've gotto say."

"No, sir. Have 'em how you like. You're the doctor."

"Well, suppose we have them fried."

Now, as they ate heartily, they said little, except to urge upon each other and accept or refuse more food. The room became warm and filled with the soft sounds of their eating and the steaming kettle on the stove. There was the humming of one or two flies about and between them recurrently. Presently a prolonged lowing was heard from back of the barn. "Cows are coming up the lane of themselves," said Brinder. "We won't have to go after them. Pretty good, eh, Len?"

Then the two men began to speak of the crops and the comparative state of the work on neighboring farms.

"We're pretty well forward with our work," said Syd, "but there's more of us for the amount of land." He referred to his two brothers who were at home. "Still, you fellows are getting along pretty well. You're getting over the ground lately, all right."

The significance came to Len of "you fellows", making him angry and sad. A great partnership it was, he told himself, wherein his share consisted of unrequited work. Then he thought that Syd had meant to be flattering or condoling, and though he imagined that he should be vexed with him for that, he could not. The conversation was sliding on over well-worn topics, with the slight necessary variations. The sun's rays were horizontal now, the raised window blind let them strike on the lower part of Syd's clean-shaven tan face. It was not every night that they had company, even in this fashion. The boy liked Syd, after all. It reminded him how, many years ago as it now seemed, Syd had known of a Hallowe'en prank which he with some of the high-school boys had played on one of the farmers thereabout. And he had never told . . . . The Hallowe'en joke had been to him, as much as anything else in his boy's world, a social due.

The three sat in the room which the flat rays from the window made to seem dusk-filled, and the two elder continued talking. Len moved his fork with the ends of his fingers, tilted his tea-cup, and thought, when he thought, and did not merely fill himself vaguely with a pleasant sense of Syd's identity, of the work to be done yet.

Presently they rose, and the boy remained in the house to do the washing-up while his father did the chores.

Slowly the dishes were assembled and slowly and thoroughly wiped. Unused to the work he took a long time to finish it. Besides, he thought, there is only more work waiting outside. "There's always work waiting outside on a farm," he reflected. "There'll be plenty of it right here when we're all dead. Wherever it's all getting us to — " But he saw some of the older farmers about him, and those who were not to that extent in neediness, still working as hard and during longer hours than anyone. They had come to like it. He envied and contemned them for that. There was so much of the world to see, so much of life to discover, to compare with what one might find in oneself! Suddenly Len was confident of this.

He went out into the dusk. Innumerable crickets joined voices to produce a trill. A wind was blowing and he sniffed it gratefully. "As fresh — as fresh, as on the sea," he muttered, slouching toward the barn. The cattle were in the yard, spotting the gloom. He could hear their windy coughing sigh, which was at once contrasted with the loud drumming snort of a horse as he burrowed about in the hay of his manger. The closed stable was loud with the grinding of jaws on the tough dried stems.

There was no sign of his father about, though he gave a shout. He wished to know which of the chores remained not done. There was no answer. The milk-pails upside down showed that the milking was not yet begun. "Likely gone home with Syd for a visit," he grunted at once, without taking any thought of the matter. He fumbled about the harnesses in the dark. "Thinks he'll lay the chores on me, I s'pose. I'll only unharness the horses and water them. If he doesn't like that he can do the other."

When he returned to the house he glanced at the alarm-clock on the shelf. A quarter past nine. He picked up a magazine and took it with a lamp into the next room. Frequently when the family went to town a magazine was brought home. Before that his reading had been restricted and this began only after Len had quit high-school. He for some time found the change grateful from his dry studies. He was drowsing with his elbows on one of the magazines when the screen-door slammed and Brinder entered the house, coming on into the room where his son was sitting. The boy, fully awake, pretended to continue his reading.

"I saw you weren't out at the barn, so I came in. You didn't get the chores all finished, did you?"

"No, I just worked 'til a little after nine, and then quit and called it a day."

"Is that so! You could have quit when you liked, if you'd asked me. I didn't order you to do the chores, remember, I asked you how many of them had been done."

"As many as I had time to do after doing the work in here."

"Well, you didn't have many hours work in here, did you? How much did you do?"

"I gave the horses water and unharnessed them."

"Oh!"

"Why, did the time seem so long over at Allrows'?"

"Over at Allrows'?"

"Yes. Didn't you go home with Syd?"

"Well, that's a joke, that is," said Brinder, turning away. "I went back to the pasture after old Belle. She wouldn't bring her calf up with the other cattle."

Len was nonplussed for an instant. His father went on, "It'll pay not to pay so much attention to the clock when a busy time's on, you'll find." He entered the kitchen, shutting the door behind him.

The boy did not try to check his anger at this. It was increased by his knowledge that his father's was controlled.

"I'll find, will I?" he shouted at the closed door. "I'll find where there's an eight-hour day to be had, you can bet on that!"

He heard his father grunting in the next room, and the creak of his lantern as he jerked it shut. Then the outside door slammed behind him.

Len was painfully awake now, but he could not keep his mind on the printing before him. His imagination ran amuck through possibilities. But he did not see them as possibilities. The actuality stood before him of every movement from now until the time he should have reached the city and entered on some transcendently congenial and remunerative occupation. The vision, with its minutiae, lasted a considerable time; then another came of his going to sea. When he judged that his father would soon be coming into the house again he took up his lamp and retired to his own room.

The next morning he came downstairs bearing the blackened lamp in his hand, to find that his father had gone out, leaving a fire for cooking the breakfast. It was half-past five by the clock on the shelf, and the boy at once began preparations for the morning meal. Before the table was set his father came in with the milk-pail. They greeted each other somewhat shamefacedly and busied themselves with straining the milk and taking the dishes from the shelves.

As they were sitting down to the table Mr. Brinder looked at the clock: "It's later than it seems; that clock's away slow." He appeared to be in a hurry, and the meal was consumed in silence. When they had finished the father said, "You clear up here. I'll not water the driver nor your team. If I'm gone to the field when you come out, you water them." He went away apparently without hearing Len's monosyllabic assent.

The morning was not yet more than faintly warm. White clouds were loitering about the sky, and dew hung in the grass beside the path worn to the barn. The boy slipped the halter from the head of Lass, the driver, pride of the farm, or at any rate very much that of himself. He drove her out into the yard, where she might go for a drink. Meanwhile he began to harness the team with which he intended to plow.

In a moment Lass entered the end of the stable in which he was working, instead of the other, containing her box-stall. For months one of the rollers on the door leading out of that end of the barn had been broken, so that it had been necessary to lead her forth from the part in which the other horses were quartered. Now, as she came in by the old way, long after the door had been repaired, there was something about the whole matter, about the inertia and preoccupation which had so long made them neglect it, more than about this unnecessary use of the old mode of entry, which enraged Len immeasurably. He could not have explained his rage with its sudden choking of his throat. He leaped at the little mare shouting, "Get out of here, you! Before I — " He reached her side and struck a blow at her muzzle. She jerked her head up, turning around, and slipping and sprawling on the cement went out. He at once became ashamed of himself, and when he had got her into the stall gave her an extra handful of oats. They watched each other while she, ears pricked, ate it. Lass did not object, as most horses did, to the impertinence of being watched while she consumed feed.

Throughout that morning the boy was nearly as tired and even more languidly bitter than the evening before. The soil seemed as hard as ever, the horses plunged, the orchard was still longer.

Wonderful high steep and billowing clouds were in the sky. They were like vast mounds and towers of tarnished well-lit silver. He sat on the side of the plow and looked over toward the part of the orchard at which he would finish his plowing. The green of an oats field beyond was visible under the apple-boughs. It was even now beginning to take on a gray misty tinge. Soon the oats field would seem an unbelievable blue-gray cloud, glimpsed from beneath the apple trees. In those days the granite of oats would call the eye throughout all the country. The heads would seem to dance in the high sunlight, and fields of wheat would bow and surge in amber-lit crests. The rows of young corn would be arching to either side and touching, black-green and healthy. The smell of it, as he cultivated and the horses nipped off pieces of the heavy leaves, would be more sweet than that of flowers, and more bland. The year would pass on, the harvesting of wheat, of barley and oats, fall-plowing again, threshings, the cutting and husking of corn, the picking of apples in this same orchard. Yes, one could see the beauty of it distantly, but when the time came he would be numbed to all with toil.

That is, this round would take place, the years pass on, if he remained on the farm. Would he, or, rather he asked himself, could he do that? Nothing very alluring was to be seen ahead in the lives of anyone about him. What was his father getting out of it?

His plow could scarcely be held in the ground at all now. The point had become worn off and rounded, and he at last went over to his father for a heavy wrench with which to break it off squarely, which would for a time postpone the necessity of replacing it with a new one. Syd was starting back to the other end of the orchard, and waved a heavy arm at him. Len pretended to be busy disengaging the wrench from his father's plow, but looked up an instant later to watch the steady progress down the field of the team of blacks; and Syd held the plow-handles with an appearance of firmness and ease.

"You needn't bother going for the water this morning, I'll go after it," his father was saying.

"Plows nice, finishing the lands up, don't it?" Len asked significantly, ignoring the remark.

"Well, if you wanted to do that, why didn't you say so in the first place?"

"Oh, don't bother changing us around now! I'm getting used to the hard part." He still looked after Syd.

"No, I won't ask him to change now."

Len walked on, more uninterruptedly now, but shouting shrilly at the horses as they jerked ahead. Stopping midway of the field he set the clevis to make the plow go deeper. It saved him some of the effort to hold it in the ground. But the horses found it still heavier going. At the hard spots at each end big blocks of cement-like earth were turned up.

He was calculating the length of the orchard and therefrom the distance walked in a day, when his father came with the drink. Pulling his watch out Sam Brinder said, "It's not as late as it seems. I've set the clock on, by my watch. It's five minutes to eleven, while the right time is twenty-five minutes to eleven. I'll holler when it's time to quit. Your team is doing all right, not sweating."

Later as he came to the end of the field he heard his father and Syd, who happened to finish at the same time, talking together.

"Yes, and she can go, all right; nice roader," his father was saying.

"Well, I think this other one would just suit you."

Were they speaking of Lass? Once or twice Brinder had considered disposing of her, and Len's dread of such a possibility was such that he would never discuss it. But she might be sold now. Anything, it came to him, might happen now. His father would just like to sell her to spite him, he knew. The ache of his anger was redoubled by the memory of what had happened that morning. He recalled now his deep-founded liking for the little horse. One evening he let her out in the field with the others. How she trotted! Proudly, with arched neck and tail streaming behind, she moved about among the other horses with great high free strides. "She can trot circles around the others," he thought. Presently she stopped, standing poised and throbbing with life, snorting, ears forward, looking at him in the doorway. And he clapped his hands and she trotted off once more. Then she became still more frolicsome. Her heels shot up again and again, and he could hear the swish of her long heavy tail as she kicked. . . . Yes, it would be just like him to sell her.

Time passed, as if in despite of itself. The boy plodded on, his mind enfolded in these thoughts, and consciously aware of only the flopping aside of the earth before him, of the dust and the hard gravel slope of the furrow-bottom. The fatal impressibility of youth was lapping chains about him. It seemed that he had never known anything else than this dolorous wrestle in the dust. The hard clamping of his hat-brim pained his forehead. He wiped it and the grime came off on his handkerchief. The ache in his legs was not to be forgotten, but his mind swung from the certainty of the loss of one of the few things — the only one it now seemed for which he could care. He began to wonder about the time. His shadow slanted a little to the east as he faced north: surely it was after noon. He could not remember whether the shadow slanted more in the spring or in the autumn: it was surely more than twelve o'clock.

Automatically he continued work after the accustomed respite. What was the meaning of this clock business? The clock had seemed accurate enough yesterday to catch the train by. But it had been slow this morning, and now, his father said, it was fast, and fast so much. There was something strange about all this.

But as it became later there ceased to be anything strange in the matter to Len. It was part of a plan, that couldn't be doubted. To pretend that they had begun later than usual and at the same stroke keep him at work later — it was sharp, all right. Indignation and a respect for his own penetration filled him. This, he reflected in bitterness, was what he must expect from his father henceforth. And the latter would regard it as no more than just discipline, probably. But he'd be shown. "He'll only try that once," the boy muttered, his face fixing and his fingers tightening on the plow-handles.

Standing at the end of the field he looked about him. Through the trees he could see his father's three square-boned horses straining onward amid the shouts of their driver. "Sitting down, having a snap," he thought, relishing the fact of taking this as a matter of course. Farther over Syd was going in the opposite direction, holding his plow as steadily it appeared as though the ground had been softened by days of rain.

"I'll not make another round," he reflected. "Or it will be a good while before I do, anyway. If he thinks he can do that sort of thing he's going to get left."

Whistling a shred of an old tune he sat down on his plow. "Have a good rest, Ned," he addressed the nigh horse, "you started early enough, anyway."

He was aware of the long barred stretch of blue-green oats now still nearer. The high sun instead of making it more vivid seemed to give its surface a hazy quality. A dragon-fly hung motionless against the mild breeze and seeming to battle with it, wings alight with a sparkle of swift motion.

"About noon when you see them things," the boy thought.

From three-quarters of a mile away came the sound of the Allrows' dinner-bell. Old-fashioned people. It was dinner-time, then, all right. Sometimes, though, they had dinner earlier, or later. He pictured the Allrow boys and their father, quitting work in various parts of the farm, and Mrs. Allrow, plump, easily pleased woman, with her grownup daughters preparing the meal. How long was it since he had been over to their place? That, he reflected, was the trouble; one didn't see anyone new for weeks at a stretch. The desire for various contacts had made him impatient of the people he might have known better, had he cared. He got through the day's work, but curiosity demanded leisure and energy. People on a farm, like the men on ship-board in the old days, saw too much of each other. That was it. But that could be remedied in his case, Len reflected with a quickening of the pulses. . . . Not an inch would he drive further. His father must learn that his little trick wouldn't work. As he sat, waiting for the call, he decided that if he discovered that the clock really had been advanced, he must leave. He pictured all the details of this, his father's queries and expostulations and his own determined silence. He would pack his suitcase, take his few dollars out of hiding and walk down the road. . . . He kicked at the side of the furrow, gazing down-ward. . . . How sore his feet had been last night! . . . But he wouldn't walk very far, only to the railway station. For he was going to the city. No, he would ask to be driven there in the buggy, drive Lass himself. If only one could keep himself unbound! But there'd be that one friend he'd always miss! . . . He would ask politely, unemotionally, and his father would not be able to refuse. . . . He'd just step to the house and 'phone central and enquire the correct time.

His father's call struck a surprise in him, and he rose stiffly and unhitched the horses. He noticed that both the others were unhitching also. They didn't intend to let him go up and prepare the dinner alone. But he'd never let that hinder him. He'd step to the 'phone in their presence and find out the truth about this matter. Robbing from both pockets at once!

He hurried toward the barn, determined to arrive there first. He came to the watering trough; and when, after waiting for the horses to drink, he had stabled them, he was so agitated that he was struck with a weak surprise to hear Syd and his father talking quietly outside while they separated their horses. He intended to go out of the building and directly to the house, having fed the team which he had been driving; but he changed his mind and went back and began to put hay in the other mangers, then made for the house and washed before them.

He heard their voices; their heavy feet scrub the grass of the yard . . . . knock against the step.

"It's a seven-foot cut, they tell me," Brinder was saying. "Now wouldn't you thought a six-foot cut would be big enough, on a farm like that."

"Old Dunc says he may as well get a big one now. Alfred'll be getting a tractor soon as he's gone, he says."

"Great old joker. He don't mind having big things around, himself."

"Then I guess he's sure he'll have the job of driving it now he's getting old." Syd laughed. "It'll make the boys hump, to shock behind it, though."

"Yes, they raise pretty good crops, just the same." Mr. Brinder was putting water in the kettle, while Syd combed his hair. "How'll we have the eggs, boys?" The voice sounded absent from the pantry, whence the regular sweep of the bread-knife could be heard.

"Well, they were pretty fair like they were last night . . . . "

Len moved from shelves to table with clean dishes. Syd sat with his arms folded on a chair tilted against the wall. He intercepted one of the rounds by asking, "Well, how you coming? Ground soft where you are, I s'pose!"

148

The boy grunted in reply and managed a half-smile.

Soon the meal was ready, and as they sat down to it he remembered that he had not gone to the 'phone as he had promised himself. He would do it as soon as the other two were gone, and he would be left alone to wash the dishes.

The two voices went on, with a calm interest, business-like inevitability, and the meal was almost over before Len realized that there was something in his mind being worn down and smoothed away, as old ice is worn away by spring rain. They talked as though they had been travellers in a desert who had become parted by accident and now met to recount all they had been through. But what they told was nothing, they meant simply to demonstrate to themselves that they were together again. Then what he thought of as the unreality of it oppressed him. A change in circumstances, the presence of strangers seemed to compel one to make little changes in one's words, in one's actions. Elements of the frank, humorous, the straightforward, of eagerness in the gallantries of conversation were there. Perhaps Syd's family would smile to recognize him. His father was different too. But weren't they both after all as much themselves in any guise as they could be?

It occurred to him that his father was seeking something in the commonplace exchange. His father had been young too, once. He tried to imagine that youth, his aims and desires and ways. The thought unaccustomed held him for a moment, but he could not imagine them as different from his own, and the idea came that his father had betrayed them. Then as he looked at the lines in the face, scars of weather, toil and the scarifications of experience, he began to descry the blind unwitting stupor of life, reaching for what it wanted, an ox setting foot on a kitten before its manger.

He wanted to rise and rush from the room. The sound of the two with their talking kept him from his own thoughts.

They continued to discuss the fallibilities and oddities of neighbors until the table began to look emptier, and then he noticed his father saying, "So you think you'll not be able to help us any more, Syd?"

"Well, not just for the present," replied Syd pleasantly, as though correcting Mr. Brinder in an important inexactitude of statement. "Maybe sometime after a while."
. . . So Syd was going; going too. They were both going, his conscious mind repeated, though something that had been fierce and silently stridulous began to shrink within him, and he began to wonder how much he meant that.

He rose and left the house. He went down the lane and along the road which led toward the corner where, on the main highway, their mail-box stood.

There was nothing but yesterday's paper, and a postcard from his sister. The latter contained only the most banal message, documenting the fact that its sender was alive and, it added, in good spirits; and that the boss said her vacation would come in the next month.

The relationship of the brother and sister was not known to any especial tenderness, and yet, as he thought of the sense of her presence in the first few days after her return, of the feeling while at work of somebody new waiting for him at mealtimes, he couldn't but look forward to it, and he realized and now admitted to himself that his struggle had found an issue. A dull quietude came upon his mind. He tramped back home, his heavy feet upon the hard rounded road.

149

He found that the men had gone to the barn when he reached the kitchen. Syd would be hitching his horses and going away.

His mother — she would be beginning her holiday among the impossible wonders of the city. He thought of the endless confidential chats she would have with her sister, his aunt Charlotte, as they would rock together in the first afternoons, and the family would be out at work or at play. Already he began to miss her. Nearly two days were gone. But he should have, though only until realization, for expectance the last one of her absence.

Then he was struck by the triviality of what he allowed to pass as excuses for abandoning the determination he had so highly taken.

Once, clearing the table, he looked at the clock, but he did not let the reminder stay with him. As he wiped the dishes slowly, he looked at it again, and said aloud and consciously:

"What's the use? What's the weary use?"

# F. R. Scott

*Frank Reginald Scott (1899- ) was born in Quebec City, the son of Archdeacon Frederick George Scott (1861-1944), himself a poet and a contemporary of the Confederation poets. Scott was educated at Bishop's College, Lennoxville, P.Q., and Oxford University, where he held a Rhodes scholarship. During the 1920s he studied law at McGill, and soon after graduation joined the Law School to teach constitutional law. From 1961 to 1964 he was Dean of the McGill Law School. Scott has been active in the CCF (now NDP) Party and the League for Social Reconstruction; he has also served on the editorial board of such magazines as* The Canadian Forum, Northern Review, *and* The Canadian Journal of Economics and Political Science. *In 1952 he acted as advisor to the United Nations Technical Assistance Program in Burma, and he was a member of the Royal Commission on Bilingualism and Biculturalism. He has translated the poetry of several French-language Canadian poets such as Saint-Denys Garneau and Ann Hébert. Among the honours he has received are election to the Royal Society of Canada (1947), the Lorne Pierce Medal (1962) for distinguished service to Canadian literature, and the Molson Prize (1965) for his contribution over the years to the arts.*

*Scott has always been best known for his satiric poems. In 1965 he explained:*

> *As I became more involved in the human society about me, particularly after the great financial crash of 1929, the ensuing depression, and the emergence of revolutionary and reform political movements in which I participated, I found that I reacted negatively in my writing and turned easily to satire. The satire was the holding up of the existing society against standards one was formulating in one's mind for a more perfect society. It was not revolutionary poetry; although somewhat allied.*[1]

*But all of Scott's poetry — the satiric poems, the apocalytic poems, the utopian poems, the humanistic poems, and the personal lyrics — are complementary aspects of the same consciousness and all are primarily about the values by which we live. Superficially, the poems have differences of style; for instance, a precise, deliberately flat, diction and an absence of metaphor are evident in the imagist landscape poems and in the satires, while the other poems are richer in diction and more inclined to metaphor and mythic allusions. Probably his early practice with the brief imagist poems taught him to compose a line whose visual, emotional, and conceptual impact is tightly unified. Scott's chief sources of metaphor are the Laurentian landscape, modern technology, evolution, and religious motifs. With these, he has made his*

151

poetry a "criticism of life", in the fullest sense of Matthew Arnold's phrase; in fact his choice of metaphors reflects a characteristic balance in Scott's writing between conservatism and radicalism.

Scott's technique in his satires is to adopt the point of view and the arguments of those whom he wishes to expose; the ridicule is thus made dramatic and ironic, as in "Efficiency". The reforming spirit behind these poems on the one hand can imagine the catastrophic consequences of our civilization, as in "Armageddon", and on the other hand, can see the possibility of a new society, socially and politically more just than the world of the 1930s. Thus "Eden", its comic tone giving an ambivalence to the religious imagery, ends by affirming a return to Eden in the future: this is an optimistic, liberal view of human nature, admitting both its flaws and its potential. Likewise, the humanist poems can be related to his political views, for they too stress the clash between fallen human nature and its efforts to remake the world. Again, the personal lyrics are fine expressions of the strength of human ties — love between a man and a woman or between the members of a family. Here Scott recognizes the importance of a fully-realized emotional life, without which any calls for a just society or for changes in human affairs are doomed to failure.

**Footnote**

[1]F. R. Scott, "The Poet in Quebec Today", in English Poetry in Quebec (Montreal: McGill University Press, 1965), p. 44.

# March Field

Now the old folded snow
Shrinks from black earth.
Now is thrust forth
Heavy and still
The field's dark furrow.

Not yet the flowing
The mound-stirring
Not yet the inevitable flow.

There is a warm wind, stealing
From blunt brown hills, loosening
Sod and cold loam
Round rigid root and stem.

But no seed stirs
In this bare prison
Under the hollow sky.
The stone is not yet rolled away
Nor the body risen.

# Efficiency

The efficiency of the capitalist system
Is rightly admired by important people.
Our huge steel mills
Operating at 25 per cent of capacity
Are the last word in organisation.
The new grain elevators
Stored with superfluous wheat
Can load a grain boat in two hours.
Marvellous card-sorting machines
Make it easy to keep track of the unemployed.
There isn't one unnecessary worker
In these textile plants
Which require a 75 per cent tariff protection.
And when our closed shoe-factories re-open
They will produce more footwear than we can possibly buy.
So don't let us start experimenting with socialism
Which everyone knows means inefficiency and waste.

# The Canadian Authors Meet*

Expansive puppets percolate self-unction
Beneath a portrait of the Prince of Wales.
Miss Crotchet's muse has somehow failed to function,
Yet she's a poetess.   Beaming, she sails

From group to chattering group, with such a dear
Victorian saintliness, as is her fashion,
Greeting the other unknowns with a cheer—
Virgins of sixty who still write of passion.

The air is heavy with Canadian topics,
And Carman, Lampman, Roberts, Campbell, Scott,
Are measured for their faith and philanthropics,
Their zeal for God and King, their earnest thought.

The cakes are sweet, but sweeter is the feeling
That one is mixing with the *literati;*
It warms the old, and melts the most congealing.
Really, it is a most delightful party.

Shall we go round the mulberry bush, or shall
We gather at the river, or shall we
Appoint a Poet Laureate this fall,
Or shall we have another cup of tea?

O Canada, O Canada, Oh can
A day go by without new authors springing
To paint the native maple, and to plan
More ways to set the selfsame welkin ringing?

*This poem had an additional final stanza when it was first published in the *McGill Fortnightly Review*, 27 April, 1927.

# Grey Morning

The moan of wind over ground
The low round palpable sound of water
Rolling down upon stone, over and down,
And birches moving in the moving air
Came to me at dawn on that grey morning
Like an unutterable, primeval warning,
Like a burden too heavy to bear.

# Saturday Sundae

The triple-decker and the double-cone
I side-swipe swiftly, suck the coke-straws dry.

Ride toadstool seat beside the slab of morgue—
Sweet corner drug-store, sweet pie in the sky.

Him of the front-flap apron, him I sing,
The counter-clockwise clerk in underalls.
Swing low, sweet chocolate, Oh swing, swing,
While cheek by juke the jitter chatter falls.

I swivel on my axle and survey
The latex tintex kotex cutex land.
Soft kingdoms sell for dimes, Life Pic Look Click
Inflate the male with conquest girly grand.

My brothers and my sisters, two by two,
Sit sipping succulence and sighing sex.
Each tiny adolescent universe
A world the vested interests annex.

Such bread and circuses these times allow,
Opium most popular, life so small and slick,
Perhaps with candy is the new world born
And cellophane shall wrap the heretic.


# Armageddon

I. THE SHOCK
Suddenly the last boundary broke
And every land was used by somebody else.
The closed world swarmed with a throng of roads
Where caterpillars span a thread of our blood
And sewed our flags into the history-quilt.
The net of tracks tangled the volunteers
So every man fastened his cuffs of steel.
The clearest call came from the citadels,
Over the churches flew the black birds,
Trumpets blew but only echoes answered
And pamphlet thought scuttled from iron heels.
A lease of fight was lent to far friends,
Prodigious ways were found through sand and ice,
Boats rolled on land while engines swam

155

And dropping men captured the centre first.
Bound in their box of hate, all were packed
In neat grades, carded and grooved. The shape
Of mind and hand fitted the single die.
Less than a horde was nothing. Zeros grew
On integers, adding an ache of size.
Off assembly lines came motor-men
Held by rivets of fear. Identical cogs
Meshed in reverse directions, gathering speed,
Knotting distance into a lace for boots
That never trod upon ground.
A single shaft could use this force, one core
For such power would magnetize a world.
But segment thought died in the private zones,
Men read their fate upon their ancient dials
And neither the pain nor vision found its goal.

II. THE INSIGHT
This foe we fight is half of our own self.
He aims our gunsight as we shoot him down,
Sings our self-righteous hymns, is our own pride,
And writes our sentence in the green baize treaty.
See our metal cannon hang in the air
Over an Asian archipelago,
Dropping the tooled death on the enemy dot
Precisely, ending a threat, and are headlined home
Till the cheers penetrate
An industrial slum.
See the façade fall
From the recent ally under the show of force,
Quislings dancing on their reddening tape,
While underneath, in the clean despair,
The scribbled slogan burns on the public wall.

This line of cleavage runs across the fronts,
Turns back on the victor foe, doubles our task and hope,
Pierces our hearts, and in the secret thought
We deal the final blows.    Out of this battle
Comes our resistance, out of this private invasion
Repelled, comes the demos flow of power.

III. THE PEOPLE'S WILL
It is white hot with our bright hurt, this torrent,
Molten will fitting our chosen mould
Shaped with the common hand in the common clay.

This is our conquest now, our enterprise,
No foreman foreign to our code or class
Takes this decision out of our union law.
We choose our leaders and select our foes
And nearest friend must pass our scrutiny.
We frame the path with the power, alter the shape
Of the overhead state to suit our solid claim.
If armies march, they are ours, if captains call
Over the Afric sands, they are our commands,
And the shouted cry heard in the jungle is ours.

We have changed this agony from our undoing
To our oncoming, the coil before the spring.


# Trans Canada

Pulled from our ruts by the made-to-order gale
We sprang upward into a wider prairie
And dropped Regina below like a pile of bones.

Sky tumbled upon us in waterfalls,
But we were smarter than a Skeena salmon
And shot our silver body over the lip of air
To rest in a pool of space
On the top storey of our adventure.

A solar peace
And a six-way choice.

Clouds, now, are the solid substance,
A floor of wool roughed by the wind
Standing in waves that halt in their fall.
A still of troughs.

The plane, our planet,
Travels on roads that are not seen or laid
But sound in instruments on pilots' ears,
While underneath
The sure wings
Are the everlasting arms of science.

Man, the lofty worm, tunnels his latest clay,
And bores his new career.

This frontier, too, is ours.
This everywhere whose life can only be led
At the pace of a rocket
Is common to man and man,
And every country below is an I land.

The sun sets on its top shelf,
And stars seem farther from our nearer grasp.

I have sat by night beside a cold lake
And touched things smoother than moonlight on still water,
But the moon on this cloud sea is not human,
And here is no shore, no intimacy,
Only the start of space, the road to suns.

# Bedside

In June I saw the withering of my mother.
Oh trees like tears, sweet fellowship of stone!
We moved as one and stared into our hearts
Till night's last round and midnight's courtesy
Was kerchief to our eyes, who found no other.

Our silent strength no help in this assault
We watched her time creep closer by the hour,
And every lengthened intake, each return,
Brought back some tender moment of her succour.
Each one of us was hers, and none his own.

The root wherein we joined at last uprooted
We lingered, reaching in our shallower soil.
What came before seemed now by time inverted,
The ground I trod was all my former home.

And five no longer integral departed.

# Lakeshore

The lake is sharp along the shore
Trimming the bevelled edge of land
To level curves; the fretted sands
Go slanting down through liquid air
Till stones below shift here and there
Floating upon their broken sky
All netted by the prism wave
And rippled where the currents are.

I stare through windows at this cave
Where fish, like planes, slow-motioned, fly.
Poised in a still of gravity
The narrow minnow, flicking fin,
Hangs in a paler, ochre sun,
His doorways open everywhere.

And I am a tall frond that waves
Its head below its rooted feet
Seeking the light that draws it down
To forest floors beyond its reach
Vivid with gloom and eerie dreams.

The water's deepest colonnades
Contract the blood, and to this home
That stirs the dark amphibian
With me the naked swimmers come
Drawn to their prehistoric womb.

They too are liquid as they fall
Like tumbled water loosed above
Until they lie, diagonal,
Within the cool and sheltered grove
Stroked by the fingertips of love.

Silent, our sport is drowned in fact
Too virginal for speech or sound
And each is personal and laned
Along his private aqueduct.

Too soon the tether of the lungs
Is taut and straining, and we rise
Upon our undeveloped wings

Toward the prison of our ground
A secret anguish in our thighs
And mermaids in our memories.

This is our talent, to have grown
Upright in posture, false-erect,
A landed gentry, circumspect,
Tied to a horizontal soil
The floor and ceiling of the soul;
Striving, with cold and fishy care
To make an ocean of the air.

Sometimes, upon a crowded street,
I feel the sudden rain come down
And in the old, magnetic sound
I hear the opening of a gate
That loosens all the seven seas.
Watching the whole creation drown
I muse, alone, on Ararat.

# A Grain of Rice

Such majestic rhythms, such tiny disturbances.
The rain of the monsoon falls, an inescapable treasure,
Hundreds of millions live
Only because of the certainty of this season,
        The turn of the wind.

The frame of our human house rests on the motion
Of earth and of moon, the rise of continents,
Invasion of deserts, erosion of hills,
        The capping of ice.

Today, while Europe tilted, drying the Baltic,
I read of a battle between brothers in anguish,
        A flag moved a mile.

And today, from a curled leaf cocoon, in the course of its rhythm,
I saw the break of a shell, the creation
Of a great Asian moth, radiant, fragile,
Incapable of not being born, and trembling
        To live its brief moment.

160

Religions build walls round our love, and science
Is equal of error and truth. Yet always we find
Such ordered purpose in cell and in galaxy,
So great a glory in life-thrust and mind-range,
Such widening frontiers to draw out our longings,
        We grow to one world
          Through enlargement of wonder.


# Eden


Adam stood by a sleeping lion
Feeling its fur with his toes.
He did not hear Eve approaching,
Like a shy fawn she crept close.

The stillness deepened. He turned.
She stood there, too solemn for speech.
He knew that something had happened
Or she never would stay out of reach.

'What is it? What have you found?'
He stared as she held out her hand.
The innocent fruit was shining.
The truth burned like a brand.

'It is good to eat,' she said,
'And pleasant to the eyes,
And — this is the reason I took it—
It is going to make us wise!'

She was like that, the beauty,
Always simple and strong.
She was leading him into trouble
But he could not say she was wrong.

Anyway, what could he do?
She'd already eaten it first.
She could not have all the wisdom.
He'd have to eat and be cursed.

161

So he ate, and their eyes were opened.
In a flash they knew they were nude.
Their ignorant innocence vanished.
Taste began shaping the crude.

This was no Fall, but Creation,
For although the Terrible Voice
Condemned them to sweat and to labour,
They had conquered the power of choice.

Even God was astonished.
'This man is become one of Us.
If he eat of the Tree of Life . . . !'
Out they went in a rush.

As the Flaming Sword receded
Eve walked a little ahead.
'If we keep on using this knowledge
I think we'll be back,' she said.


# W.L.M.K.

How shall we speak of Canada,
Mackenzie King dead?
The Mother's boy in the lonely room
With his dog, his medium and his ruins?

He blunted us.

We had no shape
Because he never took sides,
And no sides
Because he never allowed them to take shape.

He skilfully avoided what was wrong
Without saying what was right,
And never let his on the one hand
Know what his on the other hand was doing.

The height of his ambition
Was to pile a Parliamentary Committee on a Royal Commission,
To have 'conscription if necessary

But not necessarily conscription',
To let Parliament decide—
Later.

Postpone, postpone, abstain.

Only one thread was certain:
After World War I
Business as usual,
After World War II
Orderly decontrol.
Always he led us back to where we were before.

He seemed to be in the centre
Because we had no centre,
No vision
To pierce the smoke-screen of his politics.

Truly he will be remembered
Wherever men honour ingenuity,
Ambiguity, inactivity, and political longevity.

Let us raise up a temple
To the cult of mediocrity,
Do nothing by halves
Which can be done by quarters.


# All the Spikes But the Last

Where are the coolies in your poem, Ned?
Where are the thousands from China who swung
    their picks with bare hands at forty below?

Between the first and the million other spikes
    they drove, and the dressed-up act of
    Donald Smith, who has sung their story?

Did they fare so well in the land they helped to
    unite? Did they get one of the 25,000,000 CPR acres?

Is all Canada has to say to them written in the Chinese
    Immigration Act?

# A. J. M. Smith

*Arthur James Marshall Smith (1902-    ) was born in Montreal and educated at McGill University and the University of Edinburgh. Because there were few positions available in Canadian universities in the 1930s, Smith taught at several American colleges before he went to Michigan State University, East Lansing, in 1936, where he remained until his retirement in 1968. Despite his long teaching career in the United States, Smith's activity as critic, anthologist, and poet has made him a unique figure on the Canadian literary scene since the 1920s. As early as 1928 he complained of the debilitating effects of puritanism and nationalism on our literature and pleaded for frankness in poetry and higher standards in criticism. He has always attacked the double standard that operates in Canadian criticism of judging native writers leniently by overpraising them. With F.R. Scott, he contributed to and helped edit* New Provinces *(1936), the first Canadian anthology devoted to the New Poetry.[1] As anthologist, Smith is best known for* The Book of Canadian Poetry *(1943) and* The Oxford Book of Canadian Verse *(1960). In the Introduction to the former anthology, he stressed the value of the cosmopolitan, metaphysical, and anti-romantic elements in Canadian poetry in contrast to the native elements. In later editions, this polarity was minimized, but not before a critical furore had developed over Smith's statements. In 1943 Smith won the Governor General's Award for Poetry for* News of the Phoenix; *in 1966 he won the Lorne Pierce Medal for Literature.*

*Smith's importance in establishing high standards for criticism as well as for poetic craft cannot be underestimated. It is necessary, however, to cut through his critical terminology in order to determine what he is doing in his own poetry. Smith himself has said:*

> A poem is a highly organized, complex, and unified re-creation of experience in which the maximum use of meaning and suggestion in the sounds of words has been achieved with the minimum essential outlay of words. A poem is not the description of an experience, it is itself an experience, and it awakens in the mind of the alert and receptive reader a new experience analogous to the one in the mind of the poet.[2]

*For decades, Smith's critics have called his poetry "sparse", "balanced", "classic", "austere", "disciplined", "concise", and "difficult" — Smith's own favourite terms which he has drawn from T. S. Eliot's criticism, as Milton Wilson has shown.[3] We can dispense with all these terms except "difficult" when we investigate Smith's themes and techniques in order to determine what his poetry is about.*

Smith's central themes are order and value in life: these are conventional themes in any age for the poet endowed with a religious imagination. Since Smith draws on his favourite literary sources for his allusions and metaphors, the reader may have to familiarize himself with the poet's reading. Thus a knowledge of the Agamemnon tragedies, Christ's passion and death, Dante, the three seventeenth-century poets, John Donne, Henry Vaughan, and Thomas Traherne, Yeats, Eliot, and Edith Sitwell will help to clarify some of Smith's references to childhood innocence, guilt, anxiety, and death. Since the concern for order and value is usually accompanied by a need to transcend change and flux, another Smith theme is the permanence of art.

The difficulties, then, are those of identifying the allusions and determining Smith's purpose in using them. His other techniques, such as ellipsis and compression, are not in themselves unusual, although they tend to confuse readers about Smith's profundity and high seriousness. Nor are his forms such as the sonnet and ballade difficult to recognize. But Smith also likes to make parodies and pastiches, and a problem arises in identifying the sources of these poems. For example, "A Hyacinth for Edith" is a pastiche — both a compliment to Edith Sitwell by the use of her style and themes, and a means whereby Smith can comment on his own vision of childhood and this "tinsel paradise" of the twentieth century.

Like his favourite poetic models, Smith alternates between realism (as in "The Lonely Land") and symbolism (as in "A Hyacinth for Edith"), in which natural objects exist not merely for their own sake but as manifestations of a hidden world, or of the essence of a non-material reality. Thus a bird may be real enough, or as in "News of the Phoenix", it may have to be interpreted as a symbol traditionally associated with regeneration and art.

## Footnotes

[1]*The Preface which finally appeared in* New Provinces *was written by F. R. Scott* [reprinted in Dudek & Gnarowski's The Making of Modern Poetry in Canada *(Toronto: Ryerson, 1967)*] *because Smith's Preface was rejected by Pratt. This "Rejected Preface" was printed in* Canadian Literature *No. 24 (Spring 1965), pp. 6-9.*

[2]*A.J.M. Smith, "Refining Fire",* Queen's Quarterly, *LXI (Autumn 1954), p. 353.*

[3]*Milton Wilson, "Second and Third Thoughts About Smith",* Canadian Literature, *No. 15 (Winter 1963), pp. 11-12.*

# The Lonely Land

Cedar and jagged fir
uplift sharp barbs
against the gray
and cloud-piled sky;
and in the bay
blown spume and windrift
and thin, bitter spray
snap
at the whirling sky;
and the pine trees
lean one way.

A wild duck calls
to her mate,
and the ragged
and passionate tones
stagger and fall,
and recover,
and stagger and fall,
on these stones—
are lost
in the lapping of water
on smooth, flat stones.

This is a beauty
of dissonance,
this resonance
of stony strand,
this smoky cry
curled over a black pine
like a broken
and wind-battered branch
when the wind
bends the tops of the pines
and curdles the sky
from the north.

This is the beauty
of strength
broken by strength
and still strong.

# News of the Phoenix

They say the Phoenix is dying, some say dead.
Dead without issue is what one message said,
But that has been suppressed, officially denied.

I think myself the man who sent it lied.
In any case, I'm told, he has been shot,
As a precautionary measure, whether he did or not.

# Sea Cliff

Wave on wave
and green on rock
and white between
the splash and black
the crash and hiss
of the feathery fall,
the snap and shock
of the water wall
and the wall of rock:

after—
after the ebb-flow,
wet rock,
high—
high over the slapping green,
water sliding away
and the rock abiding,
new rock riding
out of the spray.

# A Hyacinth for Edith

Now that the ashen rain of gummy April
Clacks like a weedy and stain'd mill,

So that all the tall purple trees
Are pied porpoises in swishing seas,

And the yellow horses and milch cows
Come out of their long frosty house

To gape at the straining flags
The brown pompous hill wags,

I'll seek within the wood's black plinth
A candy-sweet sleek wooden hyacinth—

And in its creaking naked glaze,
And in the varnish of its blaze,

The bird of ecstasy shall sing again,
The bearded sun shall spring again—

A new ripe fruit upon the sky's high tree,
A flowery island in the sky's wide sea—

And childish cold ballades, long dead, long mute,
Shall mingle with the gayety of bird and fruit,

And fall like cool and soothing rain
On all the ardour, all the pain

Lurking within this tinsel paradise
Of trams and cinemas and manufactured ice,

Till I am grown again my own lost ghost
Of joy, long lost, long given up for lost,

And walk again the wild and sweet wildwood
Of our lost innocence, our ghostly childhood.


# The Plot Against Proteus

This is a theme for muted coronets
To dangle from debilitated heads
Of navigation, kings, or riverbeds
That rot or rise what time the seamew sets

Her course by stars among the smoky tides
Entangled. Old saltencrusted Proteus treads
Once more the watery shore that water weds
While rocking fathom bell rings round and rides.

Now when the blind king of the water thinks
The sharp hail of the salt out of his eyes
To abdicate, run thou, O Prince, and fall
Upon him. This cracked walrus skin that stinks
Of the rank sweat of a mermaid's thighs
Cast off, and nab him; when you have him, call.

# The Archer

Bend back thy bow, O Archer, till the string
Is level with thine ear, thy body taut,
Its nature art, thyself thy statue wrought
Of marble blood, thy weapon the poised wing
Of coiled and aquiline Fate. Then, loosening, fling
The hissing arrow like a burning thought
Into the empty sky that smokes as the hot
Shaft plunges to the bullseye's quenching ring.

So for a moment, motionless, serene,
Fixed between time and time, I aim and wait;
Nothing remains for breath now but to waive
His prior claim and let the barb fly clean
Into the heart of what I know and hate—
That central black, the ringed and targeted grave.

# The Sorcerer

There is a sorcerer in Lachine
Who for a small fee will put a spell
On my beloved, who has sea-green
Eyes, and on my doting self as well.

169

He will transform us, if we like, to goldfish:
We shall swim in a crystal bowl,
And the bright water will go swish
Over our naked bodies; we shall have no soul.

In the morning the syrupy sunshine
Will dance on our tails and fins.
I shall have her then all for mine,
And Father Lebeau will hear no more of her sins.

Come along, good sir, change us into goldfish.
I would put away intellect and lust,
Be but a red gleam in a crystal dish,
But kin of the trembling ocean, not of the dust.

# Business As Usual 1946

Across the craggy indigo
Come rumours of the flashing spears,
And in the clank of rancid noon
There is a tone, and such a tone.
How tender! How insidious!
The air grows gentle with protecting bosks,
And furry leaves take branch and root.
Here we are safe, we say, and slyly smile.

In this delightful forest, fluted so,
We burghers of the sunny central plain
Fable a still refuge from the spears
That clank — but gentle clank — but clank again!

# Fear As Normal 1954

But gently clank? The clank has grown
A flashing crack — the crack of doom.
It mushrooms high above our salty plain,
And plants the sea with rabid fish.

How skilful! How efficient!
The active cloud is our clenched fist.
Hysteria, dropping like the gentle dew,
Over the bent world broods with ah! bright wings.

We guess it dazzles our black foe;
But that it penetrates and chars
Our own Christ-laden lead-encaséd hearts
Our terrified fierce dreamings know.


## Universal Peace 19 —

Murder and suicide alas
The double crime our pride commends.
Too much and much too soon
The stockpile overkill condones.

The boom that boomerangs
Around the sphere and what was twi-divided
Joins — how neat! — how dead!—
A pock-marked scorched colossal Moon.

Hatred and Fear: twins locked in a dead womb.
Blind ice in orbit: heart and head
Burned, cooled, cold, killed—
*Pax mundi* singed and signed and sealed.


## The Bird

Breast-bone and ribs enmesh
A bird in a cage,
Covered for the night with flesh
To still his vocal rage,

Curb his wild ardour and
Circumscribe his wing
Till One shall unwind the band
And let the door swing.

Free then of the flesh hood
And the cage of bone,
Singing at last a good
Song, I shall be gone

Into that far and wild
Where once I sang
Before the flesh beguiled,
And the trap was sprung.

# Morley Callaghan

*Edward Morley Callaghan (1903-    ) was born in Toronto and educated at St. Michael's College in the University of Toronto and at Osgoode Hall Law School. During the summer of 1923 he worked on the Toronto* Daily Star *and there he met Ernest Hemingway, who encouraged Callaghan by praising his early pieces. Although he completed his law studies, he never practiced law. Rather, he supported himself by freelancing in order to devote full time to short story and novel writing. He first gained recognition through his short stories, which appeared each year between 1928 and 1941 in J. Edward O'Brien's annual* The Best Short Stories.[1] *Like many other young American and Canadian writers of his generation, Callaghan spent a short time in Paris, which he described in* That Summer in Paris *(1963). It was the briefest of exiles, for Callaghan rightly decided that his place for living and writing was Toronto. He told his wife "... I might have to forge my own vision in secret spiritual isolation in my native city. Joyce in exile had gone deeply, too deeply into himself. But what if he had stayed in Dublin?"[2] Although Callaghan later spent a few years in New York, his home has been primarily Toronto, where his writing career has been supplemented by journalism, and radio and television appearances. There is little disagreement today that Callaghan is the most important fiction writer in twentieth-century Canada.*

*One reason for his importance is his concern with the central issues of the twentieth century. His people inhabit a world where eroding religious values are no longer the foundations of men's view of themselves, a world where their actions create rejection and alienation. The characters and situations of his short stories (he has published three collections) are firmly rooted in the 1920s and 1930s and are almost documentaries of middle-class Toronto life. Parent-child misunderstandings, lovers' uneasy relationships, the innocent's confrontation with the world are all recurring motifs. These incidents frequently involve ambivalent sacrifices and betrayals: a sacrifice looks like a sell-out, a deception has mixed motives, and the resolution of a lovers' quarrel is not peace but truce. Callaghan cares about his characters' frustrations and sympathizes with their failures, but he is ever conscious of the spiritual vacuum which lurks behind their obsessions with material problems. He is never taken in by their North American dreams of the easy life. Hugo McPherson has described the similarity between Callaghan's vision of man and that of his contemporary, T. S. Eliot:*

> *Man's career occurs in the imperfect world of time, but its meaning (man's dignity or "place") depends finally on a larger reality out of time. To escape the first world is*

*physical death; to ignore the second is to embrace the condition of the Wasteland —
life-in-death. This tension, to which Callaghan's best fiction gives dramatic form, is the
fundamental tension of life. By exploring the relation of these two worlds — empirical
and spiritual — Callaghan has written the "little man's" Ash Wednesday and Burnt
Norton.*

Another reason for Callaghan's importance is the prose style he shaped to relate his vision of human nature. He shares with his contemporaries (Raymond Knister, W.W.E. Ross, A.J.M. Smith, F.R. Scott, and Dorothy Livesay) a common concern for finding a style for the new post-World-War I age. Callaghan explains the problem in *That Summer in Paris:*

> *Why did I dislike so much contemporary writing? . . . . I remember deciding that the
> root of the trouble with writing was that poets and storywriters used language to evade,
> to skip away from the object, because they could never bear to face the thing freshly and
> see it freshly for what it was in itself. A kind of double talk; one thing always seen in
> terms of another thing . . . . I'd be damned if the glory of literature was in the metaphor.
> Besides, it was not a time for the decorative Renaissance flight into simile. Tell the truth
> plainly.*
>
> > *I remember one time at twilight, sitting at the typewriter in the sunroom of my
> parents' home. I could smell the lilacs. A night bird cried. A woman's voice came
> from a neighbor's yard. I wanted to get it down so directly that it wouldn't feel or
> look like literature.*[4]

*This passage has been described by George Woodcock, Victor Hoar, and Brandon
Conron as Callaghan's manifesto of realism. While he has remained faithful to the
principles of realism, which in his works has the bareness of the documentary, he has
given it a characteristic note. The best realism, of course, gives more than a verbal
photograph, although this may be pleasing in itself. It evokes the essence of a character
or situation through a simple, yet appropriate, object in the external world of the
story. In Callaghan's stories, these objects — a cap, a watch, a dress, or a pair of shoes —
become central metaphors, and in at least one novel,* The Loved and the Lost *(1951),
the recurring metaphors and images invite the reader to interpret events on more than
the literal level. Indeed, all Callaghan's novels are realistic narratives constructed as
parables.*

*Furthermore, Callaghan takes another characteristic of realism — the ending that
simply stops — and gives it a special dimension. Where conventional stories ended with
a death or a wedding, Callaghan's stories are ironically open-ended. The narrative may
stop at the moment of illumination or clarity for the character (and/or the reader), but
the reader must realize that the latest problem may not be the last problem. In effect,
there is an existentialist element in the stories which pre-supposes that one crisis, even
though it may influence future situations, does not resolve a character's problems
once and for all. In the past, Callaghan was incorrectly described as a naturalistic
writer; that is, one who views man's life and actions prescribed not by his own free will
and choice, but by the forces of heredity and environment. However, a careful reading
of Callaghan will provide a view of man far subtler than the naturalistic one. Whether
the ending is happy, sad, or inconclusive, Callaghan permits his people a moral choice
in their confrontation with life, and he believes that they must ultimately accept
responsibility for their decisions and actions.*

**Footnotes**

[1]*Brandon Conron*, Morley Callaghan *(New York: Twayne, 1966), p. 33. This is the most useful critical biography of Callaghan.*
[2]*Morley Callaghan*, That Summer in Paris *(Toronto: Macmillan, 1963), p. 230.*
[3]*Hugo McPherson, "The Two Worlds of Morley Callaghan", Queen's Quarterly LXVI (Autumn 1957), p. 352.*
[4]*Callaghan, op. cit., pp. 19, 21-22.*

# A Girl With Ambition

After leaving public school when she was sixteen Mary Ross worked for two weeks with a cheap chorus at the old La Plaza, quitting when her stepmother heard the girls were a lot of toughs. Mary was a neat clean girl with short fair curls and blue eyes, looking more than her age because she had very good legs, and knew it. She got another job as cashier in the shoe department of Eaton's Store, after a row with her father and a slap on the ear from her stepmother.

She was marking time in the store, of course, but it was good fun telling the girls about imaginary offers from big companies. The older salesgirls sniffed and said her hair was bleached. The salesmen liked fooling around her cage, telling jokes, but she refused to go out with them; she didn't believe in running around with fellows working in the same department. Mary paid her mother six dollars a week for board and always tried to keep fifty cents out. Mrs. Ross managed to get the fifty cents, insisting every time that Mary would come to a bad end.

Mary met Harry Brown when he was pushing a truck on the second floor of the store, returning goods to the department. Every day he came over from the mail-order building, stopping longer than necessary in the shoe department, watching Mary in the cash cage out of the corner of his eye while he fidgeted in his brown wicker truck. Mary found out that he went to high school and worked in the store for the summer holidays. He hardly spoke to her, but once when passing, he slipped a letter written on wrapping paper under the cage wire. It was such a nice letter that she wrote a long one the next morning and dropped it in his truck when he passed. She liked him because he looked neat and had a serious face and wrote a fine letter with big words that was hard to read.

In the morning and early afternoons they exchanged wise glances that held a secret. She imagined herself talking very earnestly, all about getting on. It was good having someone to talk to like that because the neighbours on her street were always teasing her about going on the stage. If she went to the corner butcher to get a pound of round

175

steak cut thin, he saucily asked how was the village queen and the actorine. The lady next door, who had a loud voice and was on bad terms with Mrs. Ross, often called her a hussy, saying she should be spanked for staying out so late at night, waking decent people when she came in.

Mary liked to think that Harry Brown knew nothing of her home or street, for she looked up to him because he was going to be a lawyer. Harry admired her ambition but was a little shy. He thought she knew too much for him.

In the letters she called herself his sweetheart but never suggested they meet after work. Her manner implied it was unimportant that she was working in the store. Harry, impressed, liked to tell his friends about her, showing off the letters, wanting them to see that a girl who had a lot of experience was in love with him. "She's got some funny ways but I'll bet no one gets near her," he often said.

They were together the first time the night she asked him to meet her down town at 10:30 p.m. He was at the corner early and didn't ask where she had been earlier in the evening. She was ten minutes late. Linking arms they walked east along Queen Street. He was self-conscious. She was trying to be very practical, though pleased to have on her new blue suit with the short stylish coat.

Opposite the Cathedral at the corner of Church Street, she said: "I don't want you to think I'm like the people you sometimes see me with, will you now?"

"Gee no, I think you away ahead of the girls you eat with at noon hour."

"And look, I know a lot of boys, but that don't mean nothing. See?"

"Of course, you don't need to fool around with tough guys, Mary. It won't get you anywhere," he said.

"I can't help knowing them, can I?"

"I guess not."

"But I want you to know that they haven't got anything on me," she said, squeezing his arm.

"Why do you bother with them?" he said, as if he knew the fellows she was talking about.

"I go to parties, Harry. You got to do that if you're going to get along. A girl needs a lot of experience."

They walked up Parliament and turned east, talking confidentially as if many things had to be explained before they could be satisfied with each other. They came to a row of huge sewer pipes along the curb for a hundred yards to the Don River Bridge. The city was repairing the drainage. Red lights were about fifty feet apart on the pipes. Mary got up on the pipes and walked along, supporting herself with a hand on Harry's shoulder, while they talked in a silly way, laughing. A night-watchman came along and yelled at Mary, asking if she wanted to knock the lights over.

"Oh, have an apple," Mary yelled back at him.

"You better get down," Harry said, very dignified.

"Aw, let him chase me," she said. "I'll bet he's got a wooden leg," but she jumped down and held on to his arm.

For a time they stood on the bridge, looking beyond the row of short poplars lining the hill in the good district on the other side of the park. Mary asked Harry if he didn't live over there, wanting to know if they could see his house from the bridge. They

176

watched the lights on a street-car moving slowly up the hill. She felt that he was going to kiss her. He was looking down at the slow-moving water wondering if she would like it if he quoted some poetry.

"I think you are swell," he said finally.

"I'll let you walk home with me," she said.

"Gee, I wish you didn't want to be an actress," he said.

They retraced their steps until a few blocks from her home. They stood near the police station in the shadow of the firehall. He coaxed so she let him walk just one block more. In the light from the corner butcher store keeping open, they talked for a few minutes. He started to kiss her. "Oh, the butcher will see us," she said, but didn't care, for Harry was very respectable-looking and she wanted to be kissed. Harry wondered why she wouldn't let him go to the door with her. She left him and walked ahead, turning to see if he was watching her. It was necessary she walk a hundred yards before Harry went away. She turned and walked back home, one of a row of eight dirty frame houses jammed under one long caving roof.

She talked a while with her father, but was really liking the way Harry had kissed her, and talked to her, and the very respectable way he had treated her, all evening. She hoped he wouldn't meet any boys who would say bad things about her.

She might have been happy if Harry had worked on in the store. It was the end of August and his summer holidays were over. The last time he pushed his wicker truck over to the cash cage, she said he was to remember she would always be a sincere friend and would write often. They could have seen each other for he wasn't leaving the city, but they took it for granted they wouldn't.

Every week she wrote to him about offers and rehearsals that would have made a meeting awkward. She liked to think of him not because of being in love but because he seemed so respectable. Thinking of how he liked her made her feel a little better than the girls she knew.

When she quit work to spend a few weeks up at Georgian Bay with a girl friend, Hilda Heustis, who managed to have a good time without working, she forgot about Harry. Hilda had a party in a cottage on the beach and they came home the night after. It was cold and it rained all night. One of Hilda's friends, a fat man with a limp, had chased her around the house and down to the beach, shouting and swearing, and into the bush, limping and groaning. She got back to the house all right. He was drunk. A man in pajamas from the cottage to the right came and thumped on the door, shouting that they were a pack of strumpets, hussies and rotters and if they didn't clear out he would have the police on them before they could say Tom Thumb. He was shivering and looked very wet. Hilda, a little scared, said they ought to clear out next day.

Mary returned to Toronto and her stepmother was waiting, very angry because Mary had left her job. They had a big row. Mary left home, slamming the door. She went two blocks north to live with Hilda.

It was hard to get a job and the landlady was nasty. She tried to get work in a soldiers' company touring the province with a kind of musical comedy called "Mademoiselle from Courcelette", but the manager, a nice young fellow with tired eyes, said she had the looks but he wanted a dancer. After that Mary and Hilda every night practised a step dance, waiting for the show to return.

177

Mary's father one night came over to the boarding-house and coaxed her to come back home because she was really all he had in the world, and he didn't want her to turn out to be a good-for-nothing. He rubbed his brown face in her hair. She noticed for the first time that he was getting old and was afraid he was going to cry. She promised to live at home if her stepmother would mind her own business.

Now and then she wrote to Harry just to keep him thinking of her. His letters were sincere and free from slang. Often he wrote, "What is the use of trying to get on the stage?" She told herself he would be astonished if she were successful, would look up to her. She would show him.

Winter came and she had many inexpensive good times. The gang at the east-end roller-rink knew her and she occasionally got in free. There she met Wilfred Barnes, the son of a grocer four blocks east of the fire hall, who had a good business. Wilfred had a nice manner but she never thought of him in the way she thought of Harry. He got fresh with little encouragement. Sunday afternoons she used to meet him at the rink in Riverdale Park where a bunch of the fellows had a little fun. Several times she saw Harry and a boy friend walking through the park, and leaving her crowd, she would talk to him for a few minutes. He was shy and she was a little ashamed of her crowd that whistled and yelled while she was talking. These chance meetings got to mean a good deal, helping her to think a lot about Harry during the first part of the week.

In the early spring "Mademoiselle from Courcelette" returned to Toronto. Mary hurried to the man that had been nice to her and demonstrated the dance she had practised all winter. He said she was a good kid and should do well, offering her a try-out at thirty dollars a week. Even her stepmother was pleased because it was a respectable company that a girl didn't need to be ashamed of. Mary celebrated by going to a party with Wilfred and playing strip poker until four a.m. She was getting to like being with Wilfred.

When it was clear she was going on the road with the company, she phoned Harry and asked him to meet her at the roller-rink.

She was late. Harry was trying to roller-skate with another fellow, fair-haired, long-legged, wearing large glasses. They had never roller-skated before but were trying to appear unconcerned and dignified. They looked very funny because everyone else on the floor was free and easy, willing to start a fight. Mary got her skates on but the old music box stopped and the electric sign under it flashed "Reverse". The music started again. The skaters turned and went the opposite way. Harry and his friend skated off the floor because they couldn't cut corners with the left foot. Mary followed them to a bench near the soft-drink stand.

"What's your hurry, Harry?" she yelled.

He turned quickly, his skates slipping, and would have fallen, but his friend held his arm.

"Look here, Mary, this is the damnedest place," he said.

His friend said roguishly, "Hello, I know you because Harry has told me a lot about you."

"Oh, well, it's not much of a place but I know the gang," she said.

"I guess we don't have to stay here," Harry said.

"I'm not fussy. Let's go for a walk, the three of us," she said.

Harry was glad his friend was noticing her classy blue coat with the wide sleeves and her light brown fur. Taking off his skates he tore loose a leather layer on the sole of his shoe.

They left the rink and arm-in-arm the three walked up the street. Mary was eager to tell about "Mademoiselle from Courcelette". The two boys were impressed and enthusiastic.

"In some ways I don't like to think of you being on the stage, but I'll bet a dollar you get ahead," said Harry.

"Oh, baby, I'll knock them dead in the hick towns."

"How do you think she'll do, Chuck?" said Harry.

The boy with glasses could hardly say anything, he was so impressed. "Gee whiz," he said.

Mary talked seriously. She had her hand in Harry's coat pocket and kept tapping his fingers. Harry gaily beat time as they walked, flapping the loose shoe leather on the sidewalk. They felt that they should stay together after being away for a long time. When she said that it would be foolish to think she would cut up like some girls in the business did, Harry left it to Chuck if a fellow couldn't tell a mile away that she was a real good kid.

The lighted clock in the tower of the fire hall could be seen when they turned a bend in the street. Then they could make out the hands on the clock. Mary, leaving them, said she had had a swell time, she didn't know just why. Harry jerked her into the shadow of the side door of the police station and kissed her, squeezing her tight. Chuck leaned back against the wall, wondering what to do. An automobile horn hooted. Mary, laughing happily, showed the boys her contract and they shook their heads earnestly. They heard footfalls around the corner. "Give Chuck a kiss," said Harry suddenly, generously. The boy with the glasses was so pleased he could hardly kiss her. A policeman appeared at the corner and said, "All right, Mary, your mother wants you. Beat it."

Mary said, "How's your father?" After promising to write Harry she ran up the street.

The boys, pleased with themselves, walked home. "You want to hang on to her," Chuck said.

"I wonder why she is always nice to me just when she is going away," Harry said.

"Would you want her for a girl?"

"I don't know. Wouldn't she be a knock-out at the school dance? The old ladies would throw a fit."

Mary didn't write to Harry and didn't see him for a long time. After two weeks she was fired from the company. She wasn't a good dancer.

Many people had a good laugh and Mary stopped talking about her ambitions for a while. And though usually careful and fairly strict, she slipped into easy careless ways with Wilfred Barnes. She never thought of him as she thought of Harry, but he won her and became important to her. Harry was like something she used to pray for when a little girl and never really expected to get.

It was awkward when Wilfred got into trouble for tampering with the postal pillars that stood on the street corners. He had discovered a way of getting all the pennies people put in the slots for stamps. The police found a big pile of coppers hidden in his father's stable. The judge sent him to jail for only two months because his parents were very respectable people. He promised to marry Mary when he came out.

One afternoon in the late summer they were married by a Presbyterian minister. Mrs. Barnes made it clear that she didn't think much of the bride. Mr. Barnes said Wilfred would have to go on working in the store. They took three rooms in a big rooming-house on Berkeley Street.

Mary cried a little when she wrote to tell Harry she was married. She had always been too independent to cry in that way. She would be his sincere friend and still intended to be successful on the stage, she said. Harry wrote that he was surprised that she had married a fellow just out of jail even though he seemed to come from respectable people.

In the dancing-pavilion at Scarboro beach, a month later, she talked to Harry for the last time. The meeting was unexpected and she was with three frowsy girls from a circus that was in the east end for a week. Mary had on a long blue knitted cape that the stores were selling cheaply. Harry turned up his nose at the three girls but talked cheerfully to Mary. They danced together. She said that her husband didn't mind her taking another try at the stage and he wondered if he should say that he had been to the circus. Giggling and watching him closely, she said she was working for the week in the circus, for the experience. He gave her to understand that always she would do whatever pleased her, and shouldn't try for a thing that wasn't natural to her. He wasn't enthusiastic when she offered to phone him, just curious about what she might do.

Late in the fall a small part in a local company at the La Plaza for a week was offered to her. She took the job because she detested staying around the house. She wanted Harry to see her really on the stage so she phoned and asked if he would come to the La Plaza on Tuesday night. Good-humouredly, he offered to take her dancing afterward. It was funny, he said laughing, that she should be starting all over again at the La Plaza.

But Harry, sitting solemnly in the theatre, watching the ugly girls in tights on the stage, couldn't pick her out. He wondered what on earth was the matter when he waited at the stage door and she didn't appear. Disgusted, he went home and didn't bother about her because he had a nice girl of his own. She never wrote to tell him what was the matter.

But one warm afternoon in November, Mary took it into her head to sit on the front seat of the rig with Wilfred, delivering groceries. They went east through many streets until they were in the beach district. Wilfred was telling jokes and she was laughing out loud. Once he stopped his wagon, grabbed his basket and went running along a side entrance, yelling "Grocer". Mary sat on the wagon seat. Three young fellows and a woman were sitting up on a veranda opposite the wagon. She saw Harry looking at her and vaguely wondered how he got there. She didn't want him to see that she was going to have a baby. Leaning on the veranda rail, he saw that her slimness had passed into the shapelessness of her pregnancy and he knew why she had been kept off the stage that night at the La Plaza. She sat erect and strangely dignified on the seat of the grocery wagon. They didn't speak. She made up her mind to be hard up for someone to talk to before she bothered him again, as if without going any further she wasn't as good as he was. She smiled sweetly at Wilfred when he came running out of the alley and jumped on the seat, shouting "Gidup" to the horse. They drove on to a customer farther down the street.

# The Young Priest

Father Vincent Sullivan was only one of three curates at the Cathedral but he had been there long enough to understand that some men and women of the parish deserved to be cultivated more intimately than others. He had some social talent, too. At the seminary, four years ago, he had been lazy, good-natured, and very fond of telling long funny stories, and then laughing easily, showing his white teeth. He had full red lips and straight black hair. But as soon as he was ordained he became solemn, yet energetic. He never told stories. He tried to believe that he had some of the sanctity that a young priest ought to have. At his first mass, in the ordination sermon, an old priest had shouted eloquently that a very young priest was greater and holier and more worthy of respect than anyone else on earth. Father Vincent Sullivan, hearing this, couldn't believe it entirely, but it gave him courage even if it did make him more solemn and serious.

But he still had his red lips and his black hair and his clear skin and a charming, lazy, drawling voice, which was very pleasant when he was actually trying to interest someone. Since he had so much zeal and could be so charming he was a good man to send calling upon the men and women of the parish, seeking donations for various parish activities. The really important people in the congregation like Mrs. Gibbons, whom he bowed to every Sunday after eleven o'clock mass, he hardly ever met socially; they were visited usually by the priest, who sometimes even had a Sunday dinner with them or a game of cards in the evening.

Father Sullivan had a sincere admiration for Mrs. Gibbons. Her donations were frequent and generous. She went regularly to communion, always made a novena to the little flower, St. Teresa. And sometimes in the summer evenings, when he was passing down the aisle from the vestry and it was almost dark in the Cathedral, he saw this good woman saying a few prayers before the altar of the Virgin. Of course he hardly glanced at her as he passed down the aisle, his face grave and expressionless, but he thought about her when he was at the door of the church and wished that she would stop and talk to him, if he stayed there, when she passed out. She was the kind of a woman, he thought, that all priests of the parish ought to know more intimately. So he did happen to be near the door when she passed and bowed gravely, but she went by him and down to the street hardly more than nodding. She was a large, plump, well-kept woman walking erectly and slowly to the street. Her clothes were elegant.

Her skin had been pink and fine. It was very satisfactory to think that such a well-groomed, dignified, and competent woman should appreciate the necessity of strict religious practice in her daily life. If he had been older and had wanted to speak to her he could readily have found some excuse, but he was young and fully aware of his own particular dignity. Honestly, he would rather have been the youngest priest at the Cathedral at this time than be a bishop or a cardinal. It was not only that he always remembered the words of the old priest who had preached his ordination sermon, but he realized that he sometimes trembled with delight at his constant opportunity to walk upon the altar, and when hearing confessions he was scrupulous, intensely interested, and never bored by even the most tiresome old woman with idiotic notions of small sins. It exalted him further, even if it also made him a little sad, to see that older priests were more mechanical about their duties, and when he once mentioned to Father Jimmerson about it, the oldest priest at the Cathedral, the old man had smiled and sighed and said it was the inevitable lot of them all, and that the most beautiful days of his life had been when he was young and had known the ecstasy of being hesitant, timid, and full of zeal. Of course, he added, older priests were just as confident in their faith, and just as determined to be good, but they could not have the eagerness of the very young men.

One evening at about nine o'clock when Father Sullivan was sitting in the library reading a magazine, the housekeeper came into the room and said that someone, phoning from Mrs. Gibbons' house, wanted to speak to a priest.

"Was any priest in particular asked for?" Father Sullivan said.

"No. The woman — I don't know who she was — simply said she wanted to speak to a priest."

"Then I'll speak to her, of course," Father Sullivan said, putting aside his magazine and walking to the telephone. He was delighted at the opportunity of having a conversation with Mrs. Gibbons. He picked up the receiver and said "Hello".

A woman's voice, brusque, practical, said, "Who's that?"

"Father Sullivan," he said encouragingly.

"Well, I'm Mrs. Gibbons' sister-in-law, and I'm at her house now. Things have come to a pretty pass around here. If you've got any influence, you ought to use it. Just at present Mrs. Gibbons is broken up thinking she's going to die and she's been howling for a priest. There's really nothing wrong with her, but if you've got any influence you ought to use it on her. She's a terrible woman. Come over and talk to her."

"Are you sure?" he said a bit timidly.

"Sure of what?"

"Sure that you're not mistaken about Mrs. Gibbons."

"Indeed, I'm not. Are you coming?"

"Oh yes, at once," he said.

He put on his hat and mechanically looked at himself in the hall mirror. Then he glanced at his hands, which were perfectly manicured and clean. His collar was spotless. The blood showed through his clear skin and his lips were very red.

As he walked along the street he was a little nervous because the woman had sounded so abrupt, and he was wondering uneasily if Mrs. Gibbons really was a terrible

182

woman. There had been some rumours of a certain laxity in her life since her husband had either disappeared or deliberately gone away some time ago, but the parish pastor had shrugged his shoulders and spoken of scandalmongers. Insinuations against the good name of Mrs. Gibbons, who, they knew, was one of the finest women of the parish, were in a measure an insinuation against the Church. Father Sullivan had decided some time ago that Mrs. Gibbons was really a splendid woman and a credit to any community.

It was a short walk from the Cathedral to Mrs. Gibbons' home. A light was in the hall. A light was in the front room upstairs. Father Sullivan paused at the street light a moment, looking up at the house, and then walked quickly up to the door, feeling clean, aloof, dignified, and impressive, and at the same time vaguely eager.

He rang the bell. The door was opened wide by a woman, slim, brightly dressed, florid-faced, and with her hair dyed red, who stepped back and looked at him critically.

"I'm Father Sullivan," he said apologetically but seriously.

"Oh, yes, I see."

"I believe Mrs. Gibbons wanted to see me."

"Well, I don't know whether she knows you or not," the woman added a bit doubtfully. "I'm her sister-in-law. I'm the one that phoned you."

"I'll see her," he said with a kind of grave finality as he stepped into the house. He felt cool, dignified and important.

"I mean that I was going to talk to you first," the red-headed woman said. "She's a Tartar, you know — only it just happened that she feels broken up now about something, and it's time for someone to give her a talking to."

"I'll talk to her," he said. Really he didn't know what he was expected to say.

The slim woman walked ahead upstairs and Father Sullivan followed. The door of the front room was open and the slim woman stood looking into the room. The light shone on her red hair. Father Sullivan was close behind and followed her into the room. Mrs. Gibbons was lying on a divan, a purple kimono thrown loosely around her. One of her plump arms was revealed as she held her head up, resting on her elbow. Her plump body was hardly concealed under the kimono. She looked depressed and unhappy as though she had been crying. When she saw Father Sullivan she didn't even open her mouth, just shrugged her shoulders and held the same dejected expression. The red-headed slim woman stared at her alertly and then glanced at Father Sullivan, who was bending forward trying to attract Mrs. Gibbons' attention while he got ready to speak in his slow, drawling, and pleasing voice. But then he noticed a beer bottle on the table close to the divan. Mrs. Gibbons was now looking at him curiously, and then she smiled slowly. "Can't ask you to have a drink, father," she said. She was obviously thinking what a nice young fellow he was. Then she started to laugh a little, her whole body shaking.

"I thought you wanted to talk to him, Jessie," the other woman said.

"Oh, I don't think I do."

"But you said you wanted to."

"Oh, father won't mind; will you, father?"

"Go on, talk to her, father," the red-headed woman said impatiently. "I've had a row with her and I've been trying to tell her what a trollop she is. She's low, if anyone ever was. Now tell it to her."

If Mrs. Gibbons had started talking to him Father Sullivan might not have been embarrassed, but as he looked at her, waiting, and saw her stretched out so sloppily and noticed again the beer bottle on the table, he felt he was going to hear something that would disgrace her and the parish forever. She kept on looking at him, her underlip hanging a little, her eyes old and wise. The red-headed woman was standing there, one hand on her hip, her mouth drooping cynically at the corners. They were both waiting for him to say something. In the darkness of the confessional it would have been different, but now Father Sullivan felt his face flushing, for he couldn't help thinking of Mrs. Gibbons as one of the finest women of the parish, and there she was stretched out like a loose old woman. He tried to hold his full, red, lower lip with his white teeth. He felt humiliated and ashamed and they were both watching him. His nervous embarrassment began to hurt and bewilder him.

"If I can be of any assistance — " he muttered, feeling almost ready to cry.

They didn't speak to him, just kept on looking at him steadily and he had a sudden nervous feeling that the red-headed woman might go out and leave him alone with Mrs. Gibbons.

Some words did actually come into his head, but Mrs. Gibbons, sitting up suddenly, stared at him and said flatly: "Oh, he's too young. How do you expect me to talk to him?" Then she lay down again and looked away into the corner of the room.

The sister-in-law took hold of Father Sullivan firmly by the arm and led him out to the hall. "She's right about that," she said. "I thought so from the start."

"There are some things that are hard to talk about, I know," he said, flustered and ashamed. "If in her life . . . I mean I have the greatest faith in Mrs. Gibbons," he said desperately. "Please let me go back and talk to her."

"No, I sized up the situation and know that once she got talking to you she'd pull the wool over your eyes."

"I was just about to say to her — " Father Sullivan said, following her downstairs, and still trembling a little. "I know she's a good woman."

"No, you're too young for such a job. And she hasn't the morals of a tomcat."

"I ought to be able to do something."

"Oh no, never mind, thanks. She's got over the notion she's going to die. I could tell that when she shrugged her shoulders."

"But please explain what she wanted to say to me," he said. "I respect Mrs. Gibbons," he added helplessly.

"It's no use — you're too young a man," the woman said abruptly. "You wouldn't be able to do anything with her anyway."

"I'm sorry," he said. "I'm awfully sorry," he kept on saying. She had hold of his arm and was actually opening the front door. "Thanks for coming, anyway," she said. "We've been rowing all afternoon and I told her plenty and I wanted someone else she respected to take a hand in it."

"I'm sorry," he said. "Was she feeling badly?"

"Pretty badly. I came around here, as I do about once a month, to give her a piece of my mind, but she was all broken up. Something got into her."

"Something must have happened, because she's a fine woman. I know that."

"You do, eh? Her daughter Marion has gone away with her young man Peter. They must have had an awful row here earlier in the evening."

"I didn't know the daughter very well," the priest said.

"No? Well, it looks to me as if old Jess wanted to know Peter too well. That was the trouble. When I came around here she was lying down half dressed looking at herself in a hand mirror. What's the matter with her? She's got to grow old some time. Thanks, though, for coming. Good night."

"Good night. I'm sorry I couldn't help her."

As he walked down the street he had a feeling that the woman might take him by the arm and lead him down to the corner.

It was a mild warm night. He was walking very slowly. The Cathedral spire stuck up in the night sky above all the houses in the block. He was still breathing irregularly and feeling that he had been close to something immensely ugly and evil that had nearly overwhelmed him. He shook his head a little because he still wanted to go on thinking that Mrs. Gibbons was one of the finest women in the parish, for his notion of what was good in the life in the parish seemed to depend upon such a belief. And as he walked slowly he felt, with a kind of desperate clarity, that really he had been always unimportant in the life around the Cathedral. He was still ashamed and had no joy at all now in being a young priest.

# A Cap For Steve

Dave Diamond, a poor man, a carpenter's assistant, was a small, wiry, quick-tempered individual who had learned how to make every dollar count in his home. His wife, Anna, had been sick a lot, and his twelve-year-old son, Steve, had to be kept in school. Steve, a big-eyed, shy kid, ought to have known the value of money as well as Dave did. It had been ground into him.

But the boy was crazy about baseball, and after school, when he could have been working as a delivery boy or selling papers, he played ball with the kids. His failure to appreciate that the family needed a few extra dollars disgusted Dave. Around the house he wouldn't let Steve talk about baseball, and he scowled when he saw him hurrying off with his glove after dinner.

When the Phillies came to town to play an exhibition game with the home team and Steve pleaded to be taken to the ball park, Dave, of course, was outraged. Steve knew they couldn't afford it. But he had got his mother on his side. Finally Dave made a bargain with them. He said that if Steve came home after school and worked hard helping to make some kitchen shelves he would take him that night to the ball park.

Steve worked hard, but Dave was still resentful. They had to coax him to put on his good suit. When they started out Steve held aloof, feeling guilty, and they walked down the street like strangers; then Dave glanced at Steve's face and, half-ashamed, took his arm more cheerfully.

As the game went on, Dave had to listen to Steve's recitation of the batting average of every Philly that stepped up to the plate; the time the boy must have wasted learning these averages began to appal him. He showed it so plainly that Steve felt guilty again and was silent.

After the game Dave let Steve drag him onto the field to keep him company while he tried to get some autographs from the Philly players, who were being hemmed in by gangs of kids blocking the way to the club-house. But Steve, who was shy, let the other kids block him off from the players. Steve would push his way in, get blocked out, and come back to stand mournfully beside Dave. And Dave grew impatient. He was wasting valuable time. He wanted to get home; Steve knew it and was worried.

Then the big, blond Philly outfielder, Eddie Condon, who had been held up by a gang of kids tugging at his arm and thrusting their score cards at him, broke loose and made a run for the club-house. He was jostled, and his blue cap with the red peak, tilted far back on his head, fell off. It fell at Steve's feet, and Steve stooped quickly and grabbed it. "Okay, son," the outfielder called, turning back. But Steve, holding the hat in both hands, only stared at him.

"Give him his cap, Steve," Dave said, smiling apologetically at the big outfielder who towered over them. But Steve drew the hat closer to his chest. In an awed trance he looked up at big Eddie Condon. It was an embarrassing moment. All the other kids were watching. Some shouted. "Give him his cap."

"My cap, son," Eddie Condon said, his hand out.

"Hey, Steve," Dave said, and he gave him a shake. But he had to jerk the cap out of Steve's hands.

"Here you are," he said.

The outfielder, noticing Steve's white, worshipping face and pleading eyes, grinned and then shrugged. "Aw, let him keep it," he said.

"No, Mister Condon, you don't need to do that," Steve protested.

"It's happened before. Forget it," Eddie Condon said, and he trotted away to the club-house.

Dave handed the cap to Steve; envious kids circled around them and Steve said, "He said I could keep it, Dad. You heard him, didn't you?"

"Yeah, I heard him," Dave admitted. The wonder in Steve's face made him smile. He took the boy by the arm and they hurried off the field.

On the way home Dave couldn't get him to talk about the game; he couldn't get him to take his eyes off the cap. Steve could hardly believe in his own happiness. "See," he said suddenly, and he showed Dave that Eddie Condon's name was printed on the sweat-band. Then he went on dreaming. Finally he put the cap on his head and turned to Dave with a slow, proud smile. The cap was away too big for him; it fell down over his ears. "Never mind," Dave said. "You can get your mother to take a tuck in the back."

When they got home Dave was tired and his wife didn't understand the cap's importance, and they couldn't get Steve to go to bed. He swaggered around wearing the cap and looking in the mirror every ten minutes. He took the cap to bed with him.

Dave and his wife had a cup of coffee in the kitchen, and Dave told her again how they had got the cap. They agreed that their boy must have an attractive quality that showed in his face, and that Eddie Condon must have been drawn to him — why else would he have singled Steve out from all the kids?

But Dave got tired of the fuss Steve made over that cap and of the way he wore it from the time he got up in the morning until the time he went to bed. Some kid was always coming in, wanting to try on the cap. It was childish, Dave said, for Steve to go around assuming that the cap made him important in the neighbourhood, and to keep telling them how he had become a leader in the park a few blocks away where he played ball in the evenings. And Dave wouldn't stand for Steve's keeping the cap on while he was eating. He was always scolding his wife for accepting Steve's explanation that he'd forgotten he had it on. Just the same, it was remarkable what a little thing like a ball cap could do for a kid, Dave admitted to his wife as he smiled to himself.

One night Steve was late coming home from the park. Dave didn't realize how late it was until he put down his newspaper and watched his wife at the window. Her restlessness got on his nerves. "See what comes from encouraging the boy to hang around with those park loafers," he said. "I don't encourage him," she protested. "You do," he insisted irritably, for he was really worried now. A gang hung around the park until midnight. It was a bad park. It was true that on one side there was a good district with fine, expensive apartment houses, but the kids from that neighbourhood left the park to the kids from the poorer homes. When his wife went out and walked down to the corner it was his turn to wait and worry and watch at the open window. Each waiting moment tortured him. At last he heard his wife's voice and Steve's voice, and he relaxed and sighed; then he remembered his duty and rushed angrily to meet them.

"I'll fix you, Steve, once and for all," he said. "I'll show you you can't start coming into the house at midnight."

"Hold your horses, Dave," his wife said. "Can't you see the state he's in?" Steve looked utterly exhausted and beaten.

"What's the matter?" Dave asked quickly.

"I lost my cap," Steve whispered; he walked past his father and threw himself on the couch in the living-room and lay with his face hidden.

"Now, don't scold him, Dave," his wife said.

"Scold him. Who's scolding him?" Dave asked, indignantly. "It's his cap, not mine. If it's not worth his while to hang on to it, why should I scold him?" But he was implying resentfully that he alone recognized the cap's value.

"So you are scolding him," his wife said. "It's his cap. Not yours. What happened, Steve?"

Steve told them he had been playing ball and he found that when he ran the bases the cap fell off; it was still too big despite the tuck his mother had taken in the band. So the next time he came to bat he tucked the cap in his hip pocket. Someone had lifted it, he was sure.

"And he didn't even know whether it was still in his pocket," Dave said sarcastically.

"I wasn't careless, Dad," Steve said. For the last three hours he had been wandering

187

around to the homes of the kids who had been in the park at the time; he wanted to go on, but he was too tired. Dave knew the boy was apologizing to him, but he didn't know why it made him angry.

"If he didn't hang on to it, it's not worth worrying about now," he said, and he sounded offended.

After that night they knew that Steve didn't go to the park to play ball; he went to look for the cap. It irritated Dave to see him sit around listlessly, or walk in circles, trying to force his memory to find a particular incident which would suddenly recall to him the moment when the cap had been taken. It was no attitude for a growing, healthy boy to take, Dave complained. He told Steve firmly once and for all that he didn't want to hear any more about the cap.

One night, two weeks later, Dave was walking home with Steve from the shoemaker's. It was a hot night. When they passed an ice-cream parlour Steve slowed down. "I guess I couldn't have a soda, could I?" Steve said. "Nothing doing," Dave said firmly. "Come on now," he added as Steve hung back, looking in the window.

"Dad, look!" Steve cried suddenly, pointing at the window. "My cap! There's my cap! He's coming out!"

A well-dressed boy was leaving the ice-cream parlour; he had on a blue ball cap with a red peak, just like Steve's cap. "Hey, you!" Steve cried, and he rushed at the boy, his small face fierce and his eyes wild. Before the boy could back away Steve had snatched the cap from his head. "That's my cap!" he shouted.

"What's this?" the bigger boy said. "Hey, give me my cap or I'll give you a poke on the nose."

Dave was surprised that his own shy boy did not back away. He watched him clutch the cap in his left hand, half crying with excitement as he put his head down and drew back his right fist: he was willing to fight. And Dave was proud of him.

"Wait, now," Dave said. "Take it easy, son," he said to the other boy, who refused to back away.

"My boy says it's his cap," Dave said.

"Well, he's crazy. It's my cap."

"I was with him when he got this cap. When the Phillies played here. It's a Philly cap."

"Eddie Condon gave it to me," Steve said. "And you stole it from me, you jerk."

"Don't call me a jerk, you little squirt. I never saw you before in my life."

"Look," Steve said, pointing to the printing of the cap's sweatband. "It's Eddie Condon's cap. See? See, Dad?"

"Yeah. You're right, Son. Ever see this boy before, Steve?"

"No," Steve said reluctantly.

The other boy realized he might lose the cap. "I bought it from a guy," he said. "I paid him. My father knows I paid him." He said he got the cap at the ball park. He groped for some magically impressive words and suddenly found them. "You'll have to speak to my father," he said.

"Sure, I'll speak to your father," Dave said. "What's your name? Where do you live?"

"My name's Hudson. I live about ten minutes away on the other side of the park."

The boy appraised Dave, who wasn't any bigger than he was and who wore a faded blue windbreaker and no tie. "My father is a lawyer," he said boldly. "He wouldn't let me keep the cap if he didn't think I should."

"Is that a fact?" Dave asked belligerently. "Well, we'll see. Come on. Let's go." And he got between the two boys and they walked along the street. They didn't talk to each other. Dave knew the Hudson boy was waiting to get to the protection of his home, and Steve knew it, too, and he looked up apprehensively at Dave. And Dave, reaching for his hand, squeezed it encouragingly and strode along, cocky and belligerent, knowing that Steve relied on him.

The Hudson boy lived in that row of fine apartment houses on the other side of the park. At the entrance to one of these houses Dave tried not to hang back and show he was impressed, because he could feel Steve hanging back. When they got into the small elevator Dave didn't know why he took off his hat. In the carpeted hall on the fourth floor the Hudson boy said, "Just a minute," and entered his own apartment. Dave and Steve were left alone in the corridor, knowing that the other boy was preparing his father for the encounter. Steve looked anxiously at his father, and Dave said, "Don't worry, Son," and he added resolutely, "No one's putting anything over on us."

A tall balding man in a brown velvet smoking-jacket suddenly opened the door. Dave had never seen a man wearing one of those jackets, although he had seen them in department-store windows. "Good evening," he said, making a deprecatory gesture at the cap Steve still clutched tightly in his left hand. "My boy didn't get your name. My name is Hudson."

"Mine's Diamond."

"Come on in," Mr. Hudson said, putting out his hand and laughing good-naturedly. He led Dave and Steve into his living-room. "What's this about that cap?" he asked. "The way kids can get excited about a cap. Well, it's understandable, isn't it?"

"So it is," Dave said, moving closer to Steve, who was awed by the broadloom rug and the fine furniture. He wanted to show Steve he was at ease himself, and he wished Mr. Hudson wouldn't be so polite. That meant Dave had to be polite and affable, too, and it was hard to manage when he was standing in the middle of the floor in his old windbreaker.

"Sit down, Mr. Diamond," Mr. Hudson said. Dave took Steve's arm and sat him down beside him on the chesterfield. The Hudson boy watched his father. And Dave looked at Steve and saw that he wouldn't face Mr. Hudson or the other boy; he kept looking up at Dave, putting all his faith in him.

"Well, Mr. Diamond, from what I gathered from my boy, you're able to prove this cap belonged to your boy."

"That's a fact," Dave said.

"Mr. Diamond, you'll have to believe my boy bought that cap from some kid in good faith."

"I don't doubt it," Dave said. "But no kid can sell something that doesn't belong to him. You know that's a fact, Mr. Hudson."

"Yes, that's a fact," Mr. Hudson agreed. "But that cap means a lot to my boy, Mr. Diamond."

"It means a lot to my boy, too, Mr. Hudson."

189

"Sure it does. But supposing we called in a policeman. You know what he'd say? He'd ask you if you were willing to pay my boy what he paid for the cap. That's usually the way it works out," Mr. Hudson said, friendly and smiling, as he eyed Dave shrewdly.

"But that's not right. It's not justice," Dave protested. "Not when it's my boy's cap."

"I know it isn't right. But that's what they do."

"All right. What did you say your boy paid for the cap?" Dave said reluctantly.

"Two dollars."

"Two dollars!" Dave repeated. Mr. Hudson's smile was still kindly, but his eyes were shrewd, and Dave knew the lawyer was counting on his not having the two dollars; Mr. Hudson thought he had Dave sized up; he had looked at him and decided he was broke. Dave's pride was hurt, and he turned to Steve. What he saw in Steve's face was more powerful than the hurt to his pride: it was the memory of how difficult it had been to get an extra nickel, the talk he heard about the cost of food, the worry in his mother's face as she tried to make ends meet, and the bewildered embarrassment that he was here in a rich man's home, forcing his father to confess that he couldn't afford to spend two dollars. Then Dave grew angry and reckless. "I'll give you the two dollars," he said.

Steve looked at the Hudson boy and grinned brightly. The Hudson boy watched his father.

"I suppose that's fair enough," Mr. Hudson said. "A cap like this can be worth a lot to a kid. You know how it is. Your boy might want to sell — I mean be satisfied. Would he take five dollars for it?"

"Five dollars?" Dave repeated. "Is it worth five dollars, Steve?" he asked uncertainly.

Steve shook his head and looked frightened.

"No, thanks, Mr. Hudson," Dave said firmly.

"I'll tell you what I'll do," Mr. Hudson said. "I'll give you ten dollars. The cap has a sentimental value for my boy, a Philly cap, a big-leaguer's cap. It's only worth about a buck and a half really," he added. But Dave shook his head again. Mr. Hudson frowned. He looked at his own boy with indulgent concern, but now he was embarrassed. "I'll tell you what I'll do," he said. "This cap — well, it's worth as much as a day at the circus to my boy. Your boy should be recompensed. I want to be fair. Here's twenty dollars," and he held out two ten-dollar bills to Dave.

That much money for a cap, Dave thought, and his eyes brightened. But he knew what the cap had meant to Steve; to deprive him of it now that it was within his reach would be unbearable. All the things he needed in his life gathered around him; his wife was there, saying he couldn't afford to reject the offer, he had no right to do it; and he turned to Steve to see if Steve thought it wonderful that the cap could bring them twenty dollars.

"What do you say, Steve?" he asked uneasily.

"I don't know," Steve said. He was in a trance. When Dave smiled, Steve smiled too, and Dave believed that Steve was as impressed as he was, only more bewildered, and maybe even more aware that they could not possibly turn away that much money for a ball cap.

190

"Well, here you are," Mr. Hudson said, and he put the two bills in Steve's hand. "It's a lot of money. But I guess you had a right to expect as much."

With a dazed, fixed smile Steve handed the money slowly to his father, and his face was white.

Laughing jovially, Mr. Hudson led them to the door. His own boy followed a few paces behind.

In the elevator Dave took the bills out of his pocket, "See, Stevie," he whispered eagerly. "That windbreaker you wanted! And ten dollars for your bank! Won't Mother be surprised?"

"Yeah," Steve whispered, the little smile still on his face. But Dave had to turn away quickly so their eyes wouldn't meet, for he saw that it was a scared smile.

Outside, Dave said, "Here, you carry the money home, Steve. You show it to your mother."

"No, you keep it," Steve said, and then there was nothing to say. They walked in silence.

"It's a lot of money," Dave said finally. When Steve didn't answer him, he added angrily. "I turned to you, Steve. I asked you, didn't I?"

"That man knew how much his boy wanted that cap," Steve said.

"Sure. But he recognized how much it was worth to us."

"No, you let him take it away from us," Steve blurted.

"That's unfair," Dave said. "Don't dare say that to me."

"I don't want to be like you," Steve muttered, and he darted across the road and walked along on the other side of the street.

"It's unfair," Dave said angrily, only now he didn't mean that Steve was unfair, he meant that what had happened in the prosperous Hudson home was unfair, and he didn't know quite why. He had been trapped, not just by Mr. Hudson, but by his own life. Across the road Steve was hurrying along with his head down, wanting to be alone. They walked most of the way home on opposite sides of the street, until Dave could stand it no longer. "Steve," he called, crossing the street. "It was very unfair. I mean, for you to say . . . " but Steve started to run. Dave walked as fast as he could and Steve was getting beyond him, and he felt enraged and suddenly he yelled, "Steve!" and he started to chase his son. He wanted to get hold of Steve and pound him, and he didn't know why. He gained on him, he gasped for breath and he almost got him by the shoulder. Turning, Steve saw his father's face in the street light and was terrified; he circled away, got to the house, and rushed in, yelling, "Mother!"

"Son, Son!" she cried, rushing from the kitchen. As soon as she threw her arms around Steve, shielding him, Dave's anger left him and he felt stupid. He walked past them into the kitchen.

"What happened?" she asked anxiously. "Have you both gone crazy? What did you do, Steve?"

"Nothing," he said sullenly.

"What did your father do?"

"We found the boy with my ball cap, and he let the boy's father take it from us."

"No, no," Dave protested. "Nobody pushed us around. The man didn't put anything over us." He felt tired and his face was burning. He told what had happened;

191

then he slowly took the two ten-dollar bills out of his wallet and tossed them on the table and looked up guiltily at his wife.

It hurt him that she didn't pick up the money, and that she didn't rebuke him. "It is a lot of money, Son," she said slowly. "Your father was only trying to do what he knew was right, and it'll work out, and you'll understand." She was soothing Steve, but Dave knew she felt that she needed to be gentle with him, too, and he was ashamed.

When she went with Steve to his bedroom, Dave sat by himself. His son had contempt for him, he thought. His son, for the first time, had seen how easy it was for another man to handle him, and he had judged him and had wanted to walk alone on the other side of the street. He looked at the money and he hated the sight of it.

His wife returned to the kitchen, made a cup of tea, talked soothingly, and said it was incredible that he had forced the Hudson man to pay him twenty dollars for the cap, but all Dave could think of was Steve was scared of me.

Finally, he got up and went into Steve's room. The room was in darkness, but he could see the outline of Steve's body on the bed, and he sat down beside him and whispered, "Look, Son, it was a mistake. I know why. People like us — in circumstances where money can scare us. No, no," he said, feeling ashamed and shaking his head apologetically; he was taking the wrong way of showing the boy they were together; he was covering up his own failure. For the failure had been his, and it had come out of being so separated from his son that he had been blind to what was beyond the price in a boy's life. He longed now to show Steve he could be with him from day to day. His hand went out hesitantly to Steve's shoulder. "Steve, look," he said eagerly. "The trouble was I didn't realize how much I enjoyed it that night at the ball park. If I had watched you playing for your own team — the kids around here say you could be a great pitcher. We could take that money and buy a new pitcher's glove for you, and a catcher's mitt. Steve, Steve, are you listening? I could catch you, work with you in the lane. Maybe I could be your coach . . . watch you become a great pitcher." In the half-darkness he could see the boy's pale face turn to him.

Steve, who had never heard his father talk like this, was shy and wondering. All he knew was that his father, for the first time, wanted to be with him in his hopes and adventures. He said, "I guess you do know how important that cap was." His hand went out to his father's arm. "With that man the cap was — well it was just something he could buy, eh Dad?" Dave gripped his son's hand hard. The wonderful generosity of childhood — the price a boy was willing to pay to be able to count on his father's admiration and approval — made him feel humble, then strangely exalted.

# Thomas H. Raddall

*Thomas Head Raddall (1903-    ), born in England, came to Nova Scotia in 1913 when his father was posted to the Canadian Militia. In 1918 Raddall left school and entered the merchant service for five years' duty in the North Atlantic and on Sable Island as a telegrapher. In 1923 he came to Liverpool, N.S., to work. Since 1938 he has devoted his full time to writing, an arrangement few Canadian authors have been able to enjoy. Among the honours he has received are the Governor General's Awards for* The Pied Piper of Dipper Creek *(Canadian edition, 1943), for* Halifax: Warden of the North *(1948), and for* The Path of Destiny *(1957). He also received the Lorne Pierce Gold Medal for Literature, and was elected Fellow of the Royal Society of Canada (1949).[1]*

*Raddall has recorded Maritime life in a series of historical romances beginning with* His Majesty's Yankees *(1942), and with contemporary romances such as* The Nymph and the Lamp *(1950); his four collections of short stories deal with the same background. The Raddall short story is a carefully-plotted, action-centred narrative, a type (as Lord Tweedsmuir noted in his Foreword to* The Pied Piper) *"which has had many distinguished exponents from Sir Walter Scott through Stevenson and Maupassant to Kipling and Conrad. To this school Mr. Raddall belongs, and he is worthy of a great succession."[2] The kind of traditional short story which Raddall writes has received little critical notice since the 1930s, when academic critics turned their attention to the modern short story (as practiced by Chekhov and Joyce) which tends to place more emphasis on the psychological springs of character than on external action. Raddall himself has been accused of wooden characterization and too much concern for physical action. But this criticism, reflecting as it does prejudices among academics for the modern short story, has misplaced its emphasis, even if there is some truth in the accusation. Each writer must approach the truth in his own way, and that approach should be the basis for the reader's evaluation. In this regard, Raddall has said:*

> *Now, to please does not mean to pander to whatever public taste may be current. It does mean to set forth what is in the writer's or the painter's or the sculptor's mind so that it has the form, the color and the substance of the thing he saw, in the way he saw it, and because it satisfied him that way. His obligation is always to the truth. In whatever degree he falls short of that he fails in his art or his craft or whatever you wish to call it.[3]*

*Among Raddall's virtues is his crisp and elegant prose style, admirably suited to the presentation of the concrete. One sees the people talking and moving. As the narrative develops, the theme emerges out of the action; the emphasis, then, is not on character-in-depth, but on character-in-action. Furthermore, Raddall's painstaking concern for accuracy removes his historical romances from the category of conventional escapist fiction, and permits the reader to enter a long-vanished world and to watch the forces at work in our forefathers' society.[4] Raddall moreover chooses appropriate devices to piece together the facets of life in the past — letters, diaries, brief comments from town-council meetings — whereby the contemporary narrator (a* persona *of the author) can make tentative probings into the truth of those distant conflicts. These are techniques which Conrad and Faulkner also used with success.*

*Most important of all, Raddall uses historical romance to re-create a past that contains the germ of a community's identity, which is a form of conscious myth-making such as Pratt undertakes in* Brébeuf and His Brethren *and* Towards the Last Spike. *Hence, psychological truth does not reside merely in the three-dimensional character but may be found in the representative human types within the community. In "At the Tide's Turn", for example, we see in fictional form a dilemma that has faced Nova Scotians (for that matter, Canadians) for generations. This is the conflict of loyalties to the British King and to the American kinfolk. It is not a black-and-white situation, however, since both parties claiming the allegiance of the Nova Scotians have their good and bad points. A recurring motif in Raddall's stories is the dilemma which involves those physical and psychic circumstances that require a man to make the right choice, or the difficult sacrifice, for his own well-being and for that of his community.*

*In contrast to his historical romances is "Winter's Tale", an example of Raddall's use of realism in a modern setting. This story, first published in book form in 1938, may be compared with Hugh MacLennan's account of the 1917 Halifax explosion in* Barometer Rising *(1941).*

**Footnotes**

[1] *For commentary on Raddall's life and career, see W.J. Hawkins, "Thomas H. Raddall: The Man and His Work",* Queen's Quarterly, *LXXV (Spring 1968), pp. 137-146.*

[2] *John Buchan, Lord Tweedsmuir, Foreword to* The Pied Piper of Dipper Creek *(Toronto: McClelland and Stewart, 1943), p. v.*

[3] *Thomas H. Raddall, "The Literary Art",* Dalhousie Review, *XXXIV (Summer 1954), p. 141.*

[4] *Valuable discussions of Raddall's historical romances and his themes will be found in Allan Bevan's Introduction to* At the Tide's Turn *(Toronto: McClelland and Stewart, 1959) and John Matthew's Introduction to* The Nymph and the Lamp *(Toronto: McClelland and Stewart, 1963).*

# Winter's Tale

The air in the classroom was warm and rather stuffy, because it had snowed a little the night before, and Stevens the janitor had stoked up his great furnace fiercely. Grade Nine, coming in rosy-cheeked from the snow outside, found it oppressive, but nobody dared to open a window. Old Mr. Burtle, who conducted the educational fortunes of Grade Nine, was Principal of the school and a martyr to asthma.

The rest of the big brick school was empty and silent. The lower grades were not required to answer roll-call until half-past nine. It was just one minute past nine by the clock on the classroom wall when James hung his school-bag on the back of his seat and flung an arithmetic manual on the desk. He also produced two pencils and sharpened them with his jack-knife, dropping the shavings on the floor and keeping a wary eye on Old Gander Burtle, who disapproved of that procedure. All about him was a bustle of preparation. Fifty boys and girls were busy with books, pencils, and erasers.

"Attention!" demanded Old Gander, with his asthmatic cough. Everybody sat up very straight. "We shall sing the morning hymn." The class arose with a clatter, shuffled a little, and then burst raucously into "Awake my soul and with the sun" as Old Gander raised his bony forefinger. James had a point of vantage when they stood up to sing; for his desk was near the windows and he could look down into the street, two storeys below. It was certainly too nice a morning to spend indoors. The sky was blue, without a speck of cloud anywhere, sun very bright on the snow, and wisps of smoke rising straight into the air from a forest of chimneys that stretched away southward. The snow was not deep enough for sleighing. There were a few wheel-tracks in the street, and the sidewalks were a mess of brown slush already, and when the several hundred kids of the lower grades had scampered in, there would be nothing but thin black puddles. Grade Nine intoned a long "Ahhh-men!" and sat down. It was five minutes past nine by the clock on the wall.

The act of sitting down in unison always produced a clatter, but this morning the effect was astounding. The hardwood floor began to move up and down very rapidly, like a gigantic piston of some sort; the walls swayed drunkenly to and fro, so that the blackboards came down and were followed by plaster, crumbling away from the walls in lumps and whole sheets. The great clock dropped from its fastening high on the wall, missed Old Gander's head by an inch, and spewed a tangle of springs and cogs over the heaving floor. The opaque glass in the door of the boys' coat-room sprang across the classroom, sailing over James' head, and went to pieces in a mighty splatter on the wall in front of him. The windows vanished, sashes and all. Not only the inner everyday windows, but the big storm-windows that were screwed on outside every Fall and taken off in the spring. The room, the big echoing school, the whole world, were filled with tremendous sound that came in waves, each visible in breakers of plaster dust.

Then the sound was gone, as suddenly as it had come, and in its place there was a strange and awful hush that was emphasized, somehow, by distant noises of falling plaster and tinkling glass. Grade Nine was on its feet, staring at Old Gander through a

195

fog of plaster dust, and Old Gander stared back at them, with his scanty grey hair all on end, and his long seamed face the colour of snow when rain is turning it to slush. A waft of cold air came in from the street, where the windows should have been, and the fog cleared before it. A girl broke the silence, screaming shrilly. James perceived that her cheek was laid open from ear to mouth, with a great red river pouring down her chin, and that others were putting fingers to cut faces and heads, and staring strangely at the stains. Grade Nine was covered with plaster dust, and looked like a company of startled ghosts, and when James saw the thin red trickles running out of those white masks he knew he was dreaming, because things like that did not really happen. The girl with the red mask screamed again, and there was a chorus of screams, and then with one impulse the class turned and fled, as if it were Friday afternoon fire practice. James heard them clattering down the stairs into the street, with glass grinding and tinkling under their shoes. For a moment James was poised for similar flight, but in that moment he remembered the time he was frightened by a signboard groaning in the wind at night, and Dad's deep steady voice saying, "Never run from anything, son, till you've had a good look at it. Most times it's not worth running from."

Old Gander was standing beside his desk like a statue, staring at the lone survivor of his class. His watery blue eyes seemed awfully large. They looked like Mum's breakfast saucers. James moved jerkily towards him, licking plaster-dust from his lips. "What is it, Mister Burtle?" His own voice seemed queer and very far away, the way it sounded when you talked in your sleep and woke yourself up. Old Gander gazed at James in enormous surprise, as though he had never seen James before, as if James were speaking some foreign language not authorized by the School Board. Then he said in his old asthmatic voice, "James! Is that you, James?" and without waiting for a reply he added, as though it were the most ordinary thing in the world, "Some of the little boys have been playing with dynamite in the basement." James nodded slowly. Old Gander knew everything. The kids in the lower grades said he had eyes in the back of his head. He was a very wise old man.

They stood, silent, in the wrecked classroom for a space of minutes. Another gust of chill air stirred the thin hairs that stood out like a halo from the schoolmaster's head.

"You are a good boy, James," murmured Old Gander in a dazed voice. James squared his shoulders instinctively. After all, he was a sergeant in the school cadet corps. It was all right for the others to go if they wanted to. Old Gander passed a shaking hand back over his head, smoothing down the straggled hairs. Bits of plaster fell upon his dusty shoulders in a small shower, like a brittle sort of dandruff. "I think," he said vaguely, "we'd better see if there is any fire."

"Yes, sir," James said. It occurred to him that Mr. Burtle ought to look in the basement where the little boys had played with the dynamite. "I'll go through the upstairs classrooms, sir."

"Very good," murmured Old Gander, as if James were a superior officer. "I will search the lower floor and then the basement." And he added, "Don't stay up here very long, James." They separated.

James passed from room to room on the second floor. Each was like the one he had left, with blackboards tumbled off walls, heaps of plaster, doors hanging splintered in

196

the jambs. Along the south side of the school the windows had disappeared into the street, but on the north side the shattered sashes were festooned over desks, and shards of glass in the tumbled plaster gave it the glitter of snow. The big assembly hall occupied most of the north side. Miraculously, the doors were still in place, but they refused to open. One was split badly in the panel, and James peeped through at a tangle of wood, piled against the doors on the inside. He thrust an arm through the hole and pushed some of the rubbish aside. The hall was a strange sight. The tall windows which occupied almost the entire north wall had come inwards, had swept across the hall, carrying chairs with them, and the shattered sashes had wedged against the south wall and the side doors in a complete barricade. There was no trace of fire.

James walked down the stairs, along the lower hall, and out through the main entrance into the snow. The stained glass that formerly cast a prism of colours from the transom over the great main door had gone outwards, and was littered over the snow in a jig-saw puzzle of many hues. Old Gander stood there in the snow amid the coloured fragments, staring up at the mute ruins of his school. James gave him a glance, no more. Something else had caught his eye. To the north-east, over the roofs of silent houses, a mighty mushroom was growing in the sky. The stalk of the mushroom was pure white, and it extended an enormous distance upward from invisible roots in the harbour; and at the top it was unfolding, spreading out rapidly in greasy curls, brown and black, that caught the December sun and gleamed with a strange effect of varnish. An evil mushroom that writhed slightly on its stalk, and spread its eddying top until it overshadowed the whole North End, strange and terrible and beautiful. James could not take his eyes from it.

Behind him a voice was speaking, a woman's voice that penetrated the mighty singing in his ears from a great distance. Miss M'Clintock, the Grade Seven teacher, arriving early for the day's work. She was a tall woman, masterful to the point of severity. There was a wild look on her face that astonished James; for he had spent a term under her much-libelled rule and had never seen her anything but calm and dignified. " . . . all along the street. I can't tell you what I've seen this morning. Are you listening to me, Mr. Burtle?" Old Gander removed his wide gaze from the ravaged building. "My first really modern school," he murmured in that quaint asthmatic falsetto. "Dear, dear. What will the School Board say?"

James was watching that poisonous fungus in the sky again, but something Miss M'Clintock was saying made him look towards the houses about the school. They were like the school, void of window-glass, and in some cases of doors as well. There was a great silence everywhere, a dead quiet in which nothing moved except Old Gander and Miss M'Clintock and James and the mysterious mushroom that grew in the sky. But now over the whole city there came a great sigh, an odd breathless sound that was like a gasp and like a moan, and yet was neither. James saluted Old Gander awkwardly. "I — I guess I'd better go home now, sir." If Mr. Burtle heard him, he gave no sign. Miss M'Clintock said, "What a blessing the lower grades don't go in till half-past nine. All those big windows. Your hand is bleeding, James." James nodded and left them, walking out through the school gate and into the street.

Now there was a flurry of movement and a chorus of wild human sounds about the shattered houses. An oil wagon stood at the kerb, with a pair of great Percheron horses lying inert under the broken shaft. The teamster squatted beside them in the slush with his hands on their heads, addressing blood-stained people who scurried past without attention. "Dead!" he said to James in a queer surprised voice. "An' not a mark on 'em. Would you think a man could stand a Thing that killed a horse?" James began to run.

Home was not far up the street. The old brown house stood two hundred yards from the school. (Dad had said, "It'll be handy for the kids going to school. When I get back we'll look for something better.") Just now it was silent, without doors or windows. Ragged wisps of curtain dangled in the gaping window-frames fluttering with every stir of the December breeze like signals of distress. James went up the front steps shouting, "Mum! Mum!" The house was cold and still. Like a tomb. James ran, frantic, through that ominous quiet. Margery's room was empty, the bed littered with broken glass. Mum's room. His own room. Broken glass, crumbled plaster, shattered doors. Slivers of glass thrust like arrows through the panels of Margery's door. Bare laths where the plaster should have been, like the naked ribs of a skeleton. In the lower hall the long stove-pipe from the big anthracite heater lay in crumpled lengths, with soot mingled in the littered plaster, and the painting of Fujiyama that Dad brought home from a trip to the East was half-buried in the rubble, broken and forlorn. Confusion reigned, too, in the living-room; a window-sash, void of glass, was wedged against the piano, and the dusty mahogany was scored deep by invisible claws. In the wrecked kitchen he heard voices at last. Mum's voice, outside, in the garden. The rear door and the storm porch were lying, splintered, in the tiny scullery, amid a welter of broken chinaware and tumbled pots.

Mum's voice again, "James! Is that you, James?" James scrambled through the wreckage of the back door and ran into her arms, and they stood in the snow for several minutes, Mum and Margery and James, holding each other in silence. There was a bloody handkerchief about Mum's forehead, and little rivulets of blackish-red drying on her cheeks. Margery wore a coat over her nightdress.

Mum said, "I was looking out of the kitchen window, and suddenly across the way all the windows glowed red, as if they'd caught a gleam of sunset. Then our windows seemed to jump inwards." James said quickly, "Are you hurt, Mum?" but she shook her head. "Just cut a little about the forehead, I think, James. The window in Margery's room came right in on her bed, and she walked downstairs in her bare feet without a scratch. Over all that broken glass! It's a miracle, really."

"Why are you standing out here?" James demanded. It was cold, there in the snow without a coat. Mum waved her hand vaguely towards the street. "Somebody shouted, 'They're shelling the city — get behind your house!' So we came out here."

"I don't see how that could be," James considered gravely. "All the houses along the street are just like ours — doors and windows blown to pieces, and all the plaster down. The school, too. They couldn't do that. Not all at once, I mean."

There were sounds from next door. Old Mrs. Cameron appeared, embracing her husband in a strange hysterical way. He was breathing very heavily, for he was a fleshy man. Sweat made little clean streaks in the grime of his face. Mr. Cameron was something in the railway.

"Station roof came down!" he shouted across to them. "All that steel and glass!

198

Crawled out somehow! Ran all the way!" They came slowly to the garden fence, arms about each other, and Mum walked to meet them flanked by Margery and James.

"You hurt, Mrs. Gordon?" Mum shook her bandaged head again. "Nothing serious. Mr. Cameron, what does it all mean?" Mr. Cameron took an arm from his wife's waist and wiped his streaming face with a sleeve. "There was a terrible explosion in the harbour, down by the Richmond wharves. A munitions boat, they say. A French boat with two thousand tons of T.N.T. on board. She came up the harbour flying the red flag — the powder flag — and ran into another ship in the Narrows. She caught fire and blew up. It was like an earthquake. The whole North End of the city is smashed flat. Houses like bundles of toothpicks. And the boat went to pieces about the size of a plum — that big ship! When I ran up North Street the sky was raining bits of iron. I don't think many got out of the station alive."

Mum shivered. "No use standing here," James said. They went into the house and tramped silently through the shattered rooms. A motor-truck went past, soldiers leaning from the cab, shouting something urgent and incoherent. The street emerged from its dream-like silence for a second time that morning. Feet were suddenly splattering in the slush along the sidewalks, voices calling, shouting, screaming. Another truck went by, one of the olive-green army ambulances, going slowly. Soldiers hung from the doors, from the rear step, shouting up at the yawning windows. "What are they saying?" Mum said.

James said, "Sounds like, 'Get out of your houses.' " Mr. Cameron appeared on the sidewalk outside, shouting in to them through cupped hands. " . . out! Magazine's on fire! Big magazine at the Dockyard! On fire!"

"Put on your coats and overshoes first," Mum said, her mouth in a thin white line. "Where's your coat, James?"

"In school," he mumbled, embarrassed. It was hanging in the coat-room, covered with plaster dust, like all the others, and he had run away forgetting everything, like the other kids after all. "Put on your old one," Mum said. Margery went upstairs, and after a few minutes came down again, dressed in a woollen suit. They went down the street steps together, and beheld a strange and tragic procession approaching from the direction of the city. Men, women, and children in all sorts of attire, pouring along the sidewalks, choking the street itself. Some carried suit-cases and bundles. Others trundled hand-carts and perambulators laden with household treasures. Two out of three were bandaged and bloody, and all were daubed with soot and plaster. Their eyes glistened with an odd quality of fear and excitement, and they cried out to Mum as they stumbled past, "Get out! Out in the fields! There's another one coming! Dockyard's afire!"

Margery said, awed, "It's like pictures of the Belgian refugees." James looked at Mum's firm mouth and held his own chin high. They joined the exodus without words or cries. The human stream flowed westward. Every sidestreet was a tributary pouring its quota into the sad river. Open spaces began to appear between the houses, with little signboards offering "Lots for Sale." Then the open fields. The nearest fields were black with people already, standing in the snow with rapt white faces turned to the north-east, as in some exotic worship. The vanguard of the rabble halted uncertainly, like sheep confronted by a fence, and under the increasing pressure of those behind a great confusion arose. Their backs were to the stricken city. Before them lay the little valley of the Dutch Village Road, and beyond it the timbered ridges that cupped the city's water supply. Cries arose. "Here! Stop here!" And counter cries, "Too near! Move on!" At last someone shouted, "The woods! Take to the woods!" It was taken up, passed back from lip to lip. The stream moved on with a new pace, but Mum turned off the road into a field. They halted in a group of those strange expectant faces.

At the roadside was a pile of lumber. James went to the pile and pulled down some boards, made a small platform for Mum and Margery. Some of the people turned from their fearful gazing and said, "That's good. Better than standing in the snow." The lumber pile disappeared in a space of minutes. The great retreat poured past the field towards the Dutch Village Road for half an hour. Then it thinned, disintegrated into scattered groups, and was gone. The street was empty. The field was a human mass. Many of the women were in flimsy house-dresses, hatless and coatless. Two were clutching brooms in blue fingers. A blonde girl, with rouge-spots flaming like red lamps in her white cheeks, said, "Standing room only," with a catch in her voice. Nobody laughed. Most of the men were old. North-eastward rose fountains of smoke, black, white, and brown, merging in a great pall over the North End. The weird mushroom of those first tremendous minutes had shrivelled and disappeared in the new cloud. People watched the biggest of the black fountains. "That's the Dockyard," they said.

Two hours went by; long hours, cold hours. Still the people faced that black pillar of doom, braced for a mighty upheaval that did not come. There were more smoke fountains now, gaining in volume, creeping to right and left. A tall old man joined the crowd breathlessly, cried in a cracked voice, "The fire engines are smashed. The city is doomed." A murmur arose over the field, a long bitter sigh, like the stir of wind among trees. Someone said, "Nineteen days to Christmas," and laughed harshly. Three hours, and no blast from the burning Dockyard. Only the smoke poured up into the December sky. Old Mrs. Cameron came to them. She had become separated from her husband in the crowd and was weeping. "Joey! Joey!" she moaned, very softly. James thought this very strange. Joe Cameron had been killed at the Somme last year, and her other son's name was George. He was in France, too, in another regiment. But Mrs. Cameron kept moaning "Joey! Joey!" and wiping her eyes. She had no coat.

James said, "Looks as if we might be here a long time. I'll go back to the house and get some blankets, and something to eat." Mum caught him to her swiftly. "No," she said, through her teeth. Surprisingly, old Mrs. Cameron said, "That's right, James. I'll go with you. Mrs. Gordon, you stay here with Margery." Margery was not well. James looked at Mum. "Anywhere outdoors we'll be just as safe as here. I won't be in the house very long." Mum stared at him queerly. "You sound like your father, James." They set off at a brisk pace, old Mrs. Cameron clutching his arm. The snow in the field had been packed to a hard crust under a thousand feet. Farther on, where the houses stood silent rows, it was like a city of the dead. Blinds and curtains flapped lazily in gaping window-frames. Clothing, silverware, all sorts of odds and ends were littered over hallways and doorsteps, dropped in the sudden flight. There were bloody hand-prints on splintered doors, red splashes on floors and entries. The slush on the sidewalks was tinged a dirty pink in many places, where the hegira had passed.

Home at last. Smoke curled, a thin wisp, from the kitchen chimney. It was absurd, that faithful flicker in the stove, when all the doors and windows were gone and the winter breeze wandered at will through the empty rooms. They paused outside for a moment. Old Mrs. Cameron said, "We must rush in and snatch up what we want. Don't stay longer than it takes to count a hundred. Remember, James." She moved towards her doorstep, drawing a deep breath. James nodded dumbly. He clattered up the steps, making a noise that seemed tremendous in the stark silence, then along the lower hall and upstairs, where his steps were muffled in fallen plaster. All the way he counted aloud. Numbers had a sudden and enormous significance. Margery's bed was full of broken glass, cumbered with wreckage of the window-sash. He stripped a blanket from his own bed and passed into Mum's room. Mum's big eiderdown was there on the bed. Her room faced south, and the window-glass had all blown out into the street. A gust of chill air came through the empty frame, and the bedroom door slammed shockingly. The interior doors had been open at the time of the great blast, and had suffered little injury. The slam gave James a sudden feeling of suffocation and made his heart beat terribly. He went to the door quickly and twisted the handle. It came away in his hand, and the handle on the other side fell with a sharp thud, taking the shaft with it. "Hundred-'n-ten, hundred-'n-'leven." James dropped his burden and tried to force back the catch with bits of wood. They splintered and broke, without accomplishment. Outside, old Mrs. Cameron was calling, "James! James!" her voice very loud in the awful silence. Fear came to James in a rush. He fancied that sidelong earthquake again, and the big brown house tumbling into the street, a bundle of toothpicks, as Mr. Cameron had said about the houses up Richmond way. He went to the window, and debated throwing the blankets into the street and jumping after them. It looked a terrible distance down there. Mrs. Cameron caught sight of him staring down at her, and waved her arms awkwardly and shouted. She had a blanket under each arm, a loaf of bread in one hand and a pot of jam in the other. Inspiration came to James at last. Dad's rifle kit. In the bottom drawer in Mum's big chiffonier. He snatched out the drawer, brought forth a tiny screwdriver, prised back the catch with it. Freedom! He came down the stairs in four leaps, dragging blanket and eiderdown, and was out in the street, sucking in an enormous breath. Old Mrs. Cameron scolded. "I thought you were never coming, James. You should have counted."

"I couldn't get out," James said. The breeze felt very cold on his brow. He put up a hand and wiped big drops of perspiration. As they approached the field again James stopped suddenly. "I forgot to get something to eat." He was very close to tears. Old Mrs. Cameron pulled at his arm. "I have bread and jam," she said. Mum and Margery were standing on the little wooden raft in the snow. Mum clutched James against her, and held him there a long time. It was two o'clock in the afternoon.

At half-past three an olive-green truck appeared from the city, stopped in the road by the field. Soldiers came. "Any badly injured here?" There were none. All the people in the field had walked there unaided. Most of them were bandaged roughly, but nobody wanted to go to the hospital. The hospital was in the city, too near that ominous pillar of smoke. Somebody said so. A soldier said, "It's all right now. You'd better go back to your homes. You'll freeze here. The magazine's all right. Some

201

sailors went in and turned the cocks and flooded it." The truck roared away towards the city again. People stood looking at each other, with many side-glances at the smoke over burning Richmond. The old white-haired man wandered among them, shaking his bony fists at the smoke, a fierce exultation in his long face. "Woe unto ye, Sodom and Gomorrah! Alas, alas for Babylon, that mighty city! she shall be a heap." Old Mrs. Cameron muttered, "God have mercy." The girl with the rouge spots said, "You're getting your cities mixed, old man." A man cried, "Better to burn than freeze," and shouldering his bundle, walked off in the direction of the city, whistling "Tipperary." A few bold ones followed him. Then people began to move out of the field into the road in groups, walking slowly, cautiously, towards the city. The old man went with them, crying out in his wild voice. Nobody paid any attention.

Mum, James, and Margery got home at half-past four in the afternoon. Mr. Cameron was standing outside his house, staring up at the sky. The sunshine had vanished. The sky had turned grey, like steel. "It's going to snow," he said.

Mum said, "We'll have to spend the night in the kitchen." James looked at the kitchen stove-pipe. It was all right. He put coal on the faithful fire, and got the coal shovel out of the cellar and began to scoop plaster and broken glass from the kitchen floor, throwing it out into the snow. He counted the shovelfuls. There were seventy-five. "There's an awful lot of plaster in a room," Margery observed. Mum took a broom and swept up the fine stuff that escaped James' big shovel. They looked at the yawning window-frames. "That old storm-window," James said suddenly. "It's still in the cellar." They carried it up to the kitchen, and Mum and Margery steadied it while James mounted a table and drove nails to hold it in place of the vanished west window. It was meant to go on outside, of course, but there was no ladder, and it was terribly heavy. "We must have something to cover the other window," Mum said. They stared at each other. The people in the field had said you could not get glass or tarpaper in the city for love or money. James said, "The lumber — back in the field." Mum thought for a moment. "That lumber's gone by now, James. Besides, you couldn't carry a board all that way." They gathered up the living-room carpet, tugging it from under the tumbled furniture and shaking it clean of plaster. They folded it double and nailed it over the north window-frame on the inside, and James stuffed the gaps between nails with dish-cloths and towels. There were two doors to the kitchen. The one opening into the lower hall had been open at the time of the explosion, and was unhurt. The other, opening into the shattered scullery, had been blown bodily off its lock and hinges. Mum and James pushed it back into place and wedged it there tightly with pieces of wood. "The snow will drift into the house everywhere," Mum said. "But we can't help that." James nodded soberly. "The water-pipes are going to freeze and burst." They debated nailing a carpet over the bathroom window. Finally Mum said, "The hall stove is out and the stove-pipe is down. The pipes will freeze whether we cover the windows or not. We must let the taps run and hope for the best. We can get help in the morning, I hope. To-night it's everyone for himself."

Through the makeshift storm-window they could see snow falling rapidly in the winter dusk. Mum made tea, and they ate bread and butter hungrily by the light of a candle. The stove created a halo of warmth about itself, but the rising wind began to whistle through the impromptu window coverings. Margery said, "Couldn't we go somewhere for the night?" Mum shook her head. "Everybody's in the same mess," James said. "Lots of the houses looked worse than ours." Mum looked at the fingers of fine snow that were growing along the kitchen floor under the windows. "We must keep the stove going, James." James carried chairs from the living-room, grouped them close about the stove, and stuffed a towel into the crack under the hall door. The candle on the kitchen table guttered blue in the cross draught from the windows. "Thirteen hours before we see daylight again," Mum whispered, as if to herself.

There was a knocking. James opened the hall door carefully, and saw the dim figure of a soldier framed in the front doorway, rapping knuckles against the splintered jamb. "Does James Gordon live here?" Mum stepped into the hall, shielding the candle with her hand. "Colonel James Gordon lives here. But he's — away, just now." The dim figure lifted a hand in a perfunctory salute. "I mean young James Gordon that goes to the big brick school down the street." James stepped forward, but Mum caught his shoulder firmly. "What do you want with James?" The soldier made as if to salute again, but took off his fur hat and ducked his head instead. He was a young man with a uniform far too big for him, and a long solemn face, rather sheep-like in the candle-light. "We — the sergeant, I mean — has been sent up to this here school for a — well, a special kinda job, ma'am. The awf'cer telephoned to the head schoolmaster's house. He lives 'way down in the city somewheres, but he said there was a boy named James Gordon lived handy the school an' would show us how to get in the basement, an' all like that."

James moved quickly, and Mum's hand slipped from his shoulder and fell to her side. "I won't be long, Mum." The soldier mumbled, "It's only a coupla hundred yards." Mum said, "Put on your coat and overshoes, James."

It was pitch dark, and the night was thick with snow. James led the way. The soldier plodded silently behind him. It was strange to be going to school at night, and the great silent building seemed very grim and awful with its long rows of black window-holes. A dark blur in the main doorway disintegrated, came towards them. Four men in fur hats and long flapping overcoats. Soldiers. "You find the kid, Mac?" James' soldier said, "Yeah. This is him. Where's the sergeant?" One man waved a vague arm at the dim bulk of the school. "Scoutin' around in there somewheres, lightin' matches. Tryin' to find the basement door." James said, "Which door do you want? You can get in the basement from the street if you like."

"Ah," grunted the second soldier; "that's the ticket, son."

A tiny point of light appeared within the school flickered down the stairs. James wondered why the sergeant looked upstairs for a basement door. A stout figure, muffled in a khaki greatcoat, was revealed behind the feeble flame of the match. The sergeant came out into the snow swearing into a turned-up collar. With the shapeless fur hat on his head he looked strangely like a bear roused out of a winter den. "Here's the kid, Sarge." The sergeant regarded him. "Hello, son." James pointed. "The basement door is around there." He showed them. The door had been blown off its hinges and wedged, a bundle of twisted wood, in the frame. They pulled at the splintered wood stoutly, and the doorway was clear. On the basement steps the sergeant lit another match. Their voices echoed strangely in that murky cavern.

James knew them now for soldiers of the Composite Battalion, made up of detachments from various home-guard units. They wore the clumsy brown fur hats and hideous red rubber galoshes that were issued to the home guard for winter wear. Some people called them 'The Safety Firsts'; and it was common for cheeky boys to hurl snowballs after their patrols from the shadow of alleyways, chanting—

"Com-Po-Zite!
They won't fight!"

Mum had cautioned James against such pleasantry. Somebody had to stay at home, and these men were mostly physical unfits, rejected by the overseas regiments.

"Big as all Hell," declared the sergeant, after a tour of the echoing basement. "Hold a thousand, easy." The soldiers said, "Yeah." The sergeant fumbled in the big pocket of his greatcoat and brought forth a dark bottle. He took a long swig, wiped his moustache with a sweep of mittened hand, and passed the bottle around. "Gonna be a cold job," he rumbled. "All the windows gone, an' snow blowin' in everywheres. Concrete floor, too." The sheep-faced soldier said, "What-say we tear up some floorboards upstairs an' cover some of these cellar winders?" The sergeant spat, with noise. "They gotta send up a workin' party from the Engineers if they want that done. We got dirty work enough." The soldiers nodded their hats again, and said "Yeah" and "Betcha life."

Wind swirled through the gloomy basement in icy gusts. The men leaned against the wall, huddled in their greatcoats, cigarettes glowing in the darkness. James walked up the concrete steps to street level and stood inside the doorway, staring into the snowy dark. He wondered how long he was supposed to stay. A glow-worm appeared down the street, a feeble thing that swam slowly through the whirl of snow towards the school. James experienced a sudden twinge of fright. There was a great white shape behind it. Then a voice from the darkness above that ghostly shape: "Hulloa!" James cleared his throat. "Hulloa!" A man rode up to the doorway on a white horse. A lantern dangled from the horse's neck, like a luminous bell. The rider leaned over, and a face became visible in the pale glow. He was a detective of the city police, and James recognized his mount as one of the pair that used to pull the Black Maria in the days before the war. He was riding bare-back, feet hanging down, and the big policeman looked very odd, perched up there. "Anyone else around, son?" James jerked his head towards the black hole of the basement entrance. "Some soldiers. Down there, sir. Do you want them?" The policeman turned his horse awkwardly. "Just tell 'em the first wagon will be right along." He kicked the glistening side of his mount and disappeared as silently as he had come, lantern a-swing. James shouted the message down into the darkness. "Okay!" There was a lull in the wind, and the bottle gurgled in the sudden stillness.

Another glow-worm came, as silent as the first. But as it turned in towards the school James caught a faint rattle of wheels, and a hoarse voice bellowed, "Whoa-hoa!" The soldiers came stumbling up the steps in the darkness, and James went with them towards the light. It was a wagon, one of the low drays that clattered along Water Street from morn to night. A man climbed stiffly from the seat. He was crusted with snow, even to his moustache and eyebrows. "Let's have the lantern, fella," demanded the sergeant. They walked to the back of the wagon, and the sheep-faced soldier held

204

the lantern high while the sergeant whipped a long tarpaulin from the mysterious freight.

"Niggers!" rumbled the sergeant loudly. James, peering between the soldiers in astonishment, beheld six figures lying side by side on the dray: three men, two women, and a young girl. They were stiff and impassive, like the dummies you saw in shop windows. The women had dirty rags of cotton dress. One of the men wore a pair of trousers. The rest were naked. Ebony flesh gleamed in the lantern light. The snowflakes drifted lightly on the calm up-turned faces. Their eyes were closed, hands lay easily at their sides, as if they were content to sleep there, naked to the storm. "Looka!" called the sheep-faced soldier. "They bin hit, Sarge. But there's no blood!" The sergeant stooped over for a better look. Two of the dark faces were scored deeply, as if some vandal had gouged wax from the dummies with a chisel. "Concussion," announced the sergeant with immense assurance. "That's what. Drives the blood inwards. They was dead before they got hit. That boat went to pieces like shrapnel." He called it "sharpnel."

The teamster was complaining. " . . . get a move on, you guys. This snow gets much deeper I gotta go back to the barn an' shift to sleds. There's work to do." Two of the soldiers picked up a dummy by head and feet, carried it awkwardly down the basement steps, and dropped it. There was a dull 'flap' when it struck the concrete. They came up the steps quickly. "Froze?" asked Sarge. "Stiff as a board," they said. The wagon was cleared of its silent passengers and went away into the night. The sergeant struck matches while the men arranged the bodies in a neat row. "Once," a soldier said, "I worked in a meat packin' plant. In T'ronta, that was."

"Well," Sarge rumbled, "you're keeping your hand in."

Another lantern swam up the street. Another dray. More silent figures under the tarpaulin. White people this time. A man and four young women, nude, flesh gleaming like marble in the lantern light. There was blood, a lot of it, dried black like old paint. "Musta bin farther away," observed the sergeant. "Them niggers was from Africville, right by the place she went off." T'ronta said curiously, "Funny, them bein' stripped this way. Was their clo'es blowed off, would you say?" The teamster shook his head. "Nuh. These was all pulled outa the wreckage by the troops this afternoon. Clo'es caught an' tore off, I guess. Besides, lotsa people sleeps late winter mornin's. Prob'ly didn't have much on, anyway." More wagons. The intervals diminished. The sheep-faced soldier said, "The awf'cer's forgot us. We oughta bin relieved by now." "Quit beefin'," said Sarge. "All the troops is up Richmond way, pullin' stiffs outa the wreckage, huntin' for livin' ones. If it's okay for them it's okay for us." A teamster gave them a spare lantern which they stood on the basement floor, and in the fitful glow of that lonely thing the dummies lay in orderly rows, toes up, faces towards the dim ceiling. The shadows of the soldiers performed a grotesque dance on the walls as they went about their work. Sarge pulled something from his greatcoat pocket, and James gave it a sidewise glance, expecting to see the bottle. Sarge thrust it back into the pocket again, but James had seen the silver figure of a baseball pitcher, and knew it had been wrenched from the big cup his school had won last summer. He said nothing. Sarge said, "You still here, son? We don't need you no more. Better go home."

Mum greeted James anxiously in the candle-lit kitchen. "How pale you are, James!

What did they want? You've been gone three hours." James looked at the stove. "Nothing. Nothing much, Mum. I guess they — just wanted to fix up the school a bit." They sat in the cushioned chairs, huddling over the stove. Margery had her feet in the oven. James went upstairs and brought down blankets, and they muffled themselves up in the chairs. Mum said, "Don't you want something to eat, James? There's tea on the stove, and there's bread and butter." "Not hungry," James said in a low voice.

It was a long night. James had never known a night could be so long. Sometimes you would doze a little, and you would see the faces of the dead people on the drays as plain as anything. Then you would wake up with a start and find yourself sliding off the chair, and feeling terribly cold. Several times he took the hod and the candle down into the cellar and brought up more coal. When the candles burned down to the table he lit new ones and stuck them in the hot grease. After a while there was a pool of grease on the table, hard and wrinkled and dirty-white, like frozen slush in the street. Draughts came through the window-covers and under both doors, like invisible fingers of ice, and you had to keep your feet hooked in the rung of your chair, off the floor. The candles gave a thin blue light and made a continual fluttering sound, like the wings of a caged bird. Sometimes the house shook in the gusts, and twice James had to climb on the table and hammer more nails to keep the carpet in place. Snow drifted in between the carpet and the window-frame, and formed thin white dunes along the floor next the wall. The heat thrown off by the kitchen stove was lost between the bare laths of the walls and ceiling.

"There must be a lot of dead, poor souls," Mum said.

"Yes," James said.

"In the morning, James, you must go to the telegraph office and send a cable to your father. He'll be frantic."

"Yes," James said.

Mum had washed the blood from her face and tied a clean rag of bedsheet over the cuts on her forehead. James thought she looked very white and hollow, somehow. But when he looked in her eyes there was something warm and strong in them that made him feel better. When you looked in Mum's eyes you felt that everything was all right. Margery had drawn a blanket over her head, like a hood, and her head was bent, hidden in the shadow. Mum said, "Are you awake, Margery?"

"Yes," Margery said quickly.

"Are you all right?"

"Yes."

"It will be morning soon," Mum said.

But it was a long time. They sat, stiff and cramped, over the stove, and listened to the snow sweeping into the rooms upstairs, and the flap-flap of broken laths, and blinds blowing to rags in the empty window-frames; and the night seemed to go on for ever, as though the world had come to a dark end and the sun would never come back again. James thought of Sarge, and the sheep-faced man, and T'ronta, carrying frozen dummies into the school basement, and wondered if the awf'cer had remembered them. Daylight crept through the storm-window at last, a poor grey thing that gave a bleak look to everything in the kitchen. Stove, blankets — nothing could ward off the cold then. The grey light seemed to freeze everything it touched. Outside, the snow still swept fiercely against the carpet and the glass. James found potatoes in the cellar, and rescued bacon and eggs from the wreck of the pantry. Mum brushed the snow and bits of plaster from the bacon and put it in a frying-pan. It smelt good.

The telegraph office was full of people waving bits of scribbled paper. The ruins of plate-glass windows had been shovelled out into the street, and the frames boarded up. Outside, a newsboy was selling papers turned out by some miracle on battered presses in the night. They consisted of a single sheet, with "HALIFAX IN RUINS" in four-inch letters at the top. Within the telegraph office, lamps cast a yellow glow. There was a great buzz of voices and the busy clack-clack of instruments. James had to wait a long time in the line that shuffled past the counter. A broad cheerful face greeted him at last.

"What's yours, son?"

"I want to send a cable to Colonel James Gordon, in France."

The man leaned over the counter and took a better look at him. "Hello! Are you Jim Gordon's son? So you are. I'd know that chin anywhere. How old are you, son?"

"Four — going on fifteen," James said.

"Soon be old enough to fight, eh? What's your Dad's regiment?"

James paused. "That'll cost extra, won't it?" he suggested shrewdly. "Everybody in the army knows my father."

The man smiled. "Sure," he agreed reasonably. "But France is a big place, son. It's their misfortune, of course, but there's probably a lot of people in France don't know your Dad."

James said, "It's the Ninetieth."

"Ah, of course. Jim Gordon of the Ninetieth. There's an outfit will keep old Hindenburg awake nights, son, and don't you forget it. What d'you want to say?"

James placed both hands on the counter. "Just this: 'All's well. James Gordon.' That's all."

The man wrote it down, and looked up quickly. "All's well? That counts three words, son, at twenty-five cents a word. Why not just, 'All well'?"

James put his chin up. "No. 'All's well.' Send it like that."

# At the Tide's Turn

Justice Martin Bunt went down the harbour on a spring afternoon in 1778 with mingled curiosity and distaste — a trifle more distaste than curiosity. He was curious to know the meaning of the smoke and thunder which had filled the harbour mouth since mid-morning, setting all Oldport agog. And he was going to present his compliments to His Majesty's Navy, which he had no reason to love; going in fact at a peremptory command from Captain Milligan of H.M.S. *Blonde*, and in one of the frigate's boats, rowed by eight powder-stained tars and steered by a jaunty young midshipman.

There were several reasons for Mr. Bunt's discomfort. One was that he was suffering from scabies — 'that lothsome Distemper call'd the Itch,' as he wrote himself — a common ailment of the times, when people spent long winters muffled against the cold, and bathing was considered dangerous. On the previous night he and his wife had anointed themselves with the usual remedy, a mixture of brimstone, tar and tallow, to be kept on for two days and nights. The midshipman in charge of the boat had given Bunt no time to wash, change his linen or even to tell his wife where he was going.

"You smell like hell," said the midshipman wittily.

"That," answered Mr. Bunt astonishingly, for he was a pious man, "is just the way I feel."

Mr. Bunt was in his forties then, and chief magistrate of our town, a burly red-faced merchant with a smattering of New England law, a supreme honesty, a touching faith in the future of Nova Scotia, and a wistful longing to be somewhere or something else. Greatness had been thrust upon him when Silas Bradford, the founder of our town, went off to the siege of Havana and died of fever there in '62. The people of Oldport, in the New England fashion, looked to the justices for leadership, and they elected Mr. Bunt to fill Silas's big shoes — a rôle for which Martin felt inadequate.

Not that Martin Bunt lacked courage — he had fought bravely enough in the colonial militia at Louisbourg in '58. But now that he was twenty years older and a deacon of the church, and possessed a struggling trader's business and a shrewish wife, with two daughters at school in Boston, he had learned to put discretion and valour in their proper places.

The other justices we need not consider much. Justice Daggett was very old and feeble, and he left the town in the midst of its greatest troubles and went to a Heaven where presumably there was no taxation, with or without representation. As for Justice Benajah Thripps, he is a story in himself; a cold, shrewd, tireless man without fear or conscience, who played both ends against the middle throughout the American Revolution, invested in privateers on both sides, never hesitated to betray the ships and possessions of his friends, and after the war removed with his family and fortune to the neighbourhood of Salem, Massachusetts. There he lived the rest of his days like a prince, with a great house, a staff of negro servants and the finest carriage and horses in that city of wealthy freebooters. It is related that after his death his body lay in state for a week in the great hall of his house, 'embalmed' in cayenne pepper, an object of devout curiosity to the folks of Danvers and Salem. If there is any justice beyond the grave the material of his embalmment was a portent.

Two men in the Oldport of those times might be considered well educated: the Reverend Peleg Potter, a graduate of Harvard College, a godly but tipsy soul who repeatedly was asked to leave but stayed to the end of his days; and Mr. Amasa Barriman, of Yale, the schoolmaster who played the violin so charmingly, and gave singing lessons and lectures on 'musick' in the Meeting House on week-day evenings. In the midst of the Revolution Mr. Barriman left without any asking, indeed without warning, leaving an unfinished sum in the shape of debts, and a mournful male chorus of creditors.

For the rest, our townsmen were very ignorant of the great world and the machinery that was to grind them slowly in blood and tears. Their news came by letter and pamphlet and word of mouth from their friends and relatives in New England. They had the right of sending a representative to the Nova Scotia legislature — a right which they exercised indifferently because no man could spare the time or indeed the cost of his tavern bill at Halifax.

Once or twice Mr. Bunt went down, a shabby and awkward stranger amongst the legislative swells. The rest of the time our town was 'represented' by one of the Halifax merchants and lawyers who then, with the governor's favour, directed the colony's affairs, and Oldport considered itself favoured indeed if this representative addressed a note of thanks to the constituents he had never seen.

The town itself was run simply, on the New England model, a little democracy in which the justices and militia officers were selected by vote, and paid by fee or subscription — when they were paid at all. Like their pilgrim fathers (most of them came from Cape Cod) they appointed a day of prayer and fasting each spring and a day of feast and thanksgiving every fall, and observed them religiously. Christmas and Easter passed almost unnoticed, except in the way of prayer — it would have been unthrifty as well as 'Popish' to have too many holidays. But on the King's birthday the militia company straggled to Battery Point (without uniforms and with no weapons but their hunting guns, a queer collection) and fired a salute from the two 12-pounders, relics of the French wars, which then constituted the sole defence of the harbour.

For years they had watched with a shadowy disquiet the growing hostility of the older colonies towards the mother country, but they had no suspicion of the tragedy in store for themselves. Their sympathies lay where one might expect, though there was a wide and deep difference between sympathy for the cause of rebellion and agreement with what came out of it — the utter separation of the colonies in America from the rest of the British world.

It was no small part of their trial that when the Revolution began, the governor's seat at Halifax held the violent and stupid Legge, astonished to find himself head of the lone Atlantic colony not under the rebel flag. He bombarded the home authorities with petitions for troops, seeing sedition where there was only doubt, and rebellion wherever a few young hot-heads erected a 'liberty pole' or refused to take the militia oath without a reservation against fighting their New England kin. The suspect Yankee settlements, of which Oldport was the biggest, he visited with a heavy hand.

He seized the honest if poorly spelled letters of our merchants and searched them avidly for treason, took away the two sorry cannon which were Oldport's only defence against rebel privateers, forbade all intercourse with New England (where of necessity our fishermen had to buy the farm produce they could not raise themselves), and harried the inhabitants with oaths of allegiance, abjuration and supremacy.

As if this were not enough he sent a frigate to keep watch on Oldport loyalty — and Captain Dudington of *Senegal* was the contemptuous high-handed sort best fitted to arouse rebellion where there had been none. Dudington lay in our small harbour from Christmas '75 to April '76, stopping and searching every petty coaster, seizing whatever seemed contrabrand to his jaundiced eye, pressing the youngest and ablest men into the King's service as he pleased — (Justice Bunt protested as chief magistrate and was called a 'bloody rebel' for his pains) — and sailed away just at a time when privateers were swarming out of Salem and other rebel ports to harry the Nova Scotia coast.

Our town was unarmed and helpless. Rebel privateers boldly made a rendezvous of an uninhabited harbour six miles to the west. His Majesty's fleet made no effort to drive them off. But the drunken crew of a Halifax privateer, licensed by Governor Legge, made free with our town for several days, insulting the people and threatening to 'burn the rebel nest over their heads'; and a self-important lieutenant visited a sessions of the peace at Justice Bunt's house, posted sailors armed with pistols at the door, and stood over Bunt himself with a drawn cutlass 'to see that the King's justice was done, by God!'

Upon a Sunday the Reverend Peleg Potter preached a memorable sermon from Isaiah 9 — *The Syrians before, and the Philistines behind, and they shall devour Israel with open mouth. For all this his anger is not turned away, but his hand is stretched out still.* He was slightly drunk, but when the Reverend Peleg was only slightly drunk he was very eloquent indeed. Oldport came to see its tribulation as the wrath of God, a thing to be endured and not questioned. But even pious Martin Bunt wondered sometimes *whose* hand was stretched out still, and where his groping people might find it. All this and much more was in his mind as the frigate's boat carried him over the river bar and down the narrow bay on that April afternoon of 1778.

The *Duc de Choiseul* lay against the wooded east shore, on the reefs which have been known ever since as Frenchman's Ledges. Her three masts stood but she was badly holed and half full of water, careened at a sharp angle, yards acockbill, gear hanging all anyhow and the shot-riddled canvas flapping in great dismal rags. The paint of her visible port side was scarred with shotmarks. Three of the lower deck ports had been blown into one, a yawning hole that made Bunt's eyes bulge, seeing the thickness of timber and plank.

"A stern chase an' then hammer-an'-tongs for two hours," the middy said. "Then Monsoor ran her on the reefs. His flag was fouled aloft, I think. He didn't get it down quick enough to suit Old Milly, at any rate. She heeled to port first, after she struck aground, an' we fired into her again, just as a lot o' the poor devils were pourin' up from the lower deck. Barrin' that it was a jolly fine fight."

He was a pert pale youngster of fifteen or so, the pimples of adolescence enlarged and blotched by the diet of the midshipmen's berth, and he was pleased with the fight and himself and the prospect of prize money.

"Didn't know we was at war with the French," murmured Mr. Bunt.

"Pshaw! We're always at war with France."

Bunt could see the French crew, a vague human mass in the edge of the fir woods, and a number of men roosting like gulls on the rocks by the shore, watching *Blonde's* sailors swarming over the wreck, and the frigate's boats plying back and forth. The midshipman steered under *Blonde's* stern. Her ports were all open, some of the guns protruding, others run in for loading, just as they had stood when the fight finished, and her deck was a litter of ramrods, sponges, match-tubs, long wooden cartridge-boxes with their rope beckets, and linstocks stuck in the planking by their pointed iron butts. In the waist was an ever-growing mass of stuff salvaged from the Frenchman. A few splatters of blood, rope-ends, ragged holes in the bulwark, and one or two splintered grooves in the deck witnessed that *Blonde* had suffered, but it was evident that 'Monsoor's' shooting had been poor.

The midshipman led the way down a dark companionway and Bunt found himself in the captain's quarters, stooping to avoid the deck beams. The bulkhead between the main cabin and the sleeping compartment had been torn out, probably at the outbreak of war, and replaced with a canvas screen. Captain Milligan arose from a small desk in the inner compartment and greeted his visitor civilly — something new in Bunt's experience.

Besides the desk there was a cot and a twelve-pounder in that confined space. The gun had been cast loose from its frappings and run up to the open port with the train-tackles; and it had been in action, for a handspike, ramrod and sponge stood beside it and despite the breeze through the port there was a sharp smell of burnt powder. The captain was a dry alert man in white cotton stockings, a pair of stout grogram breeches and an old blue coat with tarnished buttons — evidently his battle rig. There was a black smudge on his right cheek.

"Please sit on the cot," he said, and Mr. Bunt sat down, hat in hand.

"You're the chief magistrate of the town yonder?"

"Yes," Mr. Bunt said heavily. He had been through all this before, aboard the *Senegal* and others, though with much less civility. In a moment the purser would appear and there would be a demand for fresh beef, and the town would have to provide it — at the purser's price.

"Will you drink with me? We've had a busy day, sir, and speaking for myself I can do with a stiff 'un."

"Thank ye kindly," murmured Mr. Bunt. Captain Milligan roared for his steward, a sudden clap of vocal thunder that sounded like a report of the gun at Bunt's knees. Over a pair of stiff 'uns they regarded each other.

"Shall we drink to His Majesty?" asked Captain Milligan, watching Bunt with one eye.

"Why not?" said Bunt. They stood to drink, and Mr. Bunt, unaccustomed to the low deck beams, struck his head with a violence that filled it full of sparks. Captain Milligan appeared not to notice.

"I've sent for you," he said briskly, "because we've a full two hundred prisoners on the shore yonder, some of 'em wounded. I want you to accommodate 'em in the town for a day or two, till I've stripped the wreck. Then I'll take 'em off to the hulks at Halifax."

Mr. Bunt shifted uneasily. "We've got no buildin' big enough to hold 'em, sir, barrin' the Meetin' House, which belongs to the Lord's sarvice. Add to that, sir, the town's very poor and food scarce at this time o' year. We couldn't feed twenty, let alone two hundred."

"Ah! Well, billet 'em, man, billet 'em. Two or three to a house if you like. As for food, I'll have beef and biscuit delivered from the wreck to you. Have 'em come to you each morning, say, for the day's allowance. Messes of ten, say, and ten pounds of beef and ten of biscuit to a mess. I'll make it better if we can salvage enough. They'll miss their wine most, I fancy. Tell 'em it's the fortune of war and hard lines all round." A

211

competent man, Milligan plainly expected competence in Mr. Bunt. "You understand," he added, "you'll be responsible for 'em."

There was a disconsolate lift and droop of Bunt's thick shoulders.

"We've no means of stoppin' 'em if they choose to run off, Cap'n, if that's what ye mean."

"Nonsense! Got a militia company, haven't you?"

"Yes, but no arms, no powder, no shot, nothing."

The captain regarded his visitor curiously. The stiff 'un was working within Martin Bunt. There was an odd note in his voice and a gleam in his eye.

"What's the matter?" demanded Milligan.

Mr. Bunt regarded his shabby hat and his large red hands. He wanted to talk — to talk a lot. He wanted to tell somebody the troubles of his town and people. Instinct and sour experience warned him to hold his tongue before this captain of the Royal Navy, but suddenly his tongue was past holding.

"Well," he burst out, "ye've treated me like a man, the first o' His Majesty's officers to give me a civil word in three — yes, in five years, goin' back afore the Rebellion. S'like this. We come here in '59 to make a settlement, from Cape Cod, nearly all of us. Bin a few come from Conne'ticut since, an' one or two from Boston. Every grown soul in the place today's a native o' Noo England, the heart, d'ye see, o' the — ahum! — Rebellion. All our relations live there. All our friends, barrin' a gen'leman or two in Halifax."

"I see."

"Not yet ye don't, sir. That ain't the half of it! We're mostly a fishin' people that has to git a livin' out o' the sea. The land's poor. We can't raise half, no, nor a quarter o' the grain an' roots we need. The rest we must buy in Noo England. There's no ch'ice about it. Yet the Halifax gov'nor forbids it! Ag'in, to buy we must sell — an' with us it's fish or nawthin'. Dried cod, salt alewives, smoked salmon — that's our livin', and' we have to take our pay in trade, an' trade where we can. That means a trade three-cornered like, 'tween Nova Scotia, the West Indies an' Noo England. The West Indies take our fish and give us what they've got — rum, sugar and molasses for the most part. Noo England gives us provisions an' mannafactered goods for the rum and the rest."

"Humph," Milligan said. "But taxation's at the bottom of this American trouble. What's your opinion on that?"

"I told ye we have to take our pay in trade. Cash is scarcer than . . . "

"Than loyal men in Oldport?"

"Ah, don't joke, sir," Mr. Bunt implored. He was sweating a little with emotion, or perhaps it was only the drink. "Don't ye joke about loyalty, sir. That's a serious word. S'like this. We seldom see more'n a few pounds cash in the run of a year. Consequent, we don't take taxation very kind, bein' a self-supportin' people that asks nawthin' o' gov'ment but to be let alone. When the troubles begun acrost the Bay o' Fundy we knowed Sam Adams an' John Hancock was at the bottom of it, and knew 'em for what they were. Jest the same, we didn't like the princ'ple o' the Stamp Act any more'n Boston folk. When 'twas repealed in '66 there was a celebration here in Oldport that lasted two days. We got the news June the third, an' the nex' day — 'twas the King's birthday but no harm meant — we burnt an old house for a bonfire."

"The house of a loyalist, I wager!"

"Loyalist?" Bunt turned the strange word on his tongue.

"The rebels call 'em Tories."

"Ah! No, sir. 'Twas a li'l old empty hut that was built when we come to this place in '59 along o' Silas Bradford — Bradford o' the Rangers, that died o' yeller-jack at the siege o' Havana. A mortal pity Silas ain't alive today. Silas always knowed what to do. Silas 'ud know what to do now about the way we're bein' squeezed atween the King and the rebels."

"What do you mean?" demanded Milligan.

Justice Bunt opened his big hands expressively. "The rebel privateers is ravagin' our coast, takin' up our vessels — I've lost two myself. The King's gov'nor at Halifax took away our arms an' left us helpless to defend our property. We've asked ag'in an' ag'in for protection, an' all we've got so far is accusations o' treason."

"You've the protection of His Majesty's Navy, Mr. Bunt," Milligan said stiffly.

"All we've seen o' His Majesty's ships so far," Bunt said grimly, "has been press-gangs and searchin'-parties."

There was a long silence after that.

"D'ye know any reason why the Frenchman yonder" — Captain Milligan jerked his head towards the open port — "should run in here when we overhauled him?"

"None, sir."

"Suppose, Mr. Bunt, I told you she was laden with arms and ammunition for the rebel army, and had rebel colours in her flag locker, and a letter addressed to one Morris, a member of the Congress, from Silas Read, who's Benjamin Franklin's right-hand man in Paris?"

"I know nothing of it, sir."

Their eyes met and stared hard. Captain Milligan stepped to the port with his hands beneath his coat-tails. The bowsprit and the riddled spritsail of the French ship were just visible as *Blonde* swung at anchor.

"Well, we nabbed her at any rate," he said with satisfaction. "The Chevalier de Sucay on board too, and that other mysterious fellow who calls himself Jet D'Eau, hiding in the cable tier. I believe you, Bunt. The rebel army needs this stuff too badly to risk it on a chance revolt in Nova Scotia."

He said this very innocently and shot a quick hard look at Bunt's face. It was an honest face, full of genuine perplexity. Captain Milligan prided himself on his judgment of men.

"Mr. Bunt, a man in my position's got to do his duty and ask no questions."

"Yes, sir."

"At the same time, Bunt, I'm a man and I've got my opinions. It's my opinion you've been damned poorly handled."

"Yes, sir."

"There's been nothing but stupidity in this American affair. There was no need of trouble to begin with — a group of money-grubbing merchants on both sides — and the war's only making a bad matter worse." He added gloomily, "That's not for me to say, of course."

Another silence. Martin Bunt stared at the lees in his glass.

"You understand, Mr. Bunt, I can do nothing for you — nothing absolutely."

"I understand that, Cap'n."

"I can't go shoving my oar into provincial affairs."

"No, sir."

"I am a man without influence, absolutely without influence, Bunt." Captain kept throwing these remarks over his shoulder as he stood at the port, as if to stand off a Bunt in close pursuit. "One unfortunate move and I'd find myself on the beach at half-pay."

"I understand, sir."

Captain Milligan turned and faced Bunt abruptly. "I'm going to salvage all the Frenchman's cargo that I can, and take it to Halifax with the prisoners." A pause. Then, indifferently, "After that the wreck — it'll go to pieces in the first south-east blow, mind — is anybody's as far as I'm concerned."

Mr. Bunt came to his feet. "Thankee! Thankee, Cap'n! We . . . "

"Don't thank me, man!" barked the captain of the *Blonde*. He jerked his head once more towards the wreck of the *Duc de Choiseul*, swarming with his men and boats. "You can thank," he said with a grim smile, "Mr. Silas Read, of Paris."

Three days later Martin Bunt heard that name again, but in a very different setting and in quite another voice. A small boy had brought him a mysterious message in the dusk, and he had gone to Mrs. Hewler's tavern near the fish-lots, and found in her small sanded taproom his younger brother Caleb, Justice Benajah Thripps, and a long lean man with heavy-lidded eyes and a Salem drawl.

"This," young Caleb said eagerly, "is Cap'n Jonathan Cogsley, an' wants a word wi' ye, Marty."

"Cap'n o' what?" said Justice Bunt suspiciously. They had the air of conspirators, sitting about a single candle with the curtains drawn, elbows together on a small table, with mugs of untasted beer before them.

"O' the privateer *Lizard*, in Congress service," drawled the stranger. He recited particulars in an amused voice, as if he were reading off a bill of lading. "Now lyin' an' bein' in the haven known as Port Gambier, two leagues to the west, an' ready to receive cargo duly consigned — the restraints o' princes an' rulers an' all other dangers o' the seas nothwithstandin'. Cal'lated to pay ye an official visit yes'day, Marty, but we seen that English frigate's upper yards jest in time, an' sheered off. Come overland s'afternoon, I did, shanks mare, a-purpose fer to see ye."

Mr. Bunt turned a pair of enquiring blue eyes on his fellow justice, Benajah Thripps, but the light of the coarse tallow dip came between; over the flame he could see nothing but a blurred sly smile.

"What d'ye want o' me?" he said to Cogsley.

"All the goods ye took out o' the Duck de Shozzu 'smornin', arter the frigate sailed fer Hal'fax. There was — lemme see — " Cogsley flicked his hard grey eyes towards Benajah Thripps for an instant, but Justice Thripps was staring at the ceiling — "several chists of arms, a keg or two o' powder, a keg or two o' balls, an' a box or two o' flints. Funny how that Englishman come to overlook 'em, warn't it Marty — all tucked up nice an' dry in the half-deck as they was? Yes, sirree! — an' ye salvaged 'em fer the rightful owners like the Patriot ye was — eh?"

214

"I salvaged 'em for our militia company," Bunt said stoutly.

"Bah!" snapped Justice Thripps.

"An' ain't givin' 'em up without doo authority," added Martin Bunt defiantly. "What are ye doin' here wi' this man, Caleb?"

"Caleb's j'ined my crew at Port Gambier along o' half a dozen other smart lads from your taown," Jonathan Cogsley said.

"Ye lie!" snapped Bunt, and looked at young Caleb.

"It's the truth," said Caleb Bunt. "Marty, we've been drove an' cussed an' abused, an' it's come to the point where we've got to fight one way or t'other. Might's well be this way, as I see it."

"Them guns," put in Captain Cogsley, "was consigned to us at Port Gambier by Mister Read, the Congress agent in France. 'Twas reckoned safe, up here on the coast o' Nova Scotia where nobody'd suspect, an' we could run the guns an' stuff safe into Boston where that blunderin' Frenchman was sure to git caught. How'd that nosy frigate captain git on to the game? If there's been blabbin' — well, no matter, that's all spilled milk. Marty — I'll call ye that, for we're all good friends here, ain't we? — I call upon ye to deliver up them guns or suffer the consequences."

"What consequences?" Mr. Bunt demanded bitterly. "Ye've stole half our vessels now — you an' the other privateers."

"We could take the rest."

"They could take an' burn the town, come to that," added Justice Thripps glibly. "Ye've got to think o' the town, Marty. There's twenty sail of American privateers cruisin' 'tween here an' the Cape."

"No doubt," answered Bunt. It was strange to hear that word 'American' on Benajah's lips. It seemed to set apart the people of Nova Scotia, as if the Bay of Fundy had achieved the width of the Atlantic. "On t'other hand we've now got sixty muskets, with flints, powder and ball. We'd make it a right lively burnin', we would, Benajah. Besides, Cap'n Cogsley, this ain't Port Gambier, where the men-o'-war daresn't go for fear o' the shoals, amongst the islands. Bring your privateers into this narrow bay of ours, where the first passin' frigate 'ud catch 'em like flies in a bottle? You ain't so fond o' fightin' as all that."

"There's always night," drawled the Salem man.

"Lookee here, Marty," urged Benajah Thripps. "Ye've got to figger this out like a sensible man. D'ye realise what it means — this French ship? I bin talkin' to one or two of her officers that spoke English. It means France has reckernized the independence o' the American colonies. Means France'll jine the war herself in a matter o' months. Means England'll be fightin' fer her life afore the summer's out. She'll have to call the fleet home. Take away the fleet an' what's left? A few reg'ments o' redcoats firin' muskets into a continent! Tell ye, Marty, it means the end o' the King's rule in America. Nova Scotia — yes, an' all Canady — has got to go the way o' the rest. Don't ye see that?"

"All I see," Martin Bunt said stolidly, "is you're askin' me to give up goods that belong to us by right o' salvage, under threat o' vi'lence."

"Make your ch'ice," Captain Cogsley said, sprawling in his chair.

"An' remember," Benajah warned, "this is final, Marty. It's King or Congress — no three ways about it."

"Them that ain't fer us is ag'in us," affirmed Cogsley.

"It goes deeper 'n King or Congress," Bunt said slowly. "What I see is lor on the one side — hard lor in lots o' ways; lor that's poor-conceived, lor that's administered wrong — but lor for all that, somethin' ye can depend on, put your faith in, somethin' ye can build a business on. And on t'other hand nawthin' but a lot o' Committees o' Safety, an' Sons o' Liberty, an' Patriots an' what not, all makin' lors unto theirselves an' not one knowin' or carin' what t'other's doin'.

"Some day, mebbe, the Congress'll git the upper hand o' the King's troops. Afore that, though, they'll have to git the upper hand o' the Committees o' Safety an' the rest, an' then ye'll be payin' taxes an' duties an' tidewaiters' fees an' t'other things ye think ye've scuttled fer ever, an' buyin' tea from John Hancock, say, at John Hancock's price. Then, mebbe, there'll be lor an' order south o' Fundy Bay, an' mebbe the left hand'll know what the right's doin' — but I ain't chuckin' my hat over the moon on the chance o' 'mebbe'.

"Today ye call yourself a privateer in Congress service. Where's your commission? Eh? Where's your letter-o'-marque? Ye've got none! No more has fifty other sea-thieves out o' rebel ports that's ravagin' our coast. Salem's fattenin' on stolen goods; so's Machias, Gloucester, Boston, all of 'em. D'ye tell me the Congress knows a whisper o' the thieves swarmin' acrost Fundy Bay in whaleboats, shallops, anythin' that'll float, an' lyin' in our lonely bays an' cricks for the first unsuspectin' fisherman or trader? In a week they've got a ship; an' a gun there an' a swivel there, and a bar'l o' powder somewhere else, an' away they go in the name o' Congress, robbin' and burnin' as it suits 'em, sendin' a boat to every defenceless settlement an' demandin' money an' supplies. Ye can't tell *me*! I've had to deal with your kind, talk polite to 'em, give 'em what they wanted these past three years — men that I'd ha' kicked off my wharf in or'nary times. I knew more'n one of 'em for what they were in my old days in Noo England — a lot o' gaol-birds an' wharf-rats turned pirate in the name o' Liberty! If that's liberty ye can have it an' be damned!"

"Then ye won't give up the guns?" drawled Captain Jonathan.

"Not while I can hold a gun myself," said Justice Bunt. He arose from the table, jarring the beer mugs and the candle, and slammed the tavern door behind him.

Outside, in the cool spring night, where the first frogs were piping cheerfully, a hand and a whisper caught him. Bridget Hewler, mysterious in the shawl drawn about her head, plucked him towards the stable shadow saying in her rapid Irish voice, "Wisht, Misther Bunt, sir. This way a bit if ye please!"

"Woman," Justice Bunt said sternly, "ye've harboured all kinds o' rascals in this den o' yours, but this . . . "

"Whisht!" cautioned Mrs. Hewler again. "Now don't ye come the pious deacon over me, Misther Bunt, sir, when there's matters more important. That Salem spalpeen's afther more than guns. I'll have ye know. His privateers ain't at Port Gambier by a matter o' leagues. They're layin' off Batthery P'int this minute . . . "

"What!"

"Not so loud. Wisht, for the love of God — would ye be havin' 'em burn the house over me head? There's two av 'em, the *Lizard* an' the *Civil Usage* — an' what kind av name is that for a boat? — an' anchored jist ayont the bar, they are. They've got two boat-crews lyin' at Misther Thripps' wharf, an' come moonrise an' the tide they're takin' out the Bermudy schooner that anchored in the sthream yistiddy."

"Ah!"

"An' the Bermudy captain such a gintleman, too! Gave me two shillin', he did. 'Wan for the dhrink, an' wan for the sound av a Kerry voice ag'in', says he. Now don't ye go jawin' me about harbourin' rogues an' desarters an' 'scaped rebel prisoners, Misther Bunt, when there's captains stay at me house. Besides," she chuckled, "where's the harm givin' a sup and a bite to some poor divil on the run from Halifax?"

"Hush, woman," Bunt growled. "You're one o' the kind that's made things hard for all of us. Is this a change o' heart?"

She laughed in the darkness.

"If ye must know, me poor husband was from Cape Cod, himself, an' 'Bridie', says he, 'niver thrust a Salem man.' There y'are. So help me God!"

It would be magnificent to record that Justice Bunt, mounted on his old brown horse, galloped up and down the town street on that April night in '78 crying 'To arms!' or 'The rebels are coming!' or some other shibboleth fervent and ringing that would look well in the history books. He did nothing of the sort. On foot, in his big muddy shoes, his wrinkled grey stockings, his rusty black breeches, his shabby blue coat, his old-fashioned round hat, Martin Bunt went quietly from door to door, knocking gently but insistently.

Most of the militiamen were abed, for in those simple days Oldport folk retired soon after candle-lighting. Each came blinking to the door, holding high the home-made dip of yellow tallow, showing a good deal of hairy leg below the flannel shirt, and heard a voice whispering hoarsely out of the darkness.

"It's me, Bunt. Put on your clo'es an' join me up the street. Mum's the word!"

Bunt avoided the lanes running down to the waterfront, thinking of the privateers-men lurking at Justice Thripps' wharf. He kept east along the main street, tacking from side to side as the militiamen's doors occurred, working towards the fish-lots and Battery Point. In five minutes the first aroused caught up with him and shared his labours. They assailed him with eager whispers but he told them nothing. In twenty minutes the street was full of flitting shadows and gentle knockings and the dry rustle of men's voices hushed and tense.

From the harbour not a sound. A faint mist hung over the water. In that haze lay the Bermuda schooner, further hidden by the jumbled sheds and stores and lofts of the waterfront. The moon was just rising.

Battery Point was covered in scrub spruce and fir, all gnarled and twisted by the sea winds. Great whinstone boulders stood amongst the trees. At the tip of the point was a small patch of greensward where the old cannon had stood before suspicious Governor Legge took them off to Halifax. This was where the river finally melted into the tide, and the harbour bar ran across like a threshold a few feet submerged. The ship channel lay close in with the point, a good stone's-throw, an easy musket shot.

Bunt's ox-cart was waiting in the clearing with the black man, Caesar, and Bunt's store clerk, Ogden. Caesar had taken off the ox-bells, wisely, for the big brutes stood swaying their heads in the great wooden yoke, uneasy at the presence of all these whispering men. Bunt threw off the old topsail which covered the wagon, and musket barrels gleamed in the moonlight. He and Ogden served them out. Caesar passed out flints, powder and shot.

Mr. Bunt paused with a musket in his hands, seeing an unexpected face in the queer light. "That you, Joel Thripps?"

"Yes," Joel said.

Bunt hesitated. "I might's well tell ye, Joel, we're goin' to stop some Salem picaroons from cuttin' out the Bermudy schooner. They've had two boats at your father's wharf all evenin', waitin' for the tide. They've slipped her cables by now."

"Well?" Joel said.

"Ye know your father's mind, Joel?"

"What's that to do with mine? Give me a gun!"

Bunt passed him the French musket without a further word.

"And one for my brother Zoeth."

Bunt passed down another.

"Where's your brother Reuben?" He made his voice casual. He knew all about young Reuben Thripps.

"Gone in the Salem privateer along o' your own brother Caleb."

"Um!"

The clearing was full of men in hastily donned homespuns, loading and priming the French muskets in the first flush of the moonrise. From the west, where the roofs of the wharf sheds were beginning to shine, came a distinct creak of thole-pins and the cautious dip and swirl of oars. It was not long before they saw the dim bulk of the Bermuda schooner swimming ghostlike out of the haze, with two boats ahead, towing laboriously. The Salem men had awaited full tide to get the deep-laden Bermudian over the bar, and so lost the benefit of the river current.

As the moon drank up the haze Bunt's militia could make out the privateers, a pair of schooners at anchor close in with the point, on the seaward side of the bar. There was a glimmer or two about the decks, and suddenly there came a rattle of handspikes and the rumble and shrilling of ungreased gun-trucks — the privateers casting loose their cannon for action. The militiamen grouped themselves about Bunt with expectant faces.

"Looks like our trouble's come to a head," he told them hoarsely. "But it may be we can work 'em out without bloodshed yet. Take post amongst the trees and rocks, lads, an' let me do the talkin'. My own brother's in one o' them boats. God knows I don't want his blood on my hands."

"Phoo! You reckon they'll give up the schooner without a fight?" Roger Hartley snorted.

"What's your mind on that, lads?" Bunt said quietly.

"Have it out with 'em — tonight!" demanded Bushnell, sergeant-major of the town company.

"Ay!" snapped Joel Thripps. "An end to this pull-devil pull-baker, Martin, and if hell's our portion — take it!"

"Easy to say, that," Bunt murmured. A savage note in all these voices distressed him. They had been tried too long, that was the trouble. The fanatic spirit of their

Pilgrim forefathers had welled up in them, but the Pilgrim patience was gone. Their mood was for fighting, and it mattered little whom they fought. It seemed to Martin Bunt that if the approaching boats had been a press-gang from one of His Majesty's ships they would have said the same things in the same way, with the same hard grip on the musket stocks. Upon such chances . . . but the voice of the Reverend Peleg Potter broke the silence and the trend of Bunt's thought in a stroke.

"The Philistines be upon thee!" cried the parson through his nose. He was cold sober now, and pointing a musket towards the water.

The privateers' boats were close and clearly visible in the moonlight. With their jerky efforts the tow-line rose to a taut bar, flinging a shower of glittering drops, and then drooped and dipped a long bight into the harbour again. Martin Bunt, unarmed, mounted a boulder at the waterside and hailed them.

"Ahoy!" answered a voice from the foremost boat. It was young Caleb Bunt. There was no mistaking that voice or that figure — for he stood up as he spoke. Bunt knew, with a chill at his heart, that this must have been arranged by the shrewd Cogsley in case of challenge. The boats ceased all movement and the pale faces of the oarsmen glimmered, facing all towards the dark hump of the point and the lone figure of Martin Bunt, clear against the moon.

"Caleb, tell your thievin' friends to give over towin' that vessel!"

"She's only a Bermudian," Caleb answered. "No skin off any back in Oldport."

The voice of Jonathan Cogsley spoke. "Give way ag'in, boys, hearty now!"

"I warn ye, Cap'n Cogsley, if ye don't give over we mean to stop ye!"

"You an' who else, Marty?" There was mockery in the Salem voice. The oars were dipping again.

"The town militia! Stop, I say!"

"Keep a-rowin', boys." Cogsley's voice, assured and amused. Towards the point he called, "Wouldn't fire on your own countrymen, Marty, would ye? Not you! Why, there's young Caleb in the boat astarn. Fire on your own brother? Not you, Marty! You go on home an' take the militia with ye, afore they git hurt." And he turned and hailed, "*Lizard*, ahoy!"

The nearer of the anchored schooners answered with a cheer ('a great amount of huzzaring & Strong Languige', Justice Bunt wrote afterwards) and lanterns appeared boldly on her deck, and men were plain, crouching about the cannon with glowing red dots of slow-match ready in the linstocks. She lay little more than a cable's length from the tip of the Point, with her guns trained on it and upon the looming wooden target of the lower town beyond.

"Fire a shot," Jonathan Cogsley declared, "an we'll blast ye off o' that p'int like hens off a roost, an' give your town a dose o' hot iron fer good measure. Go home, ye herrin-chokers! Home, ye Blue Noses! Home to bed an' prayers else ye suffer fer it, or my name ain't Jonathan!"

The oars were not missing a stroke. Martin turned his voice to the second boat.

"Caleb! Caleb, boy! Out o' that boat with ye, an' swim for it! On'y a few strokes to the rocks here, Caleb!"

"Not me!" Caleb cried, rowing hard with the rest.

"Caleb!" screamed the man on the rock, like a woman.

"Give way, boys, an' let the fool holler!" shouted Cogsley's voice. "Backs into it, now! Pull! Pull, my bully boys! Another cable's length an' she's over the bar an' ours. *Lizard*, there! *Lizard*, ahoy! Give us a toon!"

From the *Lizard's* deck came the rattle of a drum and the thin tweet of a fife playing *Yankee Doodle*, the old jingle of the French war that the New England rebels had made their own. It roused some thoughtful echoes in Martin Bunt. To that same tune, twenty years ago, he and his company of New England rangers had marched towards the walls of Louisbourg, fighting for King George. A jaunty song, born nobody knew where, it had a knack of picking up the feet when they were weary with the day's march and the musket heavy on the shoulder.

The words were silly, he thought. "Yengees' — that was the way the Mohawks pronounced 'English' in the early days. Now, Yankee betokened a separate race. All the story of the Revolution was summed up in the changed meaning of a word. And there was blood in that change, and sweat and tears, and all the pully-haul of ideals and greeds and passions that now convulsed the seaboard of a continent and no man yet understood.

What the outcome would be he could not guess, though he knew the deep sources of the rebel strength and saw the weakness of the King's in the very presence of these privateers, unmolested on the Nova Scotia coast. The permanent separation of the colonies and the mother country seemed no more possible than the separation of Nova Scotia and New England, or the fact that young Caleb sat yonder in the Salem boat under the menace of sixty Oldport muskets.

He had no notion that tonight's events in Oldport would prove a sign and portent for the hitherto neutral Yankees of Nova Scotia. Nor could he see the five years of fratricide to come, with a host of rebel craft raiding and pillaging the Nova Scotia coast, and a swarm of Nova-Scotiamen, keen of aim and bitter of heart, taking a savage price upon the coast of Massachusetts. Nor could he foresee the post-war hegira of loyalists from the States and their influence upon the affairs and destiny of his town and province, nor for that matter the swelling flood of Highland immigrants who would make the province truly a New Scotland in the half-century ahead.

All that was hidden in a future too uncertain and remote for a sane man's pondering. The present was problem enough, and for the present Martin Bunt could see nothing but the Bermuda schooner, her spars agleam in the moonlight, the phosphorescent swirl of busy oars, the Salem privateers beyond the bar, and somewhere above all these like a physical presence the shadow of his twin gods, Lor and Order, accusing and demanding.

"For the last time," he called resolutely, "will ye give over?"

There was no answer. The oars rose and fell. The Bermudian swam along the moon path towards the Point slowly and surely, like fate itself, and the drum and fife and the voices from the *Lizard* and *Civil Usage* began to chant again—

> *Yankee Doodle went to town,*
> *A-ridin' on a pony,*
> *He stuck a feather in his hat*
> *An' called it macaroni.*

"Fire!" said Justice Bunt, fetching the word deep from his boots. The French muskets shattered the night, and like an echo came the clash of tangled oars and a horrid chorus of screams, oaths, gasps and gurglings all mingled with a frantic splashing in the harbour water. Dimly, Bunt saw the Bermuda schooner lose way and then drift slowly into the tidal eddy within the Point, like a horse coming home instinctively to stable. The militia reloaded and fired now at random, Bushnell cursing to no purpose.

And now a ragged thunder from the anchored privateers, and a whirr and tearing in the scrub trees and bushes of the Point like a flight of woodcock driven up from cover, a voice crying out in pain amongst the rocks, a cut twig falling lightly upon Bunt's old round hat, a sound of hail on the roofs of fish-sheds and houses beyond, and torn shingles flying and falling in the silence afterwards like brittle autumn leaves. The two boats settled and vanished, oarsmen and all. Sixty well-aimed muskets at close range . . . Ah, Caleb, Caleb!

The privateers slipped their cables, well knowing the sound of their gunfire was a dangerous advertisement to seaward, where the king's ships prowled.

"We'll be back!" cried a defiant voice from the *Civil Usage* — a promise kept.

"We'll be waitin'!" answered Joel Thripps; and that promise was kept also.

Mr. Bunt had a notion to reprove Joel for this bravado, unseemly to his sober mind. But he kept silent. His cheeks were wet. The powder smoke had stung his eyes — or so he said.

# E. K. Brown

*Edward Killoran Brown (1905-1951) was born in Toronto and educated at the University of Toronto and the Sorbonne. He was Professor of English at Toronto, Manitoba, Cornell, and Chicago. His reputation as a critic is by no means confined to Canada or to his Canadian studies, for he authored three other well-received works:* Matthew Arnold: A Study in Conflict *(1948),* Willa Cather: A Critical Biography *(1953), completed by his friend Leon Edel, and* Rhythm in the Novel *(1950), a group of essays setting forth critical principles and terminology for the study of prose-fiction.*

*But Brown made two significant contributions to the development of Canadian literary studies. While he served as editor of the* University of Toronto Quarterly, *he instituted in 1936 the "Letters in Canada" series, which reviewed the year's publications by Canadians in literature, the humanities, and the social sciences. Secondly, his* On Canadian Poetry *(which won the Governor General's Award for Creative Non-Fiction in 1943) assessed the strengths and weaknesses of Canadian writing. Both the annual review and the book provided a kind of criticism of Canadian writing which had been previously lacking. Thus, they, along with A. J. M. Smith's anthology,* The Book of Canadian Poetry *(1943), helped prepare the way for both a new criticism of Canadian literature and its acceptance as part of the curriculum in Canadian high schools and universities.*

*The essay below, a preliminary version of the first chapter of* On Canadian Poetry, *describes the restricting influences of colonial, puritanical, and frontier values on both the writer and his audience. Although our society seems to be far different in this decade than it was when Brown gave this CBC Radio talk in 1938, the reader may detect around him these same attitudes in up-to-date garments.*

# The Contemporary Situation In Canadian Literature

This evening I have the pleasure of opening a series of broadcasts on the contemporary situation in Canadian literature, a series arranged by the Editorial Board of the *University of Toronto Quarterly*. In the talks which will follow, creative and critical writers will comment on the achievements and the disabilities which characterize Canadian writing in all its main types. Mr. Philip Child, the author of two moving and brilliantly executed novels, *The Village of Souls* and *God's Sparrows*, will speak of the situation in fiction; Professor W. E. Collin, who has written what I do not hesitate to call an epoch-making revaluation of Canadian poetry, will speak of the situation in poetry; Professor Arthur L. Phelps, a playwright and producer of plays as well as a critic, will speak of the situation in drama. It is a ground for special pleasure that Mr. Frederick Philip Grove, poet, novelist, critic, and one of the wisest observers of the Canadian scene, has agreed to examine that much neglected province of our literature, our criticism. Professor J. F. Macdonald will speak of Canadian humour and Professor Edgar McInnis will give an estimate of Canadian biographical writing. To Professor Watson Kirkconnell will fall what is probably the most onerous task of all: he will give a rapid view of a field about which most of us know nothing, a field of steadily growing significance in the national culture — the writings by Canadians in languages other than French or English. Unfortunately the examination of the literature of French Canada cannot come within the scope of the series. Finally, Mr. William Tyrrell, out of his long experience as a bookseller, will consider the actual taste in books of the Canadian public.

Tonight I wish to raise certain very general problems which must be reckoned with in a consideration of any type of literature in this country.

The first problem is economic. Economically the situation of our literature is and always has been unsound. No writer can live by the Canadian sales of his books. The president of one of our most active publishing companies has estimated the total profits on the sales of his Canadian books at one per cent; and I should be surprised to learn that any other Canadian publisher could tell a much more cheerful tale. The Canadian market for books is a thin one; and the market for stories and articles is little better. Our "quality" periodicals have a meagre circulation; none of them is heavily endowed; some of the best among them are unable to offer any payment whatever, and what the others pay would keep a writer in cigarettes and coffee and that is about all. Our "slick" magazines can, of course, do better; for all I know it may be true that if a writer for the "slicks" will work like an operative in a sweat-shop and if he has the rare knack of turning out exactly the right kind of story or article, he may manage to keep a roof over his head and even some butter in the pantry. But "slicks" are not literature and can do nothing to promote it; nothing more need be said of them. The essential economic fact is that, apart from them, a Canadian writer cannot earn his living by writing entirely, or even primarily, for the Canadian public.

The serious Canadian writer has a choice among three modes of combining the pursuit of literature with success in keeping alive. He may emigrate: that was the solution of Bliss Carman, and many have followed in his train. He may attempt to earn his living by some non-literary work: that was the solution of Archibald Lampman, and in our time many writers have adopted it. He may, while continuing to reside in Canada, become, economically at least, a member of another nation and civilization: that is the solution of Mr. Morley Callaghan. Each of these solutions is open to danger and objection.

The author who emigrates becomes in large part a loss to our literature. It is probable that in the end he will, like Henry James or Mr. T. S. Eliot, take out papers of citizenship in the country to which he has transferred his spiritual allegiance and in which he has found his economic security. How the powers of a writer are affected by his choice of expatriation as a solution is much too vast a problem to receive adequate consideration here. Only this I should like to say: the expatriate will find it more and more difficult to deal vigorously and vividly with the life of the country he has left. His colours will grow paler; his pictures of character and natural setting less accurate and less intimate. Sooner or later, if his work is to remain excellent, it is inevitable that he should immerse himself in the material and spiritual currents of his adopted country. Joseph Conrad did not write about Poland.

People often ask why a writer cannot satisfy himself with the solution of Archibald Lampman. Why, they inquire, with some impatience, does he not earn his living as a teacher or a clerk or a lighthouse-keeper and devote his leisure to writing? The answer to this question is an appeal to experience. Is it not true that when by a skilful economy of his leisure a man has written one or two successful books and thus has some security for a literary future he immediately gives up his unliterary job in order to have all his time for writing? Edwin Arlington Robinson preferred a cheerless hall-bedroom in New York with all his time for literature, rather than the measure of material comfort he could have had if he had retained the post Theodore Roosevelt arranged he should hold in the Customs. Time does not allow me to cite further examples. Whatever success a particular writer may have had in combining the practice of his art with earning a living in work which is more or less remote from letters, the suggestion that a literature of really commanding worth can be built up in the odd moments of busy men is an unrealistic suggestion, and one that shows alarming ignorance of the literary temper.

There remains a third solution, Mr. Callaghan's solution. It is possible to write primarily for an American or an English audience. Most of Mr. Callaghan's novels and shorter tales are about Toronto; but it seems to me at least that the Toronto which appears in them is not an individualized city, but simply a representative one. I mean that in reading Mr. Callaghan one has the sense that Toronto is being used not for the specific interest which it may have for Canadians but exclusively for the representative interest which it has for the larger North American audience. Similarly, in Miss Mazo de la Roche's novels one may well feel that the emphasis is always falling on those comparatively rare aspects of rural Ontario life which would appeal to an English audience. In the work of both these writers an alien audience has shaped the treatment of Canadian life. Whether this peculiarity has been injurious to the novelist's art as art does not concern the present question; but I do not think it even doubtful that it has been injurious to the development of literature in this country. Such fiction fails to contribute what one would hope to find in it — a stimulus to the maturing and defining of Canadian culture.

The considerations which I have been advancing all derive from the economic situation of the Canadian writer. But more serious even than the economic problem is what I shall call — loosely enough — the psychological problem. The attitude of the Canadian public towards Canadian books is far from sound. I am told that if a novel is to meet the expense of publication in this country it must sell close to two thousand copies, and that unless a novelist has had his reputation consecrated in London or New York, unless he has become a recognized purveyor of a definite kind of pleasure, he will not be able to dispose of more than one thousand copies of his novel in this country. There is a charge made against the Canadian public which I do not accept: the charge that Canadians do not buy books as generously as Americans or English people. I do not think this charge is true; but what does seem to be true is that the books Canadians buy are in the main good risks, best sellers. Reputations are not to be made in this country; they must be made somewhere else and then with our deeply engrained conservatism we ratify the judgments that more adventurous people have made.

Another vast question opens up at this point. What elements in the Canadian society are hostile to the development of a great literature? Only two such elements can be mentioned tonight. One is the colonialism which in so many ways determines the mould of our life and, for example, makes us reluctant to take risks, even in buying novels. It is a long time since in *Their Wedding Journey* William Dean Howells expressed his view of the harm done to our national life by colonial status. Howells was an accurate observer of life and he hated exaggeration; moreover he knew central and eastern Canada rather well. What he said is worth more attention than it has received. He said that any colony was and must be, in some respects, second-rate; the standard by which a colony judges is external, and therefore distorting, and, at least in part, irrelevant. I have no doubt that independence is a luxury which for reasons which have nothing to do with literature we cannot afford, and probably shall never be able to afford. On the other hand, I believe it should be frankly recognized that a colony — or a dominion (in matters of culture it is a distinction without a difference) — is not a likely nursery for a great literature. A great literature supposes that writers and readers alike have a deep interest in the kind of life which is to be found where they live. So far as I can judge, Canadians do not in the least prefer to read books about the farms of the West or the fishermen's villages of the Maritimes, or the industrial towns of Ontario, rather than books about life in Surrey or in Chicago. We are without an eager interest in the life about us; we should have that interest if we were an autonomous nation.

Colonialism is one element in our society hostile to the development of a great literature. I have time to mention one other. Most Canadians live at some distance from the frontier; but something of the frontier standards still clings to us. The effect which the standards of the frontier had on American literature of the last century has been carefully studied by literary historians. The essence of the effect can be concentrated in one sentence. Mark Twain, who was a spokesman for the frontier, used to refer to Henry James as Henrietta Maria. In that little capsule of insult he gave the frontier's summary judgment of what is too complicated, too rarefied to interest it. Walt Whitman, a man of much broader and deeper intelligence, said wisely that the

United States itself was the greatest American poem; that is to say, the literature of a country which was still in mind and temper on the frontier was in its deeds, in the raw. So it is with us today. Books are a luxury on the frontier. The test they have to meet is not a test that *Paradise Lost* or *Vanity Fair* can meet. When the day's emergency has been met and some leisure comes, a book, or as it more often is, a "slick" magazine, serves its purpose when it entertains, soothes, and relaxes for sleep. Literature has to be what Browning denied that his poems were — a substitute for a good cigar.

What I have been attempting to suggest with as little heat or bitterness as possible is that in this country the plight of literature is a painful one. People who dislike to face this truth have a facile answer. They say — and very intelligent people they often are, on other topics — : "If a Dickens begins to write in Canada, we shall greet him with a cheer, we shall buy his books by the scores of thousands, get him appointed to the Senate and ask the Crown to give him an O. M. Meanwhile don't bother us. You can't point to a single man of the quality of Dickens who has written in this country. So we haven't been neglecting any one of importance. Wait till our Dickens comes along, and then we'll show you that we know how to honour a great writer." With people who talk in some such way as I have tried to caricature, it is impossible to argue. They believe that a literature consists of the works of a few men of genius, and that you will get your literature when you catch your men of genius, and that there is no more to the problem.

Thinking of such a sort ignores an idea even more important than the idea of genius: the relation between a literature and the society in which it develops. I do not deny that at any time or in any place a single genius might emerge: no one can predict the ways of genius. But a single genius does not make a literature; he does not even help very much towards the making of a literature. I suppose it would give a strong passing stimulus to Canadian literature if a single Hardy could come to maturity in this country; but it would not be a lasting stimulus. A tradition of great literature will not emerge under social conditions which are hostile to it. In the long run it is the society which makes the literature.

I believe that a great literature is a flowering of a mature and adequate society. How the Canadian society is to become mature and adequate, a critic of literature cannot be expected to say; he must leave such considerations to the economist, the political philosopher, and others. Both for the literature and the society, however, something can be done by the nurture of a sound criticism. The literary criticism which goes on in Canada today is chiefly concerned with European subjects, and addressed to an international audience. It has little bearing on the problems of Canadian literature: and the central theme of an operative Canadian criticism must clearly be Canadian.

A recognition that in Canada we stand in need of a more effective criticism has led the editors of the *University of Toronto Quarterly* to publish an annual survey of Canadian literature. For three years now in *Letters in Canada*, to which we devote the greater part of our April issue, we have sought to supply a comprehensive survey of what is written in this country: in the course of time we hope that this undertaking may have a modest share in the diffusion of interest in Canadian literature, in the raising of aesthetic and intellectual standards in Canada,. and in the discovery of writers who might otherwise pass, for a time at least, neglected or misunderstood.

226

# Sinclair Ross

*James Sinclair Ross (1908-    ) was born near Prince Albert, Saskatchewan. He joined The Royal Bank of Canada when he finished high school and served in many Prairie towns before he was transferred to Montreal. He retired from banking in the late 1960s. His first novel,* As For Me and My House *(1941), was unfavourably received by the reviewers and the public, but since the late 1950s it has been accepted in critical circles as being among the most important Canadian novels. His collected short stories,* The Lamp at Noon and Other Stories *(1968), long-awaited in book form, have confirmed Ross's place as one of the leading craftsmen of this genre in Canadian writing.*

*These Prairie stories capture a moment in Canadian life that is now history, the tragic years of the 1930s when depression and drought made an already harsh life seem almost unbearable. The stories centre on the conflicts of interest which arise in families who live by the soil. For the men, working the land is life itself, and escape from it is never seriously questioned. The women, thinking of other lives, want a fuller life than that which they have made with their husbands. Those who can cope – with crop reverses, rain at the wrong time, and loneliness – survive by developing a right-relation to the land and to their families; those who cannot cope isolate themselves into illusion and madness. The stories about adolescents, however, end not unhappily, but rather with a sense of accomplishment in the characters' growing freedoms and greater responsibilities.*

*When Ross began writing in the 1930s, young fiction-writers were still confronted with the influences of naturalism, a philosophy which proposed that man was controlled by the forces of his biological inheritance and his social environment and claimed that he was usually a victim of his animal responses. Sandra Djwa has described several naturalistic elements in Ross's stories: human action presented as a reaction to natural events; the struggle for survival in which the tragic outcome rarely permits reconciliation between the characters; and the struggle against nature which becomes a test of endurance in which only the very strong survive.[1] Nevertheless, in spite of these elements and the sense of determinism which pervades the stories, Dr. Djwa concludes that the implied religious frame of reference, "even if only in terms of residual response",[2] suggests that Ross places significance in the endurance, dignity, and optimism with which his characters meet their reverses, and that these responses become their means of salvation. Such concerns indicate that the label "naturalistic",* applied casually to everything that Crane or Dreiser or Grove or Ross wrote, is misleading.

There are several techniques in Ross's stories which help to clarify his meaning. There is Ross's gift of capturing so accurately the speech and behaviour of his farmers and the look and feel of the landscape. Yet, this realistic description allows for metaphoric meanings as well. In the best realistic writing, the externals of life are always selected for their power of evoking the interior situation. For example, the opening paragraph of "The Lamp at Noon" sets for the reader the outer and inner "weather": the three-day wind which not only annoys Ellen, but underlines her growing inability to stay in the house with her baby. Even the sentence-rhythm conveys a mounting urgency:

> A little before noon she lit the lamp. Demented wind fled keening past the house: a wait through the eaves that died every minute or two. Three days now without respite it had held. The dust was thickening to an impenetrable fog.

Ross's use of irony suggests the complexity of character and of situation; again, in "The Lamp at Noon", the final paragraph contains ironies referring to the weather, the family group, and the relations between husband and wife. Such recurring forms of irony and ambivalence, William H. New concludes, "characterize reality in Ross's world".[3]

### Footnotes

[1] Sandra Djwa, "No Other Way: Sinclair Ross's Stories and Novels", Canadian Literature, No. 47 (Winter 1971), p. 51.
[2] Ibid., p. 63.
[3] William H. New, "Sinclair Ross's Ambivalent World", Canadian Literature, No. 40 (Spring 1969), p. 28.

# The Lamp At Noon

A little before noon she lit the lamp. Demented wind fled keening past the house: a wail through the eaves that died every minute or two. Three days now without respite it had held. The dust was thickening to an impenetrable fog.

She lit the lamp, then for a long time stood at the window motionless. In dim, fitful outline the stable and oat granary still were visible; beyond, obscuring fields and landmarks, the lower of dust clouds made the farmyard seem an isolated acre, poised aloft above a sombre void. At each blast of wind it shook, as if to topple and spin hurtling with the dust-reel into space.

From the window she went to the door, opening it a little, and peering towards the stable again. He was not coming yet. As she watched there was a sudden rift overhead, and for a moment through the tattered clouds the sun raced like a wizened orange. It shed a soft, diffused light, dim and yellow as if it were the light from the lamp reaching out through the open door.

She closed the door, and going to the stove tried the potatoes with a fork. Her eyes all the while were fixed and wide with a curious immobility. It was the window. Standing at it she had let her forehead press against the pane until the eyes were strained apart and rigid. Wide like that they had looked out to the deepening ruin of the storm. Now she could not close them.

The baby started to cry. He was lying in a home-made crib over which she had arranged a tent of muslin. Careful not to disturb the folds of it she knelt and tried to still him, whispering huskily in a sing-song voice that he must hush and go to sleep again. She would have liked to rock him, to feel the comfort of his little body in her arms, but a fear had obsessed her that in the dust-filled air he might contract pneumonia. There was dust sifting everywhere. Her own throat was parched with it. The table had been set less than ten minutes, and already a film was gathering on the dishes. The little cry continued, and with wincing, frightened lips she glanced around as if to find a corner where the air was less oppressive. But while the lips winced the eyes maintained their wide, immobile stare. "Sleep," she whispered again. "It's too soon for you to be hungry. Daddy's coming for his dinner."

He seemed a long time. Even the clock, still a few minutes off noon, could not dispel a foreboding sense that he was longer than he should be. She went to the door again — then recoiled slowly to stand white and breathless in the middle of the room. She mustn't. He would only despise her if she ran to the stable looking for him. There was too much grim endurance in his nature ever to let him understand the fear and weakness of a woman. She must stay quiet and wait. Nothing was wrong. At noon he would come — and perhaps after dinner stay with her a while.

Yesterday, and again at breakfast this morning, they had quarrelled bitterly. She wanted him now, the assurance of his strength and nearness, but he would stand aloof, wary, remembering the words she had flung at him in her anger, unable to understand it was only the dust and wind that had driven her.

Tense she fixed her eyes upon the clock, listening. There were two winds: the wind in flight, and the wind that pursued. The one sought refuge in the eaves, whimpering, in fear; the other assailed it there, and shook the eaves apart to make it flee again. Once as she listened this first wind sprang into the room, distraught like a bird that has felt the graze of talons on its wing; while furious the other wind shook the walls, and thudded tumbleweeds against the window till its quarry glanced away again in fright. But only to return — to return and quake among the feeble eaves, as if in all this dust-mad wilderness it knew no other sanctuary.

Then Paul came. At his step she hurried to the stove, intent upon the pots and frying-pan. "The worst wind yet," he ventured, hanging up his cap and smock. "I had to light the lantern in the tool shed too."

They looked at each other, then away. She wanted to go to him, to feel his arms supporting her, to cry a little just that he might soothe her, but because his presence made the menace of the wind seem less, she gripped herself and thought, "I'm in the right. I won't give in. For his sake too I won't."

He washed, hurriedly, so that a few dark welts of dust remained to indent upon his face a haggard strength. It was all she could see as she wiped the dishes and set the food before him: the strength, the grimness, the young Paul growing old and hard, buckled against a desert even grimmer than his will. "Hungry?" she asked, touched to a twinge of pity she had not intended. "There's dust in everything. It keeps coming faster than I can clean it up."

He nodded. "To-night though you'll see it go down. This is the third day."

She looked at him in silence a moment, and then as if to herself muttered broodingly, "Until the next time. Until it starts again."

There was a dark timbre of resentment in her voice now that boded another quarrel. He waited, his eyes on her dubiously as she mashed a potato with her fork. The lamp between them threw strong lights and shadows on their faces. Dust and drought, earth that betrayed alike his labor and his faith, to him the struggle had given sternness, an impassive courage. Beneath the whip of sand his youth had been effaced. Youth, zest, exuberance — there remained only a harsh and clenched virility that yet became him, that seemed at the cost of more engaging qualities to be fulfilment of his inmost and essential nature. Whereas to her the same debts and poverty had brought a plaintive indignation, a nervous dread of what was still to come. The eyes were hollowed, the lips pinched dry and colorless. It was the face of a woman that had aged without maturing, that had loved the little vanities of life, and lost them wistfully.

"I'm afraid, Paul," she said suddenly. "I can't stand it any longer. He cries all the time. You will go Paul — say you will. We aren't living here — not really living — "

The pleading in her voice now after its shrill bitterness yesterday made him think that this was only another way to persuade him. Evenly he answered, "I told you this morning, Ellen: we keep on right where we are. At least I do. It's yourself you're thinking about, not the baby."

This morning such an accusation would have stung her to rage; now, her voice swift and panting, she pressed on, "Listen, Paul — I'm thinking of all of us — you, too. Look at the sky — and your fields. Are you blind? Thistles and tumbleweeds — it's a desert, Paul. You won't have a straw this fall. You won't be able to feed a cow or a chicken. Please, Paul — say that we'll go away — "

"No, Ellen — " His voice as he answered was still remote and even, inflexibly in unison with the narrowed eyes, and the great hunch of muscle-knotted shoulder. "Even as a desert it's better than sweeping out your father's store and running his errands. That's all I've got ahead of me if I do what you want."

"And here — " she flared. "What's ahead of you here? At least we'll get enough to eat and wear when you're sweeping out his store. Look at it — look at it, you fool. Desert — the lamp lit at noon — "

"You'll see it come back," he said quietly. "There's good wheat in it yet."

"But in the meantime — year after year — can't you understand, Paul? We'll never get them back — "

He put down his knife and fork and leaned towards her across the table. "I can't go, Ellen. Living off your people — charity — stop and think of it. This is where I belong. I've no trade or education. I can't do anything else."

"Charity!" she repeated him, letting her voice rise in derision. "And this — you call this independence! Borrowed money you can't even pay the interest on — seed from the government — grocery bills — doctor bills — "

"We'll have crops again," he persisted. "Good crops — the land will come back. It's worth waiting for."

"And while we're waiting, Paul!" It was not anger now, but a kind of sob. "Think of me — and him. It's not fair. We have our lives too to live."

"And you think that going home to your family — taking your husband with you — "

"I don't care — anything would be better than this. Look at the air he's breathing. He cries all the time. For his sake, Paul. What's ahead of him here, even if you do get crops?"

He clenched his lips a minute, then with his eyes hard and contemptuous struck back, "As much as in town, growing up a pauper. You're the one who wants to go, Ellen — it's not for his sake. You think that in town you'd have a better time — not so much work — more clothes — "

"Maybe — " She dropped her head defencelessly. "I'm young still. I like pretty things."

There was silence now — a deep fastness of it enclosed by rushing wind and creaking walls. It seemed the yellow lamplight cast a hush upon them. Through the haze of dusty air the walls receded, dimmed, and came again. Listlessly at last she said, "Go on — your dinner's getting cold. Don't sit and stare at me. I've said it all."

The spent quietness in her voice was harder even than her anger to endure. It reproached him, against his will insisted that he see and understand her lot. To justify himself he tried, "I was a poor man when you married me. You said you didn't mind. Farming's never been easy, and never will be."

"I wouldn't mind the work or the scimping if there was something to look forward to. It's the hopelessness — going on — watching the land blow away."

"The land's all right," he repeated. "The dry years won't last forever."

"But it's not just dry years, Paul!" The little sob in her voice gave way suddenly to a ring of exasperation. "Will you never see? It's the land itself — the soil. You've plowed and harrowed it until there's not a root or fibre left to hold it down. That's why the soil drifts — that's why in a year or two there'll be nothing left but the bare clay. If in the first place you farmers had taken care of your land — if you hadn't been so greedy for wheat every year — "

She had taught school before she married him, and of late in her anger there had been a kind of disdain, an attitude almost of condescension, as if she no longer looked upon the farmers as her equals. He sat still, his eyes fixed on the yellow lampflame, and seeming to know how her words had hurt him she went on softly, "I want to help you Paul. That's why I won't sit quiet while you go on wasting your life. You're only thirty — you owe it to yourself as well as me."

Still he sat with his lips drawn white and his eyes on the lampflame. It seemed indifference now, as if he were ignoring her, and stung to anger again she cried, "Do you ever think what my life is? Two rooms to live in — once a month to town, and nothing to spend when I get there. I'm still young — I wasn't brought up this way."

Stolidly he answered, "You're a farmer's wife now. It doesn't matter what you used to be, or how you were brought up. You get enough to eat and wear. Just now that's all that I can do. I'm not to blame that we've been dried out five years."

"Enough to eat!" she laughed back shrilly, her eyes all the while fixed expressionless and wide. "Enough salt pork — enough potatoes and eggs. And look — " Springing to the middle of the room she thrust out a foot for him to see the scuffed old slipper. "When they're completely gone I suppose you'll tell me I can go barefoot — that I'm a farmer's wife — that it's not your fault we're dried out — "

"And look at these — " He pushed his chair away from the table now to let her see what he was wearing. "Cowhide — hard as boards — but my feet are so calloused I don't feel them any more."

Then hurriedly he stood up, ashamed of having tried to match her hardships with his own. But frightened now as he reached for his smock she pressed close to him. "Don't go yet. I brood and worry when I'm left alone. Please, Paul — you can't work on the land anyway."

"And keep on like this?" Grimly he buttoned his smock right up to his throat. "You start before I'm through the door. Week in and week out — I've troubles enough of my own."

"Paul — please stay — " The eyes were glazed now, distended a little as if with the intensity of her dread and pleading. "We won't quarrel any more. Hear it! I can't work — I just stand still and listen — "

The eyes frightened him, but responding to a kind of instinct that he must withstand her, that it was his self-respect and manhood against the fretful weakness of a woman, he answered unfeelingly, "In here safe and quiet — you don't know how well off you are. If you were out in it — fighting it — swallowing it — "

"Sometimes, Paul, I wish I were. I'm so caged — if I could only break away and run. See — I stand like this all day. I can't relax. My throat's so tight it aches — "

Firmly he loosened his smock from the clutch of her hands. "If I stay we'll only keep on like this all afternoon. To-morrow when the wind's down we can talk things over quietly."

Then without meeting her eyes again he swung outside, and doubled low against the buffets of the wind, fought his way slowly towards the stable. There was a deep hollow calm within, a vast darkness engulfed beneath the tides of moaning wind. He stood breathless a moment, hushed almost to a stupor by the sudden extinction of the storm and the incredible stillness that enfolded him. It was a long, far-reaching stillness. The first dim stalls and rafters led the way into cavern-like obscurity, into vaults and recesses that extended far beyond the stable walls. Nor in these first quiet moments did he forbid the illusion, the sense of release from a harsh, familiar world into one of immeasurable peace and darkness. The contentious mood that his stand against Ellen had roused him to, his tenacity and clenched despair before the ravages of wind, it was ebbing now, losing itself in the hover of darkness. Ellen and the wheat seemed remote, unimportant. At a whinney from the bay mare Bess he went forward and into her stall. She seemed grateful for his presence, and thrust her nose deep between his arm and body. They stood a long time thus, comforting and assuring each other.

For soon again the first deep sense of quiet and peace was shrunken to the battered

232

shelter of the stable. Instead of release or escape from the assaulting wind, the walls were but a feeble stand against it. They creaked and sawed as if the fingers of a giant hand were tightening to collapse them; the empty loft sustained a pipelike cry that rose and fell but never ended. He saw the dust-black sky again, and his fields blown smooth with drifted soil.

But always, even while listening to the storm outside, he could feel the tense and apprehensive stillness of the stable. There was not a hoof that clumped or shifted, not a rub of halter against manger. And yet, though it had been a strange stable, into which he had never set foot before, he would have known, despite the darkness, that every stall was filled. They too were all listening.

From Bess he went to the big grey gelding Prince. Prince was twenty years old, with rib-grooved sides, and high, protruding hipbones. Paul ran his hand over the ribs, and felt a sudden shame, a sting of fear that Ellen might be right in what she said. For wasn't it true — nine years a farmer now on his own land, and still he couldn't even feed his horses? What then could he hope to do for his wife and son?

There was much he planned. And so vivid was the future of his planning, so real and constant, that often the actual present was but half-felt, but half-endured. Its difficulties were lessened by a confidence in what lay beyond them. A new house for Ellen, new furniture, new clothes. Land for the boy — land and still more land — or education, whatever he might want.

But all the time was he only a blind and stubborn fool? Was Ellen right? Was he trampling on her life, and throwing away his own? The five years since he married her, were they to go on repeating themselves, five, ten, twenty, until all the brave future he looked forward to was but a stark and futile past?

She looked forward to no future. She had no faith or dream with which to make the dust and poverty less real. He understood suddenly. He saw her face again as only a few minutes ago it had begged him not to leave her. The darkness round him now was as a slate on which her lonely terror limned itself. He went from Prince to the other horses, combing their manes and forelocks with his fingers, but always still it was her face he saw, its staring eyes and twisted suffering. "See Paul — I stand like this all day. I just stand still — My throat's so tight it aches — "

And always the wind, the creak of walls, the wild lipless wailing through the loft. Until at last as he stood there, staring into the livid face before him, it seemed that this scream of wind was a cry from her parched and frantic lips. He knew it couldn't be, he knew that she was safe within the house, but still the wind persisted as a woman's cry. The cry of a woman with eyes like those that watched him through the dark. Eyes that were mad now — lips that even as they cried still pleaded, "See, Paul — I stand like this all day. I just stand still — so caged! If I could only run!"

He saw her running, pulled and driven headlong by the wind, but when at last he returned to the house, compelled by his anxiety, she was walking quietly back and forwards with the baby in her arms. Careful, despite his concern, not to reveal a fear or weakness that she might think capitulation to her wishes, he watched a moment through the window, and then went off to the tool shed to mend old harness. All afternoon he stitched and rivetted. It was easier with the lantern lit and his hands occupied. There was wind whining high past the tool shed too, but it was only wind.

He remembered the arguments with which Ellen had tried to persuade him away from the farm, and one by one he defeated them. There would be rain again — next year, or the next. Maybe she was right. Maybe in his ignorance he had farmed his land the wrong way, seeding wheat every year, working the soil till it was lifeless dust — but he would do better now. He would plant clover and alfalfa, breed cattle, acre by acre and year by year restore to his land its fibre and fertility. That was something to work for, a way to prove himself. It was ruthless wind, blackening the sky with his earth, screaming in derision of his labour, but it was not his master. Out of his land it had made a wilderness. He now, out of the wilderness, would make a farm and home again.

To-night he must talk with Ellen. Patiently, when the wind was down, and they were both quiet again. It was she who had told him to grow fibrous crops, who had called him an ignorant fool because he kept on with summer fallow and wheat. Now she might be gratified to find him acknowledging her wisdom. Perhaps she would begin to feel the power and steadfastness of the land, to take a pride in it, to understand that he was not a fool, but working for her future and their son's.

And already the wind was slackening. At four o'clock he could sense a lull. At five, straining his eyes from the tool shed doorway, he could make out a neighbour's buildings half a mile away. It was over — three days of blight and havoc like a scourge — three days so bitter and so long that for a moment he stood still, unseeing, his senses idle with a numbness of relief.

But only for a moment. Suddenly he emerged from the numbness; suddenly the fields before him struck his eyes to comprehension. They lay black, naked. Beaten and mounded smooth with dust as if a sea in gentle swell had turned to stone. And though he had tried to prepare himself for such a scene, though he had known since yesterday that not a blade would last the storm, still now, before the utter waste confronting him, he sickened and stood cold. Suddenly like the fields he was naked. Everything that had sheathed him a little from the realities of existence: vision and purpose, faith in the land, in the future, in himself — it was all rent now, all stripped away. "Desert," he heard her voice begin to sob. "Desert, you fool — the lamp lit at noon!"

In the stable again, measuring out their feed to the horses, he wondered what he would say to her to-night. For so deep were his instincts of loyalty to the land that still, even with the images of its betrayal stark upon his mind, his concern was how to withstand her, how to go on again and justify himself. It had not occurred to him yet that he might or should abandon the land. He had lived with it too long. Rather was his impulse to defend it still — as a man defends against the scorn of strangers even his most worthless kin.

He fed his horses, then waited. She too would be waiting, ready to cry at him, "Look now — that crop that was to feed and clothe us! And you'll still keep on! You'll still say 'Next year — there'll be rain next year'!"

But she was gone when he reached the house. The door was open, the lamp blown out, the crib empty. The dishes from their meal at noon were still on the table. She had perhaps begun to sweep, for the broom was lying in the middle of the floor. He tried to call, but a terror clamped upon his throat. In the wan, returning light it seemed that even the deserted kitchen was straining to whisper what it had seen. The tatters of the storm still whimpered through the eaves, and in their moaning told the desolation of

234

the miles they had traversed. On tiptoe at last he crossed to the adjoining room; then at the threshold, without even a glance inside to satisfy himself that she was really gone, he wheeled again and plunged outside.

He ran a long time — distraught and headlong as a few hours ago he had seemed to watch her run — around the farmyard, a little distance into the pasture, back again blindly to the house to see whether she had returned — and then at a stumble down the road for help.

They joined him in the search, rode away for others, spread calling across the fields in the direction she might have been carried by the wind — but nearly two hours later it was himself who came upon her. Crouched down against a drift of sand as if for shelter, her hair in matted strands around her neck and face, the child clasped tightly in her arms.

The child was quite cold. It had been her arms, perhaps, too frantic to protect him, or the smother of dust upon his throat and lungs. "Hold him," she said as he knelt beside her. "So — with his face away from the wind. Hold him until I tidy my hair."

Her eyes were still wide in an immobile stare, but with her lips she smiled at him. For a long time he knelt transfixed, trying to speak to her, touching fearfully with his fingertip the dust-grimed cheeks and eyelids of the child. At last she said, "I'll take him again. Such clumsy hands — you don't know how to hold a baby yet. See how his head falls forward on your arm."

Yet it all seemed familiar — a confirmation of what he had known since noon. He gave her the child, then, gathering them both up in his arms, struggled to his feet and turned towards home.

It was evening now. Across the fields a few spent clouds of dust still shook and fled. Beyond, as if through smoke, the sunset smouldered like a distant fire.

He walked with a long dull stride, his eyes before him, heedless of her weight. Once he glanced down and with her eyes she still was smiling. "Such strong arms, Paul — and I was so tired with carrying just him. . . "

He tried to answer, but it seemed that now the dusk was drawn apart in breathless waiting, a finger on its lips until they passed. "You were right, Paul — " Her voice came whispering, as if she too could feel the hush. "You said tonight we'd see the storm go down. So still now, and the sky burning — it means to-morrow will be fine."

# The Outlaw

She was beautiful but dangerous. She had thrown one man and killed him, had thrown another and broken his collar bone; and my parents, as if they knew what the sight of her idle in her stall was doing to me, never let a day go by without repeating details — everything from splints and stitches to the undertaker — of the painful and untimely end in store for me should I ever take it into my foolish young head to try to ride her.

"I've got troubles enough without having you laid up with broken bones and doctor's bills. She's a sly one, mind, and no good's ever come of her.

"Besides, you're only turned thirteen, and a grown man — a regular cowboy at that — would think twice before tackling her. Another year and then we'll see. You'll both be that much older. Meanwhile nobody expects it of you."

Meanwhile though, Isabel was a captive, pining her heart away. Week after week she stamped and pawed, nosed the hay out of her manger contemptuously, flung up her head and pored out wild, despairing neighs into the prairie winds and blizzards streaming past. It was mostly, of course, for my benefit. She had sized me up, evidently, as soft-hearted as well as faint-hearted, and had decided that there was just a chance that I might weaken and go riding. Her neighs, just as intended, tormented and shamed me.

She was a good horse, but a reprobate. That was how we came to own her. At the auction sale where she was put up her reputation as a killer spread among the crowd, and my father got her cheap. He was such a practical, level-headed man, and she was so obviously a poor investment, that I suspect it was because of me he bought her. As I stood at his side and watched them lead her out, poised, dramatic, radiant, some of the sudden desire that overwhelmed me must have leaped from my face and melted him.

"Anyway, she's a bargain", he explained that evening at the supper table. "I can always sell her and at least get back what I paid. But first I want to see what a taste of good hard work will do."

He tried it. His intention was to work her on the land a month or two, just till she was tamed down to make an all-round, serviceable saddle-horse, but after a painful week of half-days on the plough he let her keep her stall. She was too hard on his nerves, he said, straining ahead and pulling twice her share. She was too hard on his self-respect, actually — the slender limbs, the imperious head. For she was a very lovely reprobate. Twenty years of struggle with the land had made him a determined, often hard man, but he couldn't bring himself to break her spirit with the plough.

She was one horse: she was all horses. Thundering battle-chargers, fleet Arabians, untamed mustangs — sitting beside her on her manger, I knew and rode them all. There was history in her shapely head and burning eyes. I charged with her at Balaklava, Waterloo, scoured the deserts of Africa and the steppes of the Ukraine. Conquest and carnage, trumpets and glory! She understood, and carried me triumphantly.

To approach her meant enchantment. She was coal-black, gleaming, queenly. Her mane had a ripple and her neck an arch. And somehow, softly and mysteriously, she was always burning. The reflection of her glossy hide, whether of winter sunshine or yellow lantern light, seemed to glow from some fierce secret passion. There were moments when I felt the whole stable charged with her, as if she were the priestess of her kind, in communion with her deity.

For all that, though, she was a very dangerous horse, as my parents constantly reminded me. Facts didn't lie. A record was a record.

Isabel did her utmost to convince me that the record was a slander. With nuzzling, velvet lips she coaxed and pleaded, whispered that the delights of fantasy and dream were but as shadows beside the exhilarations of reality. Only try reality — slip her bridle on. Only be reasonable — ask myself what she would gain by throwing me. After all, I was turned thirteen. It wasn't as if I were a *small* boy.

And then, temptress, she bore me off to the mountaintop of my vanity, and with all the world spread out before my gaze, talked guilefully of prestige and acclaim.

Over there, three miles away, was the schoolhouse. What a sensation to come galloping up on her, the notorious outlaw, instead of jogging along as usual on bandy-legged old Pete. What a surprise for Millie Dickson, whose efforts to be loyal to me were always defeated by my lack of daring. For it was true: on the playground I had only a fair rating. I was butterfingers when it came to ball, and once in a fight I had cravenly turned tail and had run. How sweet to wipe out all the ignominy of my past, to be deferred to by the other boys to bask in Millie's favour.

And over there, seven miles away, was town, where fairs were sometimes held, and races run. On such a horse I naturally would win, and, for all I knew the prize might be a hundred dollars. Well then — supposing I could treat Millie to ice-cream and a movie!

Here she would pause a moment, contemptuous of one so craven, then whinny shrill in challenge to some other rider, with heart and spirit equal to her own. There was no one, of course, to hear the challenge, but still it always troubled me. Johnny Olsen, for instance, the show-off Swede who had punched my nose and had made me run — supposing he should come along and say, "I'll ride her for you — I'm not scared." What kind of figure then would I cut? What would Millie say?

Isabel's motives, in all this, were two. The first was a natural, purely equine desire to escape from her stall and stretch her legs. The second, equally strong, was a perverse, purely feminine itch to bend me to her will.

For it was a will as imperious as her head. Her pride was at stake: I had to be reduced. With the first coaxing nuzzle of her lips she had committed herself to the struggle, and since as a male I was still at such a rudimentary stage it became doubly imperative that she emerge the victor. Defeat by a man would have been bitter but endurable. Defeat by a mere boy would have been sheer humiliation.

On account of the roads and the weather, school was closed for two months after Christmas, and as the winter wore on it became increasingly difficult to resist her. A good deal of the time my father was away with wheat to town, and it was three miles to the nearest neighbour, where there was another boy. I had chores, books and the tool shop to keep me busy, but still there were long hours of idleness. Hungry for companionship, it was only natural that I should turn to Isabel. There were always her tail and mane to comb out when we wearied of each other conversationally.

My association with her, of course, was virtual disobedience, but still, despite conscience and good intentions, I lingered. Leaving her was always difficult, like leaving a fair or picnic, and going home to hunt the cows.

And then one clear sharp day, early in February, Millie Dickson and her mother drove over to spend the afternoon, and suddenly the temptation was too much for me.

They came early, country-fashion, so that Mrs. Dickson would have time for a long talk and tea, and be home again before nightfall. My father was absent, and when they drove up in their bright red cutter I hurried out to take the horse. Mrs. Dickson was generous in her thanks, and even Millie smiled invitingly from beneath her frosted yellow curls. She had always liked me well enough. It was just that my behaviour at school made it difficult for her to be my champion.

I was shy when I returned to the house, but very happy. We all sat in the kitchen, not only because it was the largest, warmest room, but also because it gave my mother a chance to entertain her guests and at the same time whip up fresh biscuits and a cake in their honour. Mrs. Dickson asked so many friendly questions that I squirmed with pleasure. What could it mean but that at home Millie did champion me, that she suppressed the discreditable and spoke only of the best!

She and I talked, too. We leafed through old magazines, gossiped about school, speculated on the new teacher, and gradually established a sense of intimacy and good-will that made me confident my past was all forgotten, my future rosy and secure. For an hour it was like that, and then, as nearly always happened when my mother had visitors, the delinquencies and scandals of the community moved in, and the kitchen became a place unfit for innocent young ears.

There must have been a considerable number of these delinquencies. It was indeed a very upright community, but it must have had its wayward side. Anyhow, surveying my entire boyhood, I am sure I could count on the fingers of one hand the times I was *not* sent out to chop wood or look for eggs when my mother and her friends got started on the neighbours. Usually, from the trend of the talk I had a fair idea who it was who had been up to what, but now, absorbed in my relationship with Millie, I heard nothing till my mother tapped my shoulder.

"Come along", she said brightly, affecting concern. "It's too fine a day for you and Millie to be sitting in the house. Run out and play in the fresh air, so you'll be ready for your tea."

But at thirteen you don't play with a girl. You can neither skin the cat up in the loft among the rafters, nor turn somersaults down a strawstack. I did suggest taking the .22 and going after rabbits, but the dear little bunnies were so sweet, she said, she couldn't bear to hurt them. Naturally, therefore, after a chilly and dispiriting turn or two around the barnyard, I took her in to visit Isabel.

Isabel rose to the occasion. She minced and pawed, strained at her halter shank to let us see how badly she wanted to be taken out, then nipped our sleeves to prove her gentle playfulness. And finally, to remind us that despite such intimacies she was by no means an ordinary horse, she lifted her head and trumpeted out one of her wild, dramatic neighs.

Millie was impressed. "The wonderful way she holds her head", she said, "just like a picture. If only you could ride her to school."

"Nobody rides her — anywhere", I replied curtly. "She's an outlaw." And then, as Millie's mouth drooped in disappointment, "At least nobody's *supposed* to ride her."

She jumped for it. "You mean you do ride her? And she doesn't throw you?"

"Of course", I conceded modestly, "she's very easy to ride. Such speed — and smooth as a rocking-chair. When you look down the ground's just like water running past. But she could throw me all right if she had a mind to."

Millie sighed. "I'd like so much, though, to *see* you ride her. To-day — isn't it a good chance, with them in there talking and your father away in town?"

I hesitated, overcome by a feeling of fright and commitment, and then Isabel joined in. She begged and wheedled, looked so innocent, at the same time so hurt and disappointed, that Millie exclaimed she felt like going for a ride herself. That settled it. "Stand at the door and see no one's coming", I commanded. "I'll put her bridle on."

Isabel practically put it on herself. She gave a shrill, excited whinny as I led her out, pranced like a circus pony, pushed me along still faster with her nose. "No", I answered Millie shortly, "I don't use the saddle. She rides easy. And in case she turns mean I won't get tangled in the stirrups."

With a flutter in her voice Millie said, "Do you really think you should?" and in response I steeled myself, nonchalantly turning up the collar of my sheepskin. "At the rate she goes", I explained, "the wind cuts through you like a knife."

But I reflected, "There's plenty of snow. At the worst it will only be a spill."

Isabel stood quite still till I was mounted. She even stood still a moment longer, letting me gather myself, take a firm grip of the reins, crouch low in readiness. Then with a plunge, a muscular spasm, she was off. And it was true: the wind cut sharp and bitter like a knife, the snow slipped past like water. Only in her motion was there a difference. She was like a rocket, not a rocking-chair.

It was nearly a mile, though, before I began to understand properly what was happening. Isabel the outlaw — the horse that had killed a man, that people talked about for fifty miles — here was I just turned thirteen, yet riding her. And an immense pride filled me. Cold as I was I pushed my sheepskin collar down and straightened recklessly to feel the rush of wind. I needed it that way, a counteracting sting of cold to steady the exhilaration.

We had gone another mile before I remembered Millie, and at once, as if sensitive to my concern, Isabel drew up short for breath. She didn't drop to a trot or walk as an ordinary horse would have done, but instead, with the clean grace and precision of a bird alighting on a branch, came smoothly to a halt. And for a moment or two, before starting home again, she rested. The prairie spread before us cold and sparkling in the winter sunlight, and poised and motionless, ears pricked forward, nostrils faintly quivering, she breathed in rapturously its loping miles of freedom.

And I, responsive to her bidding, was aware as never before of its austere, unrelenting beauty. There were the white fields and the blue, metallic sky, the little splashes here and there of yellow strawstack, luminous and clear as drops of gum on fresh pine lumber, the scattered farmsteads brave in their isolation, the gleam of sun and snow. I wanted none of it, but she insisted. Thirteen years old and riding an outlaw — naturally I wanted only that. I wanted to indulge my vanity, to drink the daring and success of my exploit in full-strength draughts, but Isabel, like a conscientious teacher at a fair, dragging you off to see instructive things, insisted on the landscape.

"Look", she said firmly, "while it's here before you, so that to the last detail it will remain clear. For you, too, some day there may be stalls and halters, and it will be a good memory."

But only for a moment or two, and then we were off again. She went even faster going home. She disdained and rebelled against her stall, but the way she whipped the wind around my ears you would have thought she suddenly had conceived a great affection for it. It was a strong wind, fiercely cold. There was a sharp sting in my ears a minute, then a sudden warmth and ease. I knew they were frozen, but there wasn't time to worry. I worked my collar up, crouched low again. Her mane blew back and lashed my face. Before the steady blast of wind my forehead felt as if the bone were wearing thin. But I didn't mind. I was riding her and holding on. I felt fearless, proud, mature. All the shame and misgivings of the past were over. I was now both her master and my own.

* * * * * *

And then she was fifteen or twenty feet away, demurely watching me, and I was picking myself up and spitting snow.

She had done it with the utmost skill, right head first into a snowdrift where I wouldn't hurt myself, less than a quarter of a mile from home.

And not even to toss her head and gallop off so that Millie would think she had done it in a fit of fright or meanness. Just to stand there, a picture of puzzled innocence, blandly transferring all the blame to me. What was wrong? Just when we were getting on so splendidly — why on earth had I deserted her?

For in her own way, despite her record, Isabel was something of a moralist. She took a firm stand against pride that wasn't justified. She considered my use of the word 'master' insufferably presumptuous. Being able to ride an outlaw was not the same thing at all as being accorded the privilege of riding one, and for the good of my soul it was high time that I appreciated the distinction.

She stood still, sniffing in my direction, until I had almost reached her, then gave a disdainful snort and trotted home. At the stable door she was waiting for me. I approached limping — not because I was hurt, but because with Millie standing back a little distance, I felt it looked better, made my tumble less an occasion for laughter — and as if believing me Isabel thrust her nose out, all condolence and touched me tenderly. From the bottom of her heart she hoped I wouldn't be so unfortunate another time. So far as she was concerned, however, she could make no promises. There had been one fall, she explained to Millie, and there might easily be another. The future was entirely up to me. She couldn't be responsible for my horsemanship.

"Your ears are frozen", Millie changed the subject. "And your mother knows everything — she's going to let your father handle you."

I looked at her accusingly, but in a self-righteous tone she explained, "She called you twice, and then came out to see why you didn't answer. Just in time to see it happen. I'll rub your ears with snow if you like before we go in for tea."

It was a good tea, but I didn't eat much. My ears were not only swelling badly and turning purple; they were also starting to drip. My mother pinned a wash-cloth to each shoulder, then sprinkled on talcum powder. She said nothing, but was ominously calm — saving herself up, I didn't doubt, until we were alone. I was in misery to escape upstairs to a mirror, but she insisted, probably as a kind of punishment, that I stay and finish my tea. Millie didn't eat much either, and kept her eyes turned fastidiously away.

When finally Mrs. Dickson and Millie were gone — and as an additional humiliation I wasn't allowed out to bring round their horse — my mother replaced the wash-cloths with towels. She was silent, still white-lipped, and it struck me that perhaps the condition of my ears was really serious. "They're smarting bad — and throbbing", I said hopefully. "It must have been colder than I thought."

240

"It must have been", she agreed. "Go up to your room now out of my way till supper time. Anyhow, I'd better talk to your father before he sees you."

I knew then that she was as afraid of what was in store for me as I was. Her expression remained stern, but there was a softness in her voice, a note of anxiety. It was a good sign, but also a bad one. It meant that she was an ally, however disappointed and indignant; it also meant that she expected my father's anger to be explosive.

Upstairs, swollen and tender as they were, I gave my ears a brisk rubbing. They were already worse — a darker, more alarming purple, and they might get me out of a hiding.

While waiting I also rehearsed a number of entrances, a number of defences, but at the last minute abandoned all of them. The heat in my ears as I went downstairs was spreading like a prairie fire, and when I entered the kitchen there was such a blaze of it across my eyes that I could make out my father only as a vague, menacing form. A desperate resolve seized me: should he so much as threaten the razor strap I would ride away on Isabel and be lost to them forever.

But instead of pouncing he looked me over critically a minute, then hitched his chair to the table and began buttering a piece of bread. "Some bronco buster!" he said at last, in a weary, disillusioned voice. "All you need now is a ten-gallon."

"I didn't have the saddle — and she stopped short and shied." My voice climbed defensively. "I had been sticking on all right, though — four miles or more."

"Anyhow", he said resignedly, "you've got yourself a pretty pair of ears."

I raised a quick, self-conscious hand to touch them, and my mother assured me, "They're still there all right — don't worry! They made a hit with Millie, too, judging by the look on her face. I think she'll be seeing them to-night in her sleep."

"But the mare", my father interrupted in a man-to-man tone, abruptly cold-shouldering my mother, "how did you find her? Mean as she's supposed to be?"

"Not mean at all. Even when I was getting on, she stood and let me."

"Next time, just the same, you'd better play safe and use a snaffle. I'll hunt one up for you. It won't hurt her so long as she behaves."

"The next time!" my mother cried. "Talking about the next time when you ought to deal with him. She's no fit horse for a boy. If nobody'll buy her you ought to give her away, before she breaks somebody else's neck."

She went on for a long time like that, but I didn't pay much attention. Pride — that was all it amounted to — pride even greater than mine had been before I landed in the snowdrift. It sent me soaring a minute, took my breath away, but it also brought a shiver of embarrassment and shame. How long, then, had I kept them waiting? How many times in the last few months had they looked at me and despaired?

"One thing", my mother declared with finality, "you're not riding her to school. The things I'd be thinking and seeing all day — I just couldn't stand it."

"You hear", my father agreed. "I'll not have you carrying on with a lot of young fools as crazy as yourself — being a good fellow, like as not, and letting them all ride her."

I was about to protest — as if any of them dared or could ride Isabel — but instead, remembering in time, went on with my supper. Outwardly impassive, I was sky-high again within. Just as Isabel herself had always said, what a sensation to ride

241

foaming up to school at a break-neck, hair-raising gallop. In the past I had indulged the prospect sparingly. Indeed, with so many threats and warnings in my ears, it had never been a prospect at all, but only a fantasy, something to be thought about wishfully, like blacking both of Johnny Olsen's eyes at once, or having five dollars to spend. Now, though, everything was going to be different. Now, in their peculiar, parental idiom, they had just given their permission, and Isabel and the future were all mine. Isabel and Millie! In accompaniment to a fervent resolve to be worthy of them both, my ears throbbed happily.

# John Glassco

*The autobiography written in early or mid-career is peculiar to twentieth-century writers and can be related to their interest in experimental forms and subjects during the 1914-1940 period. John Glassco's* Memoirs of Montparnasse *(1970) is in the company of autobiographical novels such as James Joyce's* Portrait of the Artist as a Young Man *(1914), Hemingway's* In Our Time *(1925), and Frederick Philip Grove's* A Search for America *(1927); and autobiographies such as E. E. Cumming's* The Enormous Room *(1922), Robert Graves's* Goodby to All That *(1929), and Malcolm Cowley's* Exile's Return *(1934). The "Extract from an Autobiography" appeared in the American avant-garde magazine* This Quarter *in 1929, a Paris-based journal which also published Callaghan and Knister. The writing of an autobiography at twenty naturally raises questions about the author's ego as much as the nature of his experiences. Some of the writers mentioned above are dealing with traumatic experiences such as war, death at close hand, or emigration. All of them are concerned with the role of the artist or with his relation to the world around him or to his inner world of art. Similarly, Glassco's autobiography is about the development of an artist.*

*John Glassco was born in Montreal in 1909 and educated at McGill. He left college to move to Paris where he would be able to mix with other artists and writers in exile and thus prepare himself for the literary life. His travels were cut short when he developed tuberculosis and had to return home. The "Extract" provided the first three chapters of* Memoirs of Montparnasse, *in which Glassco explains that "I wanted to compose my own* Confessions of a Young Man *à la George Moore [published in 1888 when Moore was 36] and felt I simply could not wait, as Moore did, for the onset of middle age. The rest of the book was written in the Royal Victoria Hospital in Montreal during the three months of 1932-3, when I was awaiting a crucial operation...."* [1]

*For many years Glassco has lived on a farm in Foster, in the Eastern Townships of Quebec. In his poetry,* The Deficit Made Flesh *(1958) and* A Point of Sky *(1964), a dominant theme is mutability, a favourite motif of artists through the ages who have perceived that the ravages of time and change in men's affairs may lead to despair. Glassco's attitude, however, is not pessimistic for he finds value in man's resilience and in the permanence in art. He has edited* English Poetry in Quebec *(1965), the proceedings of a poetry conference held in Foster; and he has published several novels under pseudonyms as well as completing Aubrey Beardsley's story of Tannhauser,*

Under the Hill *(1959). In 1961 Glassco won the Province of Quebec Prize for literature in English.*

*The chief problem for the youthful autobiographer is to detach himself sufficiently from his material to retain the interest and sympathy of the reader. Glassco uses the devices commonly associated with fiction — narrative, characterization, and dialogue — to create a tangible world around the* persona *(John Glassco as a character in his own writing) who tells the story. This fictional self emerges as a self-consciously sophistic- ated, good-humoured young Montrealer determined to have his apprenticeship on terms quite different from those acceptable to his parents, but very similar to those apprenticeships which other aspiring young writers of the 1920s found indispensable. Self-imposed exile to Paris was, fortunately, glamourous and essential. Our judgment of his work, then, should not be concerned with measuring how much happened to him, but with the value he gives to the experiences he selects as important to his life.*

### Footnote

[1] *John Glassco*, Memoirs of Montparnasse *(Toronto: Oxford, 1970), p. xiii.*

# Extract From An Autobiography

In the winter of 1928, George Graham and I were living in an apartment on Metcalfe Street in Montreal. We were working in the Sun Life Assurance Company of Canada, and we have many times since then agreed that that month and a half was the most wretched period of our lives. To get up at eight o'clock of a Canadian winter morning, to bathe insufficiently in a small bathtub which neither of us ever had the courage to clean, to dress without any attention to an individual appearance, and to stumble down the street with our cheekbones nipped by the frosty wind, all these things might have been endured more easily had there not been the prospect of the long day's work before us.

I had entered the employment of the Company for reasons which, at the time, seemed to justify my doing anything. The stupidity and pettiness of McGill University disgusted me greatly, and my father and mother could not understand why I was unable to ignore it all and merely bend to my books. One episode in my dealings with the teaching staff of McGill comes to my mind, when an instructor with whom I was taking a course of writing, passed criticism on a short story of mine with the words: "After all, it is only the work of a night". I did not ask him if he considered himself any the less because he owed his being to activities of an even shorter duration, but begged him to give me a fuller appreciation of the story. He then showed me that his understanding of it extended to the name and sex of the principal character.

On my telling my father that I refused to go to college any longer (I was then seventeen years old, and starting my third year), and would he allow me to write, I was told I was a great disappointment to him and to my mother, that I was ungrateful and lacking in manliness, and that I could go to work; I would be allowed to remain at home. Thus it was that at this period of my relations with my family that I decided to leave the house and live with my dearest friend. It was a fine gesture and took them quite by surprise.

In return for his services at the Sun Life Assurance Company George received ninety dollars a month, and I eighty. Neither he nor I had ever worked in an office before, but the difference of ten dollars in our monthly cheques was due to George's having attended that same university of McGill for two years longer than I had. These were miserable enough sums to live on, but our condition was bettered considerably through the financial help of two of our acquaintances, who when they heard that we were taking an apartment, put on their dark overcoats and bowler hats and visited us with a proposal — that they should each of them pay ten dollars of our rent every month for the privilege of using the room on certain nights. Their manner of making this proposal was dark and strange, as if they were plotting to overthrow the Dominion, and they rigorously avoided any vulgarity in speech. George and I were more than glad to take their money, although we found it hard to repress our smiles as these gay rounders gazed craftily around the room, surveying the shutters, curtains, locks and bolts. Indeed, in a moment of merriment I leapt upon the bed, bouncing up and down several times, and crying, "You see, it is solid and sound!" They were greatly upset, and left as soon as possible after the business had been transacted.

We found the extra twenty dollars a fine addition to our monthly income, and we were hardly discommoded by having to remain away from our apartment until late on certain nights of the week — less so than we had at first thought, when it transpired that one of the men was never in the place, undoubtedly owing to the fact that he could obtain no one who would accompany him thither. This, however, he would not admit, continuing to pay us out his money in an embarrassed silence when pressed for it. I remembered him at preparatory school many years ago, when he had won a medal for being the best boy in the school, and it amused me to reflect that in spite of all his evil intentions he was still fulfilling the role.

After a month or so I patched up a peace with my father, with whom I pleaded that I be given an allowance which he could afford, and be left to my own devices.

"But I am not going to have you doing nothing," he said to me, "because I don't believe that idleness makes for happiness. Why don't you study English Literature, or some foreign language?"

After a great deal of hypocrisy on my part, and of generosity on his, he consented to give me a hundred dollars a month allowance for seven years. I was greatly touched by this, and overcome with delight, although I do not believe that I would have been so fortunate had I not said things about myself, my ambitions and literature that make me blush when I recall them. I left the presence of my father with a mixture of joy and shame.

245

"It is awfully difficult to know what to do; I've never had any experience of bringing up boys with literary aspirations — there's never been one in the family," said my father.

After a great deal of argument and pleading I persuaded George to leave the hated offices of the Sun Life, and agree to come with me to Paris, where we could both live more cheaply than anywhere else. Before he had finally agreed, we had sat many evenings in the Traymore Cafeteria, I urging, he remaining silent and thinking of my financial good.

"But George, you know that I cannot go to Paris without you. I can go nowhere without you. To think of you living alone here, without me whom you love so much, sweating in the policy vaults of that organization down the next street, and coming in here by yourself in the evening, looking around — do you think I could enjoy myself in Paris, had I ten women in my bed every night?" I delivered this earnestly.

George sunk himself a little further in his chair, his mouth puffing out, and his eyebrows drew together with concern for my physical well-being abroad.

"But it is so ridiculous. Where will we get to eventually by doing this? You know how I would love it, but remember that you have a future ahead of you — there is no reason why you should not succeed in writing something good, and you can certainly do that without me along, to persuade you that your work is better than it is." He beamed at me, adding, "And you confess that you would like to be a celebrated 'man of letters'."

It was a long time before he came around, and I had to make out little plans and charts at the table, showing how we could both live on the money. When he finally consented I immediately fetched a newspaper and turned to the shipping page in great excitement.

"If we could only get over on a freight boat, George, run by the Canadian Government Merchant Marine — they're awfully cheap, but one has to have a lot of influence higher up to wangle a passage on them."

I was here interrupted by George, who remembered that his cousin's husband was legal advisor to the Canadian National Railways, and that it was more than probable that he could get us a cheap passage in some clever and unethical way.

O the bustle and confusion, the waiting in offices downtown, the anxiety and dread we had while strings were being pulled — I remember all these very clearly now. And I remember the note from George's brother, pushed under the door of our apartment, telling us that at last our passage had been arranged, and that we were to sail on the *Canadian Traveller*, leaving Saint John, New Brunswick, on the fourth of February, and carrying us as far as London. George received a free passage, and I was to pay a half-fare of fifty dollars.

This news so excited us that George went out and bought a black felt hat, striding out of the shop with it on his head. He hated Montreal more than even I did, I think.

We were both in the mood for fine celebration, and it happened fortunately that that night we were both taking a very beautiful girl, Mona McMaster, out to a show, and afterwards to the night-club on St. Catherine Street which is called the Venetian Gardens. As the evening was to be our last in Montreal (we were leaving the next day) we decided to do everything as nicely as possible.

246

In front of the glittering Mount Royal Hotel we hired an open sleigh, smothered in buffalo robes, with a strong white horse between the shafts. We were bundled into it by the aged French-Canadian driver, who adjusted the fur robes over our knees and stomachs and tucked them in at the sides. We gave him Mona's address in Westmount to drive to, a mile and a half away through the city, and we slid away.

The white horse trotted along the bright street, the bells on his neck jingling pleasantly, while the cold night wind made me nestle comfortably in the collar of my fur coat. The sky was full of stars, and I thought that we could not have chosen a finer night on which to call for a woman in a sleigh. Automobiles whizzed past us, many of them taxis. Had it been an ordinary night, we would have called for Mona in a taxi. In the rear window of one that passed I saw two heads, one leaning uncomfortably against the other, and I chuckled to think of the depressing country I was leaving. This common picture of two heads, in the rear window of an automobile, seemed to me the epitome of well-bred youth in Canada. Still smiling, I remembered how I had been one of them myself for a few months, some years ago when my social ambitions made me a well-known figure at coming-out dances.

The wind blew more strongly against my face, as we came into the wider streets of Westmount.

My recollections took another turn, farther back, when driving in a sleigh as a child of eight or nine I had been flushed and happy. Those drives on Sunday afternoons with my mother and my elder brother David came back to me with a fine clarity — we had driven on the mountain in the sunshine, among the crowds of people out walking, and with the ski-ers shooting down the steep snow-covered hills, and my brother and I had been pointed at as handsome children.

As I write at this moment, the memory of that night is very strong, as strong as was the memory of my childhood. I sit at the table in the apartment George and I have taken in Paris, and it is late in the evening. George, in a pair of blue pajamas, lies all humped up in bed, his face stares at me, crushed up sideways in pillow. He is sleepy, and has been waiting for a long time for me to stop writing and go to bed. As I bend again to write, his voice startles me suddenly in the silence that has not been interrupted in the last half hour.

"I saw you as an old man with whiskers, writing."

When Mona saw the sleigh in which we had called for her she did not outwardly evince the delight which most women might have, but all the way from Westmount to the theatre her face bore the expression which I am sure my own did when I was a happy child. I myself felt that it was all very pretty. George was in high spirits, having succeeded in sitting with his left side-face towards Mona. He had carefully planned this beforehand because he thinks his profile is much better when seen that way. I sat opposite to them both, my knees pressed against hers, feeling now and then a pleasant twinge of desire. She and George had known each other since their childhood, and I envied each of them for those years. George was in love with her in a fantastic way, and had written a poem the day after we had taken her to the Mount Royal Hotel to dance. I remember this much:

Now that the cabaret was in candlelight I forgot your virginal heaviness for some one said your clothes were only a week after the last style. You might as well have worn a

247

party dress and several starched petticoats, fluffed them out to sit on the floor where you ate pistochio ice-cream at twilight.

George had wanted to read the poem to her, but had thought the words 'virginal heaviness' might hurt her feelings. So he could only tell her he had written a poem.

The fare for the cab-drive came to two dollars, and when I had paid it we went into the dark theatre. The show proved rather poor, but it did not bore us as much as it might have. As for Mona I believe she was rather disappointed in the performance that had been greatly advertised in Montreal, but she kept turning from one of us to the other, smiling very charmingly. Her large dark eyes looking into mine excited me immoderately. George told me afterwards that it was an unconscious habit of hers to stare straight into the eyes of whomever she was addressing.

After the show was over we walked along St. Catherine Street for the few blocks that separated us from the Venetian Gardens, enjoying the cool air after the warmth of the theatre. Outside, on the sidewalk before the night-club, the taxi-drivers were lounging and smoking.

The Venetian Gardens was a place that had been in existence for a number of years, and at the present time was being patronised by the younger set of Montreal, together with a large sprinkling of Jews. Nevertheless it was the most beautiful room in the city for a cabaret — very large and with a low ceiling, the tables being set around the dance floor; along one entire side of the room were french windows, letting in the night sky. That night we ordered red wine and I danced the first dance with Mona.

As the evening wore on I found that the Italian wine I was drinking made me feel very well, and very charitably disposed towards those people of Montreal who for the last three years had offended my adolescent mind. At one time I walked across the floor to speak to Dodo Dawson an occasional song-and-dance man in vaudeville and at times a trader in pelts in the far North-West. His elder brother, Morris Dawson, was a devout Catholic and played the piano. Morris was often bothered by the thought that he might be taken for a Jew on account of his name and his musicianship but nothing bothered Dodo when he had someone to talk to. I told Dodo I was leaving, saying good-bye to him, and he, not to be outdone, said he was also thinking of going to Paris, to work as a gigolo. He is a beautiful dancer, and good-looking, but he has a very serious impediment in his speech.

"If you work as a gigolo," I smiled, "you might capture an American heiress. That is the conventional fairytale."

He puffed out his chest like a pigeon, but then turned tenderly to his companion, a girl in a red dress who looked like a spaniel. He took her hand, then looked at me.

"H-h-here's my only l-little hei-hei-hei-heiress," he said. I remembered someone telling me he had been trying to seduce this girl for three weeks.

George, who very seldom dances, was on this occasion stepping around the floor very nimbly. I sat and watched the dancers, and listened to the conversation going on at the tables around me. Nothing of moment occurred, except that I drank a great deal more Chianti than was good for my stomach.

In the vestibule of Mona's home in Westmount, George took his final leave of her, as he told me later. I remained in the taxi, envying them their sentimental parting; I myself had no one to sentimentalise over, because the only person I loved was coming with me. These reflections were disturbed by the gradual suspicion that I was going to be sick, and I recalled the red wine with a quiver of displeasure.

George rejoined me and we drove home through the empty, well-lit streets. Later I lay in bed, not daring to close my eyes lest things should start whirling round, as they did as soon as I tried to sleep. George was sleeping soundly, apparently with no thought of his supplemental examination in a few hours, the passing of which would determine whether or not he was to become a Bachelor of Arts. This examination he had failed to pass twice before, yet had this time paid the ten dollar fee out of his small resources for another try. He had carried with him for a week a large book on the subject, written by the best authority, but had never had the time to study it. He slept, smiling slightly and I left the room, proceeding down the hall to the w. c., which we shared with the other tenants on the ground floor.

Returning down the hall I was astonished to hear a violent knocking and banging on the street door, which caused me no little displeasure. I felt disinclined to open, wishing to seek my bed immediately, but the noise increased and I heard my name being hallooed nervously, but strenuously, from the outside.

I opened the door, and a fat little lecher whom I knew very well, entered, with a woman in a red hat at his heels. I drew my silk dressing-gown about me as a cold blast of wind blew in with them, and closed the door. Bertie was buttoned up in his coon-skin coat and his serious, circular face, above the outstanding fur collar, resembled a hen sitting on its nest. He had pushed the woman in the red hat behind him, and was explaining, in a hoarse whisper, his reason for calling in at five o'clock in the morning.

"You can get into bed with George for a bit, can't you?" he asked, "I won't be long — don't turn me down for God's sake because I haven't got the price of a room. Just for old times' sake. . . . ?"

"Why, certainly, if you wish," I replied, striving hard not to laugh frantically. I was half asleep and barely master of my limbs, but opened the door for him and his companion to enter the pitch-black room. He bundled the woman in ahead of him.

"In the same room?" I asked stupidly feeling that the whole business was rather bizarre, but he replied that the lights would be out.

I climbed into George's bed, lying like a log. For a long time they seemed to be muttering away by the other bed, and I kept wishing that they would hurry up before I fell asleep. Then I heard Bertie cursing softly with rage, and the bed creaked as they stood up.

Before I fell quite asleep I remember Bertie saying something to me about his companion being an honest woman, and she didn't like the fact that two other men were in the room as well, and so they had to go, although he didn't want to. Then they went out, and I fell asleep.

I woke late next morning, and shaved and dressed with care, for it was my last day in Montreal. While I was at my toilet, our landlady, a woman called Mrs. Casey, who looked like a witch, knocked sharply at my door and entered. I hated her very much, but bowed good morning.

"I was thinkin', Mr. Stinson," she said in her polite, but barbed, manner, her eyes shooting around the room and occasionally resting on me, "that I should receive something for the state you've got this room in. I've never had a tenant who done like you and the other gentleman does. So if you could give me something for the cleanin' up it'll require. . . "

"Yes, yes, Mrs. Casey," I said reassuringly, wishing to get her out the room on such a beautiful morning. "I will fix that up. Of course I can understand the way you feel about it, but do not bother about my settling everything in full."

After smiling ghoulishly and thanking me in the profuse and apologetic way that made her so odious, she left, making vain hints that I should pay her then.

I resolved that Mrs. Casey should not receive a cent from me that was not stipulated in the lease. She was a horrid creature, and could often be heard beating her children in the stuffy basement that she inhabited. "Get into bed now, you little bugger!" she would cry, after whipping her young son.

The loveliness of the bright morning exhilarated me. The snow, the air, the creaking underfoot on the hard-packed side-walk, and one's breath making a fine, white cloud — all is so hard and gem-like in Canada at eleven in the morning. Three blocks away, I thought, the morning is curling its edges around the thick walls of the Sun Life Assurance Company, while inside the men and women are all busy denying their dark gods. Their prospectus says that their head office staff numbers "fourteen hundred workers, beside many others in branch offices, and those carrying the banner in the field."

I was going to wait for George at the McGill Union, and hear how he had fared as a prospective Bachelor of Arts. Of course, he had no illusions about the distinction of a degree from McGill University, and placed no value on one other than its power to bring in a little more money to its bearer in the world of commerce. The fact was that George had spent four years at college, and in his dogged way had determined to have what others would consider the great reward. In addition, he had been disgustingly treated by many of the teaching staff, particularly by the head of the English Department, to whom George had imprudently revealed a taste in letters which went beyond an appreciation of Byron, Burns, Bliss Carman, Joe Howe, Stevenson and Sir James Barrie. George's relations with this backwoodsman make amusing reading, and the chapter in his book *Shadow Play*, entitled *Si tu es pot de chambre tant pis pour toi*, is a delightful treatment of the whole affair.

I strode along St. Catherine Street on my way to the Union, with groups of shop-girls, on the early lunch-hour, passing by in their closely-wrapped coats, and the young men slouching along, with varnished hair and wide-bottomed trousers. When I arrived in the Union, George was not yet come from his examination, so I sat in the lobby. Many acquaintances, and people I had been pleasant to in my charitable moments at college, came around. On hearing that I was going away they immediately inquired, practically, what I was 'going to do', and when Paris was mentioned they made appropriately stupid and disgusting remarks. I remember a very swarthy well-bred Jew who might have sat for the portrait of "Brennbaum", by Ezra Pound, saying: "Well, goodbye, and don't do anything I wouldn't do." I had once been slightly interested in him on account of his musical ability, but since then he had come to believe that the company of Christian louts and football players was more compelling a statement of his social standing than any other. I am sure that he derived great comfort from Blake's pathetic poem beginning,

My mother bore me in the southern wild,
And I am black, but O! my soul is white;
White as an angel is the English child,
But I am black, as if bereaved of light.

I rose from my seat in the lobby, deciding to wait for George on the steps of the building. Lounging there, an amusing spectacle was afforded me, when the Dean of the Faculty of Arts, because he is a Canadian, passed on the opposite side of the street, looking like a green-grocer, with his cane, gloves, and morning trousers. Unaware that anyone was watching him, he turned his head and shoulders completely round to gape lecherously at the calves of a trim co-ed who had just passed him. When he saw me, motionless on the steps, watching him, he buried his face in his collar and scurried for cover around a corner.

A little later I saw George trudging down the campus, and in front, almost obscuring him, the immense figure of Sir Arthur Currie, Principal of the University and ex-War Lord of the Canadian Expeditionary Force. I could not help but observe what a poor figure George cut behind this white-spatted symbol of the Army, attired like the editor of *Vanity Fair*. George might have a B.A., but Currie had a dozen honorary degrees and a good high-school education.

George did not know whether he had passed his examination or not, as he had twice before been sure of success and then found he had failed. But we did not bother long about the matter, as we had to pack and do many things before we caught the train for Saint John at seven o'clock that evening.

As I was midway in my packing, hurrying in a frantic haste to get everything ready before half-past six, George suddenly stopped throwing what clothes he had into an old canvas-backed trunk, and turned to me.

"Hurry," I cried, "we've got loads to do, and if we miss this train we may never get out of Canada." I confess that I was at that time quite sick with nervousness, imagining that fate was preparing some awful blow for us, to keep us in Canada.

"You know," George said with determination, "I left my fountain-pen, by mistake, with a stenographer in the Sun Life. I have had that pen for five years, and no sentimental stenographer is going to get it. It's an expensive pen, too. So I'll just run down to the office and get it from her now — we've got lots of time, it's only a quarter to six, and I'll be right back to help you finish packing your books."

In vain I protested. He bundled into his coat and his black hat and disappeared through the door.

I continued to pack, cramming all my clothes into the trunk indiscriminately, a thing I hate doing, and crushing my suits in a disgraceful manner. I kept thinking of George and his pen, and the black-haired, sensual creature who had it. George, I knew, was a queer enigma in the office he had worked in, and the women had vainly tried to rouse him to speak to them on terms of serious equality. At first his cold, Danish stare had made them giggle, and later his candid remarks, with their revelation of an antique world, set them wondering if he was not a sort of Pan. They found only momentary

251

refuge in the word "conceited", and became weirdly attracted. Then there was a conversation with a pretty Irish typist who had learnt he was going away.

"I'd love to go with you," she said, smiling slightly.

Wishing to make his situation less enviable, he replied that we would be very poor in Paris, and be in rags and tags.

"That wouldn't matter. I'd go with you, any way at all."

George burst into the room in high spirits. He had succeeded in recovering his pen from the reluctant stenographer and in addition he had met those two rogues who had used our room with the former's woman, all chatting on the steps of the Sun Life Building; in the background a stuttering fool, C.H., was capering, trying to say goodbye before George should hurry away. The former two had been a little flustered at seeing him, just when they thought they had seen the last of both of us. We, who knew their secret, were going away — although their gladness on this account was tempered, I am sure, by a feeling of loss: they had no homelike, snug apartment now, and the woman, R — W —, had looked a little sad, so George said. Then he set to work to help me pack.

All our things were finally stowed, making a great deal of luggage, and we realized that we would have to have three taxis to take us to the station. Soon the room was filled with burly taxi-drivers who fought among themselves as to who should carry the lighter articles. The smallest of the men, who was eventually left with my immense trunk to carry out, was rewarded with my overshoes, which I would need no longer, and the keys to the apartment.

"Give the keys to the landlady, won't you?" I asked, for conscience's sake, knowing very well that he probably would not. I was surprised that Mrs. Casey had not appeared before this, to demand something for the state of the room. Only when everything was loaded into the taxis did I see her. She came out on the steps, jumping up and down with rage and trying to make herself heard above the roar of the taxis. So George gave orders to proceed swiftly to the station, and we moved off. There being no room inside, George and I were forced to hang on to the side of one of the cars; thus we had a fine view of St. Catherine Street, all lighted up, as our fleet of taxis skidded and bumped over the street-car tracks in the direction of Bonaventure Station. It was a pleasant thing to be seeing the last of Montreal in this fashion.

Almost until the very moment of boarding the train I had been sick with a reasonless anxiety, but when all the business of baggage was complete, and George and I were striding along the station platform behind a porter, our arms full of overcoats, then I relaxed. Under the great roof which covered the lines of tracks, with the engines shooting off steam all around, I felt my great moment of exaltation as we walked alongside the train bound for the Port of Saint John.

# A. M. Klein

*Abraham Moses Klein (1909-     ) was born in Montreal of parents who had recently emigrated from Russia. He was educated at the Talmud Torah in preparation for the rabbinate, at Baron Byng High School (which was later immortalized in Mordecai Richler's* The Apprenticeship of Duddy Kravitz), *and at McGill University. He received his B.A. in 1930. After he was called to the bar in 1933, Klein practiced law. He served as Editor of* The Canadian Jewish Chronicle *(1939 to 1955), ran as a CCF candidate in the 1948 election, and was a visiting lecturer at McGill from 1945 to 1947. Klein was awarded the Lorne Pierce Medal in 1957 for distinguished service to Canadian literature. Since 1955 his illness has kept him in retirement.*

*Historically, A. M. Klein is the first significant Jewish poet to appear in English-Canadian writing. His importance, however, lies in the fact that he is the first Canadian poet to have written from the experience and influences of three cultural traditions — the Jewish, the English, and the Canadian.[1] His Jewish background is a religious and cultural tradition that reveres the written word; this respect pervades Klein's imagery as well as his craft. Undoubtedly some phrases and allusions will puzzle the non-Jewish reader who is unfamiliar with medieval Jewish scholarship. Even in the later poems where Klein deals with his loss of faith ("The Cripples"), his religious imagination and sensitivity remain, but these are now manifested in his concern with identity and order in the universe. Klein was influenced by the poetic styles and exotic vocabularies of three main areas of British literature: the Chaucerian period, the Elizabethan-Jacobean age, and the modern period in which James Joyce and T. S. Eliot are the chief influences. Like other poets in the 1920s and 1930s, he found in Donne's age an anxious and questioning tone which modern poets identified with their own sensibility. In Canadian literature, Klein was influenced primarily by French Canadian life, an area he turned to in the 1940s while he was still preoccupied with the Jewish troubles of the Nazi era. French-Canadian society has had a religious, political, and cultural homogeneity which the Jewish poet could appreciate and sympathize with; in fact, a tension is set up in his poems in the meeting between the member of one minority and the people of another minority. Yet the poet never forgets the historical implications for his people of the crucified "agonized Y" on Quebec walls. The poems on Quebec life are sympathetic, ironic, critical, and at times, intense to the point of being unbearable.*

*Klein's awareness of these various literary traditions explains much about his use of* language. The earlier poems have an archaic, rich diction, whereas the diction of the later poems becomes more contemporary and simple. Geometry is a favourite source of imagery, and in the later poems, there is an emphasis on space and geography. Always there is a compression of image, idea, and emotion, a technique which is characteristic of metaphysical poetry between the Wars. In a sense, language as the most important key to reality is Klein's predominant theme.[2] The poet, the "nth Adam" of "Portrait", works through language to discover, identify, and reconcile the contradictions of life. Ultimately, of course, his concern for language is a concern for humanity, always presented with compassion and fervour.

## Footnotes

[1] *This approach is used by Mariam Waddington in her fine critical study* A.M. Klein *(Toronto: Copp Clark, 1970).*
[2] *Louis Dudek relates Klein's struggles with language to similar concerns among his contemporaries: "We know that this deliberate interest in language is characteristic of our century; it has something to do with the disrupted nature of private and social experience, with the unfixed and searching character of poetry itself, with the unreality of the realities in which we live. Joyce, Gertrude Stein, Cummings, have displayed a genius for breaking language and putting its parts into a personal, beautiful order . . . . Klein therefore is in a great tradition, and in good modern company. He has been doing something that Canada badly needs: making new things with old tools, discovering the vast possibilities of poetry. What he has lacked is the criticism and understanding which would let him know when he has succeeded in this type of thing, when he has failed. His experimental poetry is exciting because it is experimental; but it is often below standard as poetry of this kind. Therefore it is often below standard simply as poetry."*
*Louis Dudek "A.M. Klein", in* A.M. Klein, *Edited by Tom Marshall (Toronto: Ryerson, 1970), p. 73.*

# *In Re* Solomon Warshawer

On Wodin's day, sixth of December, thirty-nine,
I, Friedrich Vercingetorix, attached
to the VIIth Eavesdroppers-behind-the-Line,
did cover my beat, when suddenly the crowd I watched
surrounded, in a cobbled lane one can't pass through,
a bearded man, disguised in rags, a Jew.

In the said crowd there were a number of Poles.
Mainly, however, there were Germans there;
blood-brothers of our Reich, true Aryan souls,
breathing at last — in Warsaw — Nordic air.

254

These were the words the Jew was shouting:
I took them down verbatim:

*Whom have I hurt? Against whose silk have I brushed?*
*On which of your women looked too long?*
*I tell you I have done no wrong!*
*Send home your children, lifting hardened dung,*
*And let your curs be hushed!*
*For I am beard and breathlessness, and chased enough.*
*Leave me in peace, and let me go my way.*

At this the good folk laughed. The Jew continued to say
he was no thief, he was a man for hire,
worked for his bread, artist or artisan,
a scribe, if you wished, a vendor or a buyer,
work of all kinds, and anything at all:
paint a mural, scour a latrine,
indite an ode, repair an old machine,
anything, to repeat,
anything at all,
so that he might eat
and have his straw couch in his abandoned stall.
Asked for his papers, he made a great to-do
of going through the holes in his rags, whence he withdrew
a Hebrew pamphlet and a signet ring,
herewith produced, Exhibits 1 and 2.

I said: No documents in a civilized tongue?
He replied:

*Produce, O Lord, my wretched fingerprint,*
*Bring forth, O angel in the heavenly court,*
*My dossier, full, detailed, both fact and hint,*
*Felony, misdemeanor, tort!*

I refused to be impressed by talk of that sort.

From further cross-examination, it appeared,
immediate history: a beggar in Berlin,
chased as a vagrant from the streets of Prague,
kept as a leper in forced quarantine,
shunned as the pest, avoided like a plague,
he had escaped, mysteriously come
by devious routes, and stolen frontiers, to
the *nalewkas* of Warsaw's sheenydom.

Pressed to reveal his foul identity,
He lied:

One of the anthropophagi was he,
or, if we wished, a denizen of Mars,
the ghost of my father, Conscience — aye,
the spectre of Reason, naked, and with scars;
even became insulting, said he was
Aesop the slave among the animals . . .
Sir Incognito — Rabbi Alias . . .
The eldest elder of Zion . . . said we knew
his numerous varied oriental shapes,
even as we ought to know his present guise—
the man in the jungle, and beset by apes.

It was at this point the S. S. man arrived.
The Jew was interrupted; when he was revived,
He deposed as follows:

*At low estate, a beggar, and in flight,*
*Still do I wear my pride like purple. I*
*Am undismayed by frenzy or by fright,*
*And you are those mirrored in my pitying eye.*
*For you are not the first that I have met—*
*O I have known them all,*
*The dwarf dictators, the diminutive dukes,*
*The heads of straw, the hearts of gall,*
*Th' imperial plumes of eagles covering rooks!*

*It is not necessary to name names,*
*But it may serve anon,*
*Now to evoke from darkness some dark fames,*
*Evoke,*
*Armada'd Spain, that gilded jettison;*
*And Russia's last descended Romanov,*
*Descending a dark staircase*
*To a dank cellar at Ekaterinoslov;*
*Evoke*
*The glory that was Babylon that now is gloom;*
*And Egypt, Egypt, scarcely now recalled*

*By that lone star that sentries Pharaoh's tomb;*
*And Carthage, sounded on sand, by water walled;*
*And Greece — O broken marble!—*
*And disinterred unresurrected Rome.*

256

*These several dominions hunted me;*
*They all have wished, and more than wished, me dead;*
*And now, although I do walk raggedly,*
*I walk, and they are echoes to my tread!*
*Is it by your devices I shall be undone?*

*Ah, but you are philosophers, and know*
*That what has been need not continue so;*
*The sun has risen: and the sun has set;*
*Risen again, again descended, yet*
*To-morrow no bright sun may rise to throw*
*Rays of inductive reason on Judaeophobic foe.*

*Is there great turmoil in the sparrow's nest*
*When that bright bird, the Sun, descends the west?*
*There is no fear, there is no twittering:*
*At dawn they will again behold his juvenescent wing!*

*Such is the very pattern of the world,*
*Even the sparrows understand;*
*And in that scheme of things I am enfurled,*
*Am part thereof, the whole as it was planned,*
*With increase and abatement rife,*
*Subject to sorrow, joined to joy—*
*Earth, its relenting and recurring life!*

*Yes, but the signet ring, the signet ring!*
*Since you must know, barbarian, know you shall!*
*I who now stand before you, a hunted thing,*
*Pressed and pursued and harried hither and yon,*
*I was, I am the Emperor Solomon!*

*O, to and fro upon the face of the earth,*
*I wandered, crying:* Ani Shlomo, *but—*
*But no one believed my birth.*

*For he now governs in my place and stead,*
*He who did fling me from Jerusalem*
*Four hundred parasangs;*
*Who stole the crown from off my head,*
*And robed him in my robes, beneath whose hem*
*The feet of the cock extend, the tail of the demon hangs!*
*Asmodeus!*

*Mistake me not: I am no virtuous saint;*
*Only a man, and like all men, not godly,*
*Damned by desire—*
*But I at least waged war, for holy booty,*
*Against my human taint;*
*At least sought wisdom, to discern the good;*
*Whether of man, or birds, or beasts of the wood;*
*Spread song, spread justice, ever did aspire—*
*Howbeit, man among men, I failed—*
*To lay the plan, and work upon the plan*
*To build the temple of the more-than-man!*

*But he, the unspeakable prince of malice!*
*Usurper of my throne, pretender to the Lord's!*
*Wicked, demoniac, lycanthropous,*
*Leader of hosts horrific, barbarous hordes,*
*Master of the worm, pernicious, that cleaves rocks,*
*The beast that talks,*
*Asmodeus!—*

*Who has not heard the plight of his domain?*
*Learning is banished to the hidden cave;*
*Wisdom decried, a virtue of the slave;*
*And justice, both eyes seared, goes tapping with a cane.*
*His counseler is the wolf. He counsels hate.*
*His sceptre is a claw.*
*And love is a high crime against the state.*
*The fury of the forest*
*Is the law.*

*Upon his charnel-throne, in bloodied purple,*
*Hearkening to that music where the sigh*
*Pauses to greet the groan, the groan the anguished cry,*
*Asmodeus sits;*
*And I—*

At this point the S. S. men departed.
The Jew was not revived. He was carried and carted,
and to his present gaoler brought;
awaiting higher pleasure.
     And further deponent saith not.

# The Cripples

(Oratoire de St. Joseph)

Bundled their bones, upon the ninety-nine stairs—
St. Joseph's ladder — the knobs of penance come;
the folded cripples counting up their prayers.

How rich, how plumped with blessing is that dome!
The gourd of Brother André! His sweet days
rounded! Fulfilled! Honeyed to honeycomb!

whither the heads, upon the ninety-nine trays,
the palsied, who double their aspen selves, the lame,
the unsymmetrical, the dead-limbed, raise

their look, their hope, and the *idée fixe* of their maim, —
knowing the surgery's in the heart. Are not
the ransomed crutches worshippers? And the fame

of the brother sanatorial to this plot? —
God mindful of the sparrows on the stairs?
Yes, to their faith this mountain of stairs, is not!

They know, they know, that suddenly their cares
and orthopedics will fall from them, and they
stand whole again.

*Roll empty away, wheelchairs,*
*and crutches, without armpits, hop away!*

And I who in my own faith once had faith like this,
but have not now, am crippled more than they.

# For the Sisters of the Hotel Dieu

In pairs,
as if to illustrate their sisterhood,
the sisters pace the hospital garden walks.

259

In their robes black and white immaculate hoods
they are like birds,
the safe domestic fowl of the House of God.

O biblic birds,
who fluttered to me in my childhood illnesses
—me little, afraid, ill, not of your race,—
the cool wing for my fever, the hovering solace,
the sense of angels—
be thanked, O plumage of paradise, be praised.

# Grain Elevator

Up from the low-roofed dockyard warehouses
it rises blind and babylonian
like something out of legend. Something seen
in a children's coloured book. Leviathan
swamped on our shore? The cliffs of some other river?
The blind ark lost and petrified? A cave
built to look innocent, by pirates? Or
some eastern tomb a travelled patron here makes local?

But even when known, it's more than what it is:
for here, as in a Josephdream, bow down

the sheaves, the grains, the scruples of the sun
garnered for darkness; and Saskatchewan
is rolled like a rug of a thick and golden thread.
O prison of prairies, ship in whose galleys roll
sunshines like so many shaven heads,
waiting the bushel-burst out of the beached bastille!

Sometimes, it makes me think Arabian,
the grain picked up, like tic-tacs out of time:
first one; an other; singly; one by one;—
to save life. Sometimes, some other races claim
the twinship of my thought, — as the river stirs
restless in a white Caucasian sleep,
or, as in the steerage of the elevators,
the grains, Mongolian and crowded, dream.

A box: cement, hugeness, and rightangles—
merely the sight of it leaning in my eyes
mixes up continents and makes a montage
of inconsequent time and uncontiguous space.
It's because it's bread. It's because
bread is its theme, an absolute. Because
always this great box flowers over us
with all the coloured faces of mankind. . .

# Indian Reservation: Caughnawaga

Where are the braves, the faces like autumn fruit,
who stared at the child from the coloured frontispiece?
And the monosyllabic chief who spoke with his throat?
Where are the tribes, the feathered bestiaries?—
Rank Aesop's animals erect and red,
with fur on their names to make all live things kin'—
Chief Running Deer, Black Bear, Old Buffalo Head?

Childhood, that wished me Indian, hoped that
one afterschool I'd leave the classroom chalk,
the varnish smell, the watered dust of the street,
to join the clean outdoors and the Iroquois track.
Childhood; but always, — as on a calendar,—
there stood that chief, with arms akimbo, waiting
the runaway mascot paddling to his shore.

With what strange moccasin stealth that scene is
    changed!
With French names, without paint, in overalls,
their bronze, like their nobility expunged,—
the men. Beneath their alimentary shawls
sit like black tents their squaws; while for the tourist's
brown pennies scattered at the old church door,
the ragged papooses jump, and bite the dust.

Their past is sold in a shop: the beaded shoes,
the sweetgrass basket, the curio Indian,
burnt wood and gaudy cloth and inch-canoes—
trophies and scalpings for a traveller's den.

Sometimes, it's true, they dance, but for a bribe;
after a deal don the bedraggled feather
and welcome a white mayor to the tribe.

This is a grassy ghetto, and no home.
And these are fauna in a museum kept.
The better hunters have prevailed. The game,
losing its blood, now makes these grounds its crypt.
The animals pale, the shine of the fur is lost,
bleached are their living bones. About them watch
as through a mist, the pious prosperous ghosts.

# Political Meeting

(For Camillien Houde)

On the school platform, draping the folding seats,
they wait the chairman's praise and glass of water.
Upon the wall the agonized Y initials their faith.

Here all are laic; the skirted brothers have gone.
Still, their equivocal absence is felt, like a breeze
that gives curtains the sounds of surplices.

The hall is yellow with light, and jocular;
suddenly some one lets loose upon the air
the ritual bird which the crowd in snares of singing

catches and plucks, throat, wings, and little limbs.
Fall the feathers of sound, like *alouette's*.
The chairman, now, is charming, full of asides and wit,

building his orators, and chipping off
the heckling gargoyles popping in the hall.
(Outside, in the dark, the street is body-tall,

flowered with faces intent on the scarecrow thing
that shouts to thousands the echoing
of their own wishes.) The Orator has risen!

Worshipped and loved, their favourite visitor,
a country uncle with sunflower seeds in his pockets,
full of wonderful moods, tricks, imitative talk,

he is their idol: like themselves, not handsome,
not snobbish, not of the *Grande Allee! Un homme!*
Intimate, informal, he makes bear's compliments

to the ladies; is gallant; and grins;
goes for the balloon, his opposition, with pins;
jokes also on himself, speaks of himself

in the third person, slings slang, and winks with folklore;
and knows now that he has them, kith and kin.
Calmly, therefore, he begins to speak of war,

praises the virtue of being *Canadien*,
of being at peace, of faith, of family,
and suddenly his other voice: *Where are your sons?*

He is tearful, choking tears; but not he
would blame the clever English; in their place
he'd do the same; maybe.

Where *are* your sons?
                    The whole street wears one face,
shadowed and grim; and in the darkness rises
the body-odour of race.


# Montreal

I

O city metropole, isle riverain!
Your ancient pavages and sainted routs
Traverse my spirit's conjured avenues!
Splendor erablic of your promenades
Foliates there, and there your maisonry
Of pendent balcon and escalier'd march,
Unique midst English habitat,
Is vivid Normandy!

263

## II

You populate the pupils of my eyes:
Thus, does the Indian, plumèd, furtivate
Still through your painted autumns, Ville-Marie!
Though palisades have passed, though calumet
With tabac of your peace enfumes the air,
Still do I spy the phantom, aquiline,
Genuflect, moccasin'd, behind
His statue in the square!

## III

Thus, costumed images before me pass,
Haunting your archives architectural:
*Coureur de bois,* in posts where pelts were portaged;
Seigneur within his candled manoir; Scot
Ambulant through his bank, pillar'd and vast.
Within your chapels, voyaged mariners
Still pray, and personage departed,
All present from your past!

## IV

Grand port of navigations, multiple
The lexicons uncargo'd at your quays,
Sonnant though strange to me; but chiefest, I,
Auditor of your music, cherish the
Joined double-melodied vocabulaire
Where English vocable and roll Ecossic,
Mollified by the parle of French
Bilinguefact your air!

## V

Such your suaver voice, hushed Hochelaga!
But for me also sound your potencies,
Fortissimos of sirens fluvial,
Bruit of manufactory, and thunder
From foundry issuant, all puissant tone
Implenishing your hebdomad; and then
Sanct silence, and your argent belfries
Clamant in orison!

## VI

You are a part of me, O all your quartiers—
And of dire pauvrete and of richesse—

To finished time my homage loyal claim;
You are locale of infancy, milieu
Vital of institutes that formed my fate;
And you above the city, scintillant,
Mount Royal, are my spirit's mother,
Almative, poitrinate!

### VII

Never do I sojourn in alien place
But I do languish for your scenes and sounds,
City of reverie, nostalgic isle,
Pendant most brilliant on Laurentian cord!
The coigns of your boulevards — my signiory—
Your suburbs are my exile's verdure fresh,
Your parks, your fountain'd parks—
Pasture of memory!

### VIII

City, O city, you are vision'd as
A parchemin roll of saecular exploit
Inked with the script of eterne souvenir!
You are in sound, chanson and instrument!
Mental, you rest forever edified
With tower and dome; and in these beating valves,
Here in these beating valves, you will
For all my mortal time reside!

# Lone Bather

Upon the ecstatic diving board the diver,
poised for parabolas, lets go
lets go his manshape to become a bird.
Is bird, and topsy-turvy
the pool floats overhead, and the white tiles snow
their crazy hexagons. Is dolphin. Then
is plant with lilies bursting from his heels.

Himself, suddenly mysterious and marine,
bobs up a merman leaning on his hills.

265

Plashes and plays alone the deserted pool;
as those, is free, who think themselves unseen.
He rolls in his heap of fruit,
he slides his belly over
the melonrinds of water, curved and smooth and green.
Feels good: and trains, like little acrobats
his echoes dropping from the galleries;
circles himself over a rung of water;
swims fancy and gay; taking a notion, hides
under the satins of his great big bed,—
and then comes up to float until he thinks
the ceiling at his brow, and nowhere any sides.

His thighs are a shoal of fishes: scattered: he
turns with many gloves of greeting
towards the sunnier water and the tiles.

Upon the tiles he dangles from his toes
lazily the eight reins of his ponies.

An afternoon, far from the world
a street sound throws like a stone, with paper, through
    the glass.
Up, he is chipped enamel, grained with hair.
The gloss of his footsteps follows him to the showers,
the showers, and the male room, and the towel
which rubs the bird, the plant, the dolphin back again
personable plain.

# Portrait of the Poet as Landscape

I

Not an editorial-writer, bereaved with bartlett,
mourns him, the shelved Lycidas.
No actress squeezes a glycerine tear for him.
The radio broadcast lets his passing pass.
And with the police, no record. Nobody, it appears,
either under his real name or his alias,
missed him enough to report.

266

It is possible that he is dead, and not discovered.
It is possible that he can be found some place
in a narrow closet, like the corpse in a detective story,
standing, his eyes staring, and ready to fall on his face.
It is also possible that he is alive
and amnesiac, or mad, or in retired disgrace,
or beyond recognition lost in love.

We are sure only that from our real society
he has disappeared; he simply does not count,
except in the pullulation of vital statistics—
somebody's vote, perhaps, an anonymous taunt
of the Gallup poll, a dot in a government table—
but not felt, and certainly far from eminent—
in a shouting mob, somebody's sigh.

O, he who unrolled our culture from his scroll—
the prince's quote, the rostrum-rounding roar—
who under one name made articulate
heaven, and under another the seven-circled air,
is, if he is at all, a number, an x,
a Mr. Smith in a hotel register,—
incognito, lost, lacunal.

## II

The truth is he's not dead, but only ignored—
like the mirroring lenses forgotten on a brow
that shine with the guilt of their unnoticed world.
The truth is he lives among neighbours, who, though
    they will allow
him a passable fellow, think him eccentric, not solid,
a type that one can forgive, and for that matter, forego.

Himself he has his moods, just like a poet.
Sometimes, depressed to nadir, he will think all lost,
will see himself as throwback, relict, freak,
his mother's miscarriage, his great-grandfather's ghost,
and he will curse his quintuplet senses, and their tutors
in whom he put, as he should not have put, his trust.

Then he will remember his travels over that body—
the torso verb, the beautiful face of the noun,
and all those shaped and warm auxiliaries!
A first love it was, the recognition of his own.
Dear limbs adverbial, complexion of adjective,
dimple and dip of conjugation!

And then remember how this made a change in him
affecting for always the glow and growth of his being;
how suddenly was aware of the air, like shaken tinfoil,
of the patents of nature, the shock of belated seeing,
the loneliness peering from the eyes of crowds;
the integers of thought; the cube-roots of feeling.

Thus, zoomed to zenith, sometimes he hopes again,
and sees himself as a character, with a rehearsed role:
the Count of Monte Cristo, come for his revenges;
the unsuspected heir, with papers; the risen soul;
or the chloroformed prince awaking from his flowers;
or — deflated again — the convict on parole.


III


He is alone; yet not completely alone.
Pins on a map of a colour similar to his,
each city has one, sometimes more than one;
here, caretakers of art, in colleges;
in offices, there, with arm-bands, and green-shaded;
and there, pounding their catalogued beats in libraries,—

everywhere menial, a shadow's shadow.
And always for their egos — their outmoded art.
Thus, having lost the bevel in the ear,
they know neither up nor down, mistake the part
for the whole, curl themselves in a comma,
talk technics, make a colon their eyes. They distort—

such is the pain of their frustration — truth
to something convolute and cerebral.
How they do fear the slap of the flat of the platitude!
Now Pavlov's victims, their mouths water at bell,
the platter empty.
              See they set twenty-one jewels
into their watches; the time they do not tell!

Some, patagonian in their own esteem,
and longing for the multiplying word,
join party and wear pins, now have a message,
an ear, and the convention-hall's regard.
Upon the knees of ventriloquists, they own,
of their dandled brightness, only the paint and board.

And some go mystical, and some go mad.
One stares at a mirror all day long, as if
to recognize himself; another courts
angels, — for here he does not fear rebuff;
and a third, alone, and sick with sex, and rapt,
doodles him symbols convex and concave.

O schizoid solitudes! O purities
curdling upon themselves! Who live for themselves,
or for each other, but for nobody else;
desire affection, private and public loves;
are friendly, and then quarrel and surmise
the secret perversions of each other's lives.


IV

He suspects that something has happened, a law
been passed, a nightmare ordered. Set apart,
he finds himself, with special haircut and dress,
as on a reservation. Introvert.
He does not understand this; sad conjecture
muscles and palls thrombotic on his heart.

He thinks an impostor, having studied his personal
     biography,
his gestures, his moods, now has come forward to pose
in the shivering vacuums his absence leaves.
Wigged with his laurel, that other, and faked with his
     face,
he pats the heads of his children, pecks his wife,
and is at home, and slippered, in his house.

So he guesses at the impertinent silhouette
that talks to his phone-piece and slits open his mail.
Is it the local tycoon who for a hobby
plays poet, he so epical in steel?
The orator, making a pause? Or is that man
he who blows his flash of brass in the jittering hall?

Or is he cuckolded by the troubadour
rich and successful out of celluloid?
Or by the don who unrhymes atoms? Or
the chemist death built up? Pride, lost impostor'd pride,
it is another, another, whoever he is,
who rides where he should ride.

269

## V

*Fame*, the adrenalin: to be talked about;
to be a verb; to be introduced as *The:*
to smile with endorsement from slick paper; make
caprices anecdotal; to nod to the world; to see
one's name like a song upon the marquees played;
to be forgotten with embarrassment; to be—
to be.

It has its attractions, but is not the thing;
nor is it the ape mimesis who speaks from the tree
ancestral; nor the merkin joy. . .
Rather it is stark infelicity
which stirs him from his sleep, undressed, asleep
to walk upon roofs and window-sills and defy
the gape of gravity.


## VI

Therefore he seeds illusions. Look, he is
the nth Adam taking a green inventory
in world but scarcely uttered, naming, praising,
the flowering fiats in the meadow, the
syllabled fur, stars aspirate, the pollen
whose sweet collision sounds eternally.
For to praise

the world — he, solitary man — is breath
to him. Until it has been praised, that part
has not been. Item by exciting item—
air to his lungs, and pressured blood to his heart.—
they are pulsated, and breathed, until they map,
not the world's, but his own body's chart!

And now in imagination he has climbed
another planet, the better to look
with single camera view upon this earth—
its total scope, and each afflated tick,
its talk, its trick, its tracklessness — and this,
this he would like to write down in a book!

To find a new function for the declassé craft
archaic like the fletcher's; to make a new thing;
to say the word that will become sixth sense;

perhaps by necessity and indirection bring
new forms to life, anonymously, new creeds—
O, somehow pay back the daily larcenies of the lung!

These are not mean ambitions. It is already something
merely to entertain them. Meanwhile, he
makes of his status as zero a rich garland,
a halo of his anonymity,
and lives alone, and in his secret shines
like phosphorus. At the bottom of the sea.

# Autobiographical

Out of the ghetto streets where a Jewboy
Dreamed pavement into pleasant Bible-land,
Out of the Yiddish slums where childhood met
The friendly beard, the loutish Sabbath-goy,
Or followed, proud, the Torah-escorting band,
Out of the jargoning city I regret,
Rise memories, like sparrows rising from
The gutter-scattered oats,
Like sadness sweet of synagogal hum,
Like Hebrew violins
Sobbing delight upon their Eastern notes.

Again they ring their little bells, those doors
Deemed by the tender-year'd, magnificent:
Old Ashkenazi's cellar, sharp with spice;
The widows' double-parlored candy-stores
And nuggets sweet bought for one sweaty cent;
The warm fresh-smelling bakery, its pies,
Its cakes, its navel'd bellies of black bread;
The lintels candy-poled
Of barber-shop, bright-bottled, green, blue,
    red;
And fruit-stall piled, exotic,
And the big synagogue door, with letters of
    gold.

Again my kindergarten home is full—
Saturday night — with kin and compatriot:
My brothers playing Russian card-games; my
Mirroring sisters looking beautiful,
Humming the evening's imminent fox-trot;
My uncle Mayer, of blessed memory,
Still murmuring maariv, counting holy words;
And the two strangers, come
Fiery from Volhynia's murderous hordes—
The cards and humming stop.
And I too swear revenge for that pogrom.

Occasions dear: the four-legged aleph named
And angel pennies dropping on my book;
The rabbi patting a coming scholar-head;
My mother, blessing candles, Sabbath-flamed,
Queenly in her Warsovian perruque;
My father pickabacking me to bed
To tell tall tales about the Baal Shem Tov—
Letting me curl his beard.
Oh memory of unsurpassing love,
Love leading a brave child
Through childhood's ogred corridors, unfear'd!

The week in the country at my brother's — (May
He own fat cattle in the fields of heaven!)
Its picking of strawberries from grassy ditch,
Its odor of dogrose and of yellowing hay—
Dusty, adventurous, sunny days, all seven!—
Still follow me, still warm me, still are rich
With the cow-tinkling peace of pastureland.
The meadow'd memory
Is sodded with its clover, and is spanned
By that same pillow'd sky
A boy on his back one day watched enviously.

And paved again the street: the shouting boys,
Oblivious of mothers on the stoops,
Playing the robust robbers and police,
The corncob battle — all high-spirited noise
Competitive among the lot-drawn groups.
Another day, of shaken apple trees
In the rich suburbs, and a furious dog,
And guilty boys in flight;
Hazelnut games, and games in the synagogue—

The burrs, the Haman rattle,
The Torah dance on Simchas Torah night.

Immortal days of the picture calendar
Dear to me always with the virgin joy
Of the first flowering of senses five,
Discovering birds, or textures, or a star,
Or tastes sweet, sour, acid, those that cloy;
And perfumes. Never was I more alive.
All days thereafter are a dying off,
A wandering away
From home and the familiar. The years doff
Their innocence.
No other day is ever like that day.

I am no old man fatuously intent
On memoirs, but in memory I seek
The strength and vividness of nonage days,
Not tranquil recollection of event.
It is a fabled city that I seek;
It stands in Space's vapors and Time's haze;
Thence comes my sadness in remembered joy
Constrictive of the throat;
Thence do I hear, as heard by a Jewboy,
The Hebrew violins,
Delighting in the sobbed Oriental note.

# Dorothy Livesay

*Dorothy Livesay (1909-      ) was born in Winnipeg into a literary family. Her mother was a poet and her father, J.B.F. Livesay, was Editor of the* Winnipeg Free Press *and one of the founders of* The Canadian Press. *When the Livesays lived in Clarkson, Ontario, during the 1920s, they became acquainted with Mazo de la Roche, a neighbour, and with Raymond Knister. Miss Livesay graduated from Trinity College in the University of Toronto in 1931. She spent an undergraduate year at the University of Aix-Marseilles, and in 1931-32 spent a graduate year at the Sorbonne in Paris where she completed a Master's thesis on* The Influence of French Symbolism on Modern English Poets. *Her growing concern for social conditions led her to attend the School of Social Science at the University of Toronto and to do welfare work in Montreal and Englewood, New Jersey. After her marriage in 1937, she lived in Vancouver for many years. Besides her poetry writing, she has done newspaper reporting and has held several university posts. Miss Livesay received the Governor General's Award for Poetry for* Day and Night *(1944) and for* Poems for People *(1947), and the Lorne Pierce Medal for her contribution to Canadian literature in 1947.*

*Miss Livesay immersed herself in the left-wing activities while she was doing her social work, and learned from her discovery of Auden and Spender how to combine revolutionary fervour with lyricism and personal passion, as she explains in her perceptive autobiographical comments in* The Documentaries.[1] *One poetic result was "Day and Night", which appeared in the first issue of* Canadian Poetry Magazine *in January 1936 (under E.J. Pratt's editorship) and caused a minor sensation as the first poem in Canada to preach revolution. Miss Livesay also recorded her attitudes towards unsatisfactory social conditions in "Corbin — A Company Town Fights for its Life". What is new here is the straightforward commitment to working-class interests as opposed to those of the establishment. By avoiding a strident, angry tone and presenting Corbin's crisis in a restrained manner, this documentary sketch allows the reader to make his own judgment. Frank Watt has called Dorothy Livesay one of the "best practitioners"[2] of reportage, a genre that uses the techniques of fiction to give immediacy to an historical situation and thus permits the writer to editorialize through his artistry.*

*By the 1940s, she retreated from the rigidities of left-wing doctrinaire stances and developed a humanistic, religious attitude towards life and affairs. She endured "almost an existential despair" during the 1950s Cold War Years.[3] Through the later 1950s and 1960s she continued to write her characteristic autobiographical lyrics, which are poetic accounts of her domestic and erotic life, her anxieties and inadequacies, and the fruitful discoveries she made during her three-year UNESCO teaching post in Northern Rhodesia (1960-63).*

*"Behind all poetry is the song," Miss Livesay has written. "And sometimes it is very hard to write a poem without hearing in your mind, the music behind it . . . . as far as I am concerned I am always hearing this other beat behind the ordinary spoken language, and I'm always hearing the melody."[4] Thus Miss Livesay isolates her characteristic technique, the short, flowing Skeltonic line, and the almost liquid cadence of her vers libre. These lines, usually elliptical and often impressionistic in their imagery, create a sense of time and space which is characteristic of twentieth-century writing, when poets are no longer bound by the framework of the Newtonian universe of physical measurement and sequential time, but can utilize notions like Einstein's concept of a four-dimensional universe. Indeed, many imagist poems create this effect in their depiction of a non-material reality; and in painting, the development of cubism around the First World War helped artists to achieve similar effects. Such a technique (in painting or poetry) permits the artist to shift from conscious to subconscious levels of perception as she tries to locate herself both in the physical environment and in the world of her imagination. Thus, the imagery of diving in "Fantasia" operates on these two levels. Other favourite motifs are the green world, rain, the harshness of sunlight, the womb-like world of night, the incongruities of human relations, male-female dualities, and the possibility of making a new world.*

*Miss Livesay's subjects tend to cluster around the natural world, her own life from childhood to middle age, and socialist concerns. To an extent such distinctions in subject matter become blurred, however, for she does not separate the imagery associated with the natural world from her other poems, and in some respects all her poetry is autobiographical (for example, "Prelude for Spring" or "Lorca"). Often she attempts a long poem which is not strictly speaking a narrative poem, and for which she has found an appropriate name, documentary. The documentaries are organized as a series — or mosaic, rather — of lyrics whose unity is established by means of image clusters, contrasting rhythms, refrains, and interlocking themes. With the exception of* Call My People Home, *a radio play, Miss Livesay's long poems are not dramatic, and in consequence, contain the defects as well as the virtues of an essentially lyric style.*

### Footnotes

[1]*Dorothy Livesay,* The Documentaries *(Toronto: Ryerson, 1968), p. 17.*
[2] *F. W. Watt, "Literature of Protest", in* Literary History of Canada *(Toronto: University of Toronto Press, 1965), p. 471.*
[3]*Dorothy Livesay, "Song and Dance", Canadian Literature, No. 41 (Summer 1969), p. 45.*
[4] Ibid., *p. 41.*

# Reality

Encased in the hard, bright shell of my dream,
How sudden now to wake
And find the night still passing overhead,
The wind still crying in the naked trees,
Myself alone, within a narrow bed.

# Green Rain

I remember long veils of green rain
Feathered like the shawl of my grandmother—
Green from the half-green of the spring trees
Waving in the valley.

I remember the road
Like the one which leads to my grandmother's
    house,
A warm house, with green carpets,
Geraniums, a trilling canary
And shining horsehair chairs;
And the silence, full of the rains falling
Was like my grandmother's parlour
Alive with herself and her voice rising and
    falling,
Rain and wind intermingled.

I remember that on that day
I was thinking only of my love
And of my love's house.
But now I remember the day
As I remember my grandmother.
I remember the rain as the feathery fringe
    of her shawl.

# Day and Night

I

Dawn, red and angry, whistles loud and sends
A geysered shaft of steam searching the air.
Scream after scream announces that the churn
Of life must move, the giant arm command.
Men in a stream, a moving human belt
Move into sockets, every one a bolt.
The fun begins, a humming, whirring drum—
Men do a dance in time to the machines.

II

One step forward
Two steps back
Shove the lever,
Push it back

While Arnot whirls
A roundabout
And Geoghan shuffles
Bolts about.

One step forward
Hear it crack
Smashing rhythm—
Two steps back

Your heart-beat pounds
Against your throat
The roaring voices
Drown your shout

Across the way
A writhing whack
Sets you spinning
Two steps back—

One step forward
Two steps back.

## III

Day and night are rising and falling
Night and day shift gears and slip rattling
Down the runway, shot into storerooms
Where only arms and a note-book remember
The record of evil, the sum of commitments.
We move as through sleep's revolving memories
Piling up hatred, stealing the remnants,
Doors forever folding before us—
And where is the recompense, on what agenda
Will you set love down? Who knows of peace?

Day and night
Night and day
Light rips into ribbons
What we say.

I called to love
Deep in dream:
Be with me in the daylight
As in gloom.

Be with me in the pounding
In the knives against my back
Set your voice resounding
Above the steel's whip crack.

High and sweet
Sweet and high
Hold, hold up the sunlight
In the sky!

Day and night
Night and day
Tear up all the silence
Find the words I could not say . . .

## IV

We were stoking coal in the furnaces; red hot
They gleamed, burning our skins away, his and mine.
We were working together, night and day, and knew
Each other's stroke; and without words, exchanged
An understanding about kids at home,
The landlord's jaw, wage-cuts and overtime.

We were like Buddies, see? Until they said
That nigger is too smart the way he smiles
And sauces back the foreman; he might say
Too much one day, to others changing shifts.
Therefore they cut him down, who flowered at night
And raised me up, day hanging over night—
So furnaces could still consume our withered skin.

Shadraeh, Meshach and Abednego
Turn in the furnace, whirling slow.
      Lord, I'm burnin' in the fire
      Lord, I'm steppin' on the coals
      Lord, I'm blacker than my brother
      Blow your breath down here.

      Boss, I'm smothered in the darkness
      Boss, I'm shrivellin' in the flames
      Boss, I'm blacker than my brother
      Blow your breath down here.
Shadraeh, Meshach and Abednego
Burn in the furnace, whirling slow.


V

Up in the roller room, men swing steel
Swing it, zoom; and cut it, crash.
Up in the dark the welder's torch
Makes sparks fly like lightning reel.

Now I remember storm on a field
The trees bow tense before the blow
Even the jittering sparrows' talk
Ripples into the still tree shield.

We are in storm that has no cease
No lull before, no after time
When green with rain the grasses grow
And air is sweet with fresh increase.

We bear the burden home to bed
The furnace glows within our hearts:
Our bodies hammered through the night
Are welded into bitter bread.

279

Bitter, yes:
But listen, friend:
We are mightier
In the end.

We have ears
Alert to seize
A weakness
In the foreman's ease

We have eyes
To look across
The bosses' profit
At our loss.

Are you waiting?
Wait with us
After evening
There's a hush—

Use it not
For love's slow count:
Add up hate
And let it mount

Until the lifeline
Of your hand
Is calloused with
A fiery brand!

Add up hunger,
Labor's ache
These are figures
That will make

The page grow crazy
Wheels go still,
Silence sprawling
On the till—

Add your hunger,
Brawn and bones,
Take your earnings:
Bread, not stones!

# VI

Into thy maw I commend my body
But the soul shines without
A child's hands as a leaf are tender
And draw the poison out.

Green of new leaf shall deck my spirit
Laughter's roots will spread:
Though I am overalled and silent
Boss, I'm far from dead!

One step forward
Two steps back
Will soon be over:
Hear it crack!

The wheels may whirr
A roundabout
And neighbor's shuffle
Drown your shout

The wheel must limp
Till it hangs still
And crumpled men
Pour down the hill.

Day and night
Night and day
Till life is turned
The other way!


# Lorca

*For Federico Garcia Lorca, Spanish poet shot, it was said,*
*by Franco's men.*

When veins congeal
And gesture is confounded
When pucker frowns no more
And voice's door
Is shut forever

On such a night
My bed will shrink
To single size
Sheets go cold
The heart hammer
With life-loud clamour
While someone covers up the eyes.

Ears are given
To hear the silence driven in
Nailed down.
And we descend now down from heaven
Into earth's mould down
  *While you—*
  *You hold the light*
  *Unbroken.*

When you lived
Day shone from your face:
Now the sun rays search
And find no answering torch.

If you were living now
This cliffside tree
And its embracing bough
Would speak to me.

If you were speaking now
The waves below
Would be the organ stops
For breath to blow.

And if your rigid head
Flung back its hair
Gulls in a sickle flight
Would circle there.

  *You make the flight*
  *Unshaken.*

You are alive!
O grass flash emerald sight
Dash of dog for ball
And skipping rope's bright blink
Lashing the light!

High in cloud
The sunset fruits are basketed
And fountains curl their plumes
On statue stone.

In secret thicket mold
Lovers defend their hold
Old couples hearing whisperings
Touch in a handclasp, quivering.

For you sang out aloud
Arching the silent wood
To stretch itself, tiptoe,
Above the crowd . . .

    *You hold the word*
    *Unspoken.*

You breathe. You be.
Bare, stripped light
Time's fragment flagged
Against the dark.

You dance. Explode
Unchallenged through the door
As bullets burst
Long deaths ago, your heart.

And song outsoars
The bomber's range
Serene with wind-
Manoeuvred cloud.

    *Light flight and word*
    *The unassailed, the token!*

# Prelude For Spring

These dreams abound:
Foot's leap to shore
Above the sound
Of river's roar—
Disabled door
Banged and barricaded.
Then on, on
Furrow, fawn
Through wall and wood
So fast no daring could
Tear off the hood
Unmask the soul pursued.

Slash underbrush
Tear bough and branch
Seek cover, rabbit's burrow—
Hush!

He comes. Insistent, sure
Proud prowler, this pursuer comes
Noiseless, no wind-stir
No leaf-turn over;
Together quiet creeps on twig,
Hush hovers in his hands.

How loud heart's thump—
Persistent pump
Sucks down, down sap
Then up in surge
(Axe striking stump).

How breezy breath—
Too strong a wind
Scatters a stir
Where feathers are,
Bustles a bough.

How blind two eyes
Shuttling to-fro
Not weaving light
Nor sight . . .
In darkness flow.

(Only the self is loud;
World's whisperless.)

Dive down then, scuttle under:
Run, fearless of feet's thunder.
Somehow, the road rolls back in mist
Here is the meadow where we kissed
And here the horses, galloping
We rode upon in spring . . .

   O beat of air, wing beat
   Scatter of rain, sleet,
   Resisting leaves,
   Retarding feet

   And drip of rain, leaf drip
   Sting on cheek and lip
   Tearing pores
   With lash of whip

   And hoof's away, heart's hoof
   Down greening lanes, with roof
   Of cherry blow
   And apple puff—

   O green wet, sun lit
   Soaked earth's glitter!
   Down mouth, to munch
   Up hoof, to canter

   Through willow lanes
   A gold-shaft shower,
   Embracing elms
   That lack leaf-lustre

   And copse' cool bed
   All lavendered
   With scentless, sweet
   Hepatica—

   Till side by side
   In fields' brown furrow
   Swathe sunlight over
   Every shadow!

But still
On heart's high hill
And summit of
A day's delight

Still will he swoop
From heaven's height
Soaring upspent,
Still will he stoop to brush
Wing tip on hair,
Fan mind with fear.

And now the chill
Raw sun
Goes greener still—
The sky
Cracks like an icicle:

Frozen, foot-locked
Heart choked and chafed
Wing-battered and unsafe,
Grovel to ground!
A cry
Lashes the sky—

These dreams abound.

## Fantasia

for Helena Coleman, Toronto poet

And I have learned how diving's done
How breathing air, cool wafted trees
Clouds massed above the man-made tower
How these
Can live no more in eye and ear:
And mind be dumb
To all save Undine and her comb.

Imagination's underworld! where child goes down
Light as a feather. Water pressure
Hardly holds him, diving's easy
As the flight of bird in air
Or bomber drumming to his lair.

Child goes down, and laughingly
(He's not wanted yet, you see)
Catches fishes in his hand
Burrows toe in shifting sand
Seizes all the weeds about
To make a small sub-rosa boat

Then up he bobs, as easily
As any blown balloon
To greet the bosky, brooding sky
And hunger for the sun.

.     .     .     .

And child grown taller, clothed in man's
Long limbs, and shaggy hair, his chin outthrust
Searches for years the rounded world
Climbs to its peaks, falls to its valleys green
Striding the trim and trailing towns
Fingering the fond arteries
Possessing things, and casting them
Cloakwise to earth for sleeping time . . .

Sometime the lust wanderer
Will sleep, will pause; will dream of plunging deep
Below it all, where he will need
No clock companion, thorn in flesh, no contact man
To urge him from the ground.
For flying's easy, if you do it diving
And diving is the self unmoored
Ranging and roving — man alone.

.     .     .     .

And I have learned how diving's done
Wherefore the many, many
Chose the watery stair
Down, down Virginia
With your feted hair
Following after Shelley

Or wordcarvers I knew — *
Here is the fascination
Of the salty stare:
And death is here.
Death courteous and calm, glass-smooth
His argument so suave, so water-worn
A weighted stone.

And death's deliberation, his
Most certain waiting-room
His patience with the patient, who will be
His for infinity . . .

So no astounded peerers
On the surface craft
No dragging nets, no cranes
No gnarled and toughened rope
Not any prayer nor pulley man-devised
Will shake the undersea
Or be
More than a brief torpedo, children's arrow
More than a gaudy top outspun
Its schedule done . . .

       •    •    •    •

Wise to have learned: how diving's done
How breathing air, cool wafted trees
Clouds massed above the man-made tower
How these
Can live no more in eye and ear:
And mind be dumb
To all save Undine and her comb . . .

*The 1944 version of the poem contained an additional line following "Or wordcarvers I knew":
(Bouchette; and Raymond, you)—


# In Time of War

You went, wordless; but I had not the will
Nor courage to find fanciful or plumaged phrase
To camouflage my solitude. So saying bald
Good-bye, word bouncing down each waiting step

Till out of sight and sound, I saw you turn,
Walk firm toward the iron gate. Its clang
Shattered a world. For should we greet again
This hushed horizon will have widened so
You'll not find solace walking in the Park
Or watching storm snarl over English Bay.
That night of fog, bleaching the bones of trees
Will not shroud you and me again; too wide apart
We will have grown; our thoughts too proud
Too tall for sheltering beneath these boughs.


# Of Mourners

Mourn not for man, speeding to lay waste
The essence of a countryside's most chaste
And ageless contour; her cool-breasted hills,
Purled streams, bare choirs in wood, fair daffodils—

Mourn not, as maudlin singers did, the scars
Left by the slag, industrial wars,
Men tearing fields apart for railway towns
Wresting the silly sheep from sleepy downs:

And sing no more the sentimental song
Of spinning jenny holding lads too long,
Of children toiling underground, or laws
For hanging witches, burning corn for cause.

Sing only with the gibing Chaucer's tongue
Of foible and grave fault; of words unsung,
More pungent victory than battles won:
Sing deeds neglected, desecrations done

Not on the lovely body of the world
But on man's building heart, his shaping soul.
Mourn, with me, the intolerant, hater of sun:
Child's mind maimed before he learns to run.

289

# Call My People Home

(A Documentary Poem for Radio)

ANNOUNCER:

Now after thirty years come from a far island
Of snow and cherry blossoms, holy mountains,
To make a home near water, near
The blue Pacific; newcomers and strangers
Circled again and shaped by snow-white mountains
These put down their roots, the Isseis:*
The older generation. This is their story.

> CHORUS OF ISSEIS:
>
> Home, they say, is where the heart is:
> Transplanted walls, and copper-coloured gardens
> Or where the cherry bough can blow
> Against your pain, and blow it cool again—
> This they call home.
>
> But for ourselves we learned
> How home was not
> Even the small plot, raspberry laden
> Nor shack on stilts, stooping over the water,
> Nor the brown Fraser's whirl,
> Sucking the salmon upward.
>
> Home was the uprooting:
> The shiver of separation,
> Despair for our children
> Fear for our future.
>
> Home was the finding of a dry land
> Bereft of water or rainfall
> Where water is cherished
> Where our tears made channels
> And became irrigation.
>
> Home was in watching:
> The fruit growing and pushing
> So painfully watered;
> The timber hewn down
> The mill run completed.

*Isseis — generation born in Japan.

290

Home was in waiting:
For new roots holding
For young ones branching
For our yearning fading . . .

ANNOUNCER:

His ancestors had lived near water
Been fishermen under Fujiyama's shadow.
Each season in the new land found him struggling
Against the uncertain harvest of the sea,
The uncertain temper of white fishermen
Who hungered also, who had mouths to feed.
So these men cut his share
From half to one-eighth of the fishing fleet:
But still he fished, finding the sea his friend.

THE FISHERMAN:

Home was my boat: T.K. 2930—
Wintering on the Skeena with my nets
Cast up and down the river, to lure and haul
The dogfish. (His oil, they said, was needed overseas
For children torn from home, from a blitzed town.)
We made good money, and the sockeye run
That summer had outdone all the remembered seasons.
Now I could own my boat, *Tee Kay,* the Gillnetter
The snug and round one, warm as a woman
With her stove stoked at night and her lanterns lit
And anchor cast, brooding upon the water
Settled to sleep in the lap of the Skeena.

Now after thirty years, come from an island
To make a home near water: first on a sailing vessel
Towed, each season, to the fishing grounds:
Then the small gasboat, the gillnetter, that belonged
Not to the man who fished, but to the cannery.
Now after thirty years a free man, naturalized,

A man who owned his boat! I smelt the wind
Wetting my face, waves dashing against the *Tee Kay's* sides
The grey dawn opening like a book
At the horizon's rim. I was my own master—
Must prove it now, today! Stooping over the engine
Priming the starter, opening the gas valve,
I felt her throbbing in answer; I laughed
And grasped the fly wheel, swung her over.
She churned off up the river — my own boat, my home.

That was before Pearl Harbor: before a December day
Spent on a restless sea; then anchor in the dusk
And down to bunk to have a bowl of rice.
By lantern light I turned the battery set
To hear brief messages from fishermen
From boat to shore, to learn the weather forecast.
Must have been dozing when I woke up sharp—
What was he saying? Some kind of government order?
"All fishing craft on the high seas must head at once
To the nearest port, report to authorities."

Did they not want our fish, the precious oil?
No, said the voice. Our boats were to be examined,
        searched
For hidden guns, for maps, for treachery. . . .
I heard, but could not understand. Obeyed,
But as a blind man. The numb fear about my boat
*Tee Kay* found no release in port, off shore,
Rubbing against a fleet of trollers, frail gillnetters
All heading down for Inverness and Tusk
All in the dark, with rumour flying fast.
No one knew more than his fear whispered,
No one explained.
We thought: perhaps it's all a mistake
Perhaps they'll line us up and do a search
Then leave us free for Skeena, Ucluelet—
The time is ripe, the season's fish are running.

There was no mistake. It wasn't a joke:
At every fishing port more boats fell in.
Some had no wood, no gasoline; and some
Barely a day's store of food aboard.
So we waited at the Inlet's mouth, till the 16th.

How speak about the long trip south, the last
We ever made, in the last of our boats?
The time my life turned over, love went under
Into the cold unruly sea. Those waves
Washing the cabin's walls
Lashed hate in me.

We left Rupert in two long lines of sixty boats
Strung to the Seiners, met and tugged
By *Starpoint* and the naval escort, the corvette.
All day we watched the gloomy sea roughed up
By westerlies, but had to tough it out
Glued to the wheel, weary for sleep, till 2 a.m.

Then, at Lowe Inlet, had brief anchorage.
At Milbanke Sound we ran into heavier seas
The buffeted boats like so many bobbing corks
Strung on a thin rope line that over and over
Would break, be mended by the corvette's men
And then again be snapped by snarling sea.

Day merged into night and day again
Found us with six boats broken loose; some torn
And others gashed with bumping in the dark—
If some drugged fisherman fell off to sleep
And left craft pilotless,
Smashing like blind birds through a log-strewn sea.
Some boats that had no gasoline to keep
Heart thumping in their engines, these
Were plucked aloft in fistfuls by the waves
Then brought down with a thud—
Propellers spinning helpless in mid-air.
So we proceeded into colder, rougher seas,
Seasick and sore, nodding at the wheel,
Then stamping up and down to keep the winter out.

Christmas at sea. The bitterest for me
That any year had given. Even so
Some had a celebration, pooled their funds
And bought the only chicken left in Alert Bay.
Others boiled cabbages in salt sea water,
Pulled out the playing cards and shrugged, and laughed.
So we set sail at midnight, now a thousand boats
Chained to the naval escort, steadily south
Into familiar waters where the forests cooled their feet
At rocks' end, mountains swam in mist—
As we set sail for home, and young ones, born here, swore
Not softly, into the hissing night. The old men wept.

The rest takes little telling. On the fifteenth night
We passed Point Grey's low hulk, our long line wavered
                    shoreward.
Dirty and hungry, sleep lying like a stone
Stuck in our heads, we nosed our broken craft
Into the wharf at Steveston, "Little Tokyo."
The crowd on the dock was silent. Women finding their men
Clung to them searchingly, saying never a word,
Leading them home to the *ofuro* and supper.
Others of us, like me, who knew no one,

Who had no place near the city's centre
Stood lonely on the wharf, holding the *Tee Kay's*
          line
For the last time, watching the naval men
Make a note of her number, take my name.
That was the end of my thirty years at the fishing
And the end of my boat, my home.


ANNOUNCER:

These their children, the Niseis,* were born
Into the new world, called British Columbia home
Spoke of her as mother, and beheld
Their future in her pungent evergreen.


    A YOUNG NISEI:

    *We lived unto ourselves*
    *Thinking so to be free*
    *Locked in the harbour*
    *Of father and mother*
    *The children incoming*
    *The tide inflowing.*

    Sometimes at midnight
    With burnt-out moon
    An orange eye on the river
    Or before dawn
    From a house heavy with sleepers
    The man touching my arm
    Guiding my hand through the dark
    To the boat softly bumping and sucking
    Against the wharf;
    We go out toward misty islands
    Of fog over the river
    Jockeying for position;
    Till morning steals on us, sleepy,
    And over our boat's side, leaning
    The word comes, Set the nets!
    Hiding the unannounced prayer
    Resounding in the heart's corners:
    May we have a high boat
    And the silver salmon leaping!


    *Nisei — generation born in Canada.

*We lived unto ourselves*
*Locked in the harbour.*


I remember the schoolhouse, its battered doorway
The helter-skelter of screaming children
Where the old ones went, my sisters
Soberly with books strapped over their shoulders:
Deliberately bent on learning—


(And learned, soon enough, of
The colour of their skin, and why
Their hair would never turn golden.)


But before the bell rang
For me
My turn at becoming
Before the bell rang
I was out on the hillside
Reaching high over my head for the black ones
The first plump berries of summer;
A scratch on the arm, maybe, a tumble
But filling my pail and singing my song
With the bees humming
And the sun burning.


Then no bell rang for me;
Only the siren.
Only the women crying and the men running.
Only the Mounties writing our names
In the big book; the stifled feeling
Of being caught, corralled.
Only the trucks and a scramble to find
A jacket, a ball, for the bundle.


My blackberries spilled
Smeared purple
Over the doorway.
Never again did I go
Blackberry picking on the hillside.
Never again did I know
That iron schoolbell ringing.


*The children incoming*
*The tide inflowing.*

ANNOUNCER:

From the upper islands of the coast
With only one day's notice to depart
Came these, and hundreds like them: Mariko and her mother.
In the re-allocation centre, Hastings Park
Mariko writes a letter.

THE LETTER:

I wonder where in the inner country
On what train shooting between two mountains
You fly tonight, Susumu?
When I explain to you how it is here
You will understand, perhaps,
Why I have not been able to tell my mother
About you and me.

It is this: she is continually frightened—
Never having lived so, in a horse stall before.
My bunk is above hers, and all night I lie rigid
For fear to disturb her; but she is disturbed.
She has hung her pink petticoat from my bunk rail
Down over her head, to be private; but nothing is private.
Hundreds of strangers lie breathing around us
Wakeful, or coughing; or in sleep tossing;
Hundreds of strangers pressing upon us
Like horses tethered, tied to a manger.

My mother lies wakeful with her eyes staring.
I cannot see her, but I know. She is thinking:
*This is a nightmare.* She is back in her home
Embroidering blossoms on a silk kimono
Talking to me of Yosh (the boy I mentioned,
The one I grew up with). She is making plans
To visit the go-between; to bake for a wedding.

My mother cannot believe her dream is over,
That she lies in a manger with her hands tethered.
So you will understand now, Susumu:
I have not been able to tell my mother.
It is hard for me to believe, myself,
How you said the words, how you spoke of a garden
Where my name, MARIKO, would be written in
          flowers. . . .
I wonder where in the inner country
On what train far from this animal silence

This thick night stifling my heart, my nostrils—
Where like rocket shooting between two planets
Have you flown, Susumu? Have you gone?

ANNOUNCER:

Between the fury and the fear
The window-breaking rabble and the politician's blackout,
(Wartime panic fed
On peacetime provocations)
Between the curfew rung
On Powell Street
And the rows of bunks in a public stable
Between the line-ups and the labels and the presentation
            of a one-way ticket
Between these, and the human heart—
There was in every centre one man, a white man—
A minister, a layman — even a mayor.

            THE MAYOR:

That year the snow came early, lay lightly on our hills
Cooling their colours, pointing up the evergreen
Scribbled over the ledges; at valley's end
Snow muffled with its mantle the gaunt shape,
The smokeless chimney of the copper smelter.

I stood on the station platform reading the message
Telegraphed from Vancouver: "The first contingent,
Sixty-eight persons, arriving on the night train."
Then I looked down our narrow, funneled valley
My ghost-town village, with hotels closed up
Since gold-rush days; post office perched
Upon a down-hill lurch, leaning toward empty stores.

Sixty-eight persons, and where could they find a
            pillow?
The government shacks were only half completed,
Without heat or water; there remained a hotel
Half boarded up; a church; some vacant houses
Left tenantless, standing on back streets.
These I tried first; but the neighbours protested:
They had read the newspapers, they did not want
Criminals and spies settling upon their doorsteps.
There was nothing for it but to open the creaking door,
Put stoves and straw in the Golden Gate Hotel.

297

At seven-fifteen the evening train pulled in.
I stood alone on the platform, waiting.
Slowly the aliens descended, in huddled groups,
Mothers and crying children; boys and girls
Holding a bundle of blankets, cardboard boxes,
A basket of pots and pans, a child's go-cart—
Looking bewildered up and down the platform,
The valley closing in, the hostile village. . . .

I stepped forward, urged into sudden action.
The women cowered, fell back, cried words
In panic to the old men standing surly, helpless.
I collared a young kid, bright, with his eyes snapping:
"You there, you speak English?" "Why, yah! You bet."
We eyed each other, and I smiled. "You see,"
I said, "I'm mayor here . . . your mayor.
This is your home. Can you tell the people that?
Tell them I'm here to meet them, get acquainted,
Find a place for them to sleep." The boy
Nodded. "Okay, I'll tell my mother, sure.
The rest will believe whatever she says to do."

Their conference began. I waited, tense;
Then plunged into the job of lifting crates
And scanty furnishings, getting local lads
To pile it up on trucks; until I felt
A timid touch upon my arm; I turned
And saw the Issei mother.
        Putting out my hand
I felt hers move, rest for a moment in mine—
Then we were free. We began to work together.

I remember the long looks of my neighbours
As I strode down the street the next morning
Arm in arm with a flock of Japanese kids.
I took them into the store, the post-office,
Showed them the ropes, then headed for the school,
If no one else in the town would say "hello"
There was one who would. I knew her
Inside out, like a book — the Principal.

In an hour's time she had them behind desks
Those six, of high school age, those slant-eyed
Black-haired, half-terrified children.
Then I went out to find some carpenters
To build a village in a single day. . . .

It was cold. Light snow covered the hills.
By spring, I vowed, those people would be mine!
This village would be home.

ANNOUNCER:

These were the fathers, mothers, those
Who had to choose another home, another way.
What would they choose? The questioner
Paused with his pencil lifted; gave them a day
To talk together, choose.

THE WIFE:

Either to be a ghost in mountain towns
Abandoned by the fabulous, the seekers
After gold, upon whose bones the forest and the rock
Had feasted; there to sit
With idle hands embroidering the past
Upon a window pane, fed on foreign food
And crowded together in government granted huts—
The men torn from our arms, the family parted;

Or to face the longer, stranger journey
Over the mountain ranges, barred from the sea—
To labour in uncertain soil, inclement weather
Yet labour as one — all the family together?

We looked at each other, you and I, after
So many doubtful years binding our struggles:
Our small plot grown to wider green
Pastured within the Fraser's folds, the shack
Upbuilded to a cottage, now a house—
The cherry trees abloom and strawberry fields
White with the snow of blossom, of promise.

Had it all to be done again, worked at again
By our gnarled hands, in a harsh new land
Where summer passes like a quick hot breath
And winter holds you chained for half the year?
You took my hands, and said: "It's the children's country.
Let them choose." They chafed for independence
Scenting the air of freedom in far fields.
Therefore we had no choice, but one straight way:
The eastward journey into emptiness,
A prairie place called home.

299

It was harder than hate. Home was a blueprint only.
We lived in a hen coop perched on a farmer's field
Soaked by the sudden storms, the early rains of April.
Yet there was time for ploughing, time to sow
Beet seed upon the strange black soil in rows
Of half an acre; we saw in neighbouring fields'
Bleak tableland, the stabbing green
Of the young wheat; and heard the sweet
Heart-snaring song of meadow-larks; in grass
Withered and brown saw maps move, empty patches
Purple with crocus underneath our feet.


In summer the sun's beak
Tore at our backs bending over the rows
Endless for thinning; the lumpy soil left callouses
Upon our naked knees; mosquitoes swarmed
In frenzied choruses above our heads
Sapping the neck; until a hot wind seared
The field, drove them away in clouds.


I think we had nearly given up, and wept
And gone for government help, another home—
Until, one evening lull, work done
You leaned upon the poplar gate to watch
A lime green sky rim the mauve twilight
While in the pasture fireflies danced
Like lanterns of Japan on prairie air.


Leaning the other way spoke our new friend
The neighbour from the Ukraine;
Touching your arm, using words more broken
Than yours, like scraps of bread left over.
"See how tomorrow is fine. You work
Hard, same as me. We make good harvest time."
He came from a loved land, too, the mild
Plains of the Dnieper where, in early spring
(He said) the violets hid their sweetness. "This land
Is strange and new. But clean and big
And gentle with the wheat. For children too,
Good growing."
He lifted up his hands, his praise; you heard
Over the quickening fields a fresh wind blowing.

ANNOUNCER:

This one was young, a renegade. He wanted the world
In his two hands. He would not make the choice,
But cast it back in their teeth.

NISEI VOICE:

They can't do this to me, Shig said
(Once a Jap, always a Jap)
Why, I went to school with those kids
Vancouver's my home town.

They can't do this to me, Shig said
(Once a Jap, always a Jap)
I'll spend my life in a road camp
In a freight car bunk in the bush.

They'll get tired of me, Shig said
(Once a Jap, always a Jap)
And some dark night I'll buckle my belt
And hitch-hike to the sea.

The Mounties won't get me, Shig said
(Once a Jap, always a Jap)
I'll say I'm a Chinese, see?
It's the underworld for me.

They picked Shig up on a robbery charge
(Once in jail, always in jail)
There were only a few of us such as he
But he blackened our name
Shut the gates to the sea.

ANNOUNCER:

This one was young; but he wanted the world
For others. A philosopher,
He accepted the blow, Pearl Harbor.
He learned the way of waiting.

THE PHILOSOPHER:

To be alone is grace; to see it clear
Without rancour; to let the past be
And the future become. Rarely to remember
The painful needles turning in the flesh.

301

(I had looked out of the schoolroom window
And could not see the design, held dear
Of the shaken maples; nor the rain, searing and stinging
The burning rain in the eye.

I could not see, nor hear my name called:
Tatsuo, the Pythagoras theorem!
I could not think till the ruler rapped
On the desk, and my mind snapped.

The schoolroom faded, I could not hold
A book in my hand.
It was the not knowing; the must be gone
Yet the continual fear of going.

Yes, to remember is to go back; to take
The path along the dyke, the lands of my uncle
Stretching away from the river—
The dykeside where we played

Under his fruit trees, canopied with apples,
Falling asleep under a hedgerow of roses
To the gull's shrill chatter and the tide's recurrent
Whisper in the marshland that was home. . . . )

So must I remember. It cannot be hid
Nor hurried from. As long as there abides
No bitterness; only the lesson learned
And the habit of grace chosen, accepted.

CHORUS OF NISEIS:

Home, we discover, is where life is:
Not Manitoba's wheat
Ontario's walled cities
Nor a B.C. fishing fleet.

Home is something more than harbour—
Than father, mother, sons;
Home is the white face leaning over your shoulder
As well as the darker ones.

Home is labour, with the hand and heart,
The hard doing, and the rest when done;
A rougher ocean than we knew, a tougher earth,
A more enduring sun.

# On Looking Into Henry Moore

### I

Sun, stun me, sustain me
Turn me to stone:
Stone, goad me and gall me
Urge me to run.

When I have found
Passivity in fire
And fire in stone
Female and male
I'll rise alone
Self-extending and self-known.

### II

The message of the tree is this:
Aloneness is the only bliss

Self-adoration is not in it
(Narcissus tried, but could not win it)

Rather, to extend the root
Tombwards, be at home with death

But in the upper branches know
A green eternity of fire and snow.

### III

The fire in the farthest hills
Is where I'd burn myself to bone:
Clad in the armour of the sun
I'd stand anew, alone.

Take off this flesh, this hasty dress
Prepare my half-self for myself:
One unit, as a tree or stone
Woman in man, and man in womb.

# Winter

Winter, by whom our stumbling feet were caught,
Who held us long in iron chains of cold,
Winter has turned reluctantly at last,
Unfastened the sharp snares and soberly
Moved like a dream up slopes and over hills,
Breathing a last cool sigh before he went.
Winter has gone. The marsh-hawk and the crow
Follow relentlessly his backward step.

Now you would think that spring must take his place,
Heal up the wounds, breathe freedom on the earth,
Throw all her singing on the barren air.
I tell you, no: we must be captives still
Who watch each other with the winter's look,
Touch with his hand, speak with his bitter breath.

# Ballad of Me

*i*

Misbegotten
born clumsy
bursting feet first
then topsy turvy
falling downstairs:
the fear of
joy of
falling.

*Butterfingers*
father called it
throwing the ball
which catch as catch can
I couldn't.

Was it the eyes' fault
seeing the tennis net
in two places?
the ball flying, falling
space-time team-up?

What happened was:
the world, chuckling sideways
tossed me off
left me wildly
treading air
to catch up.

ii

Everyone expected guilt
even I—
the pain was this:
to feel nothing.

Guilt? for the abortionist
who added one more line
to his flat perspective
one more cloud of dust
to his bleary eye?

For the child's
'onlie begetter'
who wanted a daughter?
He'll make another.

For the child herself
the abortive dancer?

No. Not for her
no tears.
I held the moon in my belly
nine months' duration
then she burst forth
an outcry of poems.

iii

*And what fantasies do you have?*
asked the psychiatrist
when I was running away from my husband.

305

Fantasies? fantasies?
Why surely (I might have told him)
all this living
is just that
every day dazzled
gold coins falling
                through fingers.
So I emptied my purse for the doctor
See! nothing in it
but wishes.
He sent me back home
to wash dishes.

                *iv*

Returning farther now
to childhood's *Woodlot*
I go incognito
in sandals, slacks
old sweater
and my dyed
hair

I go disarrayed
my fantasies
twist in my arms
ruffle my hair

I go wary
fearing to scare
the crow

                No one remembers Dorothy
                was ever here.


# Corbin — A Company Town Fights For Its Life

Pushing its way through the dusty mountain roads of the Crow's Nest Pass, Alberta,
the car spurts up an incline, slows to a stop. From an office at the side of the road an
officer steps out, red-faced and bull-necked, wearing the uniform of the British
Columbia Provincial Police.
    "Where you from?"

"Coleman," the driver beside me answers.

"What's your name?" The officer jots down the answers in a note book. Then he searches the driver's face, with a puzzled look. "Coming back tonight?"

"Yes."

"Going far?"

"Corbin."

"Corbin, eh? Who you going to see there?"

"My sister."

The officer gives us the onceover, appraisingly. "O.K. You can try it. But the road's in bad shape."

The car darts forward. We lean back, smiling. Plenty of other cars from the mining towns of Alberta have never got across the boundary. Leaders of the Mine Workers' Union of Canada are on a blacklist. This isn't Germany, but British Columbia, April, 1936.

The Corbin road is a narrow track skirting the edge of mountains, almost washed away in some places by snow slides. For an hour it climbs above desolate valleys, snow slashed, some green with Jackpine, others sentinelled with trees like burnt fingers. There is no one else on the road, no settlements. We push ahead under a grey sky.

"Sure, it's romantic country," my driver says. "And a rich country. Over twenty-five years ago the mine was opened, and there's still 75,000,000 tons of coal to be mined. But I wouldn't live or work up here — though I've been a miner all my life. For one thing — you have winter, and then July. But that isn't the only reason. You'll see."

Corbin lies in a narrow crescent between mountains. Three rows of identical shacks, unpainted and soot-coloured, are perched on the slope facing the tipple. There are no lanes or streets between them. An empty store and a café, a boarding-house, a school and a union hall are the main public buildings, likewise unpainted. Above the village there is only snow and burnt timber. There is no sound or activity anywhere: since the strike 15 months ago every hand has been idle. The town is living on contributions from other miners.

Today is ration day. Miners of all nationalities — Scotch, Welsh, Belgian, Czecho-slovakian — are crowding into the union hall to get the week's rations for some 200 families. The relief committee, consisting of men and women, is on hand to mark off lists and parcel up the provisions from behind a counter. One of the single men, who "batches" with his mining partner, explains how many supplies each adult is entitled to weekly. All staples are covered, such as flour (5 pounds), sugar (¾ pound), butter (½ pound), potatoes (6 pounds). Jam or peanut butter cannot be had every week, beans and cheese are likewise rare, one pound of meat has to go for ten days, eggs vary from two to eight per person per week.

"But we get along pretty good," the young man grins. "I can make such swell bread now I'm baking everybody's, almost."

"And can I wash floors," another man adds.

"Well, none of you can beat me at puttin' out a snow white washin'," says a third. I begin to wonder if the women have anything left to do, so one of the miners suggests I go up to his home and "meet the Missus."

It is one of the shacks in the middle row, with scarcely any room between houses

307

for children to play, and the front family's back yard with its ashes and garbage almost on this doorstep. The kitchen and front room are neat, but shabby, with the oil cloth worn bare and the walls askew. Mrs. W., a thin, freckled young woman, greets the visitors happily. "Well, imagine you being from the east! I was born down in Ontario. Come in and sit down."

"I see you brought the flour, Ben. Now I can make some biscuits." She laughed then. "We women had a terrible time about the flour. You see, the union had to base the rations on some budget, so they used the army list. I guess the men in the army like lots of hot cakes, so they need lots of flour. But our children don't. We had some time to convince the committee to buy more vegetables and less flour."

The supplies, she explained, were brought up every two weeks from Lethbridge by truck. Union and Corbin defence relief funds are allotted at the rate of 68 cents a week per person, and the diet expands or is restricted according to market prices.

"It's hard sometimes to make a meal seem different, especially if you have no meat. The biggest trouble is not having any fresh fruit and so few green vegetables. We can't always get the dried fruits. That's hard on the children — they aren't really under-nourished but they're not getting everything they should have. And if a person is on a diet it is impossible to get it — we couldn't ask the union for that."

Milk comes — about a pint for each family — from a dairyman who gives credit in exchange for having his hay brought for him. "But two of his cows died, and he lost two because he could not pay up for them."

Since Corbin is a company town (Corbin Collieries, Ltd., an American firm), everything in it belongs to the company. The water system was frozen all winter, and nothing done about it; electricity was turned off "so our radios are no use"; sanitation has "gone out of business"; stores are closed; rents are unpaid — "they wouldn't dare evict us because that might draw too much attention to the condition of the houses." Most irritating of all, Corbin miners are no longer taxpayers, so the school trustees are no longer elected by them, but appointed by the company. "This year there is only one, Walter Almond, who doesn't know anything about schools or teaching. He supplies fuel as well, and acts as janitor — which is against the law for a trustee. But what can we do?"

The only thing the company has been forced to do is to keep open the school and pay the two teachers. Classes only reach the eighth grade, however, and there is no way of getting children to a high school. For two months during the winter the only doctor was 15 miles away, so the government had to keep the road open. Then finally a doctor came, his salary partly paid by the government and partly by the miners themselves, who are supposed to supply rations, rent and electricity. They are greatly behind on the doctor's rent, so he is leaving at the end of April.

"Corbin is fairly healthy, except for influenza," the doctor told me. He is a military man, used to hard fare. "The diets are all that prairie children would get. The great trouble is weakness of the heart, especially among many of the women. It's due to the high altitude and of course has nothing to do with the present situation." He meant with the attitude of the company, which refuses to negotiate with the miners.

"I'm glad you want to know the truth about Corbin," another miner's wife told me. "At the beginning I used to send stories about our life up here and why we went on strike to the Nelson News. Then they began sending letters back asking, 'is your story authentic?' They would not print our facts, but lies that came from the other side. After that I quit bothering. But it makes you sore to think that people on the outside don't know what happened."

"Yes," another young woman said, with some bitterness, "some friends of mine in Lethbridge would hardly speak to me because they read I was throwing a fence post at an officer. The newspapers helped the police to frame us."

"Tell me why you went on strike?" I asked a group of miners up in the union hall, men both single and married who had been strike leaders.

"A year before then, our strike should be," a Czechoslovakian burst out.

"Yes, we must have been asleep, though we were all in the union since 1925. It wasn't the wages so much, it was the conditions we had to live under."

"Yes," agreed another, a Nova Scotian. "It got so we saw that life was dearer to us than the mine."

They told the story of those shacks built in 1909 of green lumber, costing only $175 to build and bringing in $5.00 per month rent ever since, besides $3.50 for water and light, 50 cents for radio use, 50 cents for a garbage collection that only came twice a year. The house shrunk, fell apart, and with only an outer wall it was not uncommon that snow drifted across the bed at night. Ice formed on the wall and even stuck to the beds and any effort to get the carpenter to come and do some patching was met with vague promises and a general run-around. It took one man two years to get his door lintel mended. The health officer reported that the houses were "absolutely antiquated", and he condemned 78 out of 80 houses.

Besides these conditions there was the situation in the mine itself. Nearly a mile from the village where the bath-house is the men had to walk to the mine in mid-winter clad only in their work clothes, and were often held up outside the mine to do road work. As a result they might start work soaked to the skin, and return home with the clothes frozen to their backs. In one mine there has been a fire blazing for years, and nothing done to protect the men. Pay checks went through some extraordinary gyrations, sometimes being short and taking months to get adjusted, or else being much too high. In the latter case the correct amount was pencilled in on the envelope and given to the miner, but the mistaken amount remained on the books. "Somebody was getting something."

"The company's excuse was always that they weren't making money. Yet in the B.C. mines report for three years back of 1934 it shows that Corbin was getting 5.4 tons per man, as compared with 1.1 tons on Vancouver Island and 3.0 tons at Michel. The seam is one of the richest, that's why we want a government investigation, to prove to the world the mismanagement of the company."

Mismanagement was shown most clearly in the negotiations that went on between the Mine Workers Union and the Company. In the face of an expiration of the agreement in March, 1935 and the possibility of a wage cut at that time, the union set forth its demands in January of that year. The union secretary, J. Press, had been fired by the company on the pretext that he did not work full time one day (this situation had been "fixed up" by the foreman). Reinstatement of Press was the first demand and equal to it in importance was the demand for repair of miners' houses. Equal distribution of work was requested, to stop abuses in that direction, and also it was held essential that miners taken from the working face should be paid the full rate of $5.60 per shift. The miners were willing to arbitrate these demands before calling a strike.

The company dilly-dallied but for two months after the strike was called no effort to work the mine was made. Then there were open hints that "The Big Show", which is a huge face of coal projecting from the mountainside and requiring no mining operations but only a steam shovel to work it, would be opened shortly by non-union men. Then at the beginning of April, about 6 provincial police were called for by the company and took up their residence in the town. Against all provocations the miners continued their peaceful picketing.

On Tuesday, April 16, the company met a delegation of the strike committee and appeared to be willing to sign the agreement. Then they stated that they would have to wire the head office in Spokane for a final decision. The delegation reported this to a meeting of the miners and it was agreed that they would deal with Spokane. But on returning with this decision to the company the delegation was told that they were "too late." A telegram had just come from Spokane refusing to deal with the demands.

"After that," as one of the strike leaders put it, "we knew something would happen. The police were getting restless, they had been called in to keep law and order and there wasn't a single instance of any trouble. On the morning of April 17th I walked down the road early and saw that the scabs from out of town were manning the caterpillar tractor, and filling it up with gas and water. We called out every man and woman in the town and had a mass picket line, feeling that we had to stop the tractor from taking those men up to the Big Show. The womenfolk were grouped in the middle and some were up front. Suddenly, as at a signal, the full detachment of police ran out from the hotel and grouped themselves in two squads on either side of the caterpillar, flanking the picket line .... Before we could understand anything the caterpillar was moving forward, straight at our women. And the police, instead of clearing the way, suddenly closed in, hemming us in on both sides, beating miners and their wives with pick handles and riding crops. . . . "

Mrs. W. was one of the women at the front, heading the women's auxiliary. "That morning," she said, "we didn't have any fear. We'd been told that the police were there to protect us, and we just imagined they were called out to clear the road for the tractor. Then the tractor advanced with its sharp knife edge right on us, cutting at us women in front and the cops moving forward with it. We turned to run and the police closed in, beating us .... That was when our men went wild. They had no weapons at all, for all the lies them witnesses told. They had to go down to the creek and dig up stones out of the snow to throw at the police, so as to protect us.

"There was nobody killed, though the papers made out there was. The police, some of them just youngsters, started all the violence. Before that happened I used to be patriotic. I'd stand up on my little Maple Leaf in front of anyone. But I learned my lesson. We all did. The police were sent down by the government to protect the American company — not the Canadian workers. Yet all we were asking for was a decent existence. We couldn't go on the old way any longer .... Well, one thing it done, was to bring all the miners together — solid. We've never been separated since."

310

Mrs. C. was one of the women who was badly hurt — a young, lithe European woman. "As the tractors moved down on us, Inspector Elmsie leaned over and hit me on the back of my head. I got away somehow, and was walking in the opposite direction toward the Café, when I saw a bunch of cops looking kind of queerly at me. But I was alone, and just running away, so I didn't take any notice of Inspector MacDonald coming up alongside me. All of a sudden he struck me a blow from the rear, across my right ear, it must have been from his riding crop . . . . Anyhow, I was knocked down unconscious . . . . For days after I kept fainting, and the whole side of my face and neck was swollen.

"I testified at Corbin, but not at Fernie. Maybe the lawyer thought I'd get too violent and spoil things. I felt violent, when I seen the way they lied — swearing they had seen all seventeen of the arrested men during the riot, when those same police were passing them by in the street the next morning, out with a warrant unable to identify them! And going into garbage piles to find steel bed rails which the miners were supposed to have been armed with! No one was showing the bloody pick handles the police were swinging, but we found them afterwards hidden under a mattress!

"I sure learned something about governments during those days, something I never would have believed before. My husband used to get *The Worker* and I just couldn't believe the stories I read in it. After the riot, 'You see, I was right,' he says to me . . . . Before, I never would have believed they would attack defenceless people. I guess the moral is, go armed. . . .

"Sure, right now I feel pretty bitter, I don't go to no meetings because it makes me feel too sore. Here the government is doing absolutely nothing for us and we're just living on the sweat of other miners. Maybe I shouldn't say it, but we in Corbin are just sapping the life-blood of Crow's Nest Pass miners. I figure we ought to be getting relief instead."

Getting relief is the big question in Corbin. It is not so simple as it sounds: many workers think it would be a mistake. In the first place, the doctor definitely told me he had it from the Government Inspector that Corbin could not receive provincial relief unless the families agreed to leave the town and go to a place where work might be possible. The miners feel that this would just be a move to help the company: as soon as the town is cleared of union men the company can move in scabs to work the Big Show — a very profitable operation not requiring skilled miners. Wages would go down to about $3.00 per shift and this would mark the beginning of a move to crush the union in other towns. Again, going on relief would have a bad effect on the single men, many of them union leaders, by forcing them out of the town into relief camps. For in spite of the Federal Government's promises, these camps remain open in Alberta and B.C. Lastly, relief would not be granted to all miners, as a goodly number of them have property in the shape of automobiles bought during boom days — the only means of communication with "the outside".

Possibly the greatest argument against relief is the fact that in this way the company can no longer be negotiated with, and full government inquiry into the management of the mine, the riot, and the keeping of five men in Nelson jail (even after one of those committed, David Lockart, died there on March 6), would be ignored. The report of the committee on evangelism and social service of the United

311

Church declared that "nothing less than a judicial inquiry would satisfy justice." Dr. Hugh Dobson, one of the United Church secretaries of social service, in a wire to the Provincial Secretary, urged "an impartial inquiry into all circumstances." As well as this a strong fight in Parliament has been led by Mr. T. Uphill, Labor M.L.A. and the C.C.F. members in the B.C. house. Such actions, the strikers feel, justify a further attempt for an investigation.

"Maybe we will have to go on relief, to stop draining Blairmore," one of the miners said. "But if so we will all go on relief together, and stay in our homes, and bring the real question to the fore: that of getting the mine reopened. It is still being kept in condition, though fire has burned out one mine entirely. But the equipment is still here, the upkeep continues. What are they waiting for? Spokane will give *us* no answer. But what if the Mackenzie King government should live up to its pre-election promises, and threaten confiscation of the mine if the industrial magnates refuse to co-operate? It looks as if the Canadian government and the American company are sleeping in the same bed.

"Well, the miners are together too. Not only Corbin is holding fast, but all the miners of Alberta are behind us, each man in the union from Blairmore giving $2.00 a month to keep our children alive and our union strong."

This is why Corbin is waiting. Corbin is not through fighting.

# W.P.Wilgar

W. P. Wilgar (1912-1950) was born in Canada and educated at Queen's University and Cambridge University. He taught English literature at the University of Texas, Mount Allison, Manitoba, and Carleton. "Poetry and the Divided Mind in Canada" was stimulated by Wilgar's classes in contemporary poetry.

Wilgar has not been the only teacher to speculate on the reasons why Canadian students often respond less vigorously to their own writers than they do to British and American writers. Naturally they are responding to the superb gifts of a Yeats, a Frost, an Eliot, or an Auden, but it is less clear why a Canadian poet, whose craftsmanship is of equal stature to a foreign poet's, should remain unknown in his own land. One reason has been the absence of Canadian anthologies. There has never been any lack of texts dealing with British and American writers; there was until the 1960s a dearth of Canadian texts. Indeed, most Canadian novels went out of print soon after first publication. Moreover, there has been little response to Wilgar's observation that Canadian poets occupy no place in contemporary-poetry anthologies prepared for British and American readers.

To refute Wilgar's charge that Canadian poets were not writing about the three major preoccupations of contemporary poets, the reader should turn in this anthology to Scott's "Armageddon" and "Saturday Sundae", Livesay's "Lorca" and "Day and Night", Klein's "In Re Solomon Warshawer", Pratt's "Myth and Fact", and in the succeeding anthology in this series to the work of Birney and Layton. It is more difficult, however, to answer Wilgar's other charge that Canadian poets were working "tentatively" and that their verse "contains an uncertainty which would seem to rise from indecision", for this problem is related to conditions not entirely aesthetic. The reader should consider to what extent literary and critical activity — and historical changes since 1944 — have modified Wilgar's conclusions in this wartime essay.

The ultimate subject of this essay, as in other critical writings of the period, is the Canadian identity as reflected through its literature. By pointing to the Canadian "split personality" as an explanation for the "inadequacies of . . . present Canadian poetry", Wilgar not only acknowledges the need to judge literature in its historical and social contexts, but puts his finger on some tensions in the Canadian psyche, which has had to work out its sense of reality at home in juxtaposition with versions of reality from abroad — both British and American.

313

# Poetry and the Divided Mind In Canada

Twice a week during the second term of the academic year I endeavour to arouse some interest in the poetry of to-day among a group composed largely of senior students. The class itself is typical of any similar University group in that its members have begun to think a little, and are not afraid to defend their ideas. A particularly thought-provoking aspect of the students, however, lies in the spontaneity of their response to the American poets. The Americans, as exemplified by Sandburg, Frost, MacLeish, Robinson, Millay, and the usual others, seem to establish a contact that is immediate at the same time that it is healthily questioning. For the undergraduate with some background of literary study, and an inquisitive mind about the work of the poet during, after, and re-involved in war, the writers of the United States provide a stimulus for critical discussion that is both the purpose and the blessing of such a course. The students recognize kinship with the aims and the subject-matter of the poet; they have little trouble in condoning the rhythmical and metrical departures. An average student is disposed to regard the extremists, such as E. E. Cummings, as "funny"; but even here the obvious connection with jazz rhythms reconciles the student to the rightness of the verse for the times. In some cases he will, unprompted, state the necessity for a redefinition of the word poetry, in order that it may include those aspects of the new verse which his previous training, stopping as it does with the collapse of the Victorian tradition, did not consider. This redefinition, I might add, in no way implies the complete discard of previous conceptions; rather it is prompted by a sense of the rightness of present poetry, and a wish to reorganize the older values so that this sense of rightness may be personally justified.

The poets of present-day England, however, provoke an altogether different response. When confronted with the works of Auden, Day-Lewis, MacNeice, the students openly declare themselves baffled. That part of the difficulty arises from the increased demand these poets make upon an advanced intellectual background, is obvious; but even the comparatively simple sections of their works produce an uncertain reaction, a dubiety of mind as to purpose and meaning. The stand for Traditionalism made by the Wastelanders, their despair of the present and doubt about the future, have little in common with a group of you people who, while they would experience great difficulty expressing their ideas, nevertheless feel a vigorous certainty about their own futures. In the same manner, the use of an involved and intellectual imagery, which they instinctively interpret as a vitiated attempt to prolong and to expand a literary tradition that expresses a way of life no longer suitable to them, excites negative and occasionally caustic critical comments. The lyric spirit and the choice of material of Stephen Spender is appreciated, but even here the pervading atmosphere of personal fatigue and of almost desperate loneliness, both in some way bound up with Spender's unbreakable affiliations with the Old World, cause this appreciation to be much more a purely intellectual rather than an intellectual-cum-personal thing.

Political and social issues behind large sections of such poets as W. H. Auden are recognized as important; but they are remote from the minds of those whose country has not yet begun to consider seriously the possible desirability of alternate forms of government, or whose labour problem is not only small but concerns a group not directly related to the possible collapse of a complete social order. Like the American workman, the Canadian refuses to contemplate himself as an individual moving within a caste system; therein lies the difference between the British and the Canadian attitude on labour problems; a difference which affords immediate explanation of the greater reality, for the Canadian, of American as opposed to British poetry on this subject.

As a result of the student's instinctive reactions in favour of American poetry, and of his evident desire to study and weigh values which he feels to be a part of his own civilization and which he finds reflected in this poetry, one is drawn towards a number of natural questions. Are the trends of the English Canadian's thinking laid more closely to those of the United States than they are to those of the Old World? What is lacking in the poetry of Canada that the standard textbooks of the best modern verse include so little Canadian? I believe that the answers to these two questions interlock.

The careful reader will grant the point that contemporary Canadian poets are writing tentatively, that their small bulk of verse contains an uncertainty which would seem to rise from indecision — indecision as to aim as well as to expression. There is often great delicacy of image, a certain adeptness in the handling of the line, and the communication of a very real understanding for and appreciation of nature. But Canadian poetry is cold. The most obvious criticism is that it seems much more the product of the fancy than of the imagination; in many cases, of the study rather than of the actual experience. Academically interesting as the results may be, neither do they have breadth nor do they have a sense of their own rightness.

What, then, is the matter? Everywhere the Canadian is surrounded by a wealth of natural beauty that has excited the admiration of literary visitors. Yet the poetry of nature which is being produced at present does little more than suggest that the poet is shy of his subject and avoids the full expression of any deep, sensitive reaction that he may feel. Perhaps the fault lies in the fact that nature is too close for us to view it in emotional perspective. Perhaps our accustomed acceptance of and occasional impatience with the essentially rural quality of our national life has bred a desire to escape from nature, or generated the opinion that the treatment of nature is an obvious and therefore in some way an undesirable theme for creative work. In any event, we have here the characteristic timidity, the sense of feeling for words, in place of the flow that springs from conviction and a well roused artistic excitement.

In the longer poems of the day, which not only deal with nature in connection with man but also derive a part of their value through the treatment of important national and international events, one encounters similar and further difficulties. There is frequent appearance of some of the most fortunate imagery in Canadian poetry; but the whole is seldom sustained. The experience recorded seems to be of a vicarious nature — the product of a mind that has tried but has not quite succeeded in projecting itself into the situation at hand. What is there is sound; unfortunately it is what is not there that is psychologically and poetically the more interesting. In a word, the poems lack the penetration which would give them something more than the surface appeal of narrative and the occasional excitement of fine imagery: that penetration into the inner psychological ramifications of any human experience which can bring to narrative poetry a significance that will transcend its purely narrative appeal. These poems tell a dramatic story, it is true; but the outcome is that the reader leaves the work with dissatisfaction in proportion to his sensitivity.

If one should turn aside from the nature and the narrative group, and regard those poems generally confining themselves to a reflection of artistic socialism, of the political and social issues which have captured the imagination of contemporary writers, one is struck with a sense of inadequacy that may be accounted for only in part by the conditions in the country. The industrialization of Canada has not yet expanded enough to justify a spontaneous outburst of the "smoke and steel" type of verse. In the same manner, the political situation in the Dominion, while it excites a good deal of protesting conversation, has not yet crystallized into factions which are wholly devoted to a political cause. Rather, the political character of the country is one of grumbling lassitude that watches with a fairly indifferent eye the forming or reforming of parties. Out of such inactivity poetry can arise only when the poet himself is sure of the rightness of that which he champions, and when he is willing to court social disaster by furthering it. To date, we have not produced the combination of fire and political conviction that is the mark of this particular type.

In the slightly increased speed of political thinking that the progress of this war has generated, and the inspection and resorting of personal political ideas that is being forced upon the intelligent Canadian by the magnificent stand resultant of the Russian experiment, there are signs of unrest. It is possible that this unrest may excite sensitive minds to the necessity of sharing their reactions through the medium of poetic expression. But there has been national unrest before, and the products are not noticeable. There has been a previous war; one in which the achievements of the Canadians were of sufficient nobility and self-sacrifice to inspire an equally noble literary response. The period of re-adjustment following the war, the infinite repercussions of the financial crash, the slow rise of a small but indicative interest in and understanding of the problems of labour are merely a few of the significant features of the twenties and thirties — of national importance all of them; but like the conflict which brought them in its wake, without a vigorous poetic voice.

Thus we have seen that the three major preoccupations of contemporary poets — the personal interpretation of nature, the voice of industry and the machine, and the apparent necessity for social and political change — have not yet struck fire from the Canadian stone. Nor has an alternate set of values prompted expression. We are faced, then, with the original difficulty: what lies behind this apparent ineptitude? The key, I think, may be found in the divided mind, in the inability of the Canadian to decide what he is, or, more dangerous, what he wants to be. As a member of an enormous and only partially developed country, he is certain of a momentous future; but the actual outlines of that future have been so clouded now by word combinations, such as "post-war reconstruction", "large scale internal development", "the natural link between America and Russia in the airways of the future", "the half-way house in which understanding between England and America may be maintained", and all the rest of these powerful and flattering phrases, that an actual interpretation of Canada the country as a separate and recognizable unit is almost impossible to achieve. Until such an interpretation is more fully developed in the minds of the Canadian intellectuals and its national importance more widely felt, uncertainty of aim is bound to exist, and to be reflected in the literature.

Furthermore, there is in the Canadian mentality a second internal conflict, the literary significance of which becomes apparent when we examine the attempts to communicate those ideas rising out of the contact of man with his environment, or as the result of personal struggle, or out of man's connection with God and nature; in brief, those ideas which have always acted as a stimulus to the sensitive mind. Since such poetry is of the most personal kind, it necessitates careful mental and emotional analysis on the part of the poet, together with a sorting and weighing of the values of one against the other in order to discriminate between that which is fundamental, and therefore of permanent importance, and that which is merely transitory, and therefore to be discarded. But even before these decisions are made, the poet must have a conception which he feels intellectually and sympathetically justified in expressing. Thus the division of intellect and sympathy which has long been one of the conspicuous psychological characteristics of Canadian thinking is bound to have prevented the attainment of the necessary point of view.

The Canadian is sympathetically British; his ancestral background is inextricably tangled with that of the British Isles; his loyalties are unswervingly to Empire; he is pleased with and grasps at traditionalism. But at the same time he finds himself in the curious and awkward position of respecting all that is British while he has to admit to himself that he has a far more advanced understanding of the American mind than he has of the Old World mentality. It is not for nothing that he feels at home in New York, and a self-conscious stranger in London. In brief, it is the conflict of the ideal with the fact. Under different conditions, the two would merge in artistic production; as it is, such merging is impossible, and will remain so until the Canadian has undergone careful self-examination. He must begin to evaluate actualities, to find a personal integrity, and to decide what he wishes to preserve from the culture of the Old World and from the strong movements of the New. Out of such examination and decision may be created an individual character which is no longer vacillating between two forces, or taking refuge in one side each time the other seems displeasing.

Inevitably a step in any direction will entail a certain amount of painful sacrifice; but convictions strong enough to brave the pain are of the stuff that makes literature. The divided mind cannot produce the form of concentrated expression that has always been the harbinger of literary greatness; nor can the divided mind give itself wholly to the overwhelming enthusiasm for a concept or a cause that is necessary to the highest form of poetic communication. It stands to reason that important intellectual or artistic achievement must be the product of undivided concentration. It has in the very sureness of its purpose no place for the interference of doubts. Decisions must be made constantly during its inception, and when the period of experimentation has passed, the established harmony between subject and medium should be so intricately interwoven that each complements and assists the purposes of the other. Thus a divided loyalty which is only too obviously carried over into the modes of poetic expression, a wavering between the not entirely satisfactory and

317

almost invariably unsuitable thought processes of the present-day British poets and the uncomfortable knowledge of an understanding for and a sympathy with the matter and manner of American poetry, negates the possibility of such concentration, as well as the establishment of the desired harmony.

It is on the fact of this split personality, I think, that the explanation for the inadequacies of the present Canadian poetry rests. When our poets can free themselves from the omnipresence of two powerful and conflicting voices, neither of which should be entirely right for Canada, and when they can fuse with their own convictions that which they consider relevant from both cultures, we shall see the advent of a strong and indigenous Canadian literature.

# Anne Marriott

*Joyce Anne Marriott (1913-    ) was born in Victoria, B.C., and educated at private
schools. In 1939 she published* The Wind Our Enemy *in the Ryerson Chapbooks
Series. She received the Governor General's Award for Poetry for* Calling Adventures
*(1941), and her chief collection is* Sandstone *(1945).*

*Soon after its publication,* The Wind Our Enemy *was acclaimed as one of the finest
poems to deal with the drought which struck the Prairies during the 1930s, a decade
already blighted by the consequences of the Depression. But* The Wind Our Enemy,
*sharing techniques used by Pratt, Dorothy Livesay, Earle Birney, and other Canadian
poets in their long works, is also a good example of the narrative tradition in Canadian
poetry. Rather than having the usual chronological sequence which is characteristic of
narrative poems, it is structured into episodes forming a mosaic-like pattern. These
fragmentary episodes may be lyrics, scenarios, vignettes, dialogues, even newspaper
headlines. While it lacks the unity arising from a story-line, the poem maintains its
coherence through the contrasting moods of each section, which build towards the
climactic Section VIII. Furthermore, Miss Marriott's imagist style combines the
compactness of medieval alliterative verse with the colloquial language appropriate to
her subjects and their setting. For example, note how the sound pattern in the
following lines can contribute to the coherent mood of a section:*

> *Wind*
> *flattening its gaunt furious self against*
> *the naked siding, knifing in the wounds*
> *of time. . . .*

*Or*

> *with broken wash-boiler, bucket without*
> *. . . .*

*Although her depiction of Prairie life is specifically realistic, it is also universalized.
From the tragedy of drought, Miss Marriott develops her themes of man's confrontation with the destructive, irrational forces of the natural world and man's relations
with his fellow men — whether neighbours or strangers.*

319

# The Wind Our Enemy

### I

*Wind*
*flattening its gaunt furious self against*
*the naked siding, knifing in the wounds*
*of time, pausing to tear aside the last*
*old scab of paint.*

*Wind*
*surging down the cocoa-coloured seams*
*of summer-fallow, darting in about*
*white hoofs and brown, snatching the sweaty cap*
*shielding red eyes.*

*Wind*
*filling the dry mouth with bitter dust*
*whipping the shoulders worry-bowed too soon,*
*soiling the water pail, and in grim prophecy*
*greying the hair.*

### II

The wheat in spring was like a giant's bolt of silk
Unrolled over the earth.
When the wind sprang
It rippled as if a great broad snake
Moved under the green sheet
Seeking its outward way to light.
In autumn it was an ocean of flecked gold
Sweet as a biscuit, breaking in crisp waves
That never shattered, never blurred in foam.
That was the last good year. . . .

### III

The wheat was embroidering
All the spring morning,
Frail threads needled by sunshine.like thin gold.
A man's heart could love his land,
Smoothly self-yielding,
Its broad spread promising all his granaries might hold.
A woman's eyes could kiss the soil
From her kitchen window,
Turning its black depths to unchipped cups — a silk crepe dress—

(Two-ninety-eight, Sale Catalogue)
Pray sun's touch be gentleness,
Not a hot hand scorching flesh it would caress.
But sky like a new tin pan
Hot from the oven
Seemed soldered to the earth by horizons of glare. . . .

The third day he left the fields. . . .

Heavy scraping footsteps
Spoke before his words, "Crops dried out — everywhere—"

### IV

They said, "Sure, it'll rain next year!"
When that was dry, "Well, next year anyway."
Then, "Next—"
But still the metal hardness of the sky
Softened only in mockery.
When lightning slashed and twanged
And thunder made the hot head surge with pain
Never a drop fell;
Always hard yellow sun conquered the storm.
So the soon sickly-familiar saying grew,
(Watching the futile clouds sneak down the north)
"Just empties goin' back!"
(Cold laughter bending parched lips in a smile
Bleak eyes denied.)

### V

Horses were strong so strong men might love them,
Sides groomed to copper burning the sun,
Wind tangling wild manes, dust circling wild hoofs,
*Turn the colts loose! Watch the two-year-olds run!*
Then heart thrilled fast and the veins filled with glory
The feel of hard leather a fortune more sweet
Than a girl's silky lips. He was one with the thunder,
The flying, the rhythm, of untamed, unshod feet!

*But now—*
It makes a man white-sick to see them now,
Dull — heads sagging — crowding to the trough—
No more spirit than a barren cow.
The well's pumped dry to wash poor fodder down,
Straw and salt — and endless salt and straw—
(Thank God the winter's mild so far)

Dry Russian thistle crackling in the jaw—
The old mare found the thistle pile, ate till she bulged,
Then, crazily, she wandered in the yard,
Saw a water-drum, and staggering to its rim,
Plodded around it — on and on in hard,
Madly relentless circle. Weaker — stumbling—
She fell quite suddenly, heaved once and lay.
(Nellie the kids' pet's gone, boys.
Hitch up the strongest team. Haul her away.
Maybe we should have mortgaged all we had
Though it wasn't much, even in good years, and draw
Ploughs with a jolting tractor.
Still — you can't make gas of thistles or oat-straw.)


                    VI

*Relief.*
"God, we tried so hard to stand alone!"

*Relief.*
"Well, we can't let the kids go cold."
They trudge away to school swinging half-empty lard-pails,
to shiver in the schoolhouse (unpainted seven years),
learning from a blue-lipped girl
almost as starved as they.

*Relief cars.*
"Apples, they say, and clothes!"
The folks in town get their pick first,
Then their friends—
"Eight miles for us to go so likely we
   won't get much—"
"Maybe we'll get the batteries charged up and have
   the radio to kind of brighten things—"

*Insurgents march in Spain*
*Japs bomb Chinese*
*Airliner lost*


"Maybe we're not as badly off as some—"
"Maybe there'll be a war and we'll get paid to fight—"
"Maybe—"
"See if Eddie Cantor's on to-night!"

                    322

## VII

People grew bored
Well-fed in the east and west
By stale, drought-area tales,
Bored by relief whinings,
Preferred their own troubles.
So those who still had stayed
On the scorched prairie,
Found even sympathy
Seeming to fail them
Like their own rainfall.


"Well — let's forget politics,
Forget the wind, our enemy!
Let's forget farming, boys,
Let's put on a dance to-night!
Mrs. Smith'll bring a cake.
Mrs. Olsen's coffee's swell!"


The small uneven schoolhouse floor
Scraped under big work-boots
Cleaned for the evening's fun,
Gasoline lamps whistled.
One Hungarian boy
Snapped at a shrill guitar,
A Swede from out north of town
Squeezed an accordion dry,
And a Scotchwoman from Ontario
Made the piano dance
In time to "The Mocking-Bird"
And "When I grow too Old to Dream,"
Only taking time off
To swing in a square dance,
Between ten and half-past three.


Yet in the morning
Air peppered thick with dust,
All the night's happiness
Seemed far away, unreal
Like a lying mirage,
Or the icy-white glare
Of the alkali slough.

## VIII

Presently the dark dust seemed to build a wall
That cut them off from east and west and north,
Kindness and honesty, things they used to know,
Seemed blown away and lost
In frantic soil.
At last they thought
Even God and Christ were hidden
By the false clouds.
—Dust-blinded to the staring parable,
Each wind-splintered timber like a pain-bent Cross.
Calloused, groping fingers, trembling
With overwork and fear,
Ceased trying to clutch at some faith in the dark,
Thin sick courage fainted, lacking hope.
But tightened, tangled nerves scream to the brain
If there is no hope, give them forgetfulness!
The cheap light of the beer-parlour grins out,
Promising shoddy security for an hour.
The Finn who makes bad liquor in his barn
Grows fat on groaning emptiness of souls.


## IX

The sun goes down. Earth like a thick black coin
Leans its round rim against the yellowed sky.
The air cools.   Kerosene lamps are filled and lit
In dusty windows.   Tired bodies crave to lie
In bed forever.   Chores are done at last.
A thin horse neighs drearily.   The chickens drowse,
Replete with grasshoppers that have gnawed and scraped
Shrivelled garden-leaves.   No sound from the gaunt cows.
Poverty, hand in hand with fear, two great
Shrill-jointed skeletons stride loudly out
Across the pitiful fields, none to oppose.
Courage is roped with hunger, chained with doubt.
Only against the yellow sky, a part
Of the jetty silhouette of barn and house
Two figures stand, heads close, arms locked,
And suddenly some spirit seems to rouse
And gleam, like a thin sword, tarnished, bent,
But still shining in the spared beauty of moon,
As his strained voice says to her, "We're not licked yet!
It must rain again — it *will!* Maybe —  soon—"

## X

*Wind*
*in a lonely laughterless shrill game*
*with broken wash-boiler, bucket without*
*a handle, Russian thistle, throwing up*
*sections of soil.*

*God, will it never rain again? What about*
*those clouds out west? No, that's just dust, as thick*
*and stifling now as winter underwear.*
*No rain, no crop, no feed, no faith, only*
*wind.*

# Bibliography

# Bibliography

## Primary Works

Callaghan, Morley. *Morley Callaghan's Stories.* Toronto: Macmillan, 1959.

————. *A Native Argosy.* New York: Scribner's, 1929.

————. *Now That April's Here, and Other Stories.* New York: Random, 1936.

Canadian Broadcasting Corporation. *Canadian Literature Today.* Toronto: University of Toronto Press, 1938.

De la Roche, Mazo. *The Sacred Bullock and Other Stories.* Boston: Little, Brown, 1939.

Glassco, John. *Memoirs of Montparnasse.* Toronto: Oxford, 1970.

Grove, Frederick Philip. *Over Prairie Trails.* Toronto: McClelland and Stewart, 1922.

————. *Tales from the Margin: Selected Stories of Frederick Philip Grove.* Edited by Desmond Pacey. Toronto: McGraw-Hill Ryerson, 1971.

Klein, A.M. *Poems.* Philadelphia: The Jewish Publication Society, 1944.

————. *The Rocking Chair and Other Poems.* Toronto: Ryerson, 1948.

————. *The Second Scroll.* New York: Knopf, 1951.

Knister, Raymond. *Collected Poems of Raymond Knister.* Edited, and with a Memoir by Dorothy Livesay. Toronto: Ryerson, 1949.

Livesay, Dorothy. *Call My People Home.* Toronto: Ryerson, 1950.

————. *Day and Night.* Toronto: Ryerson, 1944.

————. *Green Pitcher.* Toronto: Macmillan, 1928.

————. *Poems for People.* Toronto: Ryerson, 1947.

————. *Selected Poems.* Introduction by Desmond Pacey. Toronto: Ryerson, 1957.

————. *Signpost.* Toronto: Macmillan, 1932.

————. *The Unquiet Bed.* Toronto: Ryerson, 1967.

Marriott, Anne. *The Wind Our Enemy.* Toronto: Ryerson, 1939.

Pratt, E.J. *The Collected Poems.* Second Edition. Edited with an Introduction by Northrop Frye. Toronto: Macmillan, 1958.

————. *The Fable of the Goats and Other Poems.* Toronto: Macmillan, 1937.

————. *Many Moods.* Toronto: Macmillan, 1932.

————. *Newfoundland Verse.* Toronto: Ryerson, 1923.

————. *Selected Poems of E.J. Pratt*. Edited by Peter Buitenhuis. Toronto: Macmillan, 1968.

————. *Still Life and Other Verse*. Toronto: Macmillan, 1943.

————. *Towards the Last Spike*. Toronto: Macmillan, 1952. A Verse Panorama of the Struggle to Build the First Canadian Transcontinental from the Time of the Proposed Terms of Union with British Columbia (1870) to the Hammering of the Last Spike in the Eagle Pass (1885).

Raddall, Thomas H. *The Pied Piper of Dipper Creek and Other Tales*. Toronto: McClelland and Stewart, 1943.

————. *The Wedding Gift and Other Stories*. Toronto: McClelland and Stewart, 1947.

Ross, Sinclair. *The Lamp at Noon and Other Stories*. Introduction by Margaret Laurence. Toronto: McClelland and Stewart, 1968.

Ross, W.W.E. *Shapes and Sounds*. With a Portrait by Dennis Burton, a Memoir by Barry Callaghan, and an Editorial Note by Raymond Souster and John Robert Colombo. Toronto: Longmans, 1968.

Sandwell, B.K. *The Diversions of Duchesstown and Other Essays*. Introduction by Robertson Davies. Toronto: Dent, 1955.

Scott, F.R. *Events and Signals*. Toronto: Ryerson, 1954.

————. *The Eye of the Needle: Satires, Sorties, Sundries*. Montreal: Contact Press, 1957.

————. *Overture*. Toronto: Ryerson, 1945.

————. *Selected Poems*. Toronto: Oxford, 1966.

Scott, F.R., and Smith, A.J.M., eds. *New Provinces: Poems of Several Authors*. Toronto: Macmillan, 1936.

Smith, A.J.M. *Collected Poems*. Toronto: Oxford, 1962.

————. *News of the Phoenix and Other Poems*. Toronto: Ryerson, 1943.

————. *A Sort of Ecstasy: Poems New and Selected*. Toronto: Ryerson, 1954.

Underhill, Frank H. *In Search of Canadian Liberalism*. Toronto: Macmillan, 1960.

Wilgar, W.P. "Poetry and the Divided Mind in Canada", *Dalhousie Review*, XXIV (October 1944), pp. 266-271.

## Secondary Works

Birney, Earle. "E.J. Pratt and His Critics", in *Our Living Tradition*, Second Series. Edited by Robert L. McDougall. Toronto: University of Toronto Press, 1959.

Brown, E.K. *On Canadian Poetry*. Toronto: Ryerson, 1943.

Callaghan, Morley. *That Summer in Paris*. Toronto: Macmillan, 1963.

*The Canadian Forum*. 50th Anniversary Issue. L (April-May 1970).

Collin, W.E. *The White Savannahs*. Toronto: Macmillan, 1936.

Conron, Brandon. *Morley Callaghan*. New York: Twayne, 1966.

Creighton, Donald. *Dominion of the North*. Revised Edition. Toronto: Macmillan, 1957.

Deacon, W.A., and Reeves, Wilfred, eds. *Open House*. Ottawa: Graphic, 1931.

De la Roche, Mazo. *Delight.* Introduction by Desmond Pacey. Toronto: McClelland and Stewart, 1961.

Djwa, Sandra. "No Other Way: Sinclair Ross's Stories and Novels", *Canadian Literature,* No. 47 (Winter 1971), pp. 49-66.

Dudek, Louis. "The Role of the Little Magazines in Canada", *The Canadian Forum,* XXXVIII (July 1958), pp. 76-78.

Dudek, Louis, and Gnarowski, Michael, eds. *The Making of Modern Poetry in Canada.* Toronto: Ryerson, 1967. Essential Articles on Contemporary Canadian Poetry in English.

Frye, Northrop. *The Bush Garden: Essays on the Canadian Imagination.* Toronto: House of Anansi, 1971.

Glassco, John, ed. *Poetry in Quebec.* Proceedings of the Foster Poetry Conference, October 12-14, 1963. Montreal: McGill University Press, 1965.

Hambleton, Ronald. *Mazo de la Roche of Jalna.* Toronto: General Publishing, 1966.

Hawkins, W.J. "Thomas H. Raddall, the Man and His Work", *Queen's Quarterly,* LXXV (Spring 1968), pp. 137-146.

Hoar, Victor. *Morley Callaghan.* Toronto: Copp Clark, 1969.

Jones, D.G. *Butterfly on Rock: A Study of Themes and Images in Canadian Literature.* Toronto: University of Toronto Press, 1970.

Klinck, Carl F., ed. *Literary History of Canada.* Toronto: University of Toronto Press, 1965.

Legate, David M. *Stephen Leacock: A Biography.* Toronto: Doubleday, 1970.

Livesay, Dorothy. *The Documentaries.* Toronto: Ryerson, 1968.

—————. "The Documentary Poem: A Canadian Genre", in *Contexts of Canadian Criticism.* Edited by Eli Mandel. Chicago: University of Chicago Press, 1971.

—————. "Song and Dance", *Canadian Literature,* No. 41 (Summer 1969), pp. 40-48.

MacLennan, Hugh. "The Canadian Character", in *Cross-Country.* Toronto: Collins, 1949.

McPherson, Hugo. "The Two Worlds of Morley Callaghan: Man's Earthly Quest", *Queen's Quarterly,* LXIV (Autumn 1957), pp. 350-365.

Mandel, Eli, ed. *Contexts of Canadian Criticism.* Chicago: University of Chicago Press, 1971.

Marshall, Tom, ed. *A.M. Klein.* Critical Views on Canadian Writers. Toronto: Ryerson, 1970.

New, William H. "Sinclair Ross's Ambivalent World", *Canadian Literature,* No. 40 (Spring 1969), pp. 26-32.

Pacey, Desmond. *Creative Writing in Canada: A Short History of English-Canadian Literature.* Second Edition. Toronto: Ryerson, 1961.

—————, ed. *Frederick Philip Grove.* Critical Views on Canadian Writers. Toronto: Ryerson, 1970.

—————. *Ten Canadian Poets: A Group of Biographical and Critical Essays.* Toronto: Ryerson, 1958.

Parker, George L. "Literature, English-Language", *Encyclopedia Canadiana,* VI (1972 edition).

Pitt, D.G., ed. *On E.J. Pratt*. Critical Views on Canadian Writers. Toronto: Ryerson, 1969.

Raddall, Thomas H. *At the Tide's Turn and Other Stories*. Introduction by Allan Bevan. Toronto: McClelland and Stewart, 1959.

––––––. "The Literary Art", *Dalhousie Review*, XXXIV (Summer 1954), pp. 138-146.

––––––. *The Nymph and the Lamp*. Introduction by John Matthews. Toronto: McClelland and Stewart, 1963.

Rashley, R.E. *Poetry in Canada: The First Three Steps*. Toronto: Ryerson: 1958.

Ross, W.W.E. *Experiment*. Notes by Raymond Souster. Toronto: Contact Press, 1956.

––––––. "On National Poetry", *Canadian Forum*, XXIV (July 1944), p. 88.

Sandwell, B.K. *The Canadian Peoples*. Toronto: Oxford, 1941.

––––––. *The Gods in Twilight*. The First Hewitt Bostock Memorial Lecture in Canadian Citizenship. Vancouver: The University of British Columbia Publications, 1948.

Smith, A.J.M., ed. *The Book of Canadian Poetry: A Critical and Historical Anthology*. Chicago: University of Chicago Press, 1943.

Smith, A.J.M., ed. *Masks of Fiction: Canadian Critics on Canadian Prose*. Toronto: McClelland and Stewart, 1961.

––––––, ed. *Masks of Poetry: Canadian Critics on Canadian Verse*. Toronto: McClelland and Stewart, 1962.

––––––. "Refining Fire", *Queen's Quarterly*, LXI (Autumn 1954), pp. 353-364.

––––––. "A Rejected Preface", *Canadian Literature*, No. 24 (Spring 1965), pp. 6-9.

––––––. "Wanted–Canadian Criticism", *Canadian Forum*, VIII (April 1928), pp. 600-601.

Spettigue, Douglas. *Frederick Philip Grove*. Studies in Canadian Literature. Toronto: Copp Clark, 1969.

Stevens, Peter, ed. *The McGill Movement: A.J.M. Smith, F.R. Scott, and Leo Kennedy*. Toronto: Ryerson, 1969.

––––––. "The Old Futility of Art", *Canadian Literature*, No. 23 (Winter 1965), pp. 45-52.

––––––. "On W.W.E. Ross", *Canadian Literature*, No. 39 (Winter 1969), pp. 43-61.

Story, Norah. *The Oxford Companion to Canadian History and Literature*. Toronto: Oxford, 1967.

Sutherland, John, ed. *Other Canadians: An Anthology of the New Poetry in Canada, 1940-1946*. Montreal: First Statement Press, 1947.

Sylvestre, Guy; Conron, Brandon; and Klinck, Carl F.; *Canadian Writers/Écrivains Canadiens*. Second Edition. Toronto: Ryerson, 1966.

Waddington, Mariam, *A.M. Klein*. Studies in Canadian Literature. Toronto: Copp Clark, 1970.

Watters, R.E. "Original Relations: A Genographic Approach to the Literature of Canada and Australia", *Canadian Literature*, No. 7 (Winter 1961), pp. 6-17.

––––––. "A Special Tang: Leacock's Canadian Humour", *Canadian Literature*, No. 5 (Summer 1960), pp. 21-32.

Weaver, Robert. "Stories by Callaghan", *Canadian Literature*, No. 2 (Autumn 1959), pp. 67-70.

Whalley, George, ed. *Writing in Canada.* Proceedings of the Canadian Writers Conference, Queen's University, July 1955. Toronto: Macmillan, 1956.

Wilson, Milton. "Recent Canadian Verse", *Queen's Quarterly*, LXVI (Summer 1959), pp. 268-274.

—————. "Second and Third Thoughts about Smith", *Canadian Literature*, No. 15 (Winter 1963), pp. 11-17.

Woodcock, George. *Odysseus Ever Returning: Essays on Canadian Writers and Writing.* Toronto: McClelland and Stewart, 1970.

KD